CLASSIC
WINNERS
1980-2015

A PICTORIAL REVIEW OF THE FIVE
CLASSIC HORSE RACES IN ENGLAND

JOHN CROFTS

Miralgo Publications
30 Midland Road
Gloucester GL1 4UL

Published by Miralgo Publications 2015

ISBN 978-0-9932643-0-6

All photographs identified by a reference number are copyright of John Crofts; others are copyright as follows: **Clare Bancroft**: p161 (Derby); **Bertrand**: p99 (Blushing Groom), 119 (Vaguely Noble); **Ed Byrne**: p9 (Derby), 10, 11 (Oaks), 19 (Derby & Irish Derby), 22, 23 (Oaks lead-in), 35 (Roberto), 361 (2000 Guineas); **Steven Cargill**: p359 (Ascot Gold Cup); **Healy Racing**: p281 (Irish Oaks); **Trevor Jones**: p337 (Susan Magnier); **Jack Knight**: p31 (Golden Fleece in winner's circle at Epsom); **Peter Mooney**: p119 (Christy Roche), 342; **Keith Robinson**: p241 (Sir Neil & Lady Westbrook); **Alec Russell**: p101 (St Leger); **George Selwyn**: p15 (Jim Joel), 45 (Sir Michael Sobell), 51 (David O'Brien), 335 (Dancing Rain in winner's circle at Epsom), 355 (James Rowsell); **Unknown**: p5 (1000 Guineas & Ogden Mills Phipps), 23 (Oaks), 27 (Harry Wragg), 49 (Edward P. Taylor), 51 (Northern Dancer), 85 (Mill Reef), 121 (Robert Frankel), 275 (Aidan O'Brien), 287 (Phil Cunningham), 305 (Princess Haya of Jordan), 311 (John Oxx), 319 (Mathieu Offenstadt).

The photographs on the pedigree pages were all taken by and are copyright of the author except: **Airlie Stud**: Cut Above, Henbit; **Banstead Manor Stud**: Frankel; **Big Red Farm, Japan**: Conduit; **Ed Byrne**: Shergar, Mastery; **Calumet Farm**: Secreto; **Rex Coleman**: Quick As Lightning, Known Fact, Bireme, To-Agori-Mou, Time Charter, Sun Princess; **Coolmore**: Lomond; El Gran Senor, Don't Forget Me, Tirol, Milan, Footstepsinthesand, Scorpion, Pour Moi, Henrythenavigator; **European Racehorse**: Golden Fleece; **Bernard Gourier**: Zino; **Haras d'Etreham**: Masked Marvel; **Longholes Stud**: Minster Son; **Peter Mooney**: King's Best, Galileo, Imagine, Rock Of Gibraltar, High Chaparral, Refuse To Bend, Brian Boru, Virginia Waters, George Washington, Finsceal Beo, New Approach, Sea The Stars, Dawn Approach, Ruler of the World, Leading Light, Australia, Gleneagles, Legatissimo; **Laurie Morton**: Dancing Brave, Nashwan, Snow Bride, Generous; Commander in Chief, Bosra Sham, Reams of Verse, Wince, Oath, Love Divine; **Norman Court Stud**: Sixties Icon; **Caroline Norris**: Blue Wind, Alexandrova, Camelot, Homecoming Queen, Was; **Old Road Stud**: Arctic Cosmos; **Shadai Farm**: Workforce; **Thoroughbred Pedigree Center, Japan**: Moon Madness; **Tweenhills Stud**: Makfi; **Unknown**: Quest For Fame, King of Kings, Pennekamp, Dancing Rain.

Although the vast majority of photographs credited to the author in this book were actually taken by him, he would like to acknowledge the exceptional talent of **Jean Christophe Baudin, Tony Edenden** and especially **Genevieve Henderson**, who have all worked with him at various times over the years.

The author is very grateful to **Timeform** for permission to use the ratings published in their annual 'Racehorses' to compare and analyse the classic winners of different years and also for the quotes taken from various essays in these annuals.

Contents

Acknowledgements

I would first like to thank Tim Cox, whose idea it was that I should write a pictorial racing book about the best one hundred horses I had photographed since becoming a professional horse racing photographer in 1981. This project was shelved before it was even begun; similar books had been produced before and I was daunted by the task of selecting the best hundred out of the thousands of horses to race across my camera lens in over thirty years. No book about all the classics had been written since 1850, when George Tattersall's *Pictorial Gallery of English Race Horses* was published covering the Derby, Oaks and St Leger of the previous twenty years including portraits of all the winners by such artists as Herring, Alken and Hall. The two Newmarket Guineas races had been inaugurated in 1809 and 1814, but the idea of grouping them with the three older races to form the five classics for three year olds was not adopted until the late-1800's, after Tattersall had written his book. I thought it was perhaps time for a book about all five of the great races, and so *Classic Winners* was born.

Tim Cox not only made his library available for my use whenever needed but also took on the task of driving to the office of retired jockey Brian Rouse, to collect photographs of Quick As Lightning which Brian had kindly offered to lend me when my photo archives and those of all other photographers I contacted had failed.

Fellow photographers took the time to search their libraries for images I wanted and I would especially like to thank Ed Byrne, Laurie Morton and Peter Mooney for their help and willingness to make their images available.

I would also like to express my appreciation to Miles Bailey of The Choir Press in Gloucester for all the time and advice freely given to a first-time author and self-publisher; to Alexandra Sore of Alex Publicity, also in Gloucester, for doing such a great job of marketing for Classic Winners, and to Ross East, who designed and created the website for Miralgo Publishing.

My special friend Sharelle Wodehouse has been a constant source of encouragement and my daughter Kimberley designed the template for the pedigree pages which had proved well beyond my expertise with Word.

Thank you to all the trainers who have allowed me into their stables over the past thirty-five years to photograph their horses and to the lads and lasses who presented them so beautifully and stood them up with skill and patience and, in a few cases courage; Moonax springs immediately to mind in the latter category. This book would have been considerably the poorer without the posed conformation portraits of the classic winners sitting beside the pedigrees.

Last but not least, my thanks to Tony Morris for writing the foreword during a period when he has been feeling rather less than 100% fighting fit.

John Crofts
Gloucester 24 September 2015

Foreword

I was not yet twelve years old when I caught the racing bug. Needing some reading matter for a long train journey, I was hoping to find something cheap about soccer or cricket, my current sporting passions, on Exeter's Central Station bookstall, but no such luck. What made me invest my spare shilling on the 1956 News Chronicle Racing Annual, I shall never know. What I do know is that my life would never be the same again.

I had never been to a race meeting, had rarely even seen racing on television and if I had been asked to name all the people I knew to be involved in the sport, I would have got no further than Gordon Richards and Lester Piggott. Things had changed by the end of that train journey.

What particularly fascinated me as I leafed through that little book was the realisation that racing had such a long history. On page 26 I learnt that the Derby was first staged in 1780 – that was more than a century before the Football League was founded. There had to be more to this sport than I could ever have imagined if it had lasted so long and captured the imagination of so many generations.

My pocket money was soon being spent on other racing books, and it was the history of the sport that was my main focus. I was never going to remember the six wives of Henry VIII, but I could memorise the names of all the Derby winners from the time of George III down to that of Elizabeth II. The fact that records of all the Classic races had been kept for so long indicated that they mattered, and it followed that the current year's renewals would go down in history too.

In brief, the five Classics, re-enacted every year, represented living history, and I resolved that someday, somehow, I would contrive to be present when these additions to history took place. I had no idea then how I would earn my living, but I wanted it to be in a job which allowed me to be at the races on those five important occasions every year. I got lucky.

I am not the only one who developed and preserved an obsession about England's Classic races and though I routinely encountered my long-term friend John Crofts on significant days at Newmarket, Epsom and Doncaster, I was used to meeting him on other courses as well and I knew nothing of his plans to produce this book until he had almost completed it.

It is now my pleasure to congratulate him on an outstanding contribution to Turf literature and to thank him for reviving my memories of so many moments of living history that I have witnessed. I suspect that this work will inspire others to acquire the obsession that both John and I have maintained over many years.

Tony Morris,
Newmarket.
April 2015.

Introduction

There is little doubt in my mind that the all-consuming passion I developed in horse racing at the age of twelve, through watching the sport on BBC and ITV television during the winter of 1961/62 seriously compromised my performance at school. From being one of the top three students of my year, I slipped down the rankings at an alarming rate until I was probably rather fortunate to obtain the four GCE o-levels that I did pass. Watching re-runs of those old races on the internet now, I wonder how it generated such interest as it was virtually impossible to pick out individual horses in a large field. Perhaps that is why flashy chesnuts such as Frenchman's Cove and Miralgo became such early equine heroes of mine? They were rather easier to pick out on the fuzzy black and white screen. Ultimately the four o-levels proved superfluous to requirement as soon after leaving school I was working in racing myself, starting off with a small permit holder near Ludlow. From there I moved on to Peter Walwyn at Seven Barrows, Lambourn during the heady years for the stable 1974-78. There I had the good fortune to look after Orange Bay and came heart breakingly close to beating 1977 Derby winner The Minstrel in the King George VI and Queen Elizabeth Stakes at Ascot that year. I also had charge of Buckskin, winning the Prix du Cadran on a memorable May day at Longchamp in 1978 before Daniel Wildenstein removed all his horses to Henry Cecil at Newmarket. I followed Buckskin to Warren Place in 1979 and stayed until a neck injury necessitated a change of direction within the sport and my school-boy interest in photographs of racehorses became my profession in late-October 1981.

Readers of *Classic Winners* will discover that in the interest of continuity where possible race sponsor's names have been omitted. I have never really considered that companies which have nothing at all to do with horse racing gain much from race sponsorship. The television audience is minute compared to football, cricket or even darts. How many amongst the thousands gathered at Newmarket for the Qipco sponsored Guineas classics know, or even care, what services that company offers its clients? Die-hard racing traditionalists hate it when race names are altered to accommodate the latest new sponsor and possibly companies would achieve far greater exposure were they to donate the money to deserving charities instead. Some companies which do have strong racing connections announce how much they love British racing, yet rename long-established races they sponsor, often encouraged to do so by the individual racecourses, until the race name is completely unrecognisable from the original. Are we really so anxious to relieve sponsors of their money that we are willing to sell the tradition and heritage of our racing? It should not be permitted to completely change the names of Pattern Races (e.g. the Fred Darling and John Porter Stakes) or Heritage Handicaps, as happened in 2014 when Goodwood allowed a bookmaking company to drop the name of the Stewards' Cup, inaugurated in 1840, which was an extremely unpopular decision and probably did more harm than good for the sponsor. It is becoming ever more obvious that the B.H.A. is not the best custodian of racing as they are not looking after its heritage. So many racing people celebrated when The Jockey Club relinquished its overall responsibility for our sport. Am I the only one looking back on that time and now regarding it as a 'golden age'? Their lordships certainly did a better job than the B.H.A. which should be concentrating on finding a way of funding racing that does not involve bowing to the wishes of bookmakers. Instead they have the pie-in-the-sky target of adding 1000 extra horses in training by 2020 with the object of increasing the field sizes of their bloated race programme. All the horses fast enough to make it a worthwhile expense are already in training, so how will it benefit racing to have another 1000 horses that are too slow to pay their way? Their owners will soon tire of seeing their money slide down the drain and quit racing forever. Also, where will the 350 extra stable staff needed to look after these 1000 horses come from? Many racing yards are already under staffed and struggling to fill the vacancies. A simpler solution would be to reduce the number of races by restricting all programmes to six races, an earlier idea that seems to have been ignored by most racecourses and quietly swept under the carpet by the B.H.A.

The ill-considered and unnecessary changes to the autumn racing programme made by the B.H.A. in 2011, largely to accommodate the Qipco Challenge Series, are discussed on the pages covering Love Divine and Dancing Rain. These changes included re-scheduling many Group Races for two-year-olds not included in the Qipco Challenge. The inexplicable 2011 decision to run the six furlong Middle Park Stakes on the same day as the seven furlong Dewhurst Stakes making up a so-called 'Future Champions Day' was reversed amidst a fanfare of B.H.A. trumpets during January 2015. The B.H.A statement that they were engaged in 'an ongoing review of the autumn racing programme' (which) 'could be improved further in the years to come...with further initiatives possible', was probably received with incredulity by many racing professionals. Apparently the B.H.A. believes it is taking the initiative and improving the autumn programme for two-year-olds by returning some races to their former slots in the calendar before they interfered. One can only hope that part of this B.H.A. 'ongoing review' will be to return the Champion Stakes to its rightful home and drop the infantile race names adopted for Champions Day at Ascot, restoring the historic Jockey Club Cup, Diadem and Princess Royal Stakes. Figures released during September 2015 revealed that former B.H.A. chief executive Paul Bittar was paid a staggering £443,000 in 2014. Working on a *pro rata* basis, that probably explains why the B.H.A. are so keen to tamper with a race programme put in place many years ago by men who knew what they were doing; they have to justify their inflated salaries somehow.

Betting has always been a large part of racing's attraction to many of the people involved, not just the general public. But the extent to which bookmakers are now allowed to dictate matters within racing, even to the extent of deciding in which order the races should be run on a particular day to maximise their profits and make it more difficult for losing punters to recover their losses should be, but apparently is not, a concern for racing's governing body, the B.H.A. Racing should not be perceived by the general public as walking hand in hand with bookmakers, who have traditionally been regarded as 'the old enemy' and that state of war should be re-declared as soon as possible. The contribution to racing by bookmakers is currently calculated on their profits and this is basically wrong as it places racecourse management in the position of pandering to the wishes of bookmakers in almost everything they do.

The B.H.A. has become a bookmaker's puppet. Virtually every decision they make is designed to boost bookmaker's profits and thus their contribution to racing. This even extends to their rules relating to interference (see Sky Lantern, pages 352-3 and Leading Light, pages 358-9). The B.H.A.'s recent efforts to eliminate small fields, even going to the extreme of declaring a race void which has failed to attract what is deemed an acceptable number of runners, is totally bookmaker driven. A B.H.A. spokesman's pathetic attempt to justify this as for the good of racing should have fooled nobody. Punters are much more likely to back the winner in a race of few runners, bookmakers have to pay out, their profits are down and so is their contribution to racing. The new chief executive of the B.H.A. who took charge in January 2015, is an ex-employee of one of the biggest bookmakers, so the situation is unlikely to improve, indeed it will probably get worse. The off-course bookmaking companies would like nothing better than to stop contributing to horse racing and will not hesitate to do so, if and when the time is right. According to figures released during 2013, British bookmakers already make the lowest contribution to the sport that generates a large proportion of their profits of any country in Europe.

The Commonwealth Cup, the new six furlongs sprint for three-year-olds only, introduced at Royal Ascot in 2015, is a great idea. But why is it not run on the opening day so the possibility exists for runners from that race to contest the Diamond Jubilee Stakes on Saturday? Instead the Commonwealth Cup was run on Friday and the Diamond Jubilee closed to three-year-olds when it could have been billed as the sprint championship of the meeting.

When reference is made in *Classic Winners* to the champion jockey in Britain of a particular year it has been assumed that the jockey riding the most winners in the calendar year is champion, not the ludicrous official 'championship' which now treats winners ridden for half of each year as irrelevant.

The future of the St Leger is discussed in the pages covering Bob's Return (p140) and Camelot (p340), but despite dedicating virtually the whole of the former's essay to this subject, space restrictions limited what I was able to say. The oldest classic has become the victim of a fashion change amongst owners, trainers and breeders which can be traced back to the inauguration of the King George VI and Queen Elizabeth Stakes in 1951 and the Prix de l'Arc de Triomphe becoming a truly international race at around the same time. Formerly the only worthwhile prize for staying four-year-olds and upwards in England had been the Gold Cup at Royal Ascot and the previous year's St Leger formed part of the build-up for Gold Cup prospects amongst the classic crop as well as being a classic race that owners and trainers desperately wanted to win.

The Prix de l'Arc de Triomphe had always attracted the best French-trained horses, but in the 1950's became a target for top horses trained in England and other European countries. The 1951 running featured the St Leger runner-up Fraise Du Bois, despite his name trained in England, and two years later Premonition and Zucchero, winners respectively of the 1953 St Leger and Coronation Cup. The King George VI and Queen Elizabeth Stakes was an immediate success. The first three runnings were contested by most of the best middle-distance horses trained in Europe including the Arc winners Tantieme and Nuccio, Derby winners in Arctic Prince, Tulyar and Pinza and English classic winners

Scratch II, Belle of All, Ki Ming and Nearula. From 1951 onwards the Ascot Gold Cup was no longer the only option for the top middle-distance/staying horses kept in training after their classic year. The big prize money was now to be won in races run over twelve furlongs and with increased purses for the long-established Eclipse and Champion Stakes over ten and the Coronation Cup over twelve furlongs, suddenly few people wanted to breed or buy long-distance horses anymore.

Since Blakeney was beaten in the 1970 Gold Cup no other Derby winner has gone on to contest the Royal Ascot race. The only placed horses to do so were Derby fourths Hawkberry and Percussionist, the latter having been gelded for a hurdling career, and Fame And Glory, runner-up in Sea The Stars' Derby. Evidently Coolmore had by then given up any idea of marketing Fame And Glory as a potential sire of top flat racers and decided to stand him as what is euphemistically termed a "dual purpose" stallion, but is for all intents and purposes a sire of National Hunt horses. No other owners of horses placed in the first four in a Derby have wished to risk the value of their potential stallion by demonstrating that the horse stayed two miles, let alone two and a half. With the focus now on breeding horses with middle-distance speed, winners of the Ascot Gold Cup were no longer wanted by the best stallion studs. St Leger winners soon became tarred with the same brush as too slow to sire top ten to twelve furlong winners but it was not until the end of the 1960's that connections of the best classic colts fell out of love with the St Leger and virtually stopped running them in the race. In the thirty years 1940 to 1969, fourteen winners and forty-six horses which had been placed second, third or fourth in the Derby went on to run in the St Leger. During the next forty-five years from 1970 to 2014 only three Derby winners and twenty-eight placed horses have contested the final classic. The decline of the St Leger all started with the defeat of the 1970 winner Nijinsky in his next race, the Prix de l'Arc de Triomphe, which was widely blamed on his running in the St Leger beforehand. After Nijinsky, no Derby winner ran in the Doncaster classic until Reference Point was successful in 1987 and, as luck would have it, he was subsequently beaten in the Prix de l'Arc de Triomphe too.

The Prix Niel was inaugurated as a Group 3 race in 1972, upgraded to Group 2 in 1987 and has come to be regarded as a trial for three-year-old colts for the Prix de l'Arc de Triomphe. In most years it has been run at Longchamp on the day after the St Leger, originally over eleven furlongs, now over twelve. There are usually few runners in the Prix Niel but invariably these include top-class horses that in the years prior to 1970 would have contested the St Leger. Roberto ran in the very first Prix Niel and since then five more Derby winners have run in the French race and all except Sinndar were beaten. In the same period only two Derby winners have contested the St Leger.

It is time, way past time actually, that we stopped being stubborn about the distance over which the St Leger is run if the classic is to return to its former importance in the racing calendar. More Derby winners and placed horses would contest the St Leger if it was not such a gruelling contest run over a distance that is no longer attractive to the connections of top-class colts and, perhaps more importantly, to the owners of the stallion studs interested in standing them at the end of their racing careers. Who knows if Mill Reef, Troy and Generous might have run in a twelve furlong St Leger? Perhaps Ian Balding, Willie Carson and Paul Cole will tell me one day? Almost certainly Nashwan, Kahyasi, Sinndar, Kris Kin and Ruler of the World, which all ran the next day in the Prix Niel, would have done so.

John Hislop, writing in his 1973 book 'The Brigadier', lamented that 'One of the tragedies of modern racing and breeding is that, because of commercialism, the desire to conceal a (race) horse's possible weaknesses is far more evident than the wish to prove his qualities. Thus … horses are rushed off to stud before they have been tested against those of other generations, over varying distances and as four-year-olds'. Mr Hislop was wrong only in saying this was a 'modern' tragedy; it had actually been going on for decades, but the unrealistic surge in the value of bloodstock of the 1980's brought the early retirement trend to a new high, or low, depending upon your viewpoint. The reader will discover plenty of horses within these pages which could be auditioned for Mr Hislop's 'tragedy'.

This book was intended as a pictorial review of the English classics from 1980 to 2015, the horses and the men and women who bred, owned, trained and rode them to immortality, but gradually evolved into a critique of some of the changes that have happened in racing over that period. I make no apologies for that, or for any of the opinions expressed which are entirely my own. In closing, readers should note that the 2014 English classic winner Miss France and all those of 2015 were still in training when this book closed and their racing records may not be complete. Also remarks made about these horses in their essays may no longer be relevant.

QUICK AS LIGHTNING (USA)

Bay filly, foaled 17 March 1977
By Buckpasser (USA) out of Clear Ceiling (USA) by Bold Ruler (USA)
Owned and bred by Ogden Mills Phipps
Trained by John L. Dunlop at Castle Stables, Arundel, Sussex.

2709179

Racing Record

Year	Timeform Annual Rating	Starts	Wins	2nd	3rd	4th	U.K. Prize Money
1979	115	3	2	-	1	-	£ 15,617
1980	123	7	1	2	2	1	£ 64,605
1981	-	1	-	-	-	1	-

Principal Performances

1979 Won Fillies' Mile (G3) (2yo fillies) Ascot (8f)
1980 Won 1000 Guineas Stakes (G1) (3yo fillies) Newmarket (8f)
       4th Oaks Stakes (G1) (3yo fillies) Epsom (12f)
       2nd Coronation Stakes (G2) (3yo fillies) Royal Ascot (8f)

*****

Quick As Lightning was only an average winner of the 1000 Guineas and failed to win again after her classic victory. She disappointed when twice tried over twelve furlongs but confirmed her class over one mile when finishing a close second in the Coronation Stakes. In the autumn of 1980, Quick As Lightning was sent to America to be trained by Angel Penna. She raced there three times, finishing second and third before filling fourth place in her final start during January 1981 at Gulfstream Park in Florida. Quick As Lightning died in the U.S.A. later in 1981. Her sire Buckpasser, a champion at both two and three-years-old and U.S. Horse of the Year in 1966, died in 1978. Quick As Lightning was a half-sister to Stratospheric (1979, by Majestic Light – G3 Waterford Candelabra S, 2nd G3 Fillies Mile) and grand-daughter of the outstanding American broodmare Grey Flight, dam of nine stakes winners including U.S. champion sire What A Pleasure (1965, by Bold Ruler) and Misty Morn (1952, by

Princequillo), herself dam of two U.S. champion two-year-old colts, the brothers Bold Lad (1962, by Bold Ruler) and Successor (1964). This is also the family of Intrepid Hero (1972, by Forli - G1 Hollywood Derby).

Above: **QUICK AS LIGHTNING** (Brian Rouse) wins the 1000 Guineas beating Our Home (no.14), Mrs Penny (hidden on rail) and Millingdale Lillie (spotted cap).

0613389   1715884

Above left: **OGDEN MILLS PHIPPS** was a leading owner and breeder in the U.S. for over fifty years until his death at the age of 93 in April 2002. He owned champions Buckpasser, Personal Ensign and Easy Goer as well as English classic winners Boucher (St Leger, 1972) and Quick As Lightning. Above centre: **BRIAN ROUSE** rode his only English classic winner on Quick As Lightning. The dependable Rouse was often a jockey trainers turned to in time of trouble and John Dunlop had reportedly approached four other jockeys before asking Brian to ride Quick As Lightning. Above right: **JOHN DUNLOP** took over Castle Stables at Arundel from Gordon Smyth and trained his first winner in 1966. He went on to send out over 3000 winners in Britain before his retirement in 2012, including ten English classic winners; Quick As Lightning, Salsabil (p99) and Shadayid (p109) in the 1000 Guineas; Shirley Heights (1978) and Erhaab (p145)(Derby); Circus Plume (p49) and Salsabil (Oaks); Moon Madness (p67), Silver Patriarch (p183) and Millenary (p217) (St Leger). Dunlop also trained many more Group 1 winners and champions such as Ragstone (Ascot Gold Cup), Habibti (July Cup, Nunthorpe S), Posse (Sussex S), Bahri and Lahib (Queen Elizabeth II S), Scottish Rifle (Eclipse S), Leggera (Prix Vermeille), Black Satin and Mehthaaf (both Irish 1000 Guineas), Wassl (Irish 2000 Guineas), Elnadim (July Cup) and Golden Snake (Prix Ganay).

KNOWN FACT (USA)

Black colt, foaled 15 March 1977
By In Reality (USA) out of Tamerett (USA) by Tim Tam (USA)
Bred by Dr. William O. Reed
Owned by Khalid Abdullah
Trained by Jeremy Tree at Beckhampton, Wiltshire.

1611979

Racing Record

Year	Timeform Annual Rating	Starts	Wins	2nd	3rd	4th	Prize Money
1979	122	4	2	1	1	-	£ 36,585
1980	135	6	4	-	-	1	£ 97,310
1981	-	1	-	-	-	1	£ 769

Principal Performances

1979   3rd Mill Reef Stakes (G2) (2yo) Newbury (6f)
      Won Middle Park Stakes (G1) (2yo colts & fillies) Newmarket (6f)
1980   Won 2000 Guineas Stakes (G1) (3yo colts & fillies) Newmarket (8f)
      Won Waterford Crystal Mile (G2) Goodwood (8f)
      Won Queen Elizabeth II Stakes (G2) Ascot (8f)

*****

*K*nown Fact was purchased for Khalid Abdullah at Keeneland by Humphrey Cottrill for $225,000 and once he learned to settle, became a very high class horse. Though he owed his classic victory to the ill-judged ride of Philippe Paquet on Nureyev, Known Fact went on to prove himself a very good 2000 Guineas winner. His dam Tamerett bred other top-class winners including Tentam (1969, by Intentionally) and Secrettame (1978, by Secretariat), the dam of Gone West (1984, by Mr Prospector - G1 Dwyer S), a successful stallion in the U.S. Known Fact was originally retired to his owner's stud at Wargrave-on-Thames in Berkshire but after three seasons transferred to Whitsbury Manor Stud and

6

then to Juddmonte Farm in Kentucky. Known Fact sired three Group 1 winners in Britain, Warning (Queen Elizabeth II & Sussex S), Markofdistinction (Queen Elizabeth II S) and So Factual (Nunthorpe S). Known Fact is also the sire of Oath (G1 Spinaway S), Bold Fact (G2 July S), Teamster (G3 Sagaro S twice, G3 Henry II S) and maternal grandsire of 2000 Guineas winner Cockney Rebel (p283). Known Fact was euthanized at Juddmonte Farm on 12 July 2000 due to the infirmities of old age.

2711680

Above: French-trained favourite Nureyev (P. Paquet) is first past the post but disqualified and placed last for bumping Posse (USA) (red sleeves). The 2000 Guineas was thus awarded to Willie Carson on **KNOWN FACT** (rail) who had suffered no interference. This was a second victory in the Newmarket race for Carson, who had previously won on High Top in 1972, and the first of many English classic winners for Saudi prince, Khalid Abdullah. Philippe Paquet never did ride an English classic winner and was forced to retire from race-riding after fracturing his skull in a terrible accident on the training track in Hong Kong on 13 February 1984. The horse Paquet was riding, named Silver Star, was involved in a similar accident on 8 December of the same year which resulted in the death of English jockey Brian Taylor, who had won the Derby on Snow Knight in 1974.

2114486

1011680

0917780

Above left: Known Fact was the last English classic winner for **JEREMY TREE** in a long career at Beckhampton Stables in Wiltshire. He also trained Only For Life (2000 Guineas 1963) and the Oaks winners Juliette Marny (1975) and Scintillate (1979). Other big-race victories for Tree included Sharpo (G1 July Cup, G1 Prix de l'Abbaye, G1 Nunthorpe S three times), Rainbow Quest (see p197), champion two-year-old Double Jump (National S, Prix Robert Papin, Gimcrack S), Quiet Fling (G1 Coronation Cup), Swing Easy (King's Stand S, Nunthorpe S) and John Cherry (Chester Cup, Cesarewitch S). Jeremy Tree retired in 1989 and died on 7 March 1993.

Above centre: The drama is yet to unfold as **PHILIPPE PAQUET** on **NUREYEV** lead Posse and Pat Eddery during the parade before the 2000 Guineas. It was the first and only time in the 172 year history of this classic that a winner had been disqualified. Above right: **KNOWN FACT**'s greatest victory as he and Willie Carson beat the previous season's champion miler Kris and Joe Mercer in the Queen Elizabeth II Stakes at Ascot.

HENBIT (USA)

Bay colt, foaled 28 March 1977
By Hawaii (SAF) out of Chateaucreek (USA) by Chateaugay (USA)
Bred by Helen Drake Jones
Owned by Mrs Arpad Plesch
Trained by Major W.R. Hern at West Ilsley, Berkshire.

0013979

Racing Record

Year	Timeform Annual Rating	Starts	Wins	2nd	3rd	4th	Prize Money
1979	118	3	1	-	-	2	£ 6,107
1980	130	3	3	-	-	-	£ 186,198
1981	-	2	-	-	-	-	-

Principal Performances

1979 4th Dewhurst Stakes (G1) (2yo colts & fillies) Newmarket (7f)
1980 Won Classic Trial Stakes (G3) (3yo colts & geldings) Sandown (10f)
       Won Chester Vase (G3) (3yo) Chester (12.3f)
       Won Derby Stakes (G1) (3yo colts & fillies) Epsom (12f)

*****

A bargain $24,000 yearling purchase by George Blackwell at Keeneland, Henbit was essentially a one-paced stayer and made all the running for three of his four victories. The exception was the Derby where Henbit led with over a furlong to run and despite fracturing his off-fore cannon bone inside the final furlong, courageously held the sustained challenge of Master Willie. Brought back to the racecourse as a four-year-old, Henbit was unable to recapture his best form. His sire, Hawaii (1964, by Utrillo) was top-class over middle-distances in both South Africa and the U.S. where he was Champion Grass Horse in 1969. Chateaucreek won six races including a minor stakes, but was eventually claimed for $25,000 at Hialeah and retired after fracturing a sesamoid. Apart from Henbit, she was also dam of the minor winners Turk-O-Witz (1979, by Stop The Music) and Chateau Princess (1981, by Majestic

Prince). Her dam Mooncreek was unraced and in 1976 sold for $18,000 and exported to Venezuela. Henbit was retired to stand at Airlie Stud at Lucan in County Dublin but sired few flat race winners of any note, the best being Borromini (G2 Grand Prix de Deauville) and La Vie En Primrose (LR Pretty Polly S). Moved to Helshaw Grange Stud at Market Drayton in Shropshire, the stallion did a little better as a sire of jumpers, getting the Triumph and Champion Hurdle winner Kribensis and Sybillin, a very smart steeplechaser. Henbit died in 1997.

© Ed Byrne

Above: **HENBIT** (Willie Carson) winning the Derby beating Master Willie (left) and Rankin (green cap). It was the jockey's second successive victory in the Epsom classic. Troy's seven length romp the previous year had given him his first Derby winner after having been beaten in a photo finish by The Minstrel and Lester Piggott when riding Hot Grove in 1977.

2811180   1635182   3734089

Above left: **HENBIT** strikes a pose after winning the Classic Trial Stakes at Sandown Park. Above centre: Legendary trainer **DICK HERN**; Henbit was his second Derby winner following Troy in 1979. Above right: This was also a second Derby victory for owner **MRS ARPAD PLESCH**. Her 1961 winner Psidium, trained by Harry Wragg and ridden by Roger Poincelet, started at 66/1 and was a long way behind the leaders, with only three horses behind him rounding Tattenham Corner four furlongs from home, before staging a dramatic stretch run. Etti Plesch also owned Sassafras, winner of the Prix du Jockey-Club, Prix Royal-Oak and the Prix de l'Arc de Triomphe. In the latter race the colt became the first horse to defeat the English Triple Crown winner, Nijinsky.

BIREME (GB)

Chesnut filly, foaled 2 May 1977
By Grundy (GB) out of Ripeck (GB) by Ribot (GB)
Owned and bred by Richard D. Hollingsworth
Trained by Major W.R. Hern at West Ilsley, Berkshire.

© Ed Byrne

Racing Record

Year	Timeform Annual Rating	Starts	Wins	2nd	3rd	4th	Prize Money
1979	103	2	1	-	1	-	£ 4,974
1980	127	2	2	-	-	-	£ 84,056

Principal Performances

1980   Won Musidora Stakes (G3) (3yo fillies) York (10.5f)
       Won Oaks Stakes (G1) (3yo fillies) Epsom (12f)

*****

*T*he promising racing career of Bireme was sadly cut short when she got loose on the road shortly after winning the Oaks, sustaining injuries that necessitated retirement to her owner's Arches Hall Stud in Hertfordshire. She was the only English classic winner sired by the 1975 Derby winner Grundy in a disappointing stay at The National Stud in Newmarket before his export to Japan. Like her sire, Bireme was a beautiful mover, well suited to racing on fast ground and won her classic in a new record time for the Oaks previously held by the 1927 winner, Beam. Bireme produced several winners before her death on 10 January 2002; the best was Yawl (1990, by Rainbow Quest) winner of the Oh So Sharp and Rockfel Stakes. Bireme's other winning progeny included Trireme (1987, by Rainbow Quest), Quadrireme (1989, by Rousillon), Admiral Rous (1991, by Rousillon), Yacht (1992, by Warning) and Flagship (1994, by Rainbow Quest). Through Yawl, Bireme is the great grandam of the 2013 Oaks winner Talent and there are more details about this family on pages 354-5.

© Ed Byrne

Above: **BIREME** (Willie Carson) winning the Oaks Stakes beating Vielle (left) and The Dancer (hood) with 1000 Guineas winner Quick As Lightning (see p4) fourth. It was the first time since 1957, when Noel Murless won the Derby with Crepello and the Oaks with Carrozza, that one stable had sent out the winners of both Epsom classics in the same year.

0516194

1613789

0900475

Left: **WILLIE CARSON** was born at Stirling in 1942 and apprenticed to Gerald Armstrong at Tupgill in Yorkshire. He rode his first winner on 19 July 1962 and went on to a total of 3,828 winners in Britain. Carson was champion jockey five times between 1972 and 1983 and rode the winners of seventeen English classics; High Top (1972), Known Fact (p6), Don't Forget Me (p76) and Nashwan (p96) in the 2000 Guineas; Salsabil (p102) and Shadayid (p112)(1000 Guineas); Troy (1979), Henbit (p8), Nashwan and Erhaab (p148)(Derby); Dunfermline (1977), Bireme, Sun Princess (p44) and Salsabil (Oaks); Dunfermline, Sun Princess and Minster Son, which he also bred, (p90)(St Leger). Carson was made OBE in 1983 and retired in 1996 becoming a popular BBC television pundit.

Centre: **DICK HOLLINGSWORTH** was a successful owner and breeder whose horses were initially trained at Newmarket by George Colling and then by John Oxley. He experienced his best years when his horses were transferred to Major Hern at West Ilsley following Oxley's retirement. Bireme was his only classic winner but he also owned and bred many other high-class horses such as Buoy (Coronation Cup), Longboat (Ascot Gold Cup), Ark Royal (Yorkshire Oaks) and Hermes (Dante S, Great Voltigeur S, Jockey Club Cup). Dick Hollingsworth died at the age of eighty-two in February 2001. During 2013 Qatar Racing attempted to buy the classic Hollingsworth racing colours but their offer was rejected by Mark Dixon (p355), who had inherited them from his uncle. Qatar Racing's application for colours that were a near copy of Hollingsworth's was approved by the British Horseracing Authority, who justified their decision with the statement that it was 'in the best interests of the sport'. It seems the BHA is not averse to bending their own rules when it suits their purposes to do so.

Right: The Derby winner **GRUNDY** (1972, by Great Nephew); as well as Bireme he also sired Group 1 winners Kirtling and Little Wolf, winner of the Gold Cup at Royal Ascot in 1983. Grundy was exported to Japan in 1983 and died there in 1992.

11

LIGHT CAVALRY (GB)

Bay colt, foaled 7 February 1977
By Brigadier Gerard (GB) out of Glass Slipper (GB) by Relko (FR)
Owned and bred by H. J. Joel
Trained by Henry Cecil at Warren Place, Newmarket, Suffolk.

0517180

Racing Record

Year	Timeform Annual Rating	Starts	Wins	2nd	3rd	4th	Prize Money
1979	95	1	1	-	-	-	£ 2,052
1980	128	6	3	1	2	-	£ 107,925
1981	124	4	1	1	-	-	£ 29,167

Principal Performances

1980 Won King Edward VII Stakes (G2) (3yo colts & geldings) Royal Ascot (12f)
    2nd Great Voltigeur Stakes (G2) (3yo colts) York (12f)
    Won St Leger Stakes (G1) (3yo colts & fillies) Doncaster (14.6f)
1981 2nd Hardwicke Stakes (G2) Royal Ascot (12f)
    Won Princess of Wales's Stakes (G2) Newmarket (12f)

*****

*L*ight Cavalry was bred "in the purple". His sire was one of the very best horses to race in Britain since World War II; only Frankel (see p330) and Sea-Bird (1962, by Dan Cupid), being rated superior by Timeform. Glass Slipper (p15) came from a family notable for its excellence over several generations, developed at the Joel's Childwick Bury Stud near St Albans in Hertfordshire. She was a half-sister to Royal Palace (1964, by Ballymoss), winner of the 2000 Guineas and Derby. Light Cavalry was his dam's second foal; her third was Fairy Footsteps (p14). This is also the family of Picture Play (1941, by Donatello - 1000 Guineas), User Friendly (p130) and West Side Story (1959, by Rockefella – Yorkshire Oaks). As a four-year-old Light Cavalry was kept to races over 12 furlongs, which was a pity as a Cup campaign over two miles plus would have brought out his best qualities of courage and stamina. Light Cavalry was sold for $2.5m to stand at Crescent Farm in Kentucky. An easily*

12

predictable stud failure in America, in 1987 he was sold for export to Argentina and died in December 2004 without having excelled there either.

1317180

Above: The start of the St Leger Stakes; Joe Mercer on **LIGHT CAVALRY** sets out to make all the running and beats Water Mill (Willie Carson, centre) by four lengths. The other horses in shot are, from left to right, Saviour (Pat Eddery), Lancastrian (Freddy Head) and Grandak (Yves Saint-Martin).

1310671

3317180

Above left: One of the few truly great racehorses, **BRIGADIER GERARD** (1968, by Queens Hussar) and Joe Mercer, after beating Pat Eddery on Rarity (left) in the Champion Stakes on a horrible, wet day at Newmarket in October 1971. Light Cavalry was the only English classic winner sired by 'The Brigadier' but he also numbered the Champion Stakes winner Vayrann amongst his progeny.

Above right: **JOE MERCER** celebrates his third St Leger winner with **JIM JOEL** and **HENRY CECIL** (right). For both owner and trainer it was their first victory in the Doncaster classic. Among the smiling onlookers are Lord Manton (left), Jeremy Tree (second left) and Dick Hollingsworth (right).

FAIRY FOOTSTEPS (GB)

Bay filly, foaled 15 January 1978
By Mill Reef (USA) out of Glass Slipper (GB) by Relko (FR)
Owned and bred by Mr H.J. Joel at Childwick Bury Stud, Hertfordshire
Trained by Henry Cecil at Warren Place, Newmarket, Suffolk.

3111081

Racing Record

Year	Timeform Annual Rating	Starts	Wins	2nd	3rd	4th	Prize Money
1980	118	3	1	1	-	1	£ 7,712
1981	123	3	2	-	1	-	£ 66,363

Principal Performances

1980 Won Waterford Candelabra Stakes (Listed Race) (2yo fillies) Goodwood (7f)
1981 Won Nell Gwyn Stakes (G3) (3yo fillies) Newmarket (7f)
      Won 1000 Guineas Stakes (G1) (3yo fillies) Newmarket (8f)
      3rd Musidora Stakes (G2) (3yo fillies) York (10.5f)

*****

*H*ow could a trainer as brilliant as Henry Cecil come to the conclusion that a half-sister to his St Leger winner Light Cavalry (p12), by the Derby winner Mill Reef, did not stay beyond one mile? However, Cecil decided this was the reason for Fairy Footsteps' defeat at York in the Musidora Stakes. This writer worked at Warren Place at the time and to my way of thinking all the filly needed was a rest after a strenuous preparation for the 1000 Guineas, when she often worked with the four-year-old Belmont Bay at disadvantageous weights before the improvement in that colt became obvious with victories in the Newbury Spring Cup, carrying top-weight, and the Lockinge Stakes. Henry Cecil decided to give up and the filly was retired without even being tried again over a mile. She returned to her breeder's stud but produced only minor winners until the Joel bloodstock was dispersed at Tattersalls 1986 December Sales five years before his death on 23 March 1992. Fairy Footsteps did no better for her new owner and ultimately her first foal, Flying Fairy (1983, by Bustino) proved the best. Although she never won herself, Flying Fairy bred Desert Prince (1995, by Green Desert), winner of the Irish 2000 Guineas, Prix du Moulin and the Queen Elizabeth II Stakes.

14

2711481

Above: **FAIRY FOOTSTEPS** (Lester Piggott) wins the 1000 Guineas beating Tolmi (spots), Go Leasing (orange cap) and Marwell (dark blue sleeves). Owner **JIM JOEL** (below left) had won this classic thirty-seven years before with Picture Play (1941, by Donatello). For Piggott it was a second victory following Humble Duty (1967, by Sovereign Path).

1234985

35T0886

Above: The brilliant **MILL REEF** with stallion-man George Roth at The National Stud in Newmarket the year before the stallion's death in 1986. Above right: Only three mares were the dams of two different English classic winners during the years 1980-2015. The first of them was **GLASS SLIPPER**, a half-sister to the 1967 2000 Guineas and Derby winner Royal Palace, photographed at Childwick Bury Stud during 1986.

© George Selwyn

2711581

T110980

Above centre: The incredible **LESTER PIGGOTT**, who only seven days before had been dragged through the stalls in a horrible accident at Epsom and suffered multiple cuts and bruises as well as almost tearing an ear off, cantering Fairy Footsteps to the start before the 1000 Guineas. The jockey wore a pad under his helmet to protect his ear. Above right: Trainer **HENRY CECIL**, for whom Fairy Footsteps was a second 1000 Guineas winner in three years after One In A Million (1976, by Rarity) in 1979.

TO-AGORI-MOU (IRE)

Brown colt, foaled 22 April 1978
By Tudor Music (GB) out of Sarah Van Fleet (GB) by Cracksman (IRE)
Bred by Rathduff Stud, Golden, Co. Tipperary
Owned by Mrs Andry Muinos
Trained by Guy Harwood at Coombelands Stables, Pulborough, Sussex.

3410781

Racing Record

Year	Timeform Annual Rating	Starts	Wins	2nd	3rd	4th	U.K. Prize Money
1980	133	5	3	2	-	-	£ 28,624
1981	133	9	4	4	-	-	£ 150,278
1982	-	4	-	-	1	-	-

Principal Performances

1980   Won Solario Stakes (Listed Race) (2yo) Sandown Park (7f)
      2nd Dewhurst Stakes (G1) (2yo colts & fillies) Newmarket (7f)
1981   Won 2000 Guineas Stakes (G1) (3yo colts & fillies) Newmarket (8f)
      2nd Irish 2000 Guineas Stakes (G1) (3yo colts & fillies) Curragh (8f)
      Won St James's Palace Stakes (G2) (3yo colts) Royal Ascot (8f)
      2nd Sussex Stakes (G1) (3yo & upwards) Goodwood (8f)
      2nd Prix Jacques Le Marois (G1) (3yo & upwards) Deauville (8f)
      Won Waterford Crystal Mile (G2) (3yo & upwards) Goodwood (8f)
      Won Queen Elizabeth II Stakes (G2) (3yo & upwards) Ascot (8f)

*****

*T*o-Agori-Mou was bought cheaply by his trainer for 20,000 guineas as a yearling and was exceptionally good looking and most genuine and consistent. Top-class at both two and three-years-old and a very good winner of the 2000 Guineas, the colt held his form well throughout a busy classic season. In 1982, To-Agori-Mou was sent to race in the U.S.A. where he was trained by John Russell. He failed to win in four attempts, his best placing being third in the Laurence Armour

Handicap at Arlington and was retired after finishing unplaced at Hollywood Park in July. To-Agori-Mou attracted little interest at stud in the U.S., his classical good looks counting for little against his unfashionable pedigree; his dam was a winning hurdler by a staying handicapper. However, Sarah Van Fleet also bred the very useful sprinter Van Laser (1974, by Laser Light) and her third dam Sister Sarah (1930, by Abbots Trace) was a great grand-daughter of triple classic winner and highly influential broodmare Pretty Polly (1901, by Gallinule). Sister Sarah was the dam of Lady Sybil (1940, by Nearco – Cheveley Park S), Black Peter (1942, by Blue Peter – Jockey Club S), Welsh Abbot (1955, by Abernant – Challenge S) and Lady Angela (1944, by Hyperion), the dam of Canadian champion Nearctic (1954, by Nearco), sire of the phenomenally successful stallion Northern Dancer (1961 – Kentucky Derby, Preakness S). To-Agori-Mou was sold for only $2,000 in 1989 and the following year was sold on again for a paltry $300. One hates to speculate upon the ultimate fate of poor To-Agori-Mou. A classic tale of from rags to riches and back to rags!

1511981

Above: **TO-AGORI-MOU** (Greville Starkey) leads near the post to win the 2000 Guineas beating Mattaboy (yellow cap) and Bel Bolide (pink cap).

2513181

1911981

Above left: The duels between **TO-AGORI-MOU** and Kings Lake (1978, by Nijinsky) were one of the highlights of the 1981 flat racing season. There was a never more than a neck between them in four consecutive races. At the Curragh, Kings Lake won, was disqualified and reinstated on appeal. Then on to Royal Ascot, where To-Agori-Mou beat Kings Lake and Pat Eddery in the St James's Palace Stakes (above left). In the Sussex Stakes at Goodwood, Kings Lake got his revenge only to finish behind To-Agori-Mou again when they were both beaten at Deauville.

Above right: **GREVILLE STARKEY** and **GUY HARWOOD** with To-Agori-Mou after the 2000 Guineas. This was a first English classic victory for Harwood and a first in this race for the jockey. Starkey rode 1,989 winners in a long career including five English classic winners; Homeward Bound (1964) and Fair Salinia (1978) in the Oaks; Shirley Heights (1978 Derby); To-Agori-Mou and Dancing Brave (see p66) in the 2000 Guineas. He was champion apprentice in 1957 and retired from race-riding in 1989. Greville Starkey died on 14 April 2010, aged 70.

SHERGAR (IRE)

Bay colt, foaled 3 March 1978
By Great Nephew (GB) out of Sharmeen (FR) by Val De Loir (FR)
Owned and bred by H.H. Aga Khan
Trained by Michael R. Stoute at Beech Hurst, Newmarket, Suffolk.

3110481

Racing Record

Year	Timeform Annual Rating	Starts	Wins	2nd	3rd	4th	Prize Money
1980	122	2	1	1	-	-	£ 17,456
1981	140	6	5	-	-	1	£ 392,486

Principal Performances

1980   2nd Futurity Stakes (G1) (2yo colts & fillies) Doncaster (8f)
1981   Won Classic Trial Stakes (G3) (3yo colts & geldings) Sandown (10f)
      Won Chester Vase (G3) (3yo) Chester (12.3f)
      Won Derby Stakes (G1) (3yo colts & fillies) Epsom (12f)
      Won Irish Derby Stakes (G1) (3yo colts & fillies) The Curragh (12f)
      Won King George VI and Queen Elizabeth Stakes (G1) Ascot (12f)
      4th St Leger Stakes (G1) (3yo colts & fillies) Doncaster (14.6f)

*****

*S*hergar is regarded as one of the best middle-distance horses ever to race in Britain, but was he really as good as his wide margin victories made him appear? An old friend, long gone and much missed, used to say 'all horses run fast past trees', so perhaps it is worth examining the merit of the horses beaten by Shergar. He won the Derby by ten lengths from a field consisting of predominately non-stayers and handicappers. None of the horses that finished third, fourth or fifth ever won over the Derby trip or a Group 1 race over any distance. Runner-up Glint of Gold was twice hampered early in

18

the race and got so far behind that when he moved into second place his rider had not been close enough to see Shergar go clear and believed he was winning. Kalaglow, the only other top-class horse in the field, was injured during the race and unable to give his true running. At the Curragh, Shergar beat Cut Above, a one-paced stayer, comfortably by four lengths with no other horse of classic class in the field. Madam Gay finished second to Shergar at Ascot, a filly beaten seven lengths when second in the Oaks at Epsom and won only one race in ten attempts during 1981. The third placed horse, Fingal's Cave, said by Timeform to have 'surpassed himself', had no pretensions to being top-class and failed to win a race in varied company during the year. The Eclipse Stakes winner, Master Willie, pulled too hard owing to the slow early pace and ran below form. Light Cavalry (see p12) broke down and never ran again. I have no idea how good Shergar really was but seriously doubt he was as brilliant as many observers believe him to be. It was a shame that he was retired after the St Leger, when said by connections to be still in top form, as it would have been very informative to see him run in the Prix de l'Arc de Triomphe or Champion Stakes and also how he might have fared against Glint of Gold and a resurgent Kalaglow in 1982. Shergar descends from a family developed by the Aga Khan's grandfather from champion sprinter Mumtaz Mahal (1921, by The Tetrarch – Nunthorpe S), the seventh dam of the Derby winner. Other members of this distinguished family include his half-brother Shernazar (1981, by Busted – G2 Geoffrey Freer S, G3 September S), Mahmoud (1933, by Blenheim – Derby S), Nasrullah (1940, by Nearco – Champion S) and Abernant (1946, by Owen Tudor – Middle Park S, July Cup and Nunthorpe S twice). Shergar was stolen from Ballymany Stud on The Curragh in County Kildare on 8 February 1983 and was never recovered from his kidnappers. He left behind just one crop of foals, the best of which were Authaal (G1 Irish St Leger), Maysoon (G3 Fred Darling S, 2nd G1 1000 Guineas, 3rd G1 Oaks) and Tashtiya (G3 Princess Royal S).

© Ed Byrne   2515581

Above left: **SHERGAR** wins the Derby by ten lengths, the greatest margin of victory ever recorded in this classic. Glint of Gold (noseband) finishes second ahead of Scintillating Air (right). Nineteen-year-old Walter Swinburn was having his first ride in the Derby. Above right: A decisive four lengths defeat of Madam Gay (right) and Fingal's Cave (left) in the King George VI & Queen Elizabeth Stakes at Ascot. Swinburn is again the rider after missing the Irish Derby through suspension. Below left: SHERGAR (Lester Piggott) beating Cut Above (p24) (rail) in the Irish Derby. Below right: Dickie McCabe, who looked after the colt, leading out Shergar and **WALTER SWINBURN** before the Classic Trial at Sandown Park.

© Ed Byrne   2611181

QUICK AS LIGHTNING (USA) :
Bay 1977

Buckpasser (USA) B. 1963	Tom Fool (USA) B. 1949	Menow (USA)
		Gaga (USA)
	Busanda (USA) Bl. 1947	War Admiral (USA)
		Businesslike (USA)
Clear Ceiling (USA) B. 1968	Bold Ruler (USA) Br. 1954	Nasrullah (GB)
		Miss Disco (USA)
	Grey Flight (USA) Gr. 1945	Mahmoud (FR)
		Planetoid (USA)

KNOWN FACT (USA) : Black 1977

In Reality (USA) B. 1964	Intentionally (USA) Bl. 1956	Intent (USA)
		My Recipe (USA)
	My Dear Girl (USA) Ch. 1957	Rough'N Tumble (USA)
		Iltis (USA)
Tamerett (USA) B/br. 1962	Tim Tam (USA) B. 1955	Tom Fool (USA)
		Two Lea (USA)
	Mixed Marriage (GB) B. 1952	Tudor Minstrel (GB)
		Persian Maid (GB)

HENBIT (USA) : Bay 1977

Hawaii (SAF) B. 1964	Utrillo (ITY) Ch. 1958	Toulouse Lautrec (ITY)
		Urbinella (GB)
	Ethane (SAF) Br. 1947	Mehrali (GB)
		Ethyl (SAF)
Chateaucreek (USA) Ch. 1970	Chateaugay (USA) Ch. 1960	Swaps (USA)
		Banquet Bell (USA)
	Mooncreek (USA) Ch. 1963	Sailor (USA)
		Ouija (USA)

BIREME (GB) : Chesnut 1977

Grundy (GB) Ch. 1972	Great Nephew (GB) B. 1963	Honeyway (GB)
		Sybil's Niece (GB)
	Word From Lundy (GB) B. 1966	Worden (FR)
		Lundy Princess (GB)
Ripeck (GB) Br. 1959	Ribot (GB) B. 1952	Tenerani (ITY)
		Romanella (ITY)
	Kyak (GB) Br. 1953	Big Game (GB)
		Felucca (GB)

LIGHT CAVALRY (GB) : Bay 1977

Brigadier Gerard (GB) B. 1968	Queens Hussar (GB) B. 1960	March Past (GB)
		Jojo (GB)
	La Paiva (GB) Ch. 1956	Prince Chevalier (FR)
		Brazen Molly (GB)
Glass Slipper (GB) Br. 1969	Relko (FR) B. 1960	Tanerko (FR)
		Relance (FR)
	Crystal Palace (GB) B. 1956	Solar Slipper (GB)
		Queen of Light (GB)

FAIRY FOOTSTEPS (GB) : Bay 1978

Mill Reef (USA) B. 1968	Never Bend (USA) B. 1960	Nasrullah (GB)
		Lalun (USA)
	Milan Mill (USA) B. 1962	Princequillo (IRE)
		Virginia Water (USA)
Glass Slipper (GB) Br. 1969	Relko (FR) B. 1960	Tanerko (FR)
		Relance (FR)
	Crystal Palace (GB) B. 1956	Solar Slipper (GB)
		Queen of Light (GB)

TO-AGORI-MOU (IRE) : Brown 1978

Tudor Music (GB) Br. 1966	Tudor Melody (GB) Br. 1956	Tudor Minstrel (GB)
		Matelda (GB)
	Fran (GB) Ch. 1959	Acropolis (GB)
		Madrilene (GB)
Sarah Van Fleet (GB) B. 1966	Cracksman (IRE) Ch. 1958	Chamossaire (GB)
		Nearly (GB)
	La Rage (GB) Br. 1954	Mieuxce (FR)
		Hells Fury (GB)

SHERGAR (GB) : Bay 1978

Great Nephew (GB) B. 1963	Honeyway (GB) Br. 1941	Fairway (GB)
		Honey Buzzard (GB)
	Sybil's Niece (GB) Ch. 1951	Admiral's Walk (GB)
		Sybil's Sister (GB)
Sharmeen (FR) B. 1972	Val De Loir (FR) B. 1959	Vieux Manoir (FR)
		Vali (FR)
	Nasreen (GB) B. 1964	Charlottesville (GB)
		Ginetta (IRE)

BLUE WIND (IRE)

Chesnut filly, foaled 3 May 1978
By Lord Gayle (USA) out of Azurine (IRE) by Chamossaire (GB)
Bred by Miss E.B. Laidlaw
1980: Owned by Mrs D.M. Solomon
Trained by Patrick Prendergast, Jr. at Melitta Lodge, Kildare, Co. Kildare
1981: Owned by Mrs Bertram R. Firestone
Trained by Dermot K. Weld at Rosewell House, The Curragh, Co. Kildare.

© Ed Byrne

Racing Record

Year	Timeform Annual Rating	Starts	Wins	2nd	3rd	4th	Win Prize Money
1980	110	5	2	1	-	-	£ 6,346
1981	127	6	3	1	-	1	£ 111,897
1982	-	7	-	-	3	-	-

Principal Performances

1980   Won Silken Glider Stakes (G3) (2yo fillies) Leopardstown (8f)
1981   2nd Irish 1000 Guineas Stakes (G1) (3yo fillies) Curragh (8f)
       Won Oaks Stakes (G1) (3yo fillies) Epsom (12f)
       Won Irish Oaks Stakes (G1) (3yo fillies) Curragh (12f)
       4th Joe McGrath Memorial Stakes (G1) Leopardstown (10f)

*****

*A*fter her runaway victories in the English and Irish Oaks there was speculation that Blue Wind might be as good as Shergar, the 1981 Derby winner. Madam Gay, a distant second at Epsom, had gone on to win a French classic, the Prix de Diane and finish second, beaten only four lengths behind Shergar (see p18), in the King George VI and Queen Elizabeth Stakes. Ultimately, two decisive defeats after winning at the Curragh rather took the gloss off Blue Wind's classic victories, but she is still rated as an above average winner of the Oaks. In 1982 Blue Wind was sent to the U.S.A. to be

22

trained by Stanley Hough, but failed to win in seven attempts. Retired to her owner's stud in Virginia, Blue Wind proved a disappointing broodmare, only breeding one winner. Carefree Dancer, her 1987 colt by Nijinsky, won four minor races in Ireland. Blue Wind was extremely well-bought for 5,600 guineas as a yearling. Her dam, the prolific breeding Azurine, was placed in two Irish classics, being beaten only half-a-length in the Irish 1000 Guineas. Lord Gayle stood at the Irish National Stud; his best runner was Prix de l'Arc de Triomphe winner, Carroll House (1985).

Right: **BLUE WIND** (Lester Piggott) winning the Oaks Stakes beating Madam Gay by seven lengths with Leap Lively ten lengths behind in third place. This victory gave Piggott his fifth Oaks winner following Carrozza (1957), Petite Etoile (1959), Valoris (1966) and Juliette Marny (1975).

Below: **DIANA FIRESTONE** leading in Blue Wind and Lester Piggott after the Oaks at Epsom.

0346392   1610081

Above centre: Irish trainer **DERMOT WELD** registered his first English classic success with Blue Wind. He had to wait twenty-two years before winning his second with Refuse To Bend (p242).

Above right: The incomparable **LESTER PIGGOTT** rode his twenty-fifth English classic winner on Blue Wind after replacing the filly's regular jockey, Wally Swinburn, Sr.

CUT ABOVE (GB)

Bay colt, foaled 19 April 1978
By High Top (GB) out of Cutle (GB) by Saint Crespin III (GB)
Owned and bred by Sir John Astor
Trained by Major W.R. Hern at West Ilsley, Berkshire.

2810481

Racing Record

Year	Timeform Annual Rating	Starts	Wins	2nd	3rd	4th	U.K. Prize Money
1980	119	2	-	1	1	-	£ 6,515
1981	130	5	2	1	1	-	£ 91,004

Principal Performances

1980 2nd Horris Hill Stakes (G3) (2yo) Newbury (7.3f)
1981 Won White Rose Stakes (G3) (3yo) Ascot (10f)
       2nd Irish Derby Stakes (G1) (3yo colts & fillies) Curragh (12f)
       3rd Geoffrey Freer Stakes (G2) Newbury (13.3f)
       Won St Leger Stakes (G1) (3yo colts & fillies) Doncaster (14.6f)

*****

*I*t is regrettable that Cut Above was not given the chance to race on as a four-year-old. His trainer
was a master with this type of late maturing horse and although on pedigree Cut Above was no
certainty to stay the extended distances over which the Cup races are run, his style of racing suggested
he would have. He came from a family developed at Richard Hollingsworth's Arches Hall Stud and was
a half-brother to Sharp Edge (1970, by Silver Shark – 3rd G1 2000 Guineas, 3rd G1 Irish 2000 Guineas)
and brother to Cut Loose (1979 – LR Virginia S). Cutle was a minor winner out of Cutter (Park Hill S),
a half-sister to two more winners of that race in Ark Royal (1952, by Straight Deal) and Kyak (1953, by
Big Game). This is also the family of Bireme (p10) and Buoy (1970, by Aureole - G1 Coronation Cup, 2nd
St Leger S). Cut Above was retired to stand at Airlie Stud at Grangewilliam in County Kildare but was

24

a dismal failure and the stallion was sold for export to Brazil after four breeding seasons in Ireland. Cut Above sired very few winners on the flat and none of much merit; under National Hunt Rules his best was Nodform Wonder, the winner of eight races.

3410481

Above: The sun ducks behind a cloud in more ways than one as **CUT ABOVE** (Joe Mercer) springs a 28/1 surprise in the St Leger beating Glint of Gold and stable-mate Bustomi. Odds-on favourite Shergar (right, see p18) fails to stay the distance and is well beaten in fourth place. Joe later said that he heard Shergar 'gurgling' as they made the final turn with four furlongs to run.

3510481

1917080

Above left: Owner, **SIR JOHN ASTOR** and trainer **DICK HERN** (behind the jockey) talk to Joe Mercer in the winner's circle after the St Leger. Also in shot are Lord Oaksey (seen between Astor and Hern) and Buster Haslam (wearing a trilby, by the horse's head), Hern's long serving travelling head-lad. This was a second success in this classic for Astor following Provoke (1965) and fifth for Hern, who had won previously with Hethersett (1962), Provoke, Bustino (1974) and Dunfermline (1977). Above right: **JOE MERCER**, seen here wearing the colours of Italian owner, Carlo d'Alessio. Cut Above was the last classic winner ridden by the veteran jockey in a long career. Mercer rode his first winner in 1950 and his first classic victory was on Ambiguity in the Oaks of 1953 whilst still an apprentice. Further English classic successes followed with two winners of the 1000 Guineas, on the Queen's Highclere in 1974 and One In A Million in 1979. Cut Above was his fourth St Leger winner after Provoke, Bustino and Light Cavalry (p12). Mercer will be ever remembered as the jockey who rode the great Brigadier Gerard on which he won the 2000 Guineas in 1971. He never rode a Derby winner at Epsom but finished second on Fidalgo for Harry Wragg in 1959 and won the Irish Derby on the same horse. He was champion jockey for the only time in 1979 whilst stable jockey to Henry Cecil at Warren Place in Newmarket. Previously Joe had been stable jockey to two trainers at West Ilsley for a period spanning twenty-five years, R.J. (Jack) Colling and Dick Hern. At the time of his retirement in November 1985 Mercer had ridden 2,810 winners in Britain.

ON THE HOUSE (FR)

Bay filly, foaled 20 March 1979
By Be My Guest (USA) out of Lora (GB) by Lorenzaccio (GB)
Owned and bred by Sir Philip Oppenheimer
Trained by Harry Wragg at Abington Place, Newmarket, Suffolk.

2807182

Racing Record

Year	Timeform Annual Rating	Starts	Wins	2nd	3rd	4th	U.K. Prize Money
1981	109	4	2	1	-	-	£ 24,840
1982	125	6	2	-	1	-	£ 130,294

Principal Performances

1981   Won St Hugh's Stakes (Listed Race) (2yo fillies) Newbury (6f)
      2nd Cheveley Park Stakes (G1) (2yo fillies) Newmarket (6f)
1982   Won 1000 Guineas Stakes (G1) (3yo fillies) Newmarket (8f)
      3rd Irish 1000 Guineas Stakes (G1) (3yo fillies) Curragh (8f)
      Won Sussex Stakes (G1) (3yo & upwards) Goodwood (8f)

*****

*T*here was nothing between On The House and Chalon; the two best fillies over one mile in 1982 were both rated 125 by Timeform at the end of the season. Henry Cecil made the wrong decision to miss the 1000 Guineas with Chalon, entertaining doubts about her stamina, and On The House made the best of her opportunity for classic glory. On The House failed to reach her modest reserve when offered at Tattersalls 1980 Houghton Sales. She was from the first crop of the Coolmore stallion Be My Guest and her dam was a three-parts sister to top-class sprinter D'Urberville (1965, by Klairon – King's Stand S). Third-dam Tessa Gillian (1950, by Nearco – 2nd Cheveley Park S, 1000 Guineas) was a sister to Royal Charger (1942 – Queen Anne S, 3rd 2000 Guineas) and bred the good colts Test Case (1958, by Supreme Court – Gimcrack S) and Gentle Art (1961, by Whistler – Richmond S). On The House was a* *prolific broodmare for her owner's Hascombe and Valiant Studs, producing five winners from eleven foals, the best of which were Art Of War (1992, by Machiavellian – LR Sirenia S) and Miss Penton (1995, by Primo Dominie), a moderate runner herself but dam of Leo (2003, by Pivotal – G2 Royal Lodge S).*

2619082

Above: **ON THE HOUSE** (John Reid) wins the 1000 Guineas Stakes beating Time Charter (see p32), Dione (grey) and the French-trained favourite, Play It Safe (right).

3419082   © Unknown   2807182

Above left: **JOHN REID** returns on his first English classic winner. This was a third 1000 Guineas victory for veteran trainer **HARRY WRAGG** (centre) who retired before the start of the 1983 season. Wragg had previously won the race with Abermaid (1962) and Full Dress II (1969). Below: **ON THE HOUSE** (John Reid) confirms her class by winning the Sussex Stakes at Goodwood beating Sandhurst Prince (rail), Achieved (no.6), Tender King and Bel Bolide (no.1). Above right: Owner **SIR PHILIP OPPENHEIMER** with On The House at Goodwood.

1330882

ZINO (GB)

Bay colt, foaled 26 April 1979
By Welsh Pageant (FR) out of Cyriana (GB) by Salvo (USA)
Owned and bred by Gerald A. Oldham
Trained by Francois Boutin at Lamorlaye, Oise, France.

2619882

Racing Record

Year	Timeform Annual Rating	Starts	Wins	2nd	3rd	4th	U.K. Prize Money
1981	123	5	3	2	-	-	-
1982	127	5	2	1	1	-	£ 80,080

Principal Performances

1981   2nd Prix de la Salamandre (G1) (2yo colts & fillies) Longchamp (7f)
        Won Criterium de Maisons-Laffitte (G2) (2yo) Maisons-Laffitte (7f)
1982   Won 2000 Guineas Stakes (G1) (3yo colts & fillies) Newmarket (8f)
        2nd Prix Jean Prat (G2) (3yo) Chantilly (9f)
        3rd Prix Jacques Le Marois (G1) (3yo & upwards) Deauville (8f)

*****

Zino was a genuine and consistent racehorse who won a substandard renewal of the 2000 Guineas. By the end of 1982 only two of the first ten horses to finish had managed to win subsequently. Zino was retired to stand at Haras du Logis at Louviere-en-Auge, Normandy. His best progeny were Peckinpah's Soul (G2 Grand Prix de Deauville), Robore (G2 Prix du Conseil de Paris) and Comte Du Bourg (G2 Prix Hubert de Chaudenay). Zino's dam was a half-sister to Stintino (1967, by Sheshoon – Prix Lupin, 3rd Derby S) and Ormindo (1969, by Right Royal – G3 Chester Vase), out of Cynara, a winner of the Queen Mary Stakes. Zino was the only English classic winner sired by Welsh Pageant (Queen Elizabeth II S, Lockinge S twice, Queen Anne S), a top-class miler bred and raced by Jim Joel.

28

1219982

Above: A battle-royal between two of the best two-year-olds of 1981; victory goes to **ZINO** and Freddy Head, who catch Wind And Wuthering (Steve Cauthen) near the line and win by a head. Tender King (left) finishes third and favourite Silver Hawk (red cap) fifth.

1723882

3420792

0739494

Above left: **FREDDY HEAD** rode his first English classic winner on Zino. Centre: **FRANCOIS BOUTIN** started training in 1964 and became one of the greatest trainers in French racing history. The Prix de l'Arc de Triomphe eluded him but Boutin won every other great flat-race in France, most of them at least twice. In England, Nonoalco (1974) and Zino gave him victories in the 2000 Guineas, Miesque (see p72), the 1000 Guineas and La Lagune (1968), the Oaks. Boutin also won the Ascot Gold Cup for three successive years (1975-77) with the great stayer Sagaro. Francois Boutin suffered a fatal heart attack at the age of 58 on 1 February 1995.

Right: Owner/breeder **GERALD OLDHAM**; Zino was a second English classic winner for his Citadel Stud after Intermezzo in the St Leger of 1969. Oldham, a Geneva-based financier, was a very successful owner and breeder of racehorses. Most of his best horses were trained by Harry Wragg at Newmarket until Oldham suddenly quit English racing in the 1970's. Among the many top-class winners he owned were Talgo (Irish Derby), Fidalgo (Irish Derby, 2nd Derby S), Sovrango (Chester Vase, Ormonde S, 4th Derby S), Miralgo (Timeform Gold Cup, Hardwicke S, 2nd Eclipse S, King George VI & Queen Elizabeth S, 3rd St Leger), Espresso (Grosser Preis von Baden twice), Lacovia (Prix de Diane), Salvo (Grosser Preis von Baden, 2nd King George VI & Queen Elizabeth S, Prix de l'Arc de Triomphe), Sagaro, Chicago (Gran Premio del Jockey Club, Premio Roma), Caprera (Falmouth S), Ormindo (Chester Vase, Ormonde S), Romantica (Princess Royal S), Ileana (Falmouth S), Stintino and Cynara. Gerald Oldham died in April 2013 and his bloodstock was dispersed at Goffs October Sales in the same year.

GOLDEN FLEECE (USA)

Bay colt, foaled 1 April 1979
By Nijinsky (CAN) out of Exotic Treat (USA) by Vaguely Noble (GB)
Bred by Mr & Mrs Paul Hexter
1981: Owned by Jean-Pierre Binet
1982: Owned by Robert E. Sangster
Trained by Vincent O'Brien at Ballydoyle, Cashel, Co. Tipperary.

T104082

Racing Record

Year	Timeform Annual Rating	Starts	Wins	2nd	3rd	4th	Prize Money
1981	99	1	1	-	-	-	£ 1,242
1982	133	3	3	-	-	-	£ 164,338

Principal Performances

1982 Won Ballymoss Stakes (G2) Curragh (10f)
Won Nijinsky Stakes (G2) Leopardstown (10f)
Won Derby Stakes (G1) (3yo colts & fillies) Epsom (12f)

*****

*P*at Eddery rode Golden Fleece in the Derby as though defeat was out of the question. At Tattenham Corner he had only three horses behind him, yet Eddery appeared totally unconcerned. He was rewarded with a phenomenal burst of acceleration which took him into the lead entering the final furlong. Approaching the winning post Golden Fleece appeared to go lame behind and it was no surprise that he subsequently suffered training problems and never ran again. Had he remained sound this horse might have been remembered as one of the great Derby winners. Golden Fleece, a $775,000 yearling purchase, was retired to Coolmore Stud at Fethard in County Tipperary, but suffered from ill-health and died in March 1984 without siring any runners of note. His winning *daughter Felidia (1985, ex Exclusive Fable), is the dam of U.S. multiple graded stakes winner Lexicon (1995, by Conquistador Cielo). The unraced Exotic Treat was a grand-daughter of Rare Perfume (1947, by Eight Thirty), dam of Jaipur (1959, by Nasrullah – Belmont S) and Rare Treat (1952, by Stymie), winner of sixteen races and dam of U.S. champion What A Treat (1962, by Tudor Minstrel), herself dam of another Coolmore-based stallion, Be My Guest (1974, by Northern Dancer).*

1523782

Above: **GOLDEN FLEECE** (Pat Eddery) wins the Derby in sensational style beating Touching Wood (see p34), Silver Hawk (red cap) and Persepolis (striped sleeves). Eddery afterwards stated that Golden Fleece was the best horse he had ever sat on, although Timeform rate his first Derby winner, Grundy, as superior.

2713485

© Jack Knight, Paddock Studios

Left: Owner **ROBERT SANGSTER** was winning his second Derby following the victory of The Minstrel in 1977, ridden by Lester Piggott. Sangster's colt Assert won the Prix du Jockey-Club and the Irish Derby in 1982, an unprecedented clean-sweep of the three major Derbys in Europe. Right: With Golden Fleece in the winner's circle after the Derby are co-owners **DANNY SCHWARTZ** (left), Robert Sangster and **JEAN-PIERRE BINET** (second right). For trainer **VINCENT O'BRIEN** (centre) this was his sixth and final victory in this classic after Larkspur (1962), Sir Ivor (1968), Nijinsky (1970), Roberto (1972) and The Minstrel.

TIME CHARTER (IRE)

Bay filly, foaled 6 April 1979
By Saritamer (USA) out of Centrocon (GB) by High Line (GB)
Bred by W & R Barnett Limited : Owned by R. Barnett
Trained by Henry Candy at Kingstone Warren, Wantage, Oxfordshire.

1919082

Racing Record

Year	Timeform Annual Rating	Starts	Wins	2nd	3rd	4th	U.K. Prize Money
1981	103	5	2	-	1	-	£ 5,812
1982	131	6	4	2	-	-	£ 247,665
1983	130	5	2	1	-	1	£ 140,905
1984	125	4	1	1	-	1	£ 95,020

Principal Performances

1982   2nd 1000 Guineas Stakes (G1) (3yo fillies) Newmarket (8f)
       Won Oaks Stakes (G1) (3yo fillies) Epsom (12f)
       2nd Nassau Stakes (G2) (Fillies & mares) Goodwood (10f)
       Won Sun Chariot Stakes (G2) (3yo fillies) Newmarket (10f)
       Won Champion Stakes (G1) (3yo & upwards) Newmarket (10f)
1983   Won King George VI and Queen Elizabeth Stakes (G1) Ascot (12f)
       Won Prix Foy (G3) (4yo & upwards) Longchamp (12f)
       4th Prix de l'Arc de Triomphe (G1) (3yo & upwards) Longchamp (12f)
1984   Won Coronation Cup (G1) (4yo & upwards) Epsom (12f)
       2nd Eclipse Stakes (G1) (3yo & upwards) Sandown (10f)
       4th King George VI and Queen Elizabeth Stakes (G1) Ascot (12f)

*T*ime Charter was a good Oaks winner, talented enough to beat the top colts, winning a Group 1 race against open opposition in each of the seasons from 1982-84. Retired to her breeder's Fair Winter Farm in Buckinghamshire, Time Charter was a very successful broodmare. She produced ten foals and seven winners including By Charter (1986, by Shirley Heights), the dam of First Charter (1999, by Polish Precedent – G2 Lonsdale Cup), Zinaad (1989, by Shirley Heights - G2 Jockey Club S), sire of Kazzia (p234), Time Allowed (1983, by Sadler's Wells – G2 Jockey Club S, G3 Princess Royal S), Time Honoured (2000, by Sadler's Wells) and Time Saved (1996, by Green Desert), the dam of stakes winners Plea Bargain (2002, by Machiavellian – G2 King Edward VII S) and Lay Time (2008, by Galileo – G3 Winter Hill S). Centrocon was a talented runner, winning the Group 3 Lancashire Oaks, and a full sister to Nicholas Bill (1975, G2 Geoffrey Freer S, G2 Princess of Wales's S, G3 Jockey Club Cup) and Centroline (1978, G3 Jockey Club Cup). Saritamer (1971, by Dancer's Image) was a top-class sprinter, winner of the July Cup and Diadem Stakes. Time Charter was retired from stud duties in 2001 and died on 7 July 2005. There must have been quite a few sad faces at Fair Winter Farm that night.

32T0282

3124082

Above: **TIME CHARTER** wins the Oaks beating Slightly Dangerous (pink cap) and Last Feather (striped cap). This was the only classic winner ridden by jockey **BILLY NEWNES** (above left) in his career and the first victory in this race for an apprentice since Joe Mercer won on Ambiguity in 1953. Below left: **HENRY CANDY** has not trained a second English classic winner to date but has had charge of several high-class sprinters including Kyllachy (G1 Nunthorpe S), Airwave (G1 Cheveley Park S) and Markab (G1 Haydock Sprint Cup), as well as Master Willie (1977, by High Line – G1 Benson & Hedges Gold Cup, Coronation Cup, Eclipse S, 2nd Derby S, Champion S).

1417092

1418295

T125284

Above centre: **ROBERT BARNETT**, owner/breeder of Time Charter, also owned High Line (1966, by High Hat – G2 Princess of Wales's S twice, G3 Jockey Club Cup) and Master Willie. Above right: In a rare clash of Oaks winners, **TIME CHARTER** (Steve Cauthen) defeats Sun Princess (p44) in the 1984 Coronation Cup at Epsom.

TOUCHING WOOD (USA)

Bay colt, foaled 11 May 1979
By Roberto (USA) out of Mandera (USA) by Vaguely Noble (GB)
Bred by Pin Oak Farm, Versailles, Kentucky, U.S.A.
Owned by Sheikh Maktoum Al-Maktoum
Trained by Harry Thomson Jones at Woodlands, Newmarket, Suffolk.

13T1082

Racing Record

Year	Timeform Annual Rating	Starts	Wins	2nd	3rd	4th	Prize Money
1981	91	1	-	-	1	-	£ 731
1982	127	8	3	4	1	-	£ 199,525

Principal Performances

1982   2ⁿᵈ Derby Stakes (G1) (3yo colts & fillies) Epsom (12f)
2ⁿᵈ Gordon Stakes (G3) (3yo) Goodwood (12f)
3ʳᵈ Great Voltigeur Stakes (G2) (3yo colts) York (12f)
Won St Leger Stakes (G1) (3yo colts & fillies) Doncaster (14.6f)
Won Irish St Leger Stakes (G1) (3yo colts & fillies) Curragh (14f)

*****

*T*ouching Wood was the first horse to win both the English and Irish St Legers since Trigo in 1929. A $200,000 yearling purchase at Keeneland, the colt was the first of many bought for Sheikh Maktoum in the U.S.A. Touching Wood was yet another St Leger winner retired to stud without being given his chance in the Cup races as a four-year-old. Racing over distances in excess of two miles would have suited this dour stayer whose lack of finishing speed was exposed by his five defeats during 1982 until upped in distance for the St Leger. Touching Wood was retired to Dalham Hall Stud at Newmarket where he stood until exported to Fayette Park Stud at Cambridge in New Zealand in 1988 where he died on 31 March 2004. In Europe his best runners were Ashal (G1 Ascot Gold Cup), Great

34

Marquess (G3 Doncaster Cup, G3 Jockey Club Cup), La Tritona (G3 Prix de Flore) and Lucky Moon (G3 Goodwood Cup). For details of Touching Wood's family see Speciosa (p278-9).

21T1082

Above: **TOUCHING WOOD** wins the St Leger beating Zilos (spots) and Diamond Shoal (left) giving Dubai sheikh, Maktoum Al-Maktoum his first classic winner and **HARRY THOMSON JONES** (inset) his second St Leger victory following Athens Wood in 1971. These were the only two English classics won by the trainer in a career stretching from 1951 to 1996 during the early part of which he had charge of several high-class jumpers including Frenchman's Cove, Clever Scot and Tingle Creek. Jones switched his attentions to the flat during the 1970's and trained several Group 1 winners including Al Bahathri (Irish 1000 Guineas, Coronation S), Ashal, Fleet Wahine (Yorkshire Oaks) and At Talaq (GP de Paris). Harry Thomson Jones died on 5 December 2007, aged 82. Below left: **PAUL COOK** poses on Touching Wood after the St Leger. This was the second and last English classic winner ridden by the jockey, sixteen years after winning the 1000 Guineas on Glad Rags in 1966. He was also beaten a neck in the Derby of the same year by Scobie Breasley on Charlottown when riding Pretendre for veteran Newmarket trainer, Sir Jack Jarvis. Cook retired after sustaining injuries in a fall during the St Leger meeting at Doncaster in 1989.

26T1082

© Ed Byrne

Above right: **ROBERTO**, pictured here at the Curragh with Johnny Roe, was trained by Vincent O'Brien to win the National Stakes, the Derby Stakes, the inaugural Benson & Hedges Gold Cup (when he smashed the course record and inflicted the only defeat ever suffered by the great Brigadier Gerard) and the Coronation Cup. Roberto proved a very successful stallion and a great sire of sires. Among his progeny were Sookera (G1 Cheveley Park S), At Talaq (G1 GP de Paris, Aus-G1 McKinnon S, Aus-G1 Melbourne Cup), Lear Fan (G1 Prix Jacques le Marois), Brian's Time (G1 Florida Derby) and Sunshine Forever (G1 Man o'War S, Turf Classic S, Washington DC International S), Many sons of Roberto have proved successful stallions including Robellino (G2 Royal Lodge S, see p145), Silver Hawk (G3 Craven S, 2nd G1 Irish Derby, 3rd G1 Derby S, p209), Bob Back (G2 Prince of Wales's S), sire of Bob's Return (p140), Brian's Time (in Japan) and Dynaformer (G2 Jersey Derby), sire of classic winners in the U.S. and Britain. His daughter Slightly Dangerous was the dam of champion miler Warning and Commander in Chief (p136).

MA BICHE (USA)

Bay or brown filly, foaled 23 January 1980
By Key To The Kingdom (USA) out of Madge (FR) by Roi Dagobert (FR)
Bred by Mrs Galina Tkatch de Briones
1982: Owned by Mrs Alec Head
1983: Owned by Sheikh Maktoum Al-Maktoum
Trained by Christiane Head at Chantilly, Oise, France.

13T1383

Racing Record

Year	Timeform Annual Rating	Starts	Wins	2nd	3rd	4th	U.K. Prize Money
1982	123	6	4	-	2	-	£ 39,118
1983	125	5	3	-	-	1	£ 71,472

Principal Performances

1982   Won Prix Robert Papin (G1) (2yo) Maisons-Laffitte (5.5f)
      3rd Prix Morny (G1) (2yo) Deauville (6f)
      Won Cheveley Park Stakes (G1) (2yo fillies) Newmarket (6f)
1983   Won 1000 Guineas Stakes (G1) (3yo fillies) Newmarket (8f)
      4th Prix Jacques Le Marois (G1) (3yo & upwards) Deauville (8f)
      Won Prix de la Foret (G1) (2yo & upwards) Longchamp (7f)

*****

*F*ew fillies win the 1000 Guineas that were not among the top two-year-olds of the previous year
as the race is too early in the season for the later maturing types. Ma Biche was yet another
winner of the Cheveley Park Stakes to go on to victory in the classic but her performances overall mark
her out as average Guineas winner. Ma Biche descended from an excellent Wertheimer family. Her
grandam Midget also won the Cheveley Park Stakes, as did Mige (1966, by Saint Crespin), a half-sister

36

to Madge. This is also the family of Vimy (1952, by Wild Risk), winner of the King George VI & Queen Elizabeth Stakes in 1955. Key To The Kingdom was a stakes-winning sibling of U.S. champions Fort Marcy (1964, by Amerigo) and Key To The Mint (1969, by Graustark). At stud, Ma Biche was bred to several leading U.S. based stallions including Alydar, Danzig, Shadeed and Blushing Groom but she produced no progeny of any real merit. One notable only for his extreme mediocrity was King Henrik (2002, by King of Kings), unable to win even in selling hurdle company.

T124483

Above: **MA BICHE** wins the 1000 Guineas beating Royal Heroine (left). Champion sprinter Habibti (red cap) finishes fourth. Jockey Freddy Head was winning his first 1000 Guineas and his second English classic following Zino (see p28).

28T1383

Above: Trainer **CHRISTIANE HEAD**, sister of the winning jockey, with Ma Biche in the unsaddling ring after the 1000 Guineas. This was her first English classic victory. Inset: **MAKTOUM AL-MAKTOUM** with his trophy after his second successive classic success following the St Leger with Touching Wood (p34) the previous year.

BLUE WIND (IRE) : Chesnut 1978

	Lord Gayle (USA) B. 1965	Sir Gaylord (USA) B. 1959	Turn To (USA)
			Somethingroyal (USA)
		Sticky Case (GB) Ch. 1958	Court Martial GB
			Run Honey (GB)
	Azurine (IRE) B. 1957	Chamossaire (GB) Ch. 1942	Precipitation (GB)
			Snowberry (GB)
		Blue Dun (GB) B. 1950	Blue Train (GB)
			Dunure (GB)

CUT ABOVE (GB) : Bay 1978

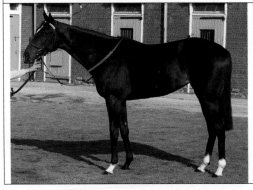

	High Top (GB) Br. 1969	Derring-do (GB) Br. 1961	Darius (GB)
			Sipsey Bridge (GB)
		Camenae (GB) B. 1961	Vimy (FR)
			Madrilene (GB)
	Cutle (GB) Ch. 1963	Saint Crespin (GB) Ch. 1956	Aureole (GB)
			Neocracy (GB)
		Cutter (GB) B. 1955	Donatello (FR)
			Felucca (GB)

ON THE HOUSE (GB) : Bay 1979

	Be My Guest (USA) Ch. 1974	Northern Dancer (CAN) B. 1961	Nearctic (CAN)
			Natalma (USA)
		What A Treat (USA) B. 1962	Tudor Minstrel (GB)
			Rare Treat (USA)
	Lora (GB) B. 1972	Lorenzaccio (GB) Ch. 1965	Klairon (FR)
			Phoenissa (GB)
		Courtessa (GB) B. 1955	Supreme Court (GB)
			Tessa Gillian (GB)

ZINO (GB) : Bay 1979

	Welsh Pageant (GB) B. 1966	Tudor Melody (GB) Br. 1956	Tudor Minstrel (GB)
			Matelda (GB)
		Picture Light (FR) B. 1954	Court Martial (GB)
			Queen of Light (GB)
	Cyriana (GB) Gr. 1972	Salvo (USA) Ch. 1963	Right Royal (FR)
			Manera (FR)
		Cynara (GB) Gr. 1958	Grey Sovereign (GB)
			Ladycroft (GB)

GOLDEN FLEECE (USA) : Bay 1979

	Nijinsky (CAN) B. 1967	Northern Dancer (CAN) B. 1961	Nearctic (CAN)
			Natalma (USA)
		Flaming Page (CAN) B. 1959	Bull Page (USA)
			Flaring Top (USA)
	Exotic Treat (USA) Ch. 1971	Vaguely Noble (IRE) B. 1965	Vienna (GB)
			Noble Lassie (GB)
		Rare Treat (USA) Ch. 1952	Stymie (USA)
			Rare Perfume (USA)

TIME CHARTER (IRE) : Bay 1979

	Saritamer (USA) Gr. 1971	Dancer's Image (USA) Gr. 1965	Native Dancer (USA)
			Noors Image (USA)
		Irish Chorus (IRE) B. 1960	Ossian (GB)
			Dawn Chorus (GB)
	Centrocon (GB) Ch. 1973	High Line (GB) Ch. 1966	High Hat (GB)
			Time Call (GB)
		Centro (GB) B. 1966	Vienna (GB)
			Ocean Sailing (GB)

TOUCHING WOOD (USA) : Bay 1979

	Roberto (USA) B. 1969	Hail To Reason (USA) Br. 1958	Turn-To (USA)
			Nothirdchance (USA)
		Bramalea (USA) B. 1959	Nashua (USA)
			Rarelea (USA)
	Mandera (USA) B. 1970	Vaguely Noble (IRE) B. 1965	Vienna (GB)
			Noble Lassie (GB)
		Foolish One (USA) B. 1957	Tom Fool (USA)
			Miss Disco (USA)

MA BICHE (USA) : Bay/brown 1980

	Key To The Kingdom (USA) B/br. 1970	Bold Ruler (USA) B. 1954	Nasrullah (GB)
			Miss Disco (USA)
		Key Bridge (USA) B. 1959	Princequillo (IRE)
			Blue Banner (USA)
	Madge (FR) B. 1975	Roi Dagobert (FR) B. 1964	Sicambre (FR)
			Dame D'Atour (FR)
		Midget (FR) Gr. 1953	Djebe (FR)
			Mimi (FR)

LOMOND (USA)

Bay colt, foaled 3 February 1980
By Northern Dancer (CAN) out of My Charmer (USA) by Poker (USA)
Bred by Warner L. Jones Jr., W.S. Farish III and W. Kilroy
Owned by Robert E. Sangster
Trained by Vincent O'Brien at Ballydoyle, Cashel, Co. Tipperary.

01T1583

Racing Record

Year	Timeform Annual Rating	Starts	Wins	2nd	3rd	4th	Prize Money
1982	109	2	1	-	1	-	£ 3,620
1983	128	5	2	1	-	-	£ 95,562

Principal Performances

1982   3rd National Stakes (G2) (2yo) Curragh (7f)
1983   Won Gladness Stakes (Listed Race) Curragh (7f)
       Won 2000 Guineas Stakes (G1) (3yo colts & fillies) Newmarket (8f)
       2nd Irish 2000 Guineas Stakes (G1) (3yo colts & fillies) Curragh (8f)

*****

*L*omond, a half-brother to the U.S. Triple Crown winner Seattle Slew (1974, by Bold Reasoning) and Seattle Dancer (1984, by Nijinsky – G2 Gallinule S), was bought from his breeders as a foal by Robert Sangster in a private deal for a reported $1.5m. His dam My Charmer was a minor stakes winner in the U.S. Lomond won the 2000 Guineas in good style, but his subsequent efforts and those of most of the horses which finished close behind him must lead one to conclude that 1983 was a substandard race. The two favourites, Diesis and Gorytus, both ran well below their two-year-old form and Wassl, winner next time out of the Irish 2000 Guineas beating Lomond, ran inexplicably badly at Newmarket. Tried in blinkers for the Sussex Stakes, Lomond followed his poor effort in the Derby with *another at Goodwood and his retirement to Coolmore Stud at Fethard in County Tipperary was announced soon after. Lomond was a fairly successful stallion siring Group 1 winners Ashayer (Prix Marcel Boussac), Dark Lomond (Irish St Leger), Flutter Away (Moyglare Stud S), Varadavour (Carleton F. Burke H.), Marling (Irish 1000 Guineas, Sussex S), Oczy Czarnie (Prix de la Salamandre) and Valanour (Grand Prix de Paris, Prix Ganay).*

T122983

Above: **LOMOND** and Pat Eddery hold the late run of Tolomeo (red cap) and win the 2000 Guineas by two lengths. Muscatite (red jacket) finishes third and co-favourite Gorytus (green cap) fifth.

18T1583

2313485

Above left: **PAT EDDERY** on Lomond, his first winner of the 2000 Guineas. Above right: **VINCENT O'BRIEN** trained sixteen English classic winners before retiring in 1994; Glad Rags (1000 Guineas 1966); Sir Ivor (1968), Nijinsky (1970), Lomond and El Gran Senor (see p48) (2000 Guineas); Larkspur (1962), Sir Ivor, Nijinsky, Roberto (1972), The Minstrel (1977) and Golden Fleece (p30) (Derby); Long Look and Valoris (Oaks 1965 and 1966); Ballymoss, Nijinsky and Boucher (St Leger 1957, 1970 and 1972). Other top-class horses handled by O'Brien include Gladness (Ascot Gold Cup), Storm Bird (Dewhurst S), Pieces of Eight (Eclipse, Champion S), Artaius (Eclipse & Sussex S), Sadler's Wells (Eclipse & Irish 2000 Guineas), Alleged (Prix de l'Arc de Triomphe twice), Thatch (July Cup, Sussex S), Caerleon (Prix du Jockey-Club, Benson & Hedges Gold Cup), Jaazeiro (Sussex S) and Royal Academy (Breeder's Cup Mile). O'Brien won all the Irish classics at least three times each. Before concentrating on the flat, he had unprecedented success as a trainer of jumpers, winning three successive Grand Nationals (1953-55) and achieving the same feat with Cottage Rake in the Cheltenham Gold Cup (1948-50) and Hatton's Grace in the Champion Hurdle (1949-51). Perennial champion trainer in Ireland as well as twice in Britain, Vincent O'Brien died on 1st June 2009, aged ninety-two.

41

TEENOSO (USA)

Bay colt, foaled 7 April 1980
By Youth (USA) out of Furioso (GB) by Ballymoss (GB)
Owned by Eric B. Moller
Bred by owner & White Lodge Stud
Trained in 1982 by Harry Wragg and 1983 - 1984 by Geoffrey Wragg,
both at Abington Place Stables, Newmarket, Suffolk.

02T5384

Racing Record

Year	Timeform Annual Rating	Starts	Wins	2nd	3rd	4th	Prize Money
1982	86	3	-	-	-	1	£ 262
1983	132	6	3	1	2	-	£ 209,150
1984	135	4	3	-	1	-	£ 242,589

Principal Performances

1983 Won Derby Trial Stakes (G3) (3yo) Lingfield (12f)
      Won Derby Stakes (G1) (3yo colts & fillies) Epsom (12f)
      3rd Irish Derby Stakes (G1) (3yo colts & fillies) Curragh (12f)
      3rd Great Voltigeur Stakes (G2) (3yo colts) York (12f)
1984 Won Ormonde Stakes (G3) Chester (13.4f)
      Won Grand Prix de Saint-Cloud (G2) Saint-Cloud (12.5f)
      Won King George VI and Queen Elizabeth Stakes (G1) Ascot (12f)

*****

*T*he heavy going that prevailed at Epsom for Teenoso's Derby caused many to doubt the value of the performance, especially after the colt was well beaten at the Curragh and York. But kept in training, Teenoso silenced his critics with two splendid victories at Saint-Cloud and Ascot which firmly established him as the best middle-distance horse in Europe during 1984. Teenoso was retired to Highclere Stud at Newbury in Berkshire but his breeding and performances were essentially that of a stayer and he struggled to attract quality mares at an unrealistic fee that was reduced all too late. His best flat performers were the minor stakes winners Young Buster and Carlton. Moved to Shade Oak

Stud in Shropshire and then to Pitts Farm Stud in Dorset, Teenoso was latterly used as a sire of jumpers, getting the Cheltenham Mildmay of Flete Steeple Chase winner, Young Spartacus. The stallion developed thrombosis and was put down on 4 October 1999 at Pitts Farm Stud. Teenoso was by far the best horse sired by Youth (1973, by Ack Ack – G1 Prix du Jockey-Club), the U.S. Turf Champion of 1976, who stood at Gainesway Farm in Lexington until his export to Brazil in 1987. Furioso also bred Topsy (1976, by Habitat – G2 Prix d'Astarte, G2 Sun Chariot S, G3 Fred Darling S) and descends from a distinguished family developed by Ralph Moller at White Lodge Stud from his foundation mare, Horama (1943, by Panorama) which includes Favoletta (p156) and Old Country (1979, by Quiet Fling).

27T2383

Above: A spectacular overnight thunderstorm threatened to wipe out the Epsom Derby meeting but a dry morning saved the day and **TEENOSO** and Lester Piggott ploughed through the mud to win in the slowest time recorded for the race since 1891. Carlingford Castle finished second and Shearwalk (grey) third. It was a record ninth Derby victory for Piggott. The legendary jockey had previously won on Never Say Die in 1954, Crepello (1957), St Paddy (1960), Sir Ivor (1968), Nijinsky (1970), Roberto (1972), Empery (1976) and The Minstrel (1977). For his trainer **GEOFFREY WRAGG** (inset), Teenoso was a solitary English classic winner. Wragg retired at the end of the 2008 season.

37T2284   T101084   2622684

Above left: **ERIC MOLLER** with his winner after the Ormonde Stakes at Chester. Teenoso was the only English classic winner Moller owned outright, although he shared 1967 1000 Guineas winner Full Dress, with his brother, Ralph; Eric Moller died in 1989. Above: **TEENOSO** and Lester Piggott beating Sadler's Wells, Tolomeo (red cap) and Time Charter (see p32) in the King George VI and Queen Elizabeth Stakes. Above right: **LESTER PIGGOTT** was still showing signs of the injuries sustained when Teenoso threw up his head, hitting him in the face during the Grand Prix de Saint-Cloud, three weeks later at the 1984 Newmarket July Meeting.

SUN PRINCESS (IRE)

Bay filly, foaled 18 May 1980
By English Prince (IRE) out of Sunny Valley (FR) by Val de Loir (FR)
Bred by Ballymacoll Stud Farm Limited
Owned by Sir Michael Sobell
Trained by Major W.R. Hern at West Ilsley, Newbury, Berkshire.

19T2583

Racing Record

Year	Timeform Annual Rating	Starts	Wins	2nd	3rd	4th	U.K. Prize Money
1982	93	1	-	1	-	-	£ 1,702
1983	130	6	3	2	1	-	£ 248,298
1984	120	3	-	1	-	-	£ 18,354

Principal Performances

1983   Won Oaks Stakes (G1) (3yo fillies) Epsom (12f)
       3rd King George VI & Queen Elizabeth Stakes (G1) Ascot (12f)
       Won Yorkshire Oaks Stakes (G1) (3yo fillies) York (12f)
       Won St Leger Stakes (G1) (3yo colts & fillies) Doncaster (14.6f)
       2nd Prix de l'Arc de Triomphe (G1) Longchamp (12f)
1984   2nd Coronation Cup (G1) Epsom (12f)

*****

S un Princess won the Oaks by twelve lengths on only her third racecourse appearance and went on prove herself one of the best winners of the Epsom classic since the war. Her sire English Prince won the Irish Derby, but proved a disappointing stallion in Europe and was exported to Japan in 1980, dying there in 1983. Sunny Valley was from an old established Ballymacoll family, the source of many top winners for this stud including Spectrum (1992, by Rainbow Quest – G1 Champion S, Irish 2000 Guineas), Sun Prince (1969, by Princely Gift – Prix Robert Papin, 3rd 2000 Guineas) and Conduit (see p306). Sun Princess was a half-sister to Saddlers' Hall (1988, by Sadler's Wells – G1 Coronation Cup).

44

She proved a good broodmare for Ballymacoll, breeding several winners the best of which were Prince of Dance (1986, by Sadler's Wells – G1 Dewhurst & G2 Champagne S) and Princely Venture (1999, by Entrepreneur – G2 Scottish Derby). The unraced Ballet Queen (1988, by Sadler's Wells), was the dam of Fusaichi Concorde (1993, by Caerleon – G1 Tokyo Yushun) and Born King (1998, by Sunday Silence – G3 Keisei Hai). Sun Princess died during 2001 and was buried at Ballymacoll Stud.

T126083

Above: **SUN PRINCESS** (Willie Carson) wins the Oaks Stakes, the first maiden to win an English classic since Asmena (Oaks 1950) and the largest winning margin since Never Say Die (St Leger 1954). Below left: **WILLIE CARSON**, **DICK HERN** and **SIR MICHAEL SOBELL** (left); Sun Princess was a third Oaks winner for the trainer and jockey following Her Majesty's Dunfermline (1977) and Bireme (p10).

© George Selwyn

3221483

Above right: SUN PRINCESS and Carson easily winning the Yorkshire Oaks beating Green Lucia. Below: Much harder this time as **SUN PRINCESS** completes her classic double in the St Leger holding the challenges of Esprit du Nord (right) and Carlingford Castle. It was a second win in this classic for Carson following Dunfermline and Hern's sixth after Hethersett (1962), Provoke (1965), Bustino (1974), Dunfermline and Cut Above (p24).

2923083

PEBBLES (GB)

Chesnut filly, foaled 27 February 1981
By Sharpen Up (GB) out of La Dolce (GB) by Connaught (GB)
Bred by Warren Hill Stud and Mimika Financiera
1983-May 1984: Owned by Captain Marcos Lemos
June 1984-1985: Owned by Sheikh Mohammed Al-Maktoum
Trained by Clive E. Brittain at Carlburg Stables, Newmarket, Suffolk.

2132985

Racing Record

Year	Timeform Annual Rating	Starts	Wins	2nd	3rd	4th	Prize Money
1983	114	6	2	1	-	1	£ 26,575
1984	124	4	2	2	-	-	£ 142,954
1985	135	5	4	1	-	-	£ 866,120

Principal Performances

1983   2nd Cheveley Park Stakes (G1) (2yo fillies) Newmarket (6f)
1984   Won Nell Gwyn Stakes (G3) (3yo fillies) Newmarket (7f)
       Won 1000 Guineas Stakes (G1) (3yo fillies) Newmarket (8f)
       2nd Coronation Stakes (G2) (3yo fillies) Royal Ascot (8f)
       2nd Champion Stakes (G1) Newmarket (10f)
1985   Won Sandown Mile (G2) Sandown (8f)
       2nd Prince of Wales's Stakes (G2) Royal Ascot (10f)
       Won Eclipse Stakes (G1) Sandown (10f)
       Won Champion Stakes (G1) Newmarket (10f)
       Won Breeders' Cup Turf (G1) Aqueduct, U.S.A. (12f)

*****

*P*ebbles was sound, tough and genuine. She improved over her three seasons of racing as she strengthened and matured and ended her career with brilliant victories at Newmarket and Aqueduct, each time producing her trademark turn of finishing speed. La Dolce was a useful filly, also

46

trained by Clive Brittain, finishing fifth in the 1979 Oaks. Pebbles' grandam Arbitrate was a stakes-placed half-sister to Doutelle (1954, by Prince Chevalier) and Above Suspicion (1956, by Court Martial) out of the Royal Studs' good mare, Above Board (1947, by Straight Deal – Yorkshire Oaks). Pebbles was a dire disappointment as a broodmare, producing nothing of any note; she was retired from breeding in 2002 and died during September 2005 at Darley's Fukumitsu Farm in Japan.

T126684

Above: Philip Robinson glances around for non-existent danger as **PEBBLES** routs the opposition in the 1000 Guineas Stakes beating Meis El-Reem (rail) and Desirable (grey).

28T1884

1817680

Above left: **CLIVE BRITTAIN, PHILIP ROBINSON** and **MARCOS LEMOS** with their 1000 Guineas trophies. Above right: **SHARPEN UP** at Side Hill Stud in Newmarket just before his export to the U.S.A. in 1980. Sharpen Up also sired Kris (G1 Sussex S), Diesis (G1 Middle Park S, Dewhurst S), Trempolino (G1 Prix de l'Arc De Triomphe), Sanglamore (G1 Prix du Jockey-Club, Prix d'Ispahan), Sharpo (G1 July Cup, Prix de l'Abbaye), Selkirk (G1 Queen Elizabeth II S) and Exactly Sharp (G1 Prix Lupin).

0333085

Above: **PEBBLES** produced arguably her best performances on the only two occasions she was ridden by Pat Eddery. Here they win the Champion Stakes, easily defeating two top colts, Slip Anchor (p62) and Palace Music (blaze). Pebbles and Eddery went on to another brilliant victory together at the Breeders' Cup.

EL GRAN SENOR (USA)

Bay colt, foaled 21 April 1981
By Northern Dancer (CAN) ex Sex Appeal (USA) by Buckpasser (USA)
Bred by Edward P. Taylor
Owned by Robert E. Sangster
Trained by Vincent O'Brien at Ballydoyle, Cashel, Co. Tipperary.

T115284

Racing Record

Year	Timeform Annual Rating	Starts	Wins	2nd	3rd	4th	Prize Money
1983	131	4	4	-	-	-	£ 85,965
1984	136	4	3	1	-	-	£ 284,128

Principal Performances

1983   Won National Stakes (G2) (2yo) Curragh (7f)
       Won Dewhurst Stakes (G1) (2yo colts & fillies) Newmarket (7f)
1984   Won 2000 Guineas Stakes (G1) (3yo colts & fillies) Newmarket (8f)
       2nd Derby Stakes (G1) (3yo colts & fillies) Epsom (12f)
       Won Irish Derby Stakes (G1) (3yo colts & fillies) Curragh (12f)

*****

*E*l Gran Senor was a brilliant winner of a very good 2000 Guineas. Runner-up Chief Singer subsequently won the G1 July Cup and Sussex Stakes and third placed Lear Fan, the Prix Jacques Le Marois, the top mile race in France by four lengths. After a rather unlucky defeat at Epsom, when beaten a whisker by Secreto (see p51), El Gran Senor made partial amends by winning the Irish Derby. A foot ailment kept him off the track afterwards. In August his connections announced that the colt would stay in training as a four-year-old. This unlikely scenario was soon remedied when in late-November El Gran Senor was retired to stud at Windfields Farm, Maryland with single nominations to him selling for $200,000. The stallion suffered from low fertility throughout his stud career and sired less than 400 foals in total. After getting only fourteen named foals in his first crop, Windfields surrendered their one-third interest in El Gran Senor and settled with their insurance companies.

48

Coolmore moved the horse to their Ashford Stud for 1986 and his fertility improved enough to enable the continuation of his stud career. The best of El Gran Senor's progeny were Al Hareb (G1 Futurity S), Belmez (G1 King George VI and Queen Elizabeth S), Saratoga Springs (G1 Racing Post Trophy), Lit de Justice (G1 Breeder's Cup Sprint), Colonel Collins (3rd G1 2000 Guineas, Derby S, Irish Derby), Toussaud (G1 Gamely S) and best of all, Rodrigo de Triano (p124). El Gran Senor was retired from stud duties in 2000 and died at Ashford Stud on 18 October 2006. The unraced Sex Appeal also bred Try My Best (1975, by Northern Dancer – G1 Dewhurst S) and Solar (1976, by Halo – G3 Railway S). The grandam Best In Show (1965, by Traffic Judge – Comely S), was the dam of Blush With Pride (1979, by Blushing Groom – G1 Kentucky Oaks) and Gielgud (1978, by Sir Ivor – G2 Champagne S).

2126083

09T2184

Above left: **EL GRAN SENOR** shows himself to be the top two-year-old of 1983 by winning the Dewhurst Stakes beating Rainbow Quest (right) and Siberian Express (grey). Above right: **EL GRAN SENOR** and Pat Eddery cruise past the post to win the 2000 Guineas beating Chief Singer (blue cap) and Lear Fan (yellow cap). After winning on Lomond (p40) in 1983, this was the jockey's second and final winner of this Newmarket classic. For Vincent O'Brien, it was a fourth victory in the race following Sir Ivor (1968), Nijinsky (1970) and Lomond and second for Robert Sangster, who also owned Lomond.

1519584

© Unknown

Above left: Future Coronation Cup and Prix de l'Arc de Triomphe winner Rainbow Quest is not ridden to best advantage by Steve Cauthen in a slowly-run race and finishes second once more as **EL GRAN SENOR** and Pat Eddery quicken impressively to victory in the Irish Derby. Cauthen had previously been Rainbow Quest's regular jockey but never rode the colt again. Above right: **EDWARD P .TAYLOR**, the breeder of El Gran Senor, pictured here with **NORTHERN DANCER**. Using this great stallion, Eddie Taylor also bred English Triple Crown winner Nijinsky (p61), Derby winners The Minstrel (p95) and Secreto (p50), Northern Taste (1971 – G1 Prix de la Foret), a champion sire in Japan, Storm Bird (1978 – G1 Dewhurst S) and Shareef Dancer (G1 Irish Derby).

SECRETO (USA)

Bay colt, foaled 12 February 1981
By Northern Dancer (CAN) ex Betty's Secret (USA) by Secretariat (USA)
Bred by Edward P. Taylor
Owned by Luigi Miglietti
Trained by David V. O'Brien at Ballydoyle, Cashel, Co. Tipperary.

T122584

Racing Record

Year	Timeform Annual Rating	Starts	Wins	2nd	3rd	4th	Prize Money
1983	83	1	1	-	-	-	£ 1,190
1984	128	3	2	-	1	-	£ 243,714

Principal Performances

1984   Won Tetrarch Stakes (G3) Curragh (7f)
    3rd Irish 2000 Guineas Stakes (G1) (3yo colts & fillies) Curragh (8f)
    Won Derby Stakes (G1) (3yo colts & fillies) Epsom (12f)

*****

*C*onsidering he was a son of the phenomenally successful stallion Northern Dancer, Secreto was a comparatively cheap buy at $340,000 at the Keeneland Select Yearling Sales. There were apparently concerns about his conformation, in particular his front legs. Less than two years later the colt was reportedly sold after the Derby in a deal which valued him at $40,000,000, an astronomical sum which basically meant that he was too valuable to race again for fear of damaging his reputation. So the colt was retired to Calumet Farm at Lexington in Kentucky having raced only four times in total. He has to be rated as a below average Derby winner, but one who showed courage and a considerable will-to-win. Secreto was a failure at Calumet and was sold to Japan during 1992 where he died in 1999. His best offspring in Europe proved to be the 2000 Guineas winner Mystiko (p114), Miss Secreto (G2 Premio Regina Elena, G2 Premio Lydia Tesio) and Palace Street (LR John of Gaunt S, LR Cammidge Trophy). In Japan his best runner was the champion two-year-old filly, Tamuro Cherry.

50

10T3384   0817784

Above: In a desperate finish, odds-on Derby favourite El Gran Senor (Pat Eddery) (p48) fails to hold the late rally of **SECRETO** (Christy Roche) and goes down by a short-head. 66/1 outsider Mighty Flutter (checks) finishes third and At Talaq (right) fourth. Above right: Venezuelan owner **LUIGI MIGLIETTI** leads in Secreto and **CHRISTY ROCHE** after the Derby. Roche also won the Oaks on Jet Ski Lady (p118) but this was Miglietti's only English classic success.

Left: The great **NORTHERN DANCER** sired 147 stakes winners including the European classic winners Nijinsky (Triple Crown 1970), The Minstrel (Derby and Irish Derby 1977), Lomond (p40), El Gran Senor (p48), Sadler's Wells (Irish 2000 Guineas), Shareef Dancer (Irish Derby), Northern Trick (Prix Diane, Prix Vermeille). Northern Dancer died on 16 November 1990 after suffering an attack of colic. Right: **DAVID O'BRIEN** trained from a neighbouring yard at his father's Ballydoyle Stables.

Left: **SECRETO** in the winner's circle at Epsom; in the foreground, David O'Brien chats to Luigi Miglietti. During a short training career, the son of Vincent O'Brien also trained Assert to win both the Prix du Jockey-Club and the Irish Derby. At age 27, David O'Brien was at that time the youngest winning trainer in Derby history. The unraced Betty's Secret was only four when she foaled Secreto and the colt became the tenth first foal to win the Derby, the latest since Blakeney in 1969. Betty's Secret was a half-sister to Carocolero (1971, by Graustark - G1 Prix du Jockey-Club). Their dam Betty Loraine (1965, by Prince John), was a useful runner, winning seven races from twenty starts in the U.S. and a half-sister to two top-class colts in Majestic Prince (1966, by Raise A Native – Kentucky Derby, Preakness S) and his brother Crowned Prince (1969 – Champagne S, Doncaster and Dewhurst S).

34T3084

CIRCUS PLUME (GB)

Bay filly, foaled 17 April 1981
By High Top (GB) out of Golden Fez (GB) by Aureole (GB)
Bred by Mrs C. Drake
Owned by Sir Robin McAlpine
Trained by John L. Dunlop at Castle Stables, Arundel, Sussex.

1718184

Racing Record

Year	Timeform Annual Rating	Starts	Wins	2nd	3rd	4th	U.K. Prize Money
1983	101	3	1	-	2	-	£ 6,175
1984	124	5	3	2	-	-	£ 165,733
1985	-	2	-	-	-	1	£ 1,359

Principal Performances

1983 3rd Fillies' Mile (G3) (2yo fillies) Ascot (8f)
1984 Won Oaks Stakes (G1) (3yo fillies) Epsom (12f)
       2nd Irish Oaks Stakes (G1) (3yo fillies) Curragh (12f)
       Won Yorkshire Oaks (G1) (3yo fillies) York (12f)
       2nd Prix Vermeille (G1) (3yo fillies) Longchamp (12f)

*****

*I*t was a moderate field of fillies that ran in the 1984 Oaks, but even so Circus Plume just scrambled home by a neck from a 66/1 outsider and would probably have been beaten had her stablemate, Out Of Shot, gone through with her effort inside the final furlong when just about to take the lead. However, Circus Plume did improve and by the end of the season was the best middle-distance three-year-old filly trained in Britain. Golden Fez won only a maiden race in France but comes from an excellent family which includes Mtoto (p173). Her dam Zabara won the 1000 Guineas, was second in the Oaks and a full sister to successful stallion Rustam (1953, by Persian Gulf - Champagne S). Golden Fez's grandam, Samovar (1940, by Caerleon) won the Queen Mary Stakes. As a broodmare, Circus Plume produced several winners although none approached her own ability. The best was Scarlet Plume (1993, by Warning - G3 Premio Dormello). Circus Plume died in 1996.*

T125784

Above: **CIRCUS PLUME** (Lester Piggott) wins the Oaks Stakes beating Media Luna (quartered cap) and Out of Shot (left). Out of Shot was disqualified for causing interference with Poquito Queen (black cap) promoted to third and Optimistic Lass to fourth place. This was a first Oaks victory for trainer **JOHN DUNLOP** (below right) and sixth for Piggott.

2018284

0314284

2716991

Above left: **SIR ROBIN McALPINE** with the Oaks trophy. Sir Robin was the breeder of Circus Plume's dam, Golden Fez, but had sold the mare in 1977. When Circus Plume was auctioned as a foal at Tattersalls December Sales in Newmarket, Sir Robin purchased her for 98,000 guineas. Above centre: **CIRCUS PLUME** lays claim to being the best middle-distance three-year-old filly in Britain, easily winning the Yorkshire Oaks ridden by Willie Carson.

1427885

Left: The 2000 Guineas winner **HIGH TOP** (1969, by Derring-do), at Woodland Stud in Newmarket during 1985. A very successful stallion, High Top sired six European classic winners; All Top (Deutsches St Leger), Cut Above (p24), Top Ville (Prix du Jockey-Club), Colorspin (Irish Oaks), My Top (Derby Italiano) and Circus Plume. Triple First (winner of five group races including G2 Nassau S), Blackadder (LR St Catherine's S), Crews Hill (Stewards' Cup), Circus Ring (G2 Lowther S), Looking For (G1 Premio Roma), Century City (Cambridgeshire H), Top Class (G2 Geoffrey Freer S), Songlines (G2 Prix Niel, G3 Prix du Lys), Kaytu (G3 Chester Vase), Aloft (G3 Princess Royal S), Miner's Lamp (G3 Oettingen Rennen) and Lofty (G3 Diomed S) were other good winners by High Top. The stallion was put down suffering from thrombosis on 9 March 1988.

53

COMMANCHE RUN (IRE)

Bay colt, foaled 1 May 1981
By Run The Gantlet (USA) out of Volley (IRE) by Ratification (GB)
Bred by Majors Racing International Limited
Owned by Ivan Allan
Trained by Luca M. Cumani at Bedford House, Newmarket, Suffolk.

0919285

Racing Record

Year	Timeform Annual Rating	Starts	Wins	2nd	3rd	4th	Prize Money
1983	95	2	-	1	-	-	£ 1,510
1984	129	7	4	-	2	-	£ 150,870
1985	133	5	3	-	1	-	£ 326,756

Principal Performances

1984 3rd King Edward VII Stakes (G2) (3yo colts & geldings) Royal Ascot (12f)
      3rd Princess of Wales's Stakes (G2) Newmarket (12f)
      Won Gordon Stakes (G3) (3yo) Goodwood (12f)
      Won St Leger Stakes (G1) (3yo colts & fillies) Doncaster (14.6f)
1985 Won Brigadier Gerard Stakes (G3) Sandown (10f)
      3rd Prince of Wales's Stakes (G2) Royal Ascot (10f)
      Won Benson & Hedges Gold Cup (G1) York (10.5f)
      Won Phoenix Champion Stakes (G1) Phoenix Park (10f)

*****

*U*nusually for a St Leger winner, Commanche Run was brought back substantially in distance as a four-year-old and won two Group 1 races over ten furlongs. Bought as a yearling on his owner's judgement for only 9,000 guineas and described by Luca Cumani as small and terribly backward, Commanche Run improved physically in mid-summer 1984 and his performances improved hand-in-

hand. His sire Run The Gantletwas a top-class U.S. runner, winning the Man O'War Stakes. Volley only ran once but is out of Mitrailleuse (1944, by Mieuxce - Park Hill S), the great-grandam of two 1000 Guineas winners, Full Dress (1966, by Shantung) and One In A Million (1976, by Rarity). Retired to Coolmore Stud at Fethard in County Tipperary, Commanche Run met with scant success and was moved to Astley Grange Stud in Leicestershire in 1999. His best progeny were Bonny Scot (G2 Great Voltigeur S, 3rd G1 St Leger), Matarun (G3 Prix Exbury) and the versatile Commanche Court (G1 Triumph Hurdle, G1 Punchestown Gold Cup Steeple Chase). Commanche Run died during March 2005.

2616884

1629285

Above: **COMMANCHE RUN** wins the St Leger beating Baynoun (green cap) and Alphabatim (pink cap). It was a first English classic victory for both owner and trainer.

Above, inset: **LESTER PIGGOTT**; Commanche Run was the brilliant jockey's twenty-eighth English classic winner beating the record of Frank Buckle between 1792 and 1827. By the end of his career in 1994, Piggott had ridden 4,493 winners in Britain including thirty classic winners; Humble Duty and Fairy Footsteps (see p14) (1000 Guineas 1970 & 1981); Crepello, Sir Ivor, Nijinsky, Shadeed (p60) and Rodrigo de Triano (p124) (2000 Guineas 1957, 1968, 1970, 1985 and 1992); nine Derby winners (p43); Carrozza, Petite Etoile, Valoris, Juliette Marny, Blue Wind (p22) and Circus Plume (p52) (Oaks 1957, 1959, 1966, 1975, 1981 and 1984); St Paddy, Aurelius, Ribocco, Ribero, Nijinsky, Athens Wood, Boucher and Commanche Run (St Leger 1960, 1961, 1967, 1968, 1970, 1971, 1972 and 1984). Piggott was a genius in the saddle, there will never be another like him.

Below: **COMMANCHE RUN** (Lester Piggott) wins the Benson & Hedges Gold Cup at York beating Steve Cauthen riding Oh So Sharp (p58).

T115385

LOMOND (USA) : Bay 1980

Northern Dancer (CAN) B. 1961	Nearctic (CAN) Br. 1954	Nearco (ITY)
		Lady Angela (GB)
	Natalma (USA) B. 1957	Native Dancer (USA)
		Almahmoud (USA)
My Charmer (USA) B. 1969	Poker (USA) B. 1963	Round Table (USA)
		Glamour (USA)
	Fair Charmer (USA) Ch. 1959	Jet Action (USA)
		Myrtle Charm (USA)

TEENOSO (USA) : Bay 1980

Youth (USA) B. 1973	Ack Ack (USA) B. 1966	Battle Joined (USA)
		Fast Turn (USA)
	Gazala (FR) B. 1964	Dark Star (USA)
		Belle Angevine (FR)
Furioso (GB) B. 1971	Ballymoss (GB) Ch. 1954	Mossborough (GB)
		Indian Call (GB)
	Violetta (ITY) B. 1958	Pinza (GB)
		Urshalim (GB)

SUN PRINCESS (IRE) : Bay 1980

English Prince (IRE) B. 1971	Petingo (GB) B. 1965	Petition (GB)
		Alcazar (FR)
	English Miss (GB) B. 1955	Bois Roussel (FR)
		Virelle (FR)
Sunny Valley (IRE) B. 1972	Val De Loir (FR) B. 1959	Vieux Manoir (FR)
		Vali (FR)
	Sunland (GB) Ch. 1965	Charlottesville (GB)
		Sunny Gulf (GB)

PEBBLES (GB) : Chesnut 1981

Sharpen Up (GB) Ch. 1969	Atan (USA) Ch. 1961	Native Dancer (USA)
		Mixed Marriage (GB)
	Rocchetta (GB) Ch. 1961	Rockefella (GB)
		Chambiges (FR)
La Dolce (GB) Ch. 1976	Connaught (GB) B. 1965	St Paddy (GB)
		Nagaika (FR)
	Guiding Light (FR) Ch. 1965	Crepello (GB)
		Arbitrate (GB)

EL GRAN SENOR (USA) : Bay 1981

Northern Dancer (CAN) B. 1961	Nearctic (CAN) Br. 1954	Nearco (ITY)
		Lady Angela (GB)
	Natalma (USA) B. 1957	Native Dancer (USA)
		Almahmoud (USA)
Sex Appeal (USA) Ch. 1970	Buckpasser (USA) Br. 1963	Tom Fool (USA)
		Busanda (USA)
	Best In Show (USA) Ch. 1965	Traffic Judge (USA)
		Stolen Hour (USA)

SECRETO (USA) : Bay 1981

Northern Dancer (CAN) B. 1961	Nearctic (CAN) Br. 1954	Nearco (ITY)
		Lady Angela (GB)
	Natalma (USA) B. 1957	Native Dancer (USA)
		Almahmoud (USA)
Betty's Secret (USA) Ch. 1977	Secretariat (USA) Ch. 1970	Bold Ruler (USA)
		Somethingroyal (USA)
	Betty Loraine (USA) Ch. 1965	Prince John (USA)
		Gay Hostess (USA)

CIRCUS PLUME (GB) : Bay 1981

High Top (IRE) Br. 1969	Derring-do (GB) Br. 1961	Darius (GB)
		Sipsey Bridge (GB)
	Camenae (GB) B. 1961	Vimy (FR)
		Madrilene (GB)
Golden Fez (GB) B. 1966	Aureole (GB) Ch. 1950	Hyperion (GB)
		Angelola (GB)
	Zabara (GB) Ch. 1949	Persian Gulf (GB)
		Samovar (GB)

COMMANCHE RUN (GB) : Bay 1981

Run The Gantlet (USA) B. 1968	Tom Rolfe (USA) B. 1962	Ribot (GB)
		Pocahontas (USA)
	First Feather (USA) Ch. 1963	First Landing (USA)
		Quill (USA)
Volley (GB) B. 1965	Ratification (GB) B. 1953	Court Martial (GB)
		Solesa (GB)
	Mitrailleuse (GB) B. 1944	Mieuxce (FR)
		French Kin (GB)

OH SO SHARP (GB)

Chestnut filly, foaled 30 March 1982
By Kris (GB) out of Oh So Fair (USA) by Graustark (USA)
Bred by Dalham Stud Farms Limited
Owned by Sheikh Mohammed Al-Maktoum
Trained by Henry R.A. Cecil at Warren Place, Newmarket, Suffolk.

3228885

Racing Record

Year	Timeform Annual Rating	Starts	Wins	2nd	3rd	4th	Prize Money
1984	114	3	3	-	-	-	£ 34,343
1985	131	6	4	2	-	-	£ 397,059

Principal Performances

1984   Won Fillies' Mile (G3) (2yo fillies) Ascot (8f)
1985   Won Nell Gwyn Stakes (G3) (3yo fillies) Newmarket (7f)
       Won 1000 Guineas Stakes (G1) (3yo fillies) Newmarket (8f)
       Won Oaks Stakes (G1) (3yo fillies) Epsom (12f)
       2nd King George VI and Queen Elizabeth Stakes (G1) Ascot (12f)
       2nd Benson & Hedges Gold Cup (G1) York (10.5f)
       Won St Leger Stakes (G1) (3yo colts & fillies) Doncaster (14.6f)

*****

O *h So Sharp was the first horse to win three English classics since Nijinsky in 1970 and only the ninth filly ever to complete the 1000 Guineas, Oaks and St Leger treble. Oh So Sharp was very genuine, consistent and versatile, effective from seven to fourteen furlongs and on any going. She was fairly successful as a broodmare. Her best foal was Rosefinch (1989, by Blushing Groom - G1 Prix Saint-Alary) and Shaima (1988, by Shareef Dancer) won the G2 Long Island Handicap at Belmont Park and was the dam of St Leger winner, Shantou (see p174). Winner and G2 placed Savoire Vivre (1997, by Sadler's Wells) has had some success as a sire in Australia. Oh So Sharp developed laminitis early in 2001 and with her condition deteriorating was put down in October.*

2514685

Above: **OH SO SHARP** and Steve Cauthen get up in the very last stride to win the 1000 Guineas beating Al Bahathri (striped cap), Bella Colora (left) and Vilikaia (right).

Left: **SHEIKH MOHAMMED** leads in a first Oaks winner for himself, Henry Cecil and Steve Cauthen. Oh So Sharp was a half-sister to Roussalka (1972, by Habitat – G2 Coronation & Nassau S), My Fair Niece (1973, by Great Nephew – LR Rous Memorial S, 3rd G2 Ribblesdale S), Etienne Gerard (1974, by Brigadier Gerard – G3 Jersey S) and Our Home (1977, by Habitat – 2nd 1000 Guineas). This family traces directly to the brilliant Mumtaz Mahal (1921, by The Tetrarch – Queen Mary S, Nunthorpe S), the grandam of Nasrullah (1940, by Nearco – Coventry & Champion S, 3rd Derby S), a champion sire in both Britain and the U.S.

3120485

Below: The first filly to win three English classics since Meld in 1955, **OH SO SHARP** and Steve Cauthen complete the treble in the St Leger beating Phardante (no.4) and Lanfranco (rail).

T117185

SHADEED (USA)

Bay colt, foaled 21 March 1982
By Nijinsky (CAN) out of Continual (USA) by Damascus (USA)
Bred by Cherry Valley Farm Inc. & The Gamely Corporation
Owned by Sheikh Maktoum Al-Maktoum
Trained by Michael R. Stoute at Beech Hurst, Newmarket, Suffolk.

2730384

Racing Record

Year	Timeform Annual Rating	Starts	Wins	2nd	3rd	4th	Prize Money
1984	101	2	1	-	1	-	£ 11,081
1985	135	5	3	-	1	-	£ 227,849

Principal Performances

1984   Won Houghton Stakes (2yo) Newmarket (7f)
1985   Won Craven Stakes (G3) (3yo colts & geldings) Newmarket (8f)
       Won 2000 Guineas Stakes (G1) (3yo colts & fillies) Newmarket (8f)
       Won Queen Elizabeth II Stakes (G2) Ascot (8f)
       3rd Breeders' Cup Mile (G1) Aqueduct, U.S.A. (8f turf)

*****

S hadeed, an $800,000 yearling purchase at the Keeneland July Select Sale, was the second foal of Continual, a winner twice from five starts in the U.S. This is the family of the Kentucky Derby and Belmont Stakes winner, Swale (1981, by Seattle Slew), Grade 1 winner Chain Bracelet (1977, by Lyphard) and the top-class Knightly Manner (1961, by Round Table). Shadeed was a very good winner of the 2000 Guineas and after a failed attempt at twelve furlongs in the Derby, after which he was found to be sick, the colt returned in September to prove himself the outstanding three-year-old miler of 1985 in Europe. Like his sire, Shadeed was very highly strung and his early departure from the 2000 Guineas parade earned his trainer a fine of £550 and caused the Stewards of the Jockey Club to issue a statement that any trainers and jockeys held responsible for a horse failing to complete an official parade could run the risk of having their licenses withdrawn. Why not simply have them flogged and *put into the stocks? Shadeed was initially retired to Three Chimneys Farm at Midway before moving to his owner's Gainsborough Farm at Versailles in Kentucky for the 1987 season. Among the many winners he sired were the English classic winners, Shadayid (see p112) and Sayyedati (p132). Shadeed was retired from stud duties in 2004 and died on 13 November 2005. He was buried at Gainsborough Farm.*

1015685

Above: **SHADEED** needs all of Lester Piggott's considerable strength to hold the challenge of Bairn (Willie Carson) and win the 2000 Guineas. Piggott, who was deputising for the suspended Walter Swinburn, was recording his fourth victory in this classic following Crepello (1957), Sir Ivor (1968) and Nijinsky (1970).

2415685

© Unknown

Above left: **MICHAEL STOUTE** poses with his first winner of the 2000 Guineas. Stoute had previously won English classics with Fair Salinia (Oaks 1978) and Shergar (p18).

Above right: Two legends, **LESTER PIGGOTT** on **NIJINSKY** (1967, by Northern Dancer), the last winner of the Triple Crown, parading at Newmarket before the 2000 Guineas. Nijinsky was also the sire of Epsom Derby winners Golden Fleece (p30), Shahrastani (p68) and Lammtarra (p160). Other Group 1 winners by Nijinsky include Caerleon (p191), Ferdinand (Kentucky Derby), Green Dancer (Poule d'Essai des Poulains) and Ile De Bourbon (p87). Nijinsky was put down in April 1992 at the age of twenty-five and was buried at Claiborne Farm in Kentucky.

SLIP ANCHOR (GB)
Bay colt, foaled 5 April 1982
By Shirley Heights (GB) out of Sayonara (GER) by Birkhahn (GER)
Owned and bred by Lord Howard de Walden
Trained by Henry R.A. Cecil at Warren Place, Newmarket, Suffolk.

2727785

Racing Record

Year	Timeform Annual Rating	Starts	Wins	2nd	3rd	4th	Prize Money
1984	91	2	1	-	-	1	£ 3,472
1985	136	6	3	2	1	-	£ 283,496
1986	-	1	-	1	-	-	£ 9,754

Principal Performances

1985   Won Derby Trial Stakes (G3) (3yo) Lingfield (12f)
       Won Derby Stakes (G1) (3yo colts & fillies) Epsom (12f)
       2nd Champion Stakes (G1) (3yo & upwards) Newmarket (10f)
1986   2nd Jockey Club Stakes (G2) Newmarket (12f)

*****

J ust how good was Slip Anchor? On the days that he won the Derby Trial easing up by ten lengths, that could have been twenty had his jockey so wished, and when he thrashed Irish Derby winner Law Society in the Derby with decent horses such as Damister, Supreme Leader and Lanfranco at least another thirteen lengths behind, he was clearly brilliant. It was an unforgettable sight watching Slip Anchor come around Tattenham Corner that day; it seemed an age before another horse came into view. The race for first place was clearly over and there was still almost half-a-mile to run! The colt jarred himself after Epsom and when he returned to the track in September was not in the same form. Sadly, his trainer was typically quick to give up on him after his defeat at Newmarket in the Jockey Club Stakes the following season. Never mind, Slip Anchor was an awesome sight at Epsom on Derby Day. His sire, Shirley Heights and paternal grandsire Mill Reef both won the Derby and his dam comes from a highly successful German family. Before Slip Anchor, Sayonara had foaled G3 Lancashire Oaks winner, Sandy Island (1981, by Mill Reef) for Lord Howard and German classic winner Swazi (1973, by

62

Herero) for her previous owners, Gestut Schlenderhan. Retired to his owner's Plantation Stud at Snailwell just outside Newmarket, Slip Anchor had his moments as a sire without really hitting the heights. His progeny included the European classic winners User Friendly (see p130) and Morshdi (Derby Italiano) as well as Posidonas (G1 Gran Premio d'Italia), Slicious (G1 Premio Roma), Three Cheers (G3 Prix de Lutece, 3rd G1 Ascot Gold Cup), Safety In Numbers (G3 Sagaro S, Prix Gladiateur), Stowaway (G2 Great Voltigeur S, G3 Gordon S), Third Watch (G2 Ribblesdale S), Up Anchor and Kaliana (both G3 St Simon S) and Give The Slip (Ebor H). Slip Anchor suffered from arthritis in his later years and was put down on 22 September 2011. His remains are buried alongside champion miler Kris at Plantation Stud.

1820185

Above: No, this is not the finish of a Grand National! It is **SLIP ANCHOR** and Steve Cauthen in splendid isolation passing the winning post in the Derby. Law Society chases in vain, seven lengths behind.

3720185

23T0485

Above left: **LORD HOWARD DE WALDEN** leading in his Derby winner. It was to prove the seventy-two years old owner/breeder's only classic winner after being involved in racing since 1945.

Above right: **HENRY CECIL** (bare-headed) admiring his first winner of the Derby. Dave Goodwin (at the colt's head) was to look after another Derby winner in Commander in Chief (p136) and Derby and St Leger runner-up Dushyantor (p173/175). Julie Cecil is in the check dress top left of picture and Lady Howard de Walden is wearing a white jacket and blue hat standing behind Henry Cecil.

MIDWAY LADY (USA)

Bay filly, foaled 14 February 1983
By Alleged (USA) out of Smooth Bore (USA) by His Majesty (USA)
Bred by Edward A. Seltzer & Shadowlawn Farm
Owned by Harold H. Ranier
Trained by Ben Hanbury at Diomed Stables, Newmarket, Suffolk.

2831885

Racing Record

Year	Timeform Annual Rating	Starts	Wins	2nd	3rd	4th	Prize Money
1985	120	4	3	1	-	-	£ 54,937
1986	126	2	2	-	-	-	£ 221,196

Principal Performances

1985   Won May Hill Stakes (G3) (2yo fillies) Doncaster (8f)
          Won Prix Marcel Boussac (G1) (2yo fillies) Longchamp (8f)
1986   Won 1000 Guineas Stakes (G1) (3yo fillies) Newmarket (8f)
          Won Oaks Stakes (G1) (3yo fillies) Epsom (12f)

*****

*M*idway Lady was a big, heavy filly and it was always likely that she might prove difficult to keep sound. Tendon trouble caused her retirement in August 1986 after just six races. Bought back as a yearling by one of her joint breeders for only $42,000, she was sold at Keeneland's 1986 November Breeding Stock Sales for $3.3m to Sheikh Hamdan Al-Maktoum's Shadwell Farm. For Sheikh Hamdan, Midway Lady bred Umniyatee (1988, by Green Desert), a winner and classic placed, the useful Haafiz (1996, by Green Desert), Eswarah (see p268), Itnab (2000, by Green Desert - G3 Princess Royal S) and the listed placed winner Ghaidaa (2005, by Cape Cross). Shumookh (2003, by Mujahid) and Sana Abel (2006, by Alhaarth) were both minor winners and although Fatehalkhair (1992, by Kris) was virtually useless on the flat he was the winner of twenty races under National Hunt rules.

2214686

Above: **MIDWAY LADY** (Ray Cochrane) wins the 1000 Guineas beating Maysoon (blue cap) and Sonic Lady (white sleeves). There had been rumours beforehand that Lester Piggott, who had been riding the winner in her work, would come out of what turned out to be temporary retirement to take the mount. But this proved premature (Piggott did not actually return to the jockey's ranks until late in 1990) and Cochrane consequently rode his first English classic winner.

1714986

1720686

Above left: **BEN HANBURY** and **RAY COCHRANE** pose with Midway Lady after the 1000 Guineas. Above right: **HAROLD RANIER** celebrates in the winner's circle after winning the Oaks with a filly bred at his Shadowlawn Farm. When trainer Ben Hanbury (right) retired in 2004 the two races won by Midway Lady were his only English classic victories. Below: A second classic for **MIDWAY LADY** as Ray Cochrane drives her to victory in the Oaks. Two Michael Stoute trained fillies, Untold (rail) and Maysoon finish second and third, as had happened in the 1000 Guineas.

T125386

65

DANCING BRAVE (USA)

Bay colt, foaled 11 May 1983
By Lyphard (USA) out of Navajo Princess (USA) by Drone (USA)
Bred by Glen Oak Farm
Owned by Khalid Abdullah
Trained by Guy Harwood at Coombelands, Pulborough, Sussex.

2835486

Racing Record

Year	Timeform Annual Rating	Starts	Wins	2nd	3rd	4th	Prize Money
1985	110	2	2	-	-	-	£ 6,767
1986	140	8	6	1	-	1	£ 980,310

Principal Performances

1986 Won Craven Stakes (G3) (3yo colts & geldings) Newmarket (8f)
Won 2000 Guineas Stakes (G1) (3yo colts & fillies) Newmarket (8f)
2nd Derby Stakes (G1) (3yo colts & fillies) Epsom (12f)
Won Eclipse Stakes (G1) Sandown (10f)
Won King George VI and Queen Elizabeth Stakes (G1) Ascot (12f)
Won Prix de l'Arc de Triomphe (G1) Longchamp (12f)

*****

D ancing Brave should be included here as a double classic winner, but Greville Starkey's ill-judged
ride caused defeat in the Derby (p69) and ultimately cost Starkey the mount on the best horse he
ever rode. Pat Eddery took over and when he and Dancing Brave swept imperiously to victory at
Longchamp we all knew that we were watching one of the best horses to ever grace the turf. His sire
Lyphard was a top-class miler, winning the Prix Jacques Le Marois. Dancing Brave's dam was good
and obviously sound, winning sixteen races, including a G2 in the U.S. This was formerly a family
notable for its durability rather than outstanding class, brought to new heights by the achievements of
Dancing Brave and his sister Jolypha (1989 – G1 Prix de Diane, Prix Vermeille). A $200,000 yearling
purchase by James Delahooke, Dancing Brave was syndicated at a valuation of £14m to stand at
Dalham Hall Stud in Newmarket. The stallion's early stud career was affected by severe illness and led
to his sale to Shizunai Stallion Station at Hokkaido, Japan in 1991. Inevitably, the good winners started

to flow after Dancing Brave's export. They included Commander in Chief (p136), Wemyss Bight (Irish Oaks), White Muzzle (Derby Italiano, 2ⁿᵈ King George VI & Queen Elizabeth S twice, 2ⁿᵈ Prix de l'Arc de Triomphe) and Cherokee Rose (G1 Sprint Cup). Dancing Brave died on 2 August 1999 in Japan.

2014886

Above: **DANCING BRAVE** (Greville Starkey) wins the 2000 Guineas with ears pricked, beating the very good colt Green Desert (Walter Swinburn) by three lengths.

2328786   3513687   3428385

Above left: Revenge for an unlucky Derby defeat; **DANCING BRAVE** wins the King George VI & Queen Elizabeth Stakes beating Shardari, Triptych and Shahrastani (see p68). Centre: **GUY HARWOOD** was a leading trainer in Britain for twenty-five years. This was his second 2000 Guineas victory following To-Agori-Mou (p16). Right: **GREVILLE STARKEY** (see p17) wearing the colours of Khalid Abdullah.

1740286

Above: **DANCING BRAVE** and Pat Eddery defeat a representative field of Europe's top middle-distance horses, producing a dazzling burst of finishing speed to win the Prix de l'Arc de Triomphe beating the Prix du Jockey-Club winner, Bering (no.14) and Triptych (hidden). Shahrastani (no.13) finishes fourth and Shardari (brown cap) fifth.

SHAHRASTANI (USA)

Chesnut colt, foaled 27 March 1983
By Nijinsky (CAN) out of Shademah (IRE) by Thatch (USA)
Owned and bred by H.H. Aga Khan
Trained by Michael R. Stoute at Beech Hurst, Newmarket, Suffolk.

1128786

Racing Record

Year	Timeform Annual Rating	Starts	Wins	2nd	3rd	4th	Prize Money
1985	104	1	-	1	-	-	£ 1,820
1986	135	6	4	-	-	2	£ 648,541

Principal Performances

1986   Won Classic Trial Stakes (G3) (3yo colts & geldings) Sandown (10f)
      Won Dante Stakes (G2) (3yo) York (10.5f)
      Won Derby Stakes (G1) (3yo colts & fillies) Epsom (12f)
      Won Irish Derby Stakes (G1) (3yo colts & fillies) Curragh (12f)
      4th King George VI and Queen Elizabeth Stakes (G1) Ascot (12f)
      4th Prix de l'Arc de Triomphe (G1) Longchamp (12f)

*****

S hahrastani is destined to be remembered as the winner of the Derby that Dancing Brave would have won but for jockey error, however he was a top classic horse in his own right. This handsome, good-moving colt subsequently won the Irish Derby and finished a gallant fourth in a vintage Prix de l'Arc de Triomphe. Shahrastani was retired to Three Chimneys Farm at Lexington in Kentucky but was disappointing as a sire moving to Ireland, France and Japan before finishing at Walton Fields Stud at Grimston in Leicestershire. Retired from stud duties in 2010, Shahrastani was put down during December 2011 at the age of twenty-eight. The best horses he sired were Dariyoun (G1 Gran Premio de Madrid), Rifapour (G2 Prix Hocquart), Cajarian (G3 Meld S, G3 Leopardstown S) and Sendoro (2nd G1 Criterium de Saint-Cloud). The Derby winner's grandam Shamim bred Shakapour (1977, by Kalamoun – G1 GP de Saint-Cloud) and Sharannpour (1980, by Busted – G1 Bowling Green H) as well as Shademah, a three-times winner for Michael Stoute in 1981. This is the family of Amante*

68

(1955, by Tehran – Irish Oaks), Opaline (1958, by Hyperion – Cheveley Park S) and Kamaraan (1971, by Tanerko – G2 Prix du Conseil de Paris, 3rd G1 Prix du Jockey-Club).

05T0186

Above: **SHAHRASTANI** (Walter Swinburn) wins the Derby beating fast-finishing Dancing Brave (pink cap) (see p66) by half-a-length. This was a second Derby victory in five years for the Aga Khan, Michael Stoute and Swinburn following Shergar (p18).

3032989   0414102   3215286

Above: A successful combination; **MICHAEL STOUTE, H.H. AGA KHAN** and **WALTER SWINBURN**. They were victorious together in three English classics with Shergar, Shahrastani and Doyoun (p84), and also the King George VI & Queen Elizabeth Stakes (Shergar), the Irish Derby (Shahrastani), the International Stakes (Shardari) and the Nassau Stakes (Kartajana). Swinburn retired early in 2000 after experiencing increasing problems keeping his weight under control. Below: Another Derby victory for **SHAHRASTANI** and Swinburn, this time in Ireland, as they defeat Bonhomie, Bakharoff and Mashkour by eight lengths, then a record winning distance in this race. Note the beautiful, uncluttered background, free of all the unsightly advertising defacing our racecourses nowadays.

0524386

69

MOON MADNESS (GB)

Bay colt, foaled 1 March 1983
By Vitiges (FR) out of Castle Moon (GB) by Kalamoun (GB)
Owned & bred by Lavinia, Duchess of Norfolk
Trained by John L. Dunlop at Castle Stables, Arundel, Sussex.

1432687

Racing Record

Year	Timeform Annual Rating	Starts	Wins	2nd	3rd	4th	Win & U.K. Prize Money
1985	80	1	-	-	-	1	-
1986	128	8	6	-	2	-	£ 157,524
1987	126	9	3	1	1	2	£ 216,089
1988	120	6	1	-	2	-	£ 49,375

Principal Performances

1986   Won Scottish Derby Stakes (Listed Race) (3yo) Ayr (11f)
      3rd Great Voltigeur Stakes (G2) (3yo colts & geldings) York (12f)
      Won St Leger Stakes (G1) (3yo colts & fillies) Doncaster (14.6f)
      3rd Europa Preis (G1) Cologne, Germany (12f)
1987   3rd Hardwicke Stakes (G2) Royal Ascot (12f)
      Won Grand Prix de Saint-Cloud (G1) Saint-Cloud (12f)
      4th King George VI and Queen Elizabeth Stakes (G1) Ascot (12f)
      Won Geoffrey Freer Stakes (G2) Newbury (13.3f)
      2nd Grosser Preis von Baden (G1) Baden-Baden (12f)
      Won Cumberland Lodge Stakes (G3) Ascot (12f)
1988   Won Yorkshire Cup (G2) York (14f)
      3rd Coronation Cup (G1) Epsom (12f)
      3rd Hardwicke Stakes (G2) Royal Ascot (12f)

*M*oon Madness was tough, sound and genuine and performed with admirable consistency at, or just below, the top level for three years until deteriorating halfway through his final season. He possessed a good turn of finishing speed and would have been an interesting contender for the Cup races, but the distance of the St Leger was the longest he ever raced over. Castle Moon won three times in maiden and handicap company and was a full sister to the useful Castle Keep (1977) and half-sister to Ragstone (1970, by Ragusa – G1 Ascot Gold Cup). A successful broodmare, Castle Moon produced at least five winners, the best of which, apart from Moon Madness, was Sheriff's Star (1985, by Posse), winner of the Coronation Cup and emulated his half-brother by adding the Grand Prix de Saint-Cloud to his victories. Moon Madness was retired to the Hokkaido Breeding Centre in Japan but attracted no interest there and was brought back to Europe during December 1994 to stand at stud in France, where he was covering National Hunt mares, but sadly achieved little impact on the French jumping scene.

1735886

Above: **MOON MADNESS** and Pat Eddery winning the St Leger. This was a first success in the Doncaster classic for owner (below left), trainer (below centre) and jockey (below right).

Right: Another view of the St Leger showing **MOON MADNESS** winning comfortably from Celestial Storm (right) with Untold and Swink (blaze) trailing. This was the only English classic success for progeny of the French-bred stallion Vitiges (1973, by Phaeton – G1 Champion S), a disappointing sire at Someries Stud in Newmarket before his export to Japan in 1984.

0536086

3535886

2139587

3013990

3335886

71

MIESQUE (USA)

Bay filly, foaled 14 March 1984
By Nureyev (USA) out of Pasadoble (USA) by Prove Out (USA)
Bred by Flaxman Holdings Limited
Owned by Stavros Niarchos
Trained by Francois Boutin at Lamorlaye, Oise, France.

3622787

Racing Record

Year	Timeform Annual Rating	Starts	Wins	2nd	3rd	4th	Win & U.K. Prize Money
1986	124	4	3	-	1	-	£ 82,394
1987	131	8	6	2	-	-	£ 736,144
1988	133	4	3	1	-	-	£ 385,585

Principal Performances

1986   3rd Prix Morny (G1) (2yo colts & fillies) Deauville (6f)
       Won Prix de la Salamandre (G1) (2yo colts & fillies) Longchamp (7f)
       Won Prix Marcel Boussac (G1) (2yo fillies) Longchamp (8f)
1987   Won 1000 Guineas Stakes (G1) (3yo fillies) Newmarket (8f)
       Won Poule d'Essai des Pouliches (G1) (3yo fillies) Longchamp (8f)
       2nd Prix de Diane (G1) (3yo fillies) Chantilly (10.5f)
       Won Prix Jacques Le Marois (G1) Deauville (8f)
       Won Prix du Moulin de Longchamp (G1) Longchamp (8f)
       2nd Queen Elizabeth II Stakes (G1) Ascot (8f)
       Won Breeders' Cup Mile (G1) Hollywood Park, U.S.A. (8f turf)
1988   Won Prix d'Ispahan (G1) Longchamp (9.2f)
       Won Prix Jacques Le Marois (G1) Deauville (8f)
       2nd Prix du Moulin de Longchamp (G1) Longchamp (8f)
       Won Breeders' Cup Mile (G1) Churchill Downs, U.S.A. (8f turf)

M *iesque was an outstanding filly at a mile, the first to complete the 1000 Guineas-Poule d'Essai des Pouliches classic double since Imprudence (1944, by Canot) and capable of beating top-class colts, Warning and Soviet Star, over the distance. Miesque was one of the best winners of the 1000 Guineas since 1950, only Petite Etoile (1959), Hula Dancer (1963) and Bosra Sham (p166) being rated above her by Timeform (p385). Pasadoble was a stakes winner in France and also bred Massaaraat (1988, by Nureyev – LR Prix Amandine), the dam of the listed winner Tessa Reef (2000, by Mark of Esteem). Grandam Santa Quilla was a half-sister to the top-class filly Comtesse de Loir (1971, by Val de Loir). Miesque was a highly successful broodmare for Niarchos producing five stakes winners including Kingmambo (1990, by Mr Prospector, p299), East of the Moon (1991, by Private Account - dual classic winner in France), Mingun (2000, by A P Indy – G3 Meld S) and Miesque's Son (1992, by Mr Prospector - G3 Prix de Ris-Orangis). Through her daughter Moon Is Up (1993, by Woodman), Miesque is also the great grandam of Karakontie (2011, by Bernstein), winner of the French classic, Poule d'Essai des Poulains. Miesque was put down at Lane's End Farm on 20 January 2011.*

0415287

Above: **MIESQUE** (Freddy Head) winning the 1000 Guineas beating Milligram (left) and Interval (centre). This was Head's second victory in this classic following that of Ma Biche (p36). Below centre: **MARIA NIARCHOS** and **FRANCOIS BOUTIN** with their 1000 Guineas trophies. This was the last of four English classics won by Boutin (for more about Francois Boutin, see p29).

2739986   2215287   1937189

Above left: **FREDDY HEAD**, here wearing the colours of Stavros Niarchos, was champion jockey in France on six occasions. Apart from the three classic winners he rode in England, Zino (p28), Ma Biche and Miesque, Head also won twenty-five French classics and the Prix de l'Arc de Triomphe on four occasions. Freddy Head is now a very successful trainer, based at Chantilly. Above right: **STAVROS NIARCHOS** was leading owner in France twice (1983-4). He also owned Nureyev (1977, by Northern Dancer), disqualified after passing the post first in the 2000 Guineas (p7). Niarchos died in Zurich in 1996 and his racing interests are perpetuated by his family.

OH SO SHARP (GB) : Chesnut 1982

Kris (GB) Ch. 1976	Sharpen Up (GB) Ch. 1969	Atan (USA)
		Rocchetta (GB)
	Doubly Sure (GB) B. 1971	Reliance (FR)
		Soft Angels (GB)
Oh So Fair (USA) B. 1967	Graustark (USA) Ch. 1963	Ribot (GB)
		Flower Bowl (USA)
	Chandelle (USA) Br. 1959	Swaps (USA)
		Malindi (IRE)

SHADEED (USA) : Bay 1982

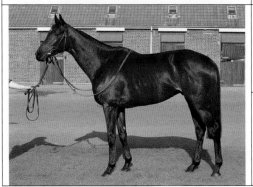

Nijinsky (CAN) B. 1967	Northern Dancer (CAN) B. 1961	Nearctic (CAN)
		Natalma (USA)
	Flaming Page (CAN) B. 1959	Bull Page (USA)
		Flaring Top (USA)
Continual (USA) B/br. 1976	Damascus (USA) B. 1964	Sword Dancer (USA)
		Kerala (USA)
	Continuation (USA) Ch. 1971	Forli (ARG)
		Continue (USA)

SLIP ANCHOR (GB) : Bay 1982

Shirley Heights (GB) B. 1975	Mill Reef (USA) B. 1968	Never Bend (USA)
		Milan Mill (USA)
	Hardiemma (GB) B. 1969	Hardicanute (GB)
		Grand Cross (GB)
Sayonara (GER) B. 1965	Birkhahn (GER) Br/bl. 1945	Alchimist (GER)
		Bramouse (FR)
	Suleika (GER) Br. 1954	Ticino (GER)
		Schwartzblaurot (GER)

MIDWAY LADY (USA) : Bay 1983

Alleged (USA) B. 1974	Hoist The Flag (USA) B. 1968	Tom Rolfe (GB)
		Wavy Navy (USA)
	Princess Pout (USA) B. 1966	Prince John (USA)
		Determined Lady (USA)
Smooth Bore (USA) Ch. 1976	His Majesty (USA) B. 1968	Ribot (GB)
		Flower Bowl (USA)
	French Leave (USA) B. 1970	Damascus (USA)
		Marche Lorraine (FR)

DANCING BRAVE (USA) : Bay 1983

		Northern Dancer (CAN) B. 1961	Nearctic (CAN)
Lyphard (USA) B. 1969			Natalma (USA)
		Goofed (USA) Ch. 1960	Court Martial (GB)
			Barra (FR)
Navajo Princess (USA) B. 1974		Drone (USA) Gr. 1966	Sir Gaylord (USA)
			Cap And Bells (USA)
		Olmec (USA) Ch. 1966	Pago Pago (AUS)
			Chocolate Beau (USA)

SHAHRASTANI (USA) : Chesnut 1983

		Northern Dancer (CAN) B. 1961	Nearctic (CAN)
Nijinsky (CAN) B. 1967			Natalma (USA)
		Flaming Page (CAN) B. 1959	Bull Page (USA)
			Flaring Top (USA)
Shademah (IRE) Ch. 1978		Thatch (USA) B. 1970	Forli (ARG)
			Thong (USA)
		Shamim (IRE) Ch. 1968	Le Haar (FR)
			Diamond Drop (GB)

MOON MADNESS (GB) : Bay 1983

		Phaeton (IRE) Gr. 1964	Sicambre (FR)
Vitiges (FR) Ch. 1973			Pasquinade (FR)
		Vale (FR) Ch. 1959	Verrieres (FR)
			Calliopsis (GB)
Castle Moon (GB) Gr. 1975		Kalamoun (GB) Gr. 1970	Zeddaan (GB)
			Khairunissa (GB)
		Fotheringay (FR) B. 1964	Right Royal (FR)
			La Fresnes (GB)

MIESQUE (USA) : Bay 1984

		Northern Dancer (CAN) B. 1961	Nearctic (CAN)
Nureyev (USA) B. 1977			Natalma (USA)
		Special (USA) B. 1969	Forli (ARG)
			Thong (USA)
Pasadoble (USA) B. 1979		Prove Out (USA) Ch. 1969	Graustark (USA)
			Equal Venture (USA)
		Santa Quilla (FR) B. 1970	Sanctus (FR)
			Neriad (USA)

DON'T FORGET ME (IRE)

Bay colt, foaled 10 April 1984
By Ahonoora (GB) out of African Doll (IRE) by African Sky (GB)
Bred by Mrs. Frances R. Hutch
Owned by James Horgan
Trained by Richard Hannon at East Everleigh Stables, Marlborough, Wiltshire.

1624986

Racing Record

Year	Timeform Annual Rating	Starts	Wins	2nd	3rd	4th	Prize Money
1986	120	4	3	-	-	1	£ 53,655
1987	127	6	2	1	-	2	£ 195,756

Principal Performances

1986   Won Vintage Stakes (G3) (2yo) Goodwood (7f)
         Won Champagne Stakes (G2) (2yo) Doncaster (7f)
1987   Won 2000 Guineas Stakes (G1) (3yo colts & fillies) Newmarket (8f)
         Won Irish 2000 Guineas Stakes (G1) (3yo colts & fillies) Curragh (8f)
         4th Prix Jacques Le Marois (G1) (3yo & upwards) Deauville (8f)

*****

*D*on't Forget Me was a very genuine colt who showed great courage to make all the running to win both the English and Irish 2000 Guineas, a double only previously achieved by Right Tack (1966, by Hard Tack). African Doll and grandam Mithril were only a minor winners but came from the same family as Rustam (see p49), Zabara (p49), Circus Plume (p49) and Mtoto (1983, by Busted). Third-dam Baraka (1955, by Souverain) was useless on the racecourse but a granddaughter of Samovar (1940, by Caerleon – Queen Mary S). A 19,000 guineas yearling bargain at Tattersalls October Sales in Newmarket, Don't Forget Me was bought by Coolmore Stud for IR£3m and stood there until his export to India in 1994. During this time the stallion was also shuttled to Australia during the southern hemisphere breeding season. His best progeny included the pattern winners, Irish Memory (LR Tyros

S, G3 Tetrarch S), My Memoirs (LR Dee S), A Smooth One (G3 Princess Margaret S), Insatiable (G2 Prix Dollar, G3 Brigadier Gerard S, G3 Blandford S) and Rudi's Pet (G3 King George S). Don't Forget Me died in India during March 2010.

0415787

Above: **DON'T FORGET ME** wins the 2000 Guineas beating Bellotto (right) and Midyan (no.8).

Below left: **WILLIE CARSON** returns to the winner's circle on his third 2000 Guineas winner. The jockey had previously been successful on High Top (1972) and Known Fact (p6).

1815487   3115487   2112179

Above centre: **RICHARD HANNON**, wearing his Don't Forget Me lucky tie, registered his second victory in this classic following Mon Fils in 1973.

Above right: **AHONOORA** was a top-class sprinter winning the King George Stakes at Goodwood (pictured) and the Nunthorpe Stakes at York. He proved a surprisingly successful sire at the Irish National Stud getting winners over a variety of distances including the English classic winners Dr Devious (p126) and Don't Forget Me. Other top-class winners by Ahonoora included Park Appeal (Cheveley Park S), Park Express (Irish Champion S), Indian Ridge (King's Stand S), Ruby Tiger (Nassau S, E.P.Taylor S) and Inchinor (Criterion S, sire of Notnowcato, Eclipse S). Ahonoora has also proved a very successful broodmare sire, with such as New Approach (p304) and Cape Cross (sire of Sea The Stars, p310) out of mares by him. Coolmore made an approach to buy Ahonoora which was rejected by the Irish National Stud, but eventually acquired him through an Australian connection. The stallion was shuttled to Segenhoe Stud in N.S.W. for the southern hemisphere breeding season but fractured a hind-leg in a paddock accident there and had to be put down in September 1989.

REFERENCE POINT (GB)

Bay colt, foaled 26 February 1984
By Mill Reef (USA) out of Home On The Range (GB) by Habitat (USA)
Owned and bred by Louis Freedman at Cliveden Stud, Maidenhead, Berkshire
Trained by Henry Cecil at Warren Place, Newmarket, Suffolk.

1720587

Racing Record

Year	Timeform Annual Rating	Starts	Wins	2nd	3rd	4th	Prize Money
1986	132	3	2	-	1	-	£ 47,660
1987	139	7	5	1	-	-	£ 726,608

Principal Performances

1986   Won Futurity Stakes (G1) (2yo) Doncaster (8f)
1987   Won Dante Stakes (G2) (3yo) York (10.5f)
          Won Derby Stakes (G1) (3yo colts & fillies) Epsom (12f)
          2nd Eclipse Stakes (G1) Sandown (10f)
          Won King George VI and Queen Elizabeth Stakes (G1) Ascot (12f)
          Won Great Voltigeur Stakes (G2) (3yo colts & geldings) York (12f)
          Won St Leger Stakes (G1) (3yo colts & fillies) Doncaster (14.6f)

*****

*R**eference Point was a brave front-runner brilliantly handled by Steve Cauthen, and proved almost impossible to pass except when pounced on close home by Mtoto (photo, p173) at Sandown. This race clearly exposed Reference Point's one weakness, an inability to quicken instantly. Reference Point was a very good horse in a below average year for staying three-year-old colts, but also proved himself by beating a useful field of older horses at Ascot. Home On The Range was a good racemare, winning the G2 Sun Chariot Stakes, bred, as was her dam Great Guns, at Cliveden Stud. Reference Point was retired to Dalham Hall Stud at Newmarket where in an undistinguished stud career he sired only one top-class winner, Ivyanna (G1 Oaks d'Italia). Reference Point was put down after fracturing a leg in an accident at Dalham Hall Stud during December 1991.*

1220787

Above: **REFERENCE POINT** (Steve Cauthen) makes all the running and wins the Derby beating Most Welcome (centre) and Bellotto (pink cap). This was a second Derby victory for trainer Henry Cecil after Slip Anchor (p62).

0429187

0537787

Above left: Winning the King George VI & Queen Elizabeth Stakes beating Celestial Storm and Triptych (rail).

Above right: **LOUIS FREEDMAN** also owned and bred Polygamy (Oaks 1974).

0614885

1237687

Above left: **STEVE CAUTHEN**; Reference Point was his second winner of both the Derby and St Leger. Above right: **REFERENCE POINT** wins his second English classic and seventh for Cauthen.

UNITE (IRE)

Chesnut filly, foaled 3 April 1984
By Kris (GB) out of Pro Patria (IRE) by Petingo (GB)
Bred by Edmund J. Loder
Owned by Sheikh Mohammed Al-Maktoum
Trained by Michael Stoute at Beech Hurst Stables, Newmarket, Suffolk.

2329087

Racing Record

Year	Timeform Annual Rating	Starts	Wins	2nd	3rd	4th	Prize Money
1986	83	1	-	1	-	-	£ 2,890
1987	126	4	3	-	-	-	£ 249,026

Principal Performances

1987   Won Oaks Stakes (G1) (3yo fillies) Epsom (12f)
       Won Irish Oaks Stakes (G1) (3yo fillies) Curragh (12f)

*****

A big, rangy filly with a powerful action and a striking resemblance to Oh So Sharp (p58), Unite, a 310,000 guineas yearling, was head and shoulders above the rest of the staying fillies of 1987, winning both the English and Irish Oaks by wide margins. After running poorly at Ascot in July she was found to have broken a blood vessel and retired. Before her death in 2001, Unite produced a few winners for Sheikh Mohammed's Darley Stud. United Kingdom (1989, by Danzig) won two minor races in 1992, Hyphenate (1990, by Lyphard) was successful in Dubai and La Confederation (1991, by Nureyev) won the G2 Sun Chariot Stakes, two other races and is the grand-dam of Veracity (G3 Jockey Club Cup). Pro Patria, a full-sister to Patris (1973 – 4th 2000 Guineas), only raced as a two-year-old, winning two small races for Peter Walwyn's Seven Barrows stables at Lambourn. Her dam Joyful was retired through injury after winning her second race, a maiden at Sandown. Lady Seymour (1972, by Tudor Melody), a half-sister to Joyful, won the Phoenix Stakes and was dam of champion sprinter Marwell (1978, by Habitat), winner of the Cheveley Park and King's Stand Stakes, the July Cup and Prix de l'Abbaye for Unite's trainer. This is the family of Paean (1983, by Bustino – G1 Ascot Gold Cup) and Be My Chief (1987, by Chief's Crown – G1 Racing Post Trophy, G3 Vintage S, Solario S).

80

0521487

Above: **UNITE** (Walter Swinburn) wins the Oaks by five lengths beating Bourbon Girl. The result was almost repeated the following month in the Irish Oaks where Bourbon Girl cut the distance between them to three lengths. This was a first Oaks victory for Swinburn and second for Michael Stoute following Fair Salinia (1978)

2233192

1221587

Above left: **SIR EDMUND LODER** of Eyrefield Lodge Stud in County Kildare, the breeder of Unite and her winning siblings Palletine (1981, by African Sky), Wahem (1990, by Lomond), Liversan (1991, by Sure Blade – LR Derby du Midi) and Spirit Willing (1996, by Fairy King – Fenwolf S). Above right: **SHEIKH MOHAMMED** in the winner's circle at Epsom with his second Oaks winner in three years following Oh So Sharp. His younger brother Sheikh Ahmed is on his right.

Right: Lord Howard de Walden's **KRIS** was champion miler in Britain in 1979, winning the Queen Elizabeth II Stakes and Sussex Stakes. Kris was syndicated at a valuation of £4m to stand at his owner's Thornton Stud in Yorkshire before moving to Plantation Stud in Newmarket during 1994. He was a very successful sire getting the European classic winners Oh So Sharp, Flash of Steel and Unite. Other group winners by Kris include Common Grounds, Reach, Fitnah, Shamshir, Sure Blade and Balisada. Kris, the champion sire in Britain in 1985, was retired from stud duties in February 2002 and found dead in his paddock during November 2004. He is buried at Plantation Stud alongside Lord Howard's Derby winner, Slip Anchor.

0113879

RAVINELLA (USA)

Bay filly, foaled 11 March 1985
By Mr Prospector (USA) out of Really Lucky (USA) by Northern Dancer (CAN)
Bred by Societe Aland
Owned by Ecurie Aland
Trained by Christiane Head at Chantilly, Oise, France.

3517488

Racing Record

Year	Timeform Annual Rating	Starts	Wins	2nd	3rd	4th	Win & U.K. Prize Money
1987	121	3	3	-	-	-	£ 53,292
1988	121	7	4	-	1	1	£ 296,204
1989	-	8	3	2	2	-	-

Principal Performances

1987 Won Prix d'Arenberg (G3) (2yo) Longchamp (5f)
      Won Cheveley Park Stakes (G1) (2yo fillies) Newmarket (6f)
1988 Won 1000 Guineas Stakes (G1) (3yo fillies) Newmarket (8f)
      Won Poule d'Essai des Pouliches (G1) (3yo fillies) Longchamp (8f)
      3rd Coronation Stakes (G1) (3yo fillies) Royal Ascot (8f)
1989 3rd Gamely Stakes (G1) (Fillies & mares) Hollywood Park, U.S.A. (9f)

*****

*R*avinella was a below average winner of the 1000 Guineas despite her winning the French
equivalent next time out. She was subsequently well beaten at Royal Ascot and when taking on
older horses for the first time in a Group 3 at Longchamp. She was the only English classic winner sired
by top U.S. stallion Mr Prospector (1970, by Raise A Native). Her dam was a minor stakes winner in
France out of top-class sprinter Realty. This is the family of Kentucky Derby winner, Believe It (1975,
by In Reality). Ravinella was sold at Tattersall's 1988 December Sales to Allen Paulson for 1.4m
guineas and raced for her new owner in the U.S.A. during 1989. Ravinella died during September 1991;
her only foal, Bodleian (1991, by Reference Point) died as a two-year-old, unraced.

0614888

Above: **RAVINELLA** (Gary Moore) winning the 1000 Guineas Stakes beating Dabaweyaa (striped cap) and Diminuendo (left, see p88). This was the Australian jockey's only English classic winner.

1814888

3414888

Above left: **GARY MOORE** with Ravinella after the 1000 Guineas. On the right is Gary's father, George Moore, the legendary Australian jockey, who had won the same race on Fleet in 1967. Above right: The 1000 Guineas trophy presentation; Gary Moore, **CHRISTIANE HEAD**, and owners **ROLAND DE CHAMBURE** and **ALEC** and **GHISLAINE HEAD**, the Ecurie Aland partnership.

Below: **RAVINELLA** (Gary Moore) triumphs in the French classic Poule d'Essai des Pouliches beating Duckling Park (Steve Cauthen).

3117788

DOYOUN (IRE)

Bay colt, foaled 8 March 1985
By Mill Reef (USA) out of Dumka (FR) by Kashmir II (GB)
Owned and bred by H.H. Aga Khan
Trained by Michael R. Stoute at Beech Hurst Stables, Newmarket, Suffolk.

2415188

Racing Record

Year	Timeform Annual Rating	Starts	Wins	2nd	3rd	4th	Prize Money
1987	101	1	1	-	-	-	£ 5,072
1988	124	6	2	-	3	-	£ 185,788

Principal Performances

1988   Won Craven Stakes (G3) (3yo colts & geldings) Newmarket (8f)
      Won 2000 Guineas Stakes (G1) (3yo colts & fillies) Newmarket (8f)
      3rd Derby Stakes (G1) (3yo colts & fillies) Epsom (12f)
      3rd Champion Stakes (G1) (3yo & upwards) Newmarket (10f)

*****

*D*oyoun ran in the 2000 Guineas having raced only twice previously. An easy win in a maiden at Newmarket in October 1987 was followed by an impressive victory over the winter 2000 Guineas favourite Warning in the Craven Stakes. The colt catapulted to the head of the betting market for the classic and on the day Doyoun started at odds-on. In a race not really run to suit him, Doyoun scrambled home from Charmer and the decision was taken to test his stamina in the Derby where the colt finished a good third behind his owner's Kahyasi (see p86). Doyoun failed to win again and was retired to Ballymany Stud on The Curragh in County Kildare. Despite getting National Stakes winner Manntari in his second crop, Doyoun's moderate early results caused his sale to Turkey in 1998. Almost inevitably the good winners came immediately. Daylami (classic winner in France, eight G1 races including the Coronation Cup, Eclipse S, King George VI and Queen Elizabeth S and Breeders' Cup Turf), Kalanisi (Champion S, Breeders' Cup Turf) and Manndar (Manhattan H) were all winners at the highest level and led to attempts being made to buy Doyoun back. The Turkish Jockey Club refused to sell and the stallion died of intestinal cancer at Izmit Central Covering Station near Istanbul on 5

December 2002. Doyoun's dam Dumka won the French classic, Poule d'Essai des Pouliches and also bred Dalsaan (1977, by Habitat – G3 Hungerford & Criterion S), Dafayna (1982, by Habitat – G3 Cork & Orrery S) and stakes winners Dayzaan (1976, by Riverman) and Dolka (1983, by Shergar). Grandam Faizebad won in France and was a half-sister to Flossy (1966, by Spy Well – Champion S), tracing back to Major Lionel Holliday's celebrated mare Lost Soul (1931, by Solario), ancestress of the English classic winners Neasham Belle (1948, by Nearco – Oaks S) and Hethersett (1959, by Hugh Lupus – St Leger S).

0315488

Above: **DOYOUN** (Walter Swinburn) wins the 2000 Guineas, holding the late challenge of Charmer (Willie Carson, right) by half-a-length. It was a first victory in this race for the Aga Khan and second for Michael Stoute following Shadeed (p60).

1915488

Left: **WALTER SWINBURN** with Doyoun after the 2000 Guineas. On the right is James Fanshawe, at that time assistant to Michael Stoute. This was the only occasion that Swinburn won this classic. He had missed the winning ride on Shadeed in 1985 through suspension.

Left: The brilliant racehorse and stallion **MILL REEF** (1968, by Never Bend), sire of Doyoun, two Derby winners, Shirley Heights (1978) and Reference Point (p78) and also Fairy Footsteps (p14). Other top-class winners by Mill Reef included Acamas (Prix du Jockey-Club), Glint of Gold (Derby Italiano), Diamond Shoal (Grand Prix de Saint-Cloud), Pas de Seul (Prix de la Foret), Milligram (Queen Elizabeth II S), Lashkari (Breeders Cup Turf), Wassl (Irish 2000 Guineas), Paris Royal (Oaks d'Italia), Ibn Bey (Preis von Europa), Star Lift (Prix Royal-Oak), Behera (Prix Saint-Alary) and Creator (Prix d'Ispahan). Mill Reef was put down in 1986 at The National Stud in Newmarket where he had been standing since 1973.

KAHYASI (IRE)

Bay colt, foaled 2 April 1985
By Ile de Bourbon (USA) out of Kadissya (USA) by Blushing Groom (FR)
Owned and bred by H.H. Aga Khan
Trained by Luca M. Cumani at Bedford House Stables, Newmarket, Suffolk.

1316388

Racing Record

Year	Timeform Annual Rating	Starts	Wins	2nd	3rd	4th	Prize Money
1987	97	1	1	-	-	-	£ 5,365
1988	130	6	4	1	-	-	£ 627,800

Principal Performances

1988 Won Derby Trial Stakes (G3) (3yo) Lingfield (12f)
      Won Derby Stakes (G1) (3yo colts & fillies) Epsom (12f)
      Won Irish Derby Stakes (G1) (3yo colts & fillies) Curragh (12f)
      2nd Prix Niel (G2) (3yo colts & fillies) Longchamp (12f)

*****

*K*ahyasi was not very big but he was tough, sound and tried his heart out. The colt was unlucky not to go into his last race unbeaten as he was inconvenienced by a slow early pace in the Prix Niel and just failed to catch the winner. His final race was the Prix de l'Arc de Triomphe, finishing sixth, only beaten about two lengths behind Tony Bin. Kadissya was a successful broodmare for the Aga Khan, also foaling Kaliana (1994, by Slip Anchor – G3 St Simon S), listed winner Kadaka (1995, Sadler's Wells – 2nd G3 Park Hill S) and Kassiyda (1986, by Mill Reef), the dam of Kassana (1994, by Shernazar – G3 Prix Minerve) and grandam of Kastoria (2001, by Selkirk, G1 Irish St Leger, G3 Curragh Cup). Retired to his owner's Ballymany Stud on The Curragh, County Kildare, Kahyasi was a moderate success at stud siring several Group 1 winners including Vereva and Zainta, both winners of the French classic Prix de Diane and Enzeli (Ascot Gold Cup), all for the Aga Khan. Other good winners by Kahyasi were Khalkevi (G1 Grand Prix de Paris), Darasim (G2 Goodwood Cup) and Nazirali (G2 San Luis Obispo H). He is also the dam-sire of the Aga Khan's Prix de l'Arc de Triomphe winner, Zarkava (2005, by Zamindar). Kahyasi was later moved to Haras de Bonneval in Normandy where he was put down in June 2008 suffering from a tumour.*

2819888

Above: **KAHYASI** (Ray Cochrane) wins the Derby beating Glacial Storm and Doyoun (see p84). The winner carried the second colours of the Aga Khan last carried to victory in this classic in 1936 by Mahmoud. It was a final English classic success for Cochrane who had previously won the 1000 Guineas and Oaks on Midway Lady (p64).

2716388

0110878

Above left: **RAY COCHRANE, LUCA CUMANI** (centre) and the **AGA KHAN** at Lingfield in May 1988.

Above right: The King George VI and Queen Elizabeth Stakes and Coronation Cup winner **ILE DE BOURBON** was a disappointing stallion in Britain and had been exported to Japan before Kahyasi won the Derby.

0424388

1419789

Above: **KAHYASI** and Ray Cochrane catch Insan (T. Quinn) in the last stride to win the Irish Derby with Glacial Storm in third place. Above right: Ulster-born **RAY COCHRANE** won three English classics and the St James's Palace Stakes, July Cup and Sussex Stakes riding Chief Singer. Cochrane received the Queen's Commendation for Bravery in 2002 for saving the life of Frankie Dettori following a plane crash during 2000.

DIMINUENDO (USA)

Chesnut filly, foaled 9 February 1985
By Diesis (GB) out of Cacti (USA) by Tom Rolfe (USA)
Bred by Nancy S. Dillman
Owned by Sheikh Mohammed Al-Maktoum
Trained by Henry R.A. Cecil at Warren Place, Newmarket, Suffolk.

1520688

Racing Record

Year	Timeform Annual Rating	Starts	Wins	2nd	3rd	4th	Prize Money
1987	120	4	4	-	-	-	£ 87,084
1988	126	8	4	2	1	-	£ 339,523

Principal Performances

1987   Won Cherry Hinton Stakes (G3) (2yo fillies) Newmarket (6f)
           Won Fillies' Mile (G2) (2yo fillies) Ascot (8f)
1988   3rd 1000 Guineas Stakes (G1) (3yo fillies) Newmarket (8f)
           Won Musidora Stakes (G3) (3yo fillies) York (10.5f)
           Won Oaks Stakes (G1) (3yo fillies) Epsom (12f)
           Won (dead-heat) Irish Oaks Stakes (G1) (3yo fillies) Curragh (12f)
           Won Yorkshire Oaks (G1) (3yo fillies) York (12f)
           2nd St Leger Stakes (G1) (3yo colts & fillies) Doncaster (14.6f)

*****

*B*ought for $125,000 at Fasig-Tipton's Summer Yearling Sale, the pony-sized Diminuendo made up for her lack of height by possessing a big heart. She also had a long fluid action and a burst of acceleration which none of her contempories among the three-year-old middle distance fillies could match. She is rated as an above average Oaks winner but well above average in popularity ratings by racegoers. Her dam was a moderate winner, but a daughter of Desert Love, a stakes winner in the U.S. Diminuendo was not a great success as a broodmare but produced the winners Carpathian (1991, by

Danzig), the winner of five races, Calando (1996, by Storm Cat - G3 May Hill S), Knight's Victory (2006, by Cape Cross) and Dimity (by Soviet Star) a minor winner in France.

0320888

Above: Steve Cauthen looks back but there is no danger to **DIMINUENDO** and her victory in the Oaks by four lengths from Sudden Love and Animatrice (left). Below left: **SHEIKH MOHAMMED** leading in his third Oaks winner in four years after Oh So Sharp (p58) and Unite (p80). For Cauthen and Henry Cecil, who rode and trained Oh So Sharp, it was a second victory in this classic.

3320688

1231088

Above right: **DIMINUENDO** thrashes Sudden Love again, this time in the Yorkshire Oaks. Below: Sheikh Mohammed's two fillies **DIMINUENDO** and Melodist run a dead-heat for the Irish Oaks with Silver Lane (centre) third.

3625888

MINSTER SON (GB)

Chesnut colt, foaled 21 March 1985
By Niniski (USA) out of Honey Bridge (GB) by Crepello (GB)
Bred by William H.F. Carson at Minster Stud, Cirencester, Glos.
Owned by the Dowager Lady Beaverbrook
1987-August 1988: Trained by Major W.R. Hern at West Ilsley, Berkshire
September 1988: Trained by Neil A. Graham at West Ilsley, Berkshire.

0920288

Racing Record

Year	Timeform Annual Rating	Starts	Wins	2nd	3rd	4th	Prize Money
1987	96	3	1	1	-	-	£ 6,236
1988	130	5	4	-	-	-	£ 156,175

Principal Performances

1988 Won Newmarket Stakes (Listed Race) (3yo colts) Newmarket (10f)
Won Predominate Stakes (Listed Race) (3yo) Goodwood (10f)
Won Gordon Stakes (G3) (3yo) Goodwood (12f)
Won St Leger Stakes (G1) (3yo colts & fillies) Doncaster (14.6f)

*****

*M*inster Son was only beaten once during 1988, when returning injured after running in the Derby. The colt was supposedly to remain in training as a four-year-old when he would have been a lively candidate for the Cup races, but was ultimately retired to Longholes Stud at Cheveley near Newmarket without racing again. His dam, a minor winner, was bought by Willie Carson at the 1978 Tattersalls December Sales and was out of the useful two-year-old Mockbridge. Minster Son was never very likely to appeal to flat racing breeders and was moved to Acrum Lodge Stud at Bishop Auckland in Durham. Under National Hunt rules he sired Rambling Minster (10 races including the G3 Haydock Gold Cup Steeple Chase), Minster Glory (16 races, £90,338), Ross Com (7 races, £76,575) and Chabrimal Minster (9 races, £62,240).

90

2334388

Above: **MINSTER SON** (Willie Carson) wins the St Leger beating Diminuendo (W.R.Swinburn). This was a third St Leger victory for Carson following Dunfermline (1977) and Sun Princess (see p44) and the first time that a jockey had ridden an English classic winner on a horse that he bred himself. Below left: **LADY BEAVERBROOK** and **WILLIE CARSON** in the winner's circle after the St Leger.

2134288

2116689

3037689

Above right: **NEIL GRAHAM** temporarily took over the training licence at West Ilsley during September 1988 after **MAJOR DICK HERN** (centre) had to undergo heart surgery.

0711080

0934288

Above right: Another view of the finish of the St Leger as **MINSTER SON** beats Diminuendo (p88) with Moon Madness' (p70) half-brother, the grey Sheriff's Star, a long-looking eight lengths behind in third place. Above left: Irish St Leger winner **NINISKI**, pictured here with Willie Carson at Newbury, also won the first open-aged Prix Royal-Oak. He was a great success at Lanwades Stud at Moulton near Newmarket siring Hernando (Prix du Jockey-Club, Prix Lupin), Caitano (G1 Melbourne Cup H), Lomitas (Grosser Preis von Baden), Assessor (Prix Royal-Oak, Prix du Cadran), Vialli (G1 winner in Japan), Alflora (Queen Anne S), San Sebastian (Prix du Cadran) and Kala Dancer (Dewhurst S).

DON'T FORGET ME (IRE) :
Bay 1984

Ahonoora (GB) Ch. 1975	Lorenzaccio (GB) Ch. 1965	Klairon (FR)
		Phoenissa (GB)
	Helen Nichols (GB) Ch. 1966	Martial (IRE)
		Quaker Girl (GB)
African Doll (IRE) B. 1978	African Sky (GB) B. 1970	Sing Sing (GB)
		Sweet Caroline (GB)
	Mithril (GB) Ch. 1966	Princely Gift (GB)
		Baraka (GB)

REFERENCE POINT (GB) : Bay 1984

Mill Reef (USA) B. 1968	Never Bend (USA) B/br. 1960	Nasrullah (GB)
		Lalun (USA)
	Milan Mill (USA) B. 1962	Princequillo (IRE)
		Virginia Water (USA)
Home On The Range (GB) Br. 1978	Habitat (USA) B. 1966	Sir Gaylord (USA)
		Little Hut (USA)
	Great Guns (GB) B. 1971	Busted (GB)
		Byblis (GB)

UNITE (GB) : Chesnut 1984

Kris (GB) Ch. 1976	Sharpen Up (GB) Ch. 1969	Atan (USA)
		Rocchetta (GB)
	Doubly Sure (GB) B. 1971	Reliance (FR)
		Soft Angels (GB)
Pro Patria (IRE) B. 1976	Petingo (GB) B. 1965	Petition (GB)
		Alcazar (FR)
	Joyful (GB) B. 1962	Princely Gift (GB)
		My Game (IRE)

RAVINELLA (USA) : Bay 1985

Mr Prospector (USA) B. 1970	Raise A Native (USA) Ch. 1961	Native Dancer (USA)
		Raise You (USA)
	Gold Digger (USA) B. 1962	Nashua (USA)
		Sequence (USA)
Really Lucky (USA) Ch. 1978	Northern Dancer (CAN) B. 1961	Nearctic (CAN)
		Natalma (USA)
	Realty (USA) Ch. 1972	Sir Ivor (USA)
		Reveille (AUS)

DOYOUN (IRE) : Bay 1985

		Never Bend (USA) B/br. 1960	Nasrullah (GB)
Mill Reef (USA) B. 1968			Lalun (USA)
		Milan Mill (USA) B. 1962	Princequillo (IRE)
			Virginia Water (USA)
Dumka (FR) Br. 1971		Kashmir (IRE) B/br. 1963	Tudor Melody (GB)
			Queen of Speed (GB)
		Faizebad (FR) Br. 1962	Prince Taj (FR)
			Floralie (FR)

KAHYASI (IRE) : Bay 1985

		Nijinsky (CAN) B. 1967	Northern Dancer (CAN)
Ile De Bourbon (USA) Br. 1975			Flaming Page (CAN)
		Roseliere (FR) B/br. 1965	Misti (FR)
			Peace Rose (FR)
Kadissya (USA) B. 1979		Blushing Groom (FR) Ch. 1974	Red God (USA)
			Runaway Bride (GB)
		Kalkeen (IRE) B. 1974	Sheshoon (GB)
			Gioia (GB)

DIMINUENDO (USA) : Chesnut 1985

		Sharpen Up (GB) Ch. 1969	Atan (USA)
Diesis (GB) Ch. 1980			Rocchetta (GB)
		Doubly Sure (GB) B. 1971	Reliance (FR)
			Soft Angels (GB)
Cacti (USA) Ch. 1977		Tom Rolfe (USA) B. 1962	Ribot (GB)
			Pocahontas (USA)
		Desert Love (USA) B. 1962	Amerigo (GB)
			Desert Vision (USA)

MINSTER SON (GB) : Chesnut 1985

		Nijinsky (CAN) B. 1967	Northern Dancer (CAN)
Niniski (USA) B. 1976			Flaming Page (CAN)
		Virginia Hills (USA) B. 1971	Tom Rolfe (USA)
			Ridin' Easy (USA)
Honey Bridge (GB) Ch. 1975		Crepello (GB) Ch. 1954	Donatello (FR)
			Crepuscule (GB)
		Mockbridge (GB) Ch. 1969	Bleep-Bleep (GB)
			Greenbridge (GB)

93

MUSICAL BLISS (USA)

Bay filly, foaled 25 February 1986
By The Minstrel (CAN) out of Bori (USA) by Quadrangle (USA)
Bred by Sterlingbrook Farm, Canandaigua, New York, U.S.A.
Owned by Sheikh Mohammed Al-Maktoum
Trained by Michael R. Stoute at Beech Hurst Stables, Newmarket, Suffolk.

0739288

Racing Record

Year	Timeform Annual Rating	Starts	Wins	2nd	3rd	4th	Prize Money
1988	112	2	2	-	-	-	£ 8,556
1989	117	3	1	-	-	-	£ 98,260

Principal Performances

1988   Won Rockfel Stakes (G3) (2yo fillies) Newmarket (7f)
1989   Won 1000 Guineas Stakes (G1) (3yo fillies) Newmarket (8f)

*****

*M*usical Bliss won a 1000 Guineas which was run at a muddling, false pace and as she performed poorly in her two subsequent races, in the first of which she failed to stay twelve furlongs, it is difficult to judge her true ability. All one can say is that on Guineas day she was given a brilliant ride by an inspired Walter Swinburn and was the best horse in the race as it was run. However, she has to be rated as a well below average winner of the 1000 Guineas. Sheikh Mohammed paid $350,000 for Musical Bliss at the Keeneland Select Sale as a yearling. Her dam had previously bred the high-class, Safe Play (1978, by Sham), herself dam of Defensive Play (1987, by Fappiano – G1 Man O'War S). Bori was still a maiden after two seasons racing but was a grand-daughter of Arietta (see opposite page). Retained by her owner as a broodmare, Musical Bliss was a prolific breeder and produced one stakes winner and a few minor winners. Her best runner was Muscadel (1994, by Nashwan - LR Prix de Liancourt) and Raneem (1998, by Gone West) won 3 minor races in France and Dubai.

0715889

Above: **MUSICAL BLISS** and Walter Swinburn win the sprint after a slowly-run race, beating stable-mate Kerrera (left) and Aldbourne (2nd right); the favourite, Ensconse (right) finishes fourth. The first, second and fourth placed fillies were all owned by Sheikh Mohammed.

1016289

0106377

Above left: **MICHAEL STOUTE**, having saddled six runners-up, including one that was later disqualified, and two fillies that had finished third, finally won the 1000 Guineas with Musical Bliss.

Above right: **THE MINSTREL** and Lester Piggott winning the 1977 Derby beating Hot Grove (right) and Blushing Groom (right). Musical Bliss was the only English classic winner sired by the Kentucky based stallion. The Minstrel died during September 1990 and is buried at Overbrook Farm in Lexington.

Right: The founder of Timeform, **PHIL BULL** (pictured with Steve Cauthen), was the breeder of Arietta (1953, by Tudor Minstrel), third in the 1000 Guineas and dam of the champion miler of 1962, Romulus (1959, by Ribot - Queen Elizabeth II S, Sussex S, Prix du Moulin), the brilliant but unsound Ebor winner Sostenuto (1958, by Never Say Die) and great grandam of Musical Bliss. Bull had sold Arietta for export to the U.S.A. in 1962.

3414685

95

NASHWAN (USA)

Chesnut colt, foaled 1 March 1986
By Blushing Groom (FR) out of Height of Fashion (FR) by Bustino (GB)
Owned and bred by Sheikh Hamdan Al-Maktoum
Trained by Major W.R. Hern at West Ilsley, Berkshire
Sep-Oct 1988 Trained by Neil A. Graham at West Ilsley, Berkshire.

0623789

Racing Record

Year	Timeform Annual Rating	Starts	Wins	2nd	3rd	4th	Prize Money
1988	106	2	2	-	-	-	£ 14,310
1989	135	5	4	-	1	-	£ 778,938

Principal Performances

1989   Won 2000 Guineas Stakes (G1) (3yo colts & fillies) Newmarket (8f)
       Won Derby Stakes (G1) (3yo colts & fillies) Epsom (12f)
       Won Eclipse Stakes (G1) (3yo & upwards) Sandown (10f)
       Won King George VI and Queen Elizabeth Stakes (G1) Ascot (12f)

*****

N ashwan lit up the spring and summer of 1989 as he powered his way to four successive Group 1 victories, the first time these races had been won by the same horse in a single season. Sections of the media hailed Nashwan as a wonder horse and then criticised Sheikh Hamdan for not running him in the last leg of the classic Triple Crown, the St Leger. That Nashwan would probably not have stayed the distance of the race was overlooked as they rushed to deplore the owner's decision. The colt was retired to Sheikh Hamdan's Nunnery Stud at Thetford in Norfolk where he stood until his death in 2002. The best of his offspring were Bago (G1 Prix de l'Arc de Triomphe, Prix Ganay, Grand Prix de Paris, Prix Jean Prat), Swain (G1 Coronation Cup, King George VI & Queen Elizabeth S twice, Irish Champion S), Wandesta (G1 Santa Ana H), Aqaarid (G1 Fillies' Mile, G3 Fred Darling S, 2nd 1000 Guineas) and One So Wonderful (G1 International S). Nashwan's very successful dam (p313) also bred the full-brothers Alwasmi (1984, by Northern Dancer – G3 John Porter S) and Unfuwain (p213).

2416789

Above: **NASHWAN** (Willie Carson) wins the 2000 Guineas beating Exbourne (right) and Danehill (left, see p261). This was the first English classic victory for Sheikh Hamdan Al-Maktoum. Below: The fun, excitement and tradition of Derby Day as NASHWAN collects a second classic.

3123489

Below left: **SHEIKH HAMDAN** leads in Willie Carson on his third Derby winner following Troy (1979) and Henbit (p8). This was also a third Derby victory for Major Hern, who trained Troy and Henbit.

Below right: **NASHWAN** fights off Cacoethes to win the King George VI and Queen Elizabeth Stakes.

Right: **DICK HERN** and **WILLIE CARSON** were victorious in nine English classics together between 1977 and 1989.

2128089

0630789

SNOW BRIDE (USA)

Chesnut filly, foaled 28 February 1986
By Blushing Groom (FR) out of Awaasif (CAN) by Snow Knight (GB)
Bred by Darley Stud Management
1988: Owned by Sheikh Mohammed Al-Maktoum
1989: Owned by Saeed Maktoum Al-Maktoum
Trained by Henry R.A. Cecil at Warren Place, Newmarket, Suffolk.

1824289

Racing Record

Year	Timeform Annual Rating	Starts	Wins	2nd	3rd	4th	Prize Money
1988	102	2	2	-	-	-	£ 12,282
1989	121	5	3	-	-	1	£ 164,906

Principal Performances

1989   Won Musidora Stakes (G3) (3yo fillies) York (10.5f)
       Won Oaks Stakes (G1) (3yo fillies) Epsom (12f)
       Won Princess Royal Stakes (G3) (Fillies & mares) Ascot (12f)

*****

S *now Bride was a very fortunate winner of the Oaks and never actually passed the post first in any race above Group 3 level. She was the lowest rated Oaks winner of the decade, but went on to breed Lammtarra (see p160) from a mating with the 1970 Triple Crown hero Nijinsky. Her dam is a half-sister to the 1000 Guineas second, Konafa (1973, by Damascus), herself dam of Proskona (1981, by Mr Prospector – G2 Premio Umbra), Keos (1994, by Riverman – G2 Goldene Peitsche) and Korveya (1982, by Riverman), dam of French classic winner, Hector Protector (1988) and Bosra Sham (p168), both by Woodman (p169). Snow Bride bred two good fillies in Saytarra (1996, by Seeking The Gold – G3 Prix d'Aumale) and Abhisheka (2003, by Sadler's Wells), the winner of three minor races and second at Listed Race level in Dubai. Concordia (2006, by Pivotal) was the last of seven winners foaled by Snow Bride before the mare was put down on 10 June 2009.*

2724189

Above: **SNOW BRIDE** (Steve Cauthen) is beaten three lengths by the comfortable winner Aliysa in the Oaks with Roseate Tern a short-head behind in third. Aliysa failed a post-race dope test and was subsequently disqualified with the classic victory awarded to Snow Bride.

© Bertrand

1724082

Above left: The brilliant two-year-old **BLUSHING GROOM** sired 92 stakes winners, including the English classic winners, Nashwan (p96) and Snow Bride, making him the first stallion to sire the winners of the Derby and Oaks in the same season since Solario in 1937. Also among Blushing Groom's progeny were Rainbow Quest (p197), Arazi, champion two-year-old in both the U.S. and France, Al Bahathri (p253), Baillamont (G1 Prix Ganay), Blushing John (G1 Poule d'Essai des Poulains) and Crystal Glitters (G1 Prix d'Ispahan). Blushing Groom died in 1992 and is buried at Gainesway Farm in Kentucky. Above right: Snow Bride's dam, **AWAASIF**, was a much better racehorse than her daughter winning the Yorkshire Oaks and was third in the Prix de l'Arc de Triomphe in 1982.

Left: **SHEIKH MOHAMMED**, whose Darley Stud bred Snow Bride, with **HENRY CECIL** for whom the filly was a third Oaks winner following Oh So Sharp (p58) and Diminuendo (p88), both owned by Sheikh Mohammed, who removed all his horses from Cecil's Warren Place stables in 1995. Henry had trained the winners of four English classics for Sheikh Mohammed and other G1 winners including Indian Skimmer (Prix de Diane, Champion S), Old Vic (Prix du Jockey-Club, Irish Derby), Kissing Cousin (Coronation S), King's Theatre and Belmez (both King George VI & Queen Elizabeth S), Salse (Prix de la Foret) and El Cuite (Prix Royal-Oak).

1920888

MICHELOZZO (USA)

Bay colt, foaled 1 January 1986
By Northern Baby (CAN) out of Tres Agreable (FR) by Luthier (FR)
Bred by Charles Rowe
1988-91: Owned by Charles A.B. St. George
1988-90: Trained by Henry R.A. Cecil at Sefton Lodge, Newmarket
1992-93: Owned by Edward St. George
1991-92: Trained by John E. Hammond at Chantilly, Oise, France
July 1992-93: Trained by Richard Hannon at East Everleigh Stables, Marlborough.

1428989

Racing Record

Year	Timeform Annual Rating	Starts	Wins	2nd	3rd	4th	U.K. Prize Money
1988	-	0	-	-	-	-	-
1989	127	4	3	-	1	-	£ 192,720
1990	117	5	-	2	-	1	£ 10,595
1991	-	6	2	1	-	2	-
1992	109	6	1	-	1	1	£ 4,996
1993	-	3	-	-	1	-	£ 1,246

Principal Performances

1989 3rd Princess of Wales's Stakes (G2) Newmarket (12f)
      Won March Stakes (Listed Race) (3yo) Goodwood (14f)
      Won St Leger Stakes (G1) (3yo) Ayr (14.6f)
1990 2nd Ormonde Stakes (G3) Chester (13.4f)
      4th Prix Royal-Oak (G1) Longchamp (15.5f)
1991 4th Prix Royal-Oak (G1) Longchamp (15.5f)
      Won Prix Touffier (Listed Race) Marseille (13.5f)
1992 4th Geoffrey Freer Stakes (G2) Newbury (13.5f)
      3rd Prix Kergorlay (G2) Deauville (15f)

*T*he 1989 St Leger was postponed and transferred to Ayr after subsidence was discovered at Doncaster the day before the race was originally scheduled. The delay caused the defection of two leading contenders, Aliysa (1986, by Darshaan) and Cacoethes (1986, by Alydar), (the connections of both preferring to take their outside chances in the Prix de l'Arc de Triomphe, a sad indication of how far the St Leger has fallen in importance) but was a blessing for Michelozzo. The horse had injured a foot travelling from Newmarket and may not have been able to run had the classic gone ahead as planned. Michelozzo had been bought as a foal for $90,000 by a partnership including Charles St George and when the colt went back to auction a year later to dissolve the partnership, St George bought him for $180,000. Michelozzo is the first foal of his dam, a minor winner in France and a half-sister to El Cuite (1983, by Vaguely Noble – G1 Prix Royal-Oak). Their dam was Assez Cuite, a G3 stakes winner in France and second in the now defunct Group 1 Prix de la Salamandre. Tres Agreable also bred Micheletti (1988, by Critique – 3rd G1 St Leger S). This is a family developed by the Earls of Derby, tracing back to the wartime 1000 Guineas and St Leger winner, Herringbone (1940, by King Salmon) which includes Ragstone, Moon Madness (p70) and Sheriff's Star (p71). The best horse sired by Michelozzo was Run For Paddy (G3 Scottish Grand National Steeple Chase).

© Alec Russell Photography

Above: **MICHELOZZO** and Steve Cauthen win the St Leger by an official eight lengths from Sapience. This was the last English classic winner ridden by Kentuckian Cauthen, who moved to England in 1979 and rode ten English classic winners before his retirement in 1992; Tap On Wood (1976, by Sallust - 2000 Guineas), Oh So Sharp (p58), Slip Anchor (p62), Reference Point (p78), Diminuendo (p88) and Snow Bride (p98). Cauthen also won the American Triple Crown on Affirmed (1975, by Exclusive Native) and was champion jockey in Britain on three occasions, 1984, 1985 and 1987.

3220787   3728789   3214079

Above left: **HENRY CECIL** and **STEVE CAUTHEN**; Michelozzo was the last classic winner for the most successful team of the decade. Centre: **CHARLES ST. GEORGE** owned three English classic winners; Ginevra (1969, by Shantung - Oaks 1972), Bruni (1972, by Sea Hawk - St Leger 1975) and Michelozzo. He is best remembered as the owner of champion stayer, Ardross (1976, by Run The Gantlet). Right: Champion Stakes winner **NORTHERN BABY** (1976, by Northern Dancer) stood at Stone Farm in Kentucky for twenty-six years and sired forty-seven stakes winners. The stallion was retired in 2002 and died at the age of thirty-one in 2007. Michelozzo was his only English classic winner.

SALSABIL (IRE)

Bay filly, foaled 18 January 1987
By Sadler's Wells (USA) out of Flame of Tara (IRE) by Artaius (USA)
Bred by Kilcarn Stud, Navan, Co. Meath
Owned by Sheikh Hamdan Al-Maktoum
Trained by John L. Dunlop at Castle Stables, Arundel, Sussex.

0941989

Racing Record

Year	Timeform Annual Rating	Starts	Wins	2nd	3rd	4th	Prize Money
1989	116	3	2	1	-	-	£ 73,551
1990	130	6	5	-	-	-	£ 653,273

Principal Performances

1989   Won Prix Marcel Boussac (G1) (2yo fillies) Longchamp (8f)
1990   Won Fred Darling Stakes (G3) (3yo fillies) Newbury (7.3f)
      Won 1000 Guineas Stakes (G1) (3yo fillies) Newmarket (8f)
      Won Oaks Stakes (G1) (3yo fillies) Epsom (12f)
      Won Irish Derby Stakes (G1) (3yo colts & fillies) Curragh (12f)
      Won Prix Vermeille (G1) (3yo fillies) Longchamp (12f)

*****

S *alsabil was at 440,000 guineas the highest-priced filly at Tattersalls 1988 Highflyer Yearling Sale. Flame of Tara (G2 Coronation S) was also the dam of Marju (1988, by Last Tycoon – G1 St James's Palace S, 2nd Derby S), Danse Royale (1990, by Caerleon – G3 Prix de Psyche) and Flame of Athens (1993, by Royal Academy – G3 Railway S). Her half-sister Fruition (1978, by Rheingold) bred the good stayer Kneller (1985, by Lomond – G3 Doncaster & Jockey Club Cups) and Northern Spur (1991, by Sadler's Wells – G1 Breeders Cup Turf). This is the family of Alcide (1955, by Alycidon – St Leger & King George VI & Queen Elizabeth S) and Parthia (1956, by Persian Gulf – Derby S). Salsabil became the first filly to win the Irish Derby since 1900, winning four classics in three countries in a sequence of six races that included five Group 1 events. A disappointing finale in Paris did little to tarnish her illustrious career and Salsabil retired to stud regarded as one of the best fillies to win an*

102

English classic in the period 1980-2015. Salsabil was put down in October 1996 suffering from cancer of the colon. Her five years at Shadwell Stud had yielded five foals which all won except Firdous (1992, by Nashwan). The winners were Bint Salsabil (1993, by Nashwan - G3 Rockfel S), Sahm (1994, by Mr Prospector - G3 Knickerbocker H, Aqueduct), Muhaba (1995, by Mr Prospector) and Alabaq (1996, by Riverman - G2 Premio Bagutta, LR Pretty Polly S).

0915990

Above: **SALSABIL** (Willie Carson) and Heart of Joy (rails) battle for the winning post in the 1000 Guineas. Salsabil won by three-quarters of a length to give Carson his first victory in this classic and second for John Dunlop following Quick As Lightning (see p4).

Right: Much easier this time as **SALSABIL** and Carson win the Oaks by five lengths beating Game Plan (yellow cap) and Knight's Baroness (right). It was a second victory in this classic for John Dunlop after Circus Plume (p52) and fourth for Willie Carson following Dunfermline (1977), Bireme (p10) and Sun Princess (p44).

2221990

1725690

2937490

Above: SALSABIL and **WILLIE CARSON** added two more classics to their collection; the Irish Derby, pictured here (left) after the race with owner **HAMDAN AL-MAKTOUM**, for whom Salsabil was a first winner of the 1000 Guineas and Oaks, and (right) the Prix Vermeille at Longchamp in Paris, beating Miss Alleged.

TIROL (GB)

Brown colt, foaled 16 March 1987
By Thatching (IRE) out of Alpine Niece (GB) by Great Nephew (GB)
Bred by Mrs R.D. Peacock at Manor House Stud, Middleham, Yorks.
Owned by John Horgan
Trained by Richard Hannon at East Everleigh Stables, Marlborough, Wiltshire.

3013690

Racing Record

Year	Timeform Annual Rating	Starts	Wins	2nd	3rd	4th	Prize Money
1989	112	4	2	1	1	-	£ 31,706
1990	127	5	3	-	1	-	£ 292,105

Principal Performances

1989   Won Horris Hill Stakes (G3) (2yo colts & geldings) Newbury (7.3f)
1990   Won Craven Stakes (G3) (3yo colts & geldings) Newmarket (8f)
       Won 2000 Guineas Stakes (G1) (3yo colts & fillies) Newmarket (8f)
       Won Irish 2000 Guineas Stakes (G1) (3yo colts & fillies) Curragh (8f)
       3rd Grand Prix de Paris (G1) (3yo colts & fillies) Longchamp (10f)

*****

T irol, a 13,000 guineas foal and at 52,000 guineas a typical Richard Hannon bargain buy at Tattersalls Highflyer Sale as a yearling, was the first horse bred in Yorkshire to win the 2000 Guineas for nearly a century. The colt went on to victory in the Irish equivalent, a relatively rare double only achieved previously by Right Tack (1969) and Don't Forget Me (see p76). Tirol was unable to win again and was syndicated at IR £27,500 a share to stand at Coolmore Stud at Fethard in County Tipperary. The syndication terms placed a valuation of IR£1.1m on him at an initial covering fee of IR 7,500 guineas. One has to go back to the Derby and St Leger winner, Airborne (1943, by Precipitation), to find another top-class horse on the distaff side of Tirol's pedigree. Alpine Niece failed to win and her dam Fragrant Morn, won only a small maiden race at Folkestone. Tirol was a first European Group 1

104

winner for champion sprinter Thatching, who also stood at Coolmore and sired many winners without being a source for much in the way of class. So Tirol took an unfashionable pedigree with him to stud and was not well supported with high-class mares but still managed to sire the winners of over six hundred races in Europe. The best of these were Miss Tahiti (G1 Prix Marcel Boussac, 2nd Prix de Diane, Prix Saint-Alary and dam of Miss France, p364), Princess Ellen (LR Sweet Solera S, 2nd G1 1000 Guineas, Coronation S), Tarascon (G1 Moyglare Stud S, Irish 1000 Guineas), Saratan (G3 Prix du Palais-Royal), Pipe Major (G3 Criterion S) and Softly Tread (G3 Gladness S), the dam of Pether's Moon (2010, by Dylan Thomas – G1 Coronation Cup). During 1997 Tirol was sold to stand at Capricorn Stud at Pune in India and sired several important winners there before dying of colic in August 2007. On hearing of Tirol's death, Richard Hannon said 'he was one of the best horses that we ever had here. We always held him in high regard, as he was a good, sound horse to have anything to do with and had a very good turn of foot'.

1616690

Above: **TIROL** (Mick Kinane) wins the 2000 Guineas beating Machiavellian and Anshan (left). It was a first classic success in England for the Irish jockey.

2416790

3216690

Above left: Mrs Horgan and **RICHARD HANNON** with Tirol and **MICK KINANE** after the 2000 Guineas. This was the trainer's third victory in this race following Mon Fils (1973) and Don't Forget Me.

Above right: **JOHN HORGAN** and his sons with Tirol in the Newmarket winner's circle.

QUEST FOR FAME (GB)

Bay colt, foaled 15 February 1987
By Rainbow Quest (USA) out of Aryenne (FR) by Green Dancer (USA)
Bred by Juddmonte Farms
Owned by Khalid Abdullah
1989: Trained by Jeremy Tree and 1990-91: Trained by Roger Charlton at Beckhampton,
Marlborough, Wiltshire.
1992: Trained by Robert Frankel in the U.S.A.

0221590

Racing Record

Year	Timeform Annual Rating	Starts	Wins	2nd	3rd	4th	U.K. Prize Money
1989	89	1	-	1	-	-	£ 2,688
1990	127	4	2	1	-	-	£ 367,678
1991	124	6	-	2	2	1	£ 69,871
1992	-	8	3	-	2	-	-

Principal Performances

1990   2nd Chester Vase (3yo) (G3) Chester (12.3f)
     Won Derby Stakes (G1) (3yo colts & fillies) Epsom (12f)
1991   4th Coronation Cup (G1) Epsom (12f)
     2nd International Stakes (G1) York (10.4f)
     2nd September Stakes (G3) Kempton (11.1f)
     3rd Breeders' Cup Turf (G1) Churchill Downs, U.S.A. (12f)
1992   Won San Luis Obispo Handicap (G3) Santa Anita, U.S.A. (12f turf)
     Won Hollywood Invitational Turf Handicap (G1) Hollywood Park, U.S.A. (10f)
     3rd Breeders' Cup Turf (G1) Gulfstream Park, U.S.A. (12f)

*T*en years after his first English classic victory with Known Fact, Khalid Abdullah won the Derby with Quest For Fame, a colt bred at his own Juddmonte Farms. Aryenne won the Group 1 Criterium des Pouliches as a two-year-old and the classic Poule d'Essai des Pouliches in 1980; she was bought by Juddmonte Farms at the end of her racing days. Her dam Americaine was a half-sister to Adamastor (1959, by Norseman – Poule d'Essai des Poulains). This is the family of the outstanding French filly Roseliere (1965, by Misti), winner of the Prix de Diane and Prix Vermeille and dam of Rose Bowl (1972, by Habitat – G1 Champion S, Queen Elizabeth II S twice) and Ile De Bourbon (1975, by Nijinsky, p87). After sustaining an injury to his near foreleg during the Irish Derby, Quest For Fame missed the remainder of his classic season, returning in June 1991, but failed to recapture his best form. This precipitated his transfer to Robert Frankel in the U.S.A., where he became the first English Derby winner to win a major race as a five-year-old since St Gatien in 1886. Quest For Fame was retired to stand at Gainesway Farm in Kentucky, shuttling to Woodland Stud in NSW, Australia during the southern hemisphere breeding season. Unsurprisingly, he did much better 'down under' and sired there Viscount (3 x G1 & £526,519), Sarrera (2 x G1 & £352,842), De Beers (G1 Rosehill Guineas), Dracula (G1 George Main S), Tributes (G1 Crown Oaks) and Unworldly (G1 Flight S). In Britain, his best winners were Perfect Sunday (G3 Lingfield Derby Trial) and Shot To Fame (G3 Ascot Silver Trophy). Quest For Fame was retired from stud duties in April 2010.

0921590

Above: **QUEST FOR FAME** (Pat Eddery) wins the Derby Stakes beating Blue Stag (centre) and Elmaamul (right). It was Eddery's third and last winner of this classic, following Grundy (1975) and Golden Fleece (p30). Photo opposite: Quest For Fame cantering to the start on Derby Day, watched by The Queen and Prince Philip, a tradition now sadly discontinued.

2421390

Right: **KHALID ABDULLAH** leading in Pat Eddery and Quest For Fame at Epsom. Abdullah has to date won eleven English classics; the 2000 Guineas with Known Fact (p6), Dancing Brave (p66), Zafonic (p134) and Frankel (p330); the 1000 Guineas with Wince (p202) and Special Duty (p320); the Derby with Commander in Chief (p136), Quest For Fame and Workforce (p324); the Oaks with Reams of Verse (p180) and the St Leger with Toulon (p120). He was leading owner in Britain in 2003, 2010 and 2011 and made an honorary member of The Jockey Club in 1983.

ROGER CHARLTON (right) thus trained a Derby winner in his first season after taking over Beckhampton from his mentor, Jeremy Tree. He also won the Prix du Jockey-Club in 1990 with another Prince Khalid Abdullah owned colt, Sanglamore.

SNURGE (IRE)

Chesnut colt, foaled 12 March 1987
By Ela-Mana-Mou (IRE) out of Finlandia (FR) by Faraway Son (USA)
Bred by Kilcarn Stud, Navan, Co. Meath, Ireland
Owned by Martin Arbib
Trained by Paul F.I. Cole at Whatcombe, Wantage, Oxfordshire.

1436790

Racing Record

Year	Timeform Annual Rating	Starts	Wins	2nd	3rd	4th	Prize Money
1989	118	3	-	2	1	-	£ 20,944
1990	130	4	1	2	1	-	£ 280,908
1991	125	6	4	-	1	-	£ 387,015
1992	122	9	1	4	1	-	£ 415,296
1993	123	6	1	-	-	2	£ 75,566
1994	121	6	-	2	1	1	£ 101,805

Principle Performances

1989   Won Criterium de Saint-Cloud (G1) (2yo colts & fillies) Saint-Cloud (10f)
       (disqualified and placed second for interference)
1990   2nd Great Voltigeur Stakes (G2) (3yo colts & geldings) York (12f)
       Won St Leger Stakes (G1) (3yo colts & fillies) Doncaster (14.6f)
       3rd Prix de l'Arc de Triomphe (G1) Longchamp (12f)
1991   Won Aston Park Stakes (Listed Race) Newbury (13.3f)
       Won Gran Premio di Milano (G1) San Siro (12f)
       Won Grand Prix de Deauville (G2) Deauville (12.5f)
       3rd Gran Premio del Jockey Club e Coppa d'Oro (G1) San Siro (12f)
       Won Premio Roma Vecchia (G3) Rome (14f)
1992   2nd Preis der Privatbankiers Merck, Finck & Co (G1) Dusseldorf (12f)
       2nd Aral-Pokal (G1) Gelsenkirchen-Horst (12f)
       2nd Irish St Leger Stakes (G1) Curragh (14f)

Won Rothmans International (G1) Woodbine, Canada (12f turf)
1993   Won Grand Prix de Deauville (G2) Deauville (12.5f)
1994   2nd Gran Premio di Milano (G1) San Siro (12f)
      3rd Aral-Pokal (G1) Gelsenkirchen-Horst (12f)

*****

S nurge, a bargain IR36,000 yearling, was a good St Leger winner and the first maiden to win the race since Night Hawk in 1913. When he was retired after sustaining a foot injury during the Cumberland Lodge Stakes at Ascot, Snurge's earnings of officially £1,283,794 made him the highest prize-money winner in European history. Finlandia, a half-sister to Musicienne (1968, by Sicambre), the dam of Horage (1980, by Tumble Wind - Gimcrack S), was useless on the racecourse but came from an excellent family; her grandam Musidora (1946, by Nasrullah), won the 1000 Guineas and Oaks. Snurge stood as a stallion at Haras du Val Henry at Livarot before being moved to Ireland where he was based at the Arctic Tack Stud at Newbawn in County Wexford and then at Coolmore's Grange Stud at Fermoy in County Cork, where he died of colic at the age of nineteen in November 2006. Snurge sired the winners of more than 300 National Hunt races, but none at the highest level. His best winners were Samson, twice winner of the Prix Lutteur III at Auteuil, Perle De Puce (G2 Kennel Gate Hurdle), The Disengager (LR Lord Mildmay Memorial Chase), Kilkrea Kim (G3 Heroes Hurdle) and on the flat, Rhodesian Winner (LR Premio Coppa D'Oro).

1036990   2941890   0336990

Above left: **MARTIN ARBIB** won his only English classic with Snurge. Above centre: Snurge was a first English classic winner for **PAUL COLE**, who went on to train 1991 Derby winner, Generous (see p116). Above right: The finish of the St Leger with **SNURGE** and **RICHARD QUINN** (below right) beating Hellenic and River God (right). This was also a first English classic victory for the jockey.

1110678   3544191

Above left: Snurge was the only English classic winner sired by **ELA-MANA-MOU** (1976, by Pitcairn – G1 Eclipse S, King George VI and Queen Elizabeth S, G2 RoyalLodge S, King Edward VII S, Prince of Wales's S, G3 Earl of Sefton S, 3rd G1 Prix de l'Arc de Triomphe, 4th Derby S).

MUSICAL BLISS (USA) : Bay 1986

The Minstrel (CAN) Ch. 1974	Northern Dancer (CAN) B. 1961	Nearctic (CAN)
		Natalma (USA)
	Fleur (CAN) B. 1964	Victoria Park (CAN)
		Flaming Page (CAN)
Bori (USA) B. 1972	Quadrangle (USA) B. 1961	Cohoes (USA)
		Tap Day (USA)
	Lucretia Bori (USA) B. 1965	Bold Ruler (USA)
		Arietta (GB)

NASHWAN (USA) : Chesnut 1986

Blushing Groom (FR) Ch. 1974	Red God (USA) Ch. 1954	Nasrullah (GB)
		Spring Run (USA)
	Runaway Bride (GB) B. 1962	Wild Risk (FR)
		Aimee (GB)
Height of Fashion (FR) B. 1979	Bustino (GB) B. 1971	Busted (GB)
		Ship Yard (GB)
	Highclere (GB) B. 1971	Queens Hussar (GB)
		Highlight (GB)

SNOW BRIDE (USA) : Chesnut 1986

Blushing Groom (FR) Ch. 1974	Red God (USA) Ch. 1954	Nasrullah (GB)
		Spring Run (USA)
	Runaway Bride (GB) B. 1962	Wild Risk (FR)
		Aimee (GB)
Awaasif (CAN) B. 1979	Snow Knight (GB) Ch. 1971	Firestreak (GB)
		Snow Blossom (GB)
	Royal Statute (CAN) B. 1969	Northern Dancer (CAN)
		Queen's Statute (GB)

MICHELOZZO (USA) : Bay 1986

Northern Baby (CAN) B. 1976	Northern Dancer (CAN) B. 1961	Nearctic (CAN)
		Natalma (USA)
	Two Rings (USA) B. 1970	Round Table (USA)
		Allofthem (USA)
Tres Agreable (FR) B. 1980	Luthier (FR) Br. 1965	Klairon (FR)
		Flute Enchantee (FR)
	Assez Cuite (USA) B. 1974	Graustark (USA)
		Clinkers (GB)

SALSABIL (IRE) : Bay 1987

		Northern Dancer (CAN) B. 1961	Nearctic (CAN)
	Sadler's Wells (USA) B. 1981		Natalma (USA)
		Fairy Bridge (USA) B. 1975	Bold Reason (USA)
			Special (USA)
	Flame of Tara (IRE) B. 1980	Artaius (USA) B. 1974	Round Table (USA)
			Stylish Pattern (USA)
		Welsh Flame (GB) B. 1973	Welsh Pageant (FR)
			Electric Flash (GB)

TIROL (GB) : Brown 1987

		Thatch (USA) B. 1970	Forli (ARG)
	Thatching (IRE) B. 1975		Thong (USA)
		Welsh Flame (GB) B. 1973	Welsh Pageant (FR)
			Electric Flash (GB)
	Alpine Niece (GB) B. 1972	Great Nephew (GB) B. 1963	Honeyway (GB)
			Sybil's Niece (GB)
		Fragrant Morn (GB) Ch. 1966	Mourne (FR)
			Alpine Scent (GB)

QUEST FOR FAME (USA) : Brown 1987

		Blushing Groom (FR) Ch. 1974	Red God (USA)
	Rainbow Quest (USA) B. 1981		Runaway Bride (GB)
		I Will Follow (USA) B. 1975	Herbager (FR)
			Where You Lead (USA)
	Aryenne (FR) Br. 1977	Green Dancer (USA) B. 1972	Nijinsky (CAN)
			Green Valley (FR)
		Americaine (FR) Ch. 1968	Cambremont (FR)
			Alora (FR)

SNURGE (IRE) : Chesnut 1987

		Pitcairn (IRE) Br. 1971	Petingo (GB)
	Ela-Mana-Mou (IRE) B. 1976		Border Bounty (GB)
		Rose Bertin (GB) Ch. 1970	High Hat (GB)
			Wide Awake (GB)
	Finlandia (FR) B. 1977	Faraway Son (USA) B. 1967	Ambiopoise (USA)
			Locust Time (USA)
		Musical (FR) Ch. 1961	Prince Chevalier (FR)
			Musidora (IRE)

SHADAYID (USA)

Grey filly, foaled 10 April 1988
By Shadeed (USA) out of Desirable (IRE) by Lord Gayle (USA)
Bred by Shadwell Farm Inc.
Owned by Sheikh Hamdan Al-Maktoum
Trained by John L. Dunlop at Castle Stables, Arundel, Sussex.

3541890

Racing Record

Year	Timeform Annual Rating	Starts	Wins	2nd	3rd	4th	Prize Money
1990	117	3	3	-	-	-	£ 104,894
1991	122	8	2	2	3	-	£ 296,868

Principal Performances

1990   Won Prix Marcel Boussac (G1) (2yo fillies) Longchamp (8f)
1991   Won Fred Darling Stakes (G3) (3yo fillies) Newbury (7.3f)
      Won 1000 Guineas Stakes (G1) (3yo fillies) Newmarket (8f)
      3rd Oaks Stakes (G1) (3yo fillies) Epsom (12f)
      2nd Coronation Stakes (G1) (3yo fillies) Royal Ascot (8f)
      2nd Sussex Stakes (G1) (3yo & upwards) Goodwood (8f)
      3rd Sprint Cup (G1) (3yo & upwards) Haydock (6f)
      3rd Queen Elizabeth II Stakes (G1) (3yo & upwards) Ascot (8f)

*****

Although Shadayid was in terms of ability only an average winner of the 1000 Guineas, for toughness and versatility she had few superiors. She ran in eight Group 1 races from six to twelve furlongs and only once finished out of the first three. Shadayid was retained as a broodmare and produced several winners the best of which were Bint Shadayid (1993, by Nashwan - G3 Prestige S, 3rd 1000 Guineas), Imtiyaz (1999, by Woodman - LR Foundation S, Glasgow S, 2nd G1 Prix Jean Prat) and Alshadiyah (1998, by Danzig - LR Firth of Clyde S). Shadayid died on 27 April 2002 after rupturing a uterine artery giving birth to a healthy foal by Seeking The Gold, subsequently named Teeba and another winner for her admirable dam. Desirable descended from a very successful family, more details of which can be found within the pages about To-Agori-Mou (p16) and Russian Rhythm (p244).

1341990

Above: **SHADAYID** (Willie Carson) wins the Prix Marcel Boussac at Longchamp in Paris. Below: Shadayid and Carson extend their unbeaten run to five races in the 1000 Guineas beating Kooyonga (second left) and Crystal Gazing (extreme right), a second victory in this classic for Carson (below left with Shadayid in the winner's circle after the race) and third for trainer John Dunlop.

1517091

2416991

2112993

3107193

Above centre: **SHEIKH HAMDAN AL-MAKTOUM** has owned twelve English classic winners between 1989 and 2014; Nashwan (see p96) and Haafhd (p252) in the 2000 Guineas; Salsabil (p102), Shadayid, Harayir (p156), Lahan (p212) and Ghanaati (p312) in the 1000 Guineas; Salsabil, Eswarah (p268) and Taghrooda (p366), the Oaks; and Nashwan and Erhaab (p148) in the Derby. All of these winners except Salsabil were bred at one of Sheikh Hamdan's studs in England, Ireland or the U.S.A. He has been notably loyal to all his jockeys and trainers, his support invariably lasting until they retire. Above right: **WILLIE CARSON** rode six English classic winners for Sheikh Hamdan on Nashwan, Salsabil, Erhaab and Shadayid.

113

MYSTIKO (USA)

Grey colt, foaled 22 February 1988
By Secreto (USA) out of Caracciola (FR) by Zeddaan (GB)
Bred by Kingston Park Stud Inc., Victoria, Australia
Owned by The Dowager Lady Beaverbrook
Trained by Clive E. Brittain at Carlburg Stables, Newmarket, Suffolk.

0637992

Racing Record

Year	Timeform Annual Rating	Starts	Wins	2nd	3rd	4th	Prize Money
1990	97	3	1	1	1	-	£ 13,636
1991	124	6	3	-	-	1	£ 181,310
1992	-	4	-	-	-	-	-

Principal Performances

1990   3rd Gimcrack Stakes (G2) (2yo colts & geldings) York (6f)
1991   Won European Free Handicap (Listed Race) (3yo) Newmarket (7f)
   Won 2000 Guineas Stakes (G1) (3yo) Newmarket (8f)
   4th Sprint Cup (G1) (3yo & upwards) Haydock Park (6f)
   Won Challenge Stakes (G2) (3yo & upwards) Newmarket (7f)

*****

*M*ystiko was bred in America by an Australian stud and sold as a yearling for $150,000 at Keeneland. His dam was a poor maiden raced in France, but grandam Cendres Bleues was a winning half-sister to the unbeaten Italian Group 1 winner, Claude (1964, by Hornbeam), a champion sire in Italy. Cendres Bleues was also dam of Pasakos (1985, by Nureyev - G3 Prix La Rochette), second three times at Group 1 level in France and Calderina (1975, by Lyphard - G2 Prix de Malleret), runner-up in the classic Prix de Diane. Mystiko was an excitable colt who tended to sweat and get on edge before his races and never won other than at his home track at Newmarket. Retired to Barton Stud at

114

Bury St Edmunds in Suffolk, Mystiko had a poor record as a stallion, siring the winners of fewer than one hundred races, with no stakes winners among them.

1717791

Above: **MYSTIKO** and Michael Roberts lead all the way close to the stand-side rail and hold off the challenge of Steve Cauthen riding Lycius to win the 2000 Guineas. This was the only English classic winner sired by the 1984 Derby winner, Secreto (see p50).

1224092   1817891   1439291

Above left: Popular Newmarket trainer **CLIVE BRITTAIN** registered his third English classic victory with the mercurial Mystiko. Clive had previously won the St Leger (Julio Mariner, 1978) and the 1000 Guineas (Pebbles (p46). He went on to win the Oaks and another St Leger with User Friendly (p130) and when Sayyedati (p132) gave him a second 1000 Guineas, Clive had won three English classic races in succession.

Above centre: **LADY BEAVERBROOK** was a big spender at the yearling sales usually buying British-bred horses. She enjoyed other classic successes with Bustino (1974 St Leger) and Minster Son (p90) and also owned Boldboy (Lockinge S), two Derby runners-up in Relkino (Benson & Hedges Gold Cup) and Terimon (International S), Niniski (Irish St Leger, Prix Royal-Oak) and Petoski (King George VI & Queen Elizabeth S). A noted philanthropist, Lady Beaverbrook died in October 1994.

Above right: South African-born jockey **MICHAEL ROBERTS** won his first English classic on Mystiko. Roberts was champion jockey in Great Britain in 1992 and enjoyed another classic success, winning the Oaks on Intrepidity (p138) in 1993 for Sheikh Mohammed and trainer Andre Fabre. He also won the King George VI and Queen Elizabeth Stakes and the Eclipse Stakes twice on Mtoto (1983, by Busted - p173).

GENEROUS (IRE)

Chesnut colt, foaled 8 February 1988
By Caerleon (USA) out of Doff The Derby (USA) by Master Derby (USA)
Bred by Barronstown Stud, Grange Con, Co. Wicklow
Owned by Fahd Salman
Trained by Paul F.I. Cole at Whatcombe, Wantage, Oxfordshire.

3029791

Racing Record

Year	Timeform Annual Rating	Starts	Wins	2nd	3rd	4th	Prize Money
1990	115	6	3	1	1	-	£ 141,447
1991	139	5	3	-	-	1	£ 975,384

Principal Performances

1990   Won Dewhurst Stakes (G1) (2yo colts & fillies) Newmarket (7f)
1991   4th 2000 Guineas Stakes (G1) (3yo colts & fillies) Newmarket (8f)
       Won Derby Stakes (G1) (3yo colts & fillies) Epsom (12f)
       Won Irish Derby Stakes (G1) (3yo colts & fillies) Curragh (12f)
       Won King George VI and Queen Elizabeth Stakes (G1) Ascot (12f)

*****

*G*enerous was sold at Goffs December Sales as a foal for IR80,000 guineas and again as a yearling at Goffs Cartier Million Sale, where he was bought on behalf of Fahd Salman for IR200,000 guineas. Doff The Derby was an unraced half-sister to Trillion (1974, by Hail To Reason), a champion in both France and the U.S. and dam of the outstanding racemare Triptych (1982, by Riverman). Doff The Derby died in 1999, but bred a second English classic winner in Imagine (see p226), Wedding Bouquet (1987, by Kings Lake – G3 Park S, 2nd G1 National S), herself the grandam of Moonlight Cloud (2008, by Invincible Spirit, G1 Prix Maurice de Gheest, Prix du Moulin, Prix Jacques Le Marois, Prix de la Foret), Osumi Tycoon (1991, by Last Tycoon), a stakes winner in Japan, and Strawberry Roan (1994, by Sadler's Wells), a listed winner and classic placed in Ireland. Generous was a good two-year-old and trained on to become the outstanding colt of his generation in 1991 winning two classics and the King George VI & Queen Elizabeth Stakes by wide margins. Given a rest, he was

116

brought back in October but ran well below his best at Longchamp. Generous was retired to Banstead Manor Stud at Cheveley near Newmarket in a deal which reportedly placed a value on the colt of £7.875m. His first crop were not yet three years old when Generous was sold to Japan in 1996, moving on to New Zealand three years later. The stallion was brought back to Europe in 2002 to stand at Scarvagh Stud in County Down and Sandley Stud at Gillingham in Dorset, where he died on 15 January 2013. The best of his offspring were Catella (G1 Grosser Erdgas-Preis), Generous Rosi (G3 Gordon Richards S), Fahris (G3 Select S), Bahr (G2 Ribblesdale S, G3 Musidora S, 2nd G1 Oaks S) and Blueprint (G2 Jockey Club S).

1022091

Above: **GENEROUS** (Alan Munro) wins the Derby by five lengths from Marju. Below left: **PRINCE FAHD SALMAN** with Generous, his first English classic winner, after the Derby. Salman (below right) suffered a fatal heart attack at the age of 46 in July 2001. Above centre: **ALAN MUNRO** registered his sole English classic victory on Generous at Epsom.

2722191

3643591

3143591

Below: An easy victory for **GENEROUS** in the King George VI and Queen Elizabeth Stakes beating Sanglamore.

JET SKI LADY (USA)

Chesnut filly, foaled 20 February 1988
By Vaguely Noble (IRE) out of Bemissed (USA) by Nijinsky (CAN)
Bred by Ryehill Farm, U.S.A.
Owned by Maktoum Al-Maktoum
Trained by James S. Bolger at Glebe House, Coolcullen, Co. Carlow.

1022991

Racing Record

Year	Timeform Annual Rating	Starts	Wins	2nd	3rd	4th	Prize Money
1990	106	4	2	-	1	-	£ 10,405
1991	122	6	2	2	-	1	£ 220,654

Principal Performances

1991   Won Ballysax Stakes (Listed Race) (3yo) Curragh (10f)
       Won Oaks Stakes (G1) (3yo fillies) Epsom (12f)
       2nd Irish Oaks Stakes (G1) (3yo fillies) Curragh (12f)
       2nd Yorkshire Oaks (G1) (Fillies & mares) York (12f)

*****

*J*et Ski Lady won the Oaks in sensational style but proved unable to confirm her superiority over the middle-distance fillies of her classic year and was subsequently beaten in the Oaks races at the Curragh and York. At Epsom, Jet Ski Lady had been an unconsidered 50/1 shot, the longest priced winner since Vespa started at the same odds in 1833. Bemissed won the G1 Selima Stakes and finished third in the Kentucky Oaks. Jet Ski Lady's grandam Bemis Heights was also a graded stakes winner in the U.S. Very few members of this family had raced in Europe recently, but one which did was Tuscarora (1972, by Herbager – 2nd G1 Irish Oaks), a grand-daughter of Salt Lake, the fourth dam of the Oaks winner. Jet Ski Lady was bought for $335,000 at the dispersal sale of Ryehill Farm and was the second and last English classic winner sired by Vaguely Noble following Empery (Derby S, 1976). Jet Ski Lady bred Legaya (1994, by Shirley Heights), Lucky Lady (1997, by Nashwan) and Colorado Ski (2007, by Western Winter), all minor winners, respectively in Ireland, Britain and South Africa.*

1422991

Above: **JET SKI LADY** (C.Roche) romps to a stunning ten lengths victory in the Oaks beating Shamshir (white sleeves) and the non-staying hot favourite Shadayid (see p112). Only Sun Princess (p44) had won this classic by further and none of its winners had started at longer odds. This was a first English classic success for **JAMES BOLGER** (below left), a second **for CHRISTY ROCHE** (below right), who had previously won the 1984 Derby on Secreto (p50) and fourth English classic and first Oaks for **MAKTOUM AL-MAKTOUM** (below centre) following Touching Wood (p34), Ma Biche (p36) and Shadeed (p60).

3514192

2312902

© Peter Mooney

© Bertrand

Right: **VAGUELY NOBLE** was a brilliant winner of the Prix de l'Arc de Triomphe in 1968. He changed hands for the then record price for a horse in training of 136,000 guineas at Tattersalls 1967 December Sales, a transaction that would never have taken place had his breeder Major Lionel Holliday not died two years earlier, when the colt was still a foal. Retired to Gainesway Farm in Kentucky, Vaguely Noble was an equally brilliant stallion siring many top winners including Empery (Derby S), Dahlia (Irish Oaks, King George VI & Queen Elizabeth S twice), Exceller (Prix Royal-Oak, Coronation Cup), Noble Decree (Observer Gold Cup), Ace of Aces (Sussex S), Estrapade (Arlington Million), Gay Mecene (GP de St-Cloud), Nobiliary (Prix St. Alary, 2nd Derby S), Mississipian (Grand Criterium), El Cuite (Prix Royal-Oak) and Sporting Yankee (Futurity S). Vaguely Noble suffered a fatal heart attack at Gainesway Farm on 19th of April 1989.

TOULON (GB)

Bay colt, foaled 15 April 1988
By Top Ville (IRE) out of Green Rock (FR) by Mill Reef (USA)
Bred by Juddmonte Farms
Owned by Khalid Abdullah
1990-1992: Trained by Andre Fabre at Chantilly, Oise, France
1993: Trained by Robert Frankel in the U.S.A.

0125292

Racing Record

Year	Timeform Annual Rating	Starts	Wins	2nd	3rd	4th	Win & U.K. Prize Money
1990	-	1	1	-	-	-	-
1991	125	6	3	-	1	1	£ 245,782
1992	117	4	-	-	1	2	£ 6,080
1993	-	3	1	-	-	-	-

Principal Performances

1991   3rd Prix Greffulhe (G2) (3yo colts & fillies) Longchamp (10.5f)
       Won Chester Vase (G3) (3yo) Chester (12.3f)
       Won Prix Maurice de Nieuil (G2) Maisons-Laffitte (12.5f)
       Won St Leger Stakes (G1) (3yo colts & fillies) Doncaster (14.6f)
       4th Prix de l'Arc de Triomphe (G1) Longchamp (12f)
1992   3rd Jockey Club Stakes (G2) Newmarket (12f)
1993   Won Jim Murray Memorial Handicap (G2) Hollywood Park, U.S.A. (12f)

*****

*A*fter an impressive victory at Chester, Toulon went to Epsom well fancied to give his trainer a first English classic success. But unsuited by the very firm ground the colt finished well beaten, his one poor effort in 1991. As a four-year-old Toulon was very disappointing and in an effort to rekindle his enthusiasm was sent to be trained in America. After two poor runs at Santa Anita, Toulon won at Hollywood Park before being retired to stud in Ireland. Toulon died in 1998 leaving only four crops of *foals, which included the good steeplechaser Kingscliff (G1 Lancashire Chase), Too Forward (G2 hurdles winner, £135,367), Xenophon (G3 Coral Cup, Cheltenham) and Solerina, a mare successful in twenty-two races including the G1 Hatton's Grace Hurdle three times and £466,471 in prize money. Green Rock won only two minor races, but was a daughter of Infra Green (G1 Prix Ganay), the dam of Green Reef (1980, by Mill Reef – G3 Prix de Psyche), Greensmith (1986, by Known Fact – 2nd G1 St James's Palace S) and Ecologist (1988, by Rainbow Quest – G3 Prix Berteux). Green Rock also bred Aquamarine (1989, by Shardari – LR Cheshire Oaks) for Khalid Abdullah's Juddmonte Farms.*

2339391

Above: **TOULON** (Pat Eddery) wins the St Leger beating Saddlers' Hall. This was a second victory in this race for Eddery following Moon Madness (p70) and his ninth English classic success. Owner **KHALID ABDULLAH** (below left) had never previously won the St Leger, but this was his fourth English classic victory after Known Fact (p6), Dancing Brave (p66) and Quest For Fame (p106).

3517990

© Unknown

Above centre: Perennial champion trainer in France, **ANDRE FABRE** won his first English classic with Toulon. Above right: **ROBERT FRANKEL** was champion trainer in U.S.A. in 2002 and 2003 and won several Eclipse Awards for best trainer. One of the many good horses trained by him was Empire Maker, winner of the classic Belmont Stakes. Frankel died in November 2009 and the great colt Frankel (p330) was named in his honour.

HATOOF (USA)
Chesnut filly, foaled 26 January 1989
By Irish River (FR) out of Cadeaux d'Amie (USA) by Lyphard (USA)
Bred by Gainsborough Farm Inc.
Owned by Sheikh Maktoum Al-Maktoum
Trained by Christiane Head at Chantilly, Oise, France.

0521293

Racing Record

Year	Timeform Annual Rating	Starts	Wins	2nd	3rd	4th	Prize Money
1991	110	3	1	2	-	-	£ 48,881
1992	120	7	3	1	1	-	£ 276,386
1993	124	6	3	-	-	2	£ 300,297
1994	121	5	2	1	-	1	£ 417,227

Principal Performances

1991 2nd Prix Marcel Boussac (G1) (2yo fillies) Longchamp (8f)
1992 Won 1000 Guineas Stakes (G1) (3yo fillies) Newmarket (8f)
      3rd Prix du Moulin de Longchamp (G1) Longchamp (8f)
      Won Prix de l'Opera (G2) (Fillies & mares) Longchamp (9.3f)
      Won E.P. Taylor Stakes (G2) (Fillies & mares) Woodbine, Canada (10f turf)
1993 Won Prix du Muguet (G3) Saint-Cloud (8f)
      4th Prix d'Ispahan (G1) Longchamp (9.3f)
      Won La Coupe de Maisons-Laffitte (G3) Maisons-Laffitte (10f)
      Won Champion Stakes (G1) Newmarket (10f)
1994 4th Prix d'Ispahan (G1) Longchamp (9.3f)
      Won Prix d'Astarte (G2) (Fillies & mares) Deauville (8f)
      Won Beverly D. Stakes (G1) (Fillies & mares) Arlington, U.S.A. (9.5f turf)
      2nd Breeders' Cup Turf (G1) Churchill Downs, U.S.A. (12f)

H *atoof was tough, sound, genuine and versatile, fully effective from eight to twelve furlongs and winning in four different countries spread over four years, racing predominately in open competition. She was rated as a below average winner of the 1000 Guineas in her classic season, but improved the following year to win the all-aged Champion Stakes. Hatoof won again at Group 1 level in 1994 before retiring to her owner's Gainsborough Farm. Her dam, a stakes placed winner in France and a half-sister to Mrs Penny (1977, by Great Nephew – G1 Prix de Diane, Prix Vermeille, Cheveley Park S), also bred Irish Prize (1996, by Irish River – G1 Shoemaker Breeders Cup Mile S) and the French Listed Race winners Insijaam (1990, by Secretariat) and Fasateen (1991, by Alysheba). Hatoof has foaled nothing of any real class, her winners being Prospects Of Glory (1996, by Mr Prospector), Mighty Isis (1998, by Pleasant Colony), Dubai Edition (1999, by Mr Prospector) and Loulou (2006, by El Prado). Her seventh foal Bochinche (2004, by Kingmambo), only ran twice without winning.*

1916892

Above: **HATOOF** (Walter Swinburn) wins the 1000 Guineas beating Marling (left) and Kenbu. It was the jockey's second victory in this classic following Musical Bliss (see p94) and also for owner, Sheikh Maktoum Al-Maktoum, who had previously triumphed with Ma Biche (p36).

30T0485

2541793

3341793

Above right: **WALTER SWINBURN** won the sixth of his eight English classics on Hatoof. A tactically sound jockey with lovely 'hands', Swinburn also rode Sayyedati (p132) to victory in the 1000 Guineas, Shergar (p18), Shahrastani (p68) and Lammtarra (p160) in the Derby, Unite (p80)(Oaks) and Doyoun (p84) in the 2000 Guineas.

Above centre: **HATOOF** and Swinburn cruise to victory in a second Newmarket Group 1 event, the Champion Stakes; Dernier Empereur and Ezzoud (left) chase in vain. Above right: **CHRISTIANE HEAD** with Hatoof, her third winner of the 1000 Guineas after Ma Biche and Ravinella (p82). Head won the race for a fourth time in 2010 with Special Duty (p320). She has yet to win any other English classic.

RODRIGO DE TRIANO (USA)

Chesnut colt, foaled 27 May 1989
By El Gran Senor (USA) out of Hot Princess (IRE) by Hot Spark (IRE)
Bred by Swettenham Stud
Owned by Robert E. Sangster
Trained by Peter W. Chapple-Hyam at Manton, Marlborough, Wiltshire.

2023292

Racing Record

Year	Timeform Annual Rating	Starts	Wins	2nd	3rd	4th	Prize Money
1991	120	5	5	-	-	-	£ 141,031
1992	130	8	4	-	-	2	£ 608,052

Principal Performances

1991   Won Champagne Stakes (G2) (2yo colts & geldings) Doncaster (7f)
       Won Middle Park Stakes (G1) (2yo colts) Newmarket (6f)
1992   Won 2000 Guineas Stakes (G1) (3yo colts & fillies) Newmarket (8f)
       Won Irish 2000 Guineas Stakes (G1) (3yo colts & fillies) Curragh (8f)
       Won International Stakes (G1) York (10.4f)
       Won Champion Stakes (G1) Newmarket (10f)

*****

*I*f anyone ever doubted the skill of trainer Peter Chapple-Hyam, then Rodrigo de Triano is a *testament to it. At Royal Ascot, the colt was very stirred up beforehand and it seemed as though the mental and physical strain of the unsuccessful trip to Epsom for the Derby had finished him. But Chapple-Hyam had Rodrigo back in top form by August and two decisive victories in Group 1 company at York and Newmarket firmly established both horse and trainer in the very top-class. Rodrigo de Triano was retired to stud in Japan where he stood from 1993 until retiring from stud duties in 2013. His best progeny included Erimo Excel (G1 Yushun Himba-Japan Oaks), Super Hornet (G2 Milers Cup, Swan S, Mianichi Okan, Keio Hai Spring Cup, 2nd G1 Yasuda Kinen), Meiner Condor (G3 Sapporo*

Sansai S), Grace Namura (G3 Kyoto Himba S), Ibuki Yamano O (G3 Diamond S) and Miyagi Rodrigo (G3 Fukushima Kinen). Rodrigo was spending his retirement at the JBBA Shizunai Stallion Station where he died on 5 August 2014. His dam Hot Princess was a listed winner in Ireland, but descended from a modest family. The grandam Aspara was a moderate maiden but bred numerous winners, though none better than Hot Princess. Third dam Courtside (1965, by Court Martial) and fourth dam Omelet Souffle (1953, by Eight Thirty), produced nothing of note between them.

2117692

Above: **RODRIGO DE TRIANO** wins the 2000 Guineas beating Lucky Lindy (right) and Pursuit Of Love (left). This was a first classic success for trainer, Peter Chapple-Hyam. Owner Robert Sangster was recording his third victory in the 2000 Guineas following Lomond (p40) and El Gran Senor (p48). For the great jockey **LESTER PIGGOTT** (below left) it was his thirtieth and final English classic. He rode his first winner, aged twelve, in 1948 and his first classic winner in 1954 (see p43 and 55 for a complete list of Piggott's English classic winners). He had initially retired at the end of the 1985 season and began training from his Eve Lodge Stables at Newmarket. Jailed for tax evasion in 1987, Piggott served one year of a three year sentence and returned to the saddle at the age of fifty-four during mid-October 1990, scoring an incredible victory in the Breeders' Cup Mile on Royal Academy. He finally retired in 1995. It was the end of a remarkable career.

Below centre: Two brilliant jockeys; **LESTER PIGGOTT** on Rodrigo de Triano beating Pat Eddery and All At Sea in the International Stakes at York. Below right: **PETER CHAPPLE-HYAM** trained a 2000 Guineas and a Derby winner in 1992, only his second season with a training licence.

2326391   1036492   3430691

125

DR DEVIOUS (IRE)

Chesnut colt, foaled 10 March 1989
By Ahonoora (GB) out of Rose of Jericho (USA) by Alleged (USA)
Bred by Lyonstown Stud, Cashel, Co. Tipperary
1991: Owned by Robert E. Sangster
October 1991: Owned by Luciano Gaucci
1992: Owned by Sidney H. Craig
Trained by Peter W. Chapple-Hyam at Manton, Marlborough, Wiltshire.

1641791

Racing Record

Year	Timeform Annual Rating	Starts	Wins	2nd	3rd	4th	Prize Money
1991	117	6	4	2	-	-	£ 187,872
1992	127	9	2	2	-	2	£ 624,422

Principal Performances

1991 Won Superlative Stakes (Listed Race) (2yo) Newmarket (7f)
Won Vintage Stakes (G3) (2yo) Goodwood (7f)
Won Dewhurst Stakes (G1) (2yo colts & fillies) Newmarket (7f)
1992 Won Derby Stakes (G1) (3yo colts & fillies) Epsom (12f)
2nd Irish Derby Stakes (G1) (3yo colts & fillies) Curragh (12f)
4th International Stakes (G1) York (10.4f)
Won Irish Champion Stakes (G1) Leopardstown (10f)
4th Breeders' Cup Turf (G1) Gulfstream, U.S.A. (12f)

*****

*H*as there ever been a Derby winner that changed hands so often as Dr Devious? The colt was twice sold by Tattersalls at Newmarket, as a foal for 52,000 guineas and as a yearling for 56,000 guineas. He raced first in the colours of Robert Sangster and was then sold to Luciano Gaucci, who passed him on, reportedly for $2.5m, to Mrs Sidney Craig as a sixtieth birthday present for her husband. The superbly tough and genuine Dr Devious is the only horse ever to triumph in the Epsom Derby after having previously run in the Kentucky Derby and the first sired by a sprinter since Hard

126

Ridden in 1958. His sire Ahonoora (see p77) was best at five furlongs and renowned for blistering early pace. The unraced Rose of Jericho also bred Archway (1988, by Thatching – G3 Greenlands S, 3rd G2 King's Stand S) and Royal Court (1993, by Sadler's Wells – G3 Ormonde S, 3rd G2 Great Voltigeur S) and came from the family of Princesse Lida (1977, by Nijinsky – G1 Prix Morny, Prix de la Salamandre), Critique (1978, by Roberto – G2 Hardwicke S) and Markofdistinction (1986, by Known Fact - G1 Queen Elizabeth II S). Further back, Dr Devious' fourth dam was Torbella (1955, by Tornado), winner of the Dewhurst Stakes and dam of Carlemont (1962, by Charlottesville - Sussex S). Dr Devious was retired to stud at Shadai Farm in Hokkaido, but was a failure in Japan, siring only two minor graded stakes winners, Takeichi Kento and Over The Wall. The stallion was brought back to Europe in 1997 since when his best winner has been the remarkable gelding Collier Hill (G1 Irish St Leger, Canadian International, Hong Kong Vase, G2 Gerling-Preis, G3 Stockholm Cup), who started his racing career as a four-year-old running in a National Hunt Flat Race and finished by winning two Group 1 stakes as an eight-year-old. Other notable progeny have included Kinnaird (G1 Prix de l'Opera, G2 May Hill S), London Bridge (2nd G1 Oka Sho-Japan 1000 Guineas), Olive Crown (3rd G1 Yushun Himba-Japan Oaks), Demophilos (2nd G1 St Leger S), Duca D'Atri (G2 Premio Ribot), Day Walker (G3 Furstenberg-Rennen), Devious Indian (G3 Prix Quincey) and Dr Greenfield (LR Dee S). Dr Devious has sired racehorses as tough, sound and genuine as himself, without getting any of his own ability. The latter part of his stud career has been spent at Allavamenti della Berardenga in Italy, where he has topped the General Sires list on more than one occasion.

2623092

Above: **DR DEVIOUS** wins the Derby beating St Jovite (rail) and Silver Wisp (blaze). For County Down born jockey, John Reid, this was a second English classic victory following On The House (p26) and also the second for trainer Peter Chapple-Hyam, who had saddled Rodrigo De Triano to win the 2000 Guineas earlier in the year.

0346591

2723392

Above left: **DR DEVIOUS**, with Willie Carson wearing the colours of his second owner Luciano Gaucci, wins the Dewhurst Stakes beating Great Palm (grey). Above right: **SIDNEY CRAIG** and his wife on Derby Day at Epsom.

SHADAYID (USA) : Grey 1988

Shadeed (USA) B. 1982	Nijinsky (CAN) B. 1967	Northern Dancer (CAN)
		Flaming Page (CAN)
	Continual (USA) B/br. 1976	Damascus (USA)
		Continuation (USA)
Desirable (GB) Gr. 1981	Lord Gayle (USA) B. 1965	Sir Gaylord (USA)
		Sticky Case (USA)
	Balidaress (IRE) Gr. 1973	Balidar (GB)
		Innocence (GB)

MYSTIKO (USA) : Grey 1988

Secreto (USA) B. 1981	Northern Dancer (CAN) B. 1961	Nearctic (CAN)
		Natalma (USA)
	Betty's Secret (USA) Ch. 1977	Secretariat (USA)
		Betty Loraine (USA)
Caracciola (FR) Gr. 1978	Zeddaan (GB) Gr. 1965	Grey Sovereign (GB)
		Vareta (FR)
	Cendres Bleues (FR) B. 1968	Charlottesville (GB)
		Aigue-Vive (FR)

GENEROUS (IRE) : Chesnut 1988

Caerleon (USA) B. 1980	Nijinsky (CAN) B. 1967	Northern Dancer (CAN)
		Flaming Page (CAN)
	Foreseer (USA) B/br. 1969	Round Table (USA)
		Regal Gleam (USA)
Doff The Derby (USA) B. 1981	Master Derby (USA) Ch. 1972	Dust Commander (USA)
		Madam Jerry (USA)
	Margarethan (USA) B. 1962	Tulyar (IRE)
		Russ-Marie (USA)

JET SKI LADY (USA) : Chesnut 1988

Vaguely Noble (IRE) B. 1965	Vienna (GB) Ch. 1957	Aureole (GB)
		Turkish Blood (GB)
	Noble Lassie (GB) B. 1956	Nearco (ITY)
		Belle Sauvage (GB)
Bemissed (USA) B. 1980	Nijinsky (CAN) B. 1967	Northern Dancer (CAN)
		Flaming Page (CAN)
	Bemis Heights (USA) B. 1975	Herbager (FR)
		Orissa (USA)

TOULON (GB) : Bay 1988

		High Top (GB) B. 1969	Derring-do (GB)
Top Ville (IRE) B. 1976			Camenae (GB)
		Sega Ville (FR) B. 1968	Charlottesville (GB)
			La Sega (FR)
Green Rock (FR) Ch. 1981		Mill Reef (USA) B. 1968	Never Bend (USA)
			Milan Mill (USA)
		Infra Green (IRE) Ch. 1972	Laser Light (GB)
			Greenback (FR)

HATOOF (USA) : Chesnut 1989

		Riverman (USA) Br. 1969	Never Bend (USA)
Irish River (FR) Ch. 1976			River Lady (USA)
		Irish Star (FR) B. 1960	Klairon (FR)
			Botany Bay (FR)
Cadeaux d'Amie (FR) Ch. 1984		Lyphard (USA) B. 1969	Northern Dancer (CAN)
			Goofed (USA)
		Tananarive (GB) B. 1970	Le Fabuleux (FR)
			Ten Double (USA)

RODRIGO DE TRIANO (USA) : Chesnut 1989

		Northern Dancer (CAN) B. 1961	Nearctic (CAN)
El Gran Senor (USA) B. 1981			Natalma (USA)
		Sex Appeal (USA) Ch. 1970	Buckpasser (USA)
			Best In Show (USA)
Hot Princess (GB) Ch. 1980		Hot Spark (IRE) Ch. 1972	Habitat (USA)
			Garvey Girl (IRE)
		Aspara (USA) B. 1972	Crimson Satan (USA)
			Courtside (USA)

DR DEVIOUS (IRE) : Chesnut 1989

		Lorenzaccio (GB) Ch. 1965	Klairon (FR)
Ahonoora (GB) Ch. 1975			Phoenissa (GB)
		Helen Nichols (GB) Ch. 1966	Martial (IRE)
			Quaker Girl (GB)
Rose of Jericho (USA) B. 1984		Alleged (USA) B. 1974	Hoist The Flag (USA)
			Princess Pout (USA)
		Rose Red (USA) Ch. 1979	Northern Dancer (CAN)
			Cambrienne (FR)

USER FRIENDLY (GB)

Bay filly, foaled 4 February 1989
By Slip Anchor (GB) out of Rostova (GB) by Blakeney (GB)
Bred by Stetchworth Park Stud Limited
Owned by William J. Gredley
Trained by Clive E. Brittain at Carlburg Stables, Newmarket, Suffolk.

1740492

Racing Record

Year	Timeform Annual Rating	Starts	Wins	2nd	3rd	4th	Prize Money
1991	-	0	-	-	-	-	-
1992	128	8	6	1	-	-	£ 721,539
1993	123	5	1	-	1	2	£ 219,388
1994	-	2	1	-	-	-	£ 20,439

Principal Performances

1992   Won Oaks Trial Stakes (Listed Race) (3yo fillies) Lingfield (11.5f)
       Won Oaks Stakes (G1) (3yo fillies) Epsom (12f)
       Won Irish Oaks Stakes (G1) (3yo fillies) Curragh (12f)
       Won Yorkshire Oaks (G1) (Fillies & mares) York (11.9f)
       Won St Leger Stakes (G1) (3yo colts & fillies) Doncaster (14.6f)
       2nd Prix de l'Arc de Triomphe (G1) Longchamp (12f)
1993   4th Coronation Cup (G1) Epsom (12f)
       Won Grand Prix de Saint-Cloud (G1) Saint-Cloud (12f)
       4th King George VI & Queen Elizabeth Stakes (G1) Ascot (12f)
       3rd Yorkshire Oaks (G1) (Fillies & mares) York (11.9f)

*****

*U*ser Friendly was sent to be trained by Rodney Rash in the USA during 1994 where in two outings she won an allowance race at Del Mar and was unplaced at Arlington. In foal to Mr Prospector, User Friendly was sold for $2.5m at the November 1995 Keeneland Breeding Stock Sale to Kazuo Nakamura. The mare was sold again at the same sale in 1999 for $1.7m to David Nagle of Barronstown Stud. User Friendly was a prolific breeder producing eleven foals between 1996 and

2007, but none approached her own ability. Downtown (2004, by Danehill - G3 Give Thanks S) was the best and Two Miles West (2001, by Sadler's Wells) was G3 placed as well as winning on the flat and also over hurdles and fences, as did Streets Of Gold (2002, by Sadler's Wells). User Friendly descended from a family developed by Jim Joel at his Childwick Bury Stud from the 1944 1000 Guineas winner Picture Play. For more details about this classic family see Light Cavalry (p12).

T012013   3023892   3536692

Above left: **GEORGE DUFFIELD** rode the only two English classic winners of his career on User Friendly. Above centre: **USER FRIENDLY** wins the Oaks beating All At Sea. Above right: **BILL GREDLEY** with his home-bred filly after the Yorkshire Oaks.

Right and opposite: A third classic and a fourth successive Group 1 as **USER FRIENDLY** powers to victory in the St Leger beating Sonus (right) and Bonny Scot. This was the second victory in this classic for trainer Clive Brittain, having previously won with Julio Mariner (1975, by Blakeney), a full brother to Juliette Marny (1972 – Oaks S) and half-brother to Scintillate (1976, by Sparkler – Oaks S).

1040392

1026993

Above: A consolation prize for **USER FRIENDLY** in a disappointing 1993 season; victory in the Grand Prix de Saint-Cloud beating Apple Tree (left) and Modhish.

SAYYEDATI (GB)

Bay filly, foaled 26 January 1990
By Shadeed (USA) out of Dubian (GB) by High Line (GB)
Bred by Gainsborough Stud Management Limited
Owned by Mohamed Obaida
Trained by Clive E. Brittain at Carlburg Stables, Newmarket, Suffolk.

0516593

Racing Record

Year	Timeform Annual Rating	Starts	Wins	2nd	3rd	4th	Prize Money
1992	116	4	3	1	-	-	£ 179,194
1993	122	6	2	1	1	1	£ 274,676
1994	121	6	-	1	1	1	£ 145,423
1995	122	6	1	2	1	1	£ 256,406

Principal Performances

1992   Won Cherry Hinton Stakes (G3) (2yo fillies) Newmarket (6f)
      Won Moyglare Stud Stakes (G1) (2yo fillies) Curragh (7f)
      Won Cheveley Park Stakes (G1) (2yo fillies) Newmarket (6f)

1993   Won 1000 Guineas Stakes (G1) (3yo fillies) Newmarket (8f)
      2nd Sussex Stakes (G1) Goodwood (8f)
      Won Prix Jacques Le Marois (G1) Deauville (8f)
      4th Queen Elizabeth II Stakes (G1) Ascot (8f)

1994   4th Sussex Stakes (G1) Goodwood (8f)
      2nd Prix Jacques Le Marois (G1) Deauville (8f)

1995   Won Sussex Stakes (G1) Goodwood (8f)
      2nd Prix Jacques Le Marois (G1) Deauville (8f)
      4th Prix du Moulin de Longchamp (G1) Longchamp (8f)
      3rd Breeders' Cup Mile (G1) Belmont Park, U.S.A. (8f turf)

S ayyedati achieved a high level of form in each of her four seasons racing and was good enough to twice beat the top colts in the very competitive Group 1 mile events. Attractive and rangy with a long fluent action, Sayyedati was an admirable filly in every way. Her dam was a good runner, winning a Group 1 in Italy and placing in both the English and Irish Oaks; she was a half-sister to the triple champion hurdler, See You Then (1980, by Royal Palace) and several other useful winners. Sayyedati's grandam Melodina won the Seaton Delaval Stakes and was a half-sister to Celina (1965, by Crepello – Irish Oaks), out of Rose of Medina (1956, by Never Say Die), winner of the Princess Elizabeth Stakes and placed in both the 1000 Guineas and Oaks. This is also the family of the Irish St Leger winner, Ommeyad (1954, by Hyperion), Neolight (1943, by Nearco – Cheveley Park S, Coronation S) and Golden Snake (1996, by Danzig), a half-brother to Sayyedati and winner of four Group 1 events including the Prix Jean Prat and the Prix Ganay. Sayyedati died during August 2007 after having foaled several winners. Almushahar (2000, by Silver Hawk) was the best, winning the Group 2 Champagne Stakes. Djebel Amour (1998, by Mt Livermore), Cunas (1999, by Irish River) and Hyper Delight (2001, by Silver Hawk) also won, as did Lonely Ahead (2003, by Rahy), a filly placed fourth in the G2 Lowther Stakes.

0616493

Above: The 1000 Guineas: Lester Piggott on Niche (blaze) glances across and has the beating of third placed Ajfan (centre) but cannot catch **SAYYEDATI** and Walter Swinburn. This was Swinburn's third win in this classic following Musical Bliss (p94) and Hatoof (p122). For trainer Clive Brittain it was a second 1000 Guineas victory after Pebbles (p46). Sayyedati was the only English classic winner to race in the colours of **MOHAMED OBAIDA** (below left).

Below right: After a somewhat unlucky defeat in the Sussex Stakes, when the run of the race went against her, **SAYYEDATI** (Walter Swinburn) made amends by winning the Prix Jacques Le Marois at Deauville beating Ski Paradise (grey) and Miesque's (p72) first foal, Kingmambo (no.2).

1728395

1931893

133

ZAFONIC (USA)

Bay colt, foaled 1 April 1990
By Gone West (USA) out of Zaizafon (USA) by The Minstrel (CAN)
Bred by Juddmonte Farms Incorporated
Owned by Khalid Abdullah
Trained by Andre Fabre at Chantilly, Oise, France.

0837392

Racing Record

Year	Timeform Annual Rating	Starts	Wins	2nd	3rd	4th	Prize Money
1992	126	4	4	-	-	-	£ 257,436
1993	130	3	1	1	-	-	£ 116,606

Principal Performances

1992   Won Prix Morny (G1) (2yo colts & fillies) Deauville (6f)
      Won Prix de la Salamandre (G1) (2yo colts & fillies) Longchamp (7f)
      Won Dewhurst Stakes (G1) (2yo colts & fillies) Newmarket (7f)
1993   Won 2000 Guineas Stakes (G1) (3yo colts & fillies) Newmarket (8f)

*****

A fter two deeply impressive performances at Longchamp and Newmarket, at 5/4 Zafonic was made the shortest-priced winter favourite for the 2000 Guineas since Tudor Minstrel in 1946/7. Like that great horse, Zafonic won with devastating ease and looked set to prove himself an outstanding miler. But the colt ran well below his best at Goodwood in late-July, was found to have bled internally and only days later came the announcement that he had been retired to his owner's Banstead Manor Stud at Cheveley near Newmarket. Zafonic died in a freak paddock accident on 7 September 2002 at Arrowfield Stud in NSW, where he had been due to stand during the southern hemisphere breeding season. Among the best of his progeny were Xaar (G1 Prix de la Salamandre, Dewhurst S), Iffraaj (G2 Lennox S, Park S, 2nd G1 July Cup), Zafeen (G1 St James's Palace S, G2 Mill Reef S, 2nd G1 Prix Morny, 2000 Guineas), Zee Zee Top (G1 Prix de l'Opera), Flashy Wings (G2 Queen Mary S, Lowther S, 2nd G1 Coronation S), Zipping (G2 Prix Robert Papin, 2nd G1 Prix Morny, Middle Park S, 4th 2000 Guineas), Dupont and Pacino (both G2 Mehl-Mullens Rennen) and Trade Fair (G3

134

Criterion S, Minstrel S). Zaizafon won the Group 3 Seaton Delaval Stakes and also bred Choice Spirit (1996, by Danzig – LR Prix de la Calonne). She was out of the tough and talented Mofida, the winner of eight races and group placed from forty starts and also dam of Modena (1983, by Roberto), the dam of Elmaamul (1987, by Diesis – G1 Eclipse S) and Reams of Verse (p180). Since Zafonic, Zaizafon has bred his full-brother Zamindar (1994, G3 Prix de Cabourg, 2ⁿᵈ G1 Prix Morny, Prix de la Salamandre).

2717193

Above: **ZAFONIC** and Pat Eddery brighten a dismal Newmarket day, winning the 2000 Guineas with a magnificent burst of speed. Top-class colt Barathea is left trailing in his wake.

1927695

3217093

2337392

Above left: **ANDRE FABRE**, for whom Zafonic was a first 2000 Guineas winner and third for **KHALID ABDULLAH** (centre) following Known Fact (p6) and Dancing Brave (p66). Above right: The first of three Group 1 wins in 1992 as Pat Eddery drives **ZAFONIC** to victory in the Prix Morny. Right: Better ground and an impressive performance from Zafonic in the Prix de la Salamandre, beating Kingmambo and Splendent (right).

0940992

135

COMMANDER IN CHIEF (GB)

Bay or brown colt, foaled 18 May 1990
By Dancing Brave (USA) out of Slightly Dangerous (USA) by Roberto (USA)
Bred by Juddmonte Farms
Owned by Khalid Abdullah
Trained by Henry R.A. Cecil at Warren Place, Newmarket, Suffolk.

3113193

Racing Record

Year	Timeform Annual Rating	Starts	Wins	2nd	3rd	4th	Prize Money
1992	-	0	-	-	-	-	-
1993	128	6	5	-	1	-	£ 844,823

Principal Performances

1993   Won Derby Stakes (G1) (3yo colts & fillies) Epsom (12f)
        Won Irish Derby Stakes (G1) (3yo colts & fillies) Curragh (12f)
        3rd King George VI and Queen Elizabeth Stakes (G1) Ascot (12f)

*****

*C*ommander in Chief was the first since Morston in 1973 to win the Derby after being unraced as a two-year-old. The colt made rapid progress in the seven weeks between his debut in a maiden at Newmarket and the Derby and won the classic comfortably beating two 150/1 outsiders. With Tenby and Bob's Return (p140) running below form and Barathea failing to stay it looked a below standard race, but Commander in Chief went on to win the Irish Derby and confirm his class. The double Derby winner came from a top-class family; both his dam and grandam Where You Lead finished second in the Oaks. His great grandam, Noblesse (1960, by Mossborough) was a most impressive ten lengths Oaks winner. This is also the family of Rainbow Quest (p197) and Derby and St Leger runner-up, Dushyantor (1993, by Sadler's Wells). Commander in Chief was retired to stud in Japan in 1994 and stood there until his death in a paddock accident at the Yushun Stallion Station in June 2007. He sired over six hundred winners, the best of which were Ein Bride (G1 Hanshin Sansai Himba S), Regular Member (G1 Derby Grand Prix), Meiner Combat (G1 Japan Dirt Derby), Top Commander (G2 Nikkei Shinshun Hai) and Courir Cyclone (G2 Spring S).

136

2122093

Above: **COMMANDER IN CHIEF** (Mick Kinane) wins the Derby beating Blue Stag (left) and Blues Traveller (rail). Kinane was presented with his first Derby winner when Pat Eddery, Khalid Abdullah's retained jockey, chose to ride the unplaced odds-on favourite, stable-companion Tenby. Below right: **KHALID ABDULLAH** won his second Epsom Derby in four years following Quest For Fame in 1990 (see p106).

1125993

1326293

2414302

Above left: Reunited with Eddery, who had ridden him in all his races prior to Epsom, **COMMANDER IN CHIEF** wins his second Derby beating Prix du Jockey-Club victor Hernando at the Curragh. Above centre: **HENRY CECIL** with his second winner of the Irish Derby after the race.

Right: **MICHAEL J. KINANE** was born at Killenaule, County Tipperary and was champion jockey in Ireland on thirteen occasions between 1984 and 2003. He rode ten English classic winners before retiring aged fifty in December 2009; 2000 Guineas four times, Tirol (p104), Entrepreneur (p176), King Of Kings (p188) and Sea The Stars (p310); the Oaks twice on Shahtoush (p192) and Imagine (p226). The Derby on three occasions on Commander in Chief, Galileo (p228), Sea The Stars and the St Leger on Milan (p230). Kinane also won the King George VI and Queen Elizabeth Stakes five times, the Eclipse Stakes and Sussex Stakes on four occasions, the Prix de l'Arc de Triomphe, Ascot Gold Cup and International Stakes three times. He was victorious in many more top international races including the Melbourne Cup, the Belmont Stakes, Japan Cup and all the Irish classics at least twice each.

0442489

INTREPIDITY (IRE)

Bay filly, foaled 19 February 1990
By Sadler's Wells (USA) out of Intrepid Lady (USA) by Bold Ruler (USA)
Bred by Michael J. Ryan
Owned by Sheikh Mohammed Al-Maktoum
Trained by Andre Fabre at Chantilly, Oise, France.

3020493

Racing Record

Year	Timeform Annual Rating	Starts	Wins	2nd	3rd	4th	Prize Money
1992	94	1	1	-	-	-	-
1993	124	7	4	-	-	2	£ 409,877
1994	119	5	-	2	-	1	£ 107,712

Principal Performances

1993 Won Prix Saint-Alary (G1) (3yo fillies) Longchamp (10f) (photo above)
Won Oaks Stakes (G1) (3yo fillies) Epsom (12f)
4th Irish Oaks Stakes (G1) (3yo fillies) The Curragh (12f)
Won Prix Vermeille (G1) (3yo fillies) Longchamp (12f)
4th Prix de l'Arc de Triomphe (G1) Longchamp (12f)
1994 2nd Prix Ganay (G1) Longchamp (10.5f)
4th Breeders' Cup Turf (G1) Churchill Downs, U.S.A. (12f)

*****

*I*ntrepidity was a good Oaks winner, winning three G1 races and looking slightly unlucky not to finish even closer than fourth in the Prix de l'Arc de Triomphe. Her rivalry with stablemate Wemyss Bight was one of the highlights of the season in 1993, the fillies meeting in four successive races in which Intrepidity came out on top three times. Intrepid Lady, a minor winner in France, was twenty years old when foaling Intrepidity, the oldest dam of an Oaks winner since 1945. She had previously bred Calandra (1977, by Sir Ivor – G2 Pretty Polly S, 4th G1 Irish Oaks) and Acushla (1983, by Storm Bird – G3 Phoenix Sprint S twice). Her dam, the unraced Stepping Stone, bred U.S. stakes winner, High Bid (1956, by To Market), the dam of U.S. champion, Bold Bidder (1962, by Bold Ruler). Intrepidity proved a very disappointing broodmare, her best foal was Deodatus (1998, by Darshaan), a winner*

138

seven times in Dubai. Wild Geese (2007, by Cape Cross) has won three races under National Hunt rules to date. Intrepidity was retired from stud in October 2011.

2422393

Above: **INTREPIDITY** (Michael Roberts) wins the Oaks beating Royal Ballerina (centre) and Oakmead (yellow cap). Wemyss Bight is on the right of shot (pink cap). This was a second English classic victory for Roberts following Mystiko (p114) and third for Andre Fabre after Toulon (p120) and Zafonic (p134).

SADLER'S WELLS, pictured here with Pat Eddery at Phoenix Park in 1984, was by no means the best of his classic generation, but became one of the greatest stallions ever. Much of the success of the Coolmore Stud operation has been due to the dominance of Sadler's Wells and his stallion sons, Galileo (p228) and Montjeu (Prix du Jockey-Club, Prix de l'Arc de Triomphe, King George VI & Queen Elizabeth S). Other successful offspring include In The Wings (Coronation Cup), Old Vic (Prix du Jockey-Club, Irish Derby), Opera House (King George VI & Queen Elizabeth S, Eclipse S), Salsabil (p102), Carnegie (Prix de l'Arc de Triomphe), Kayf Tara (Ascot Gold Cup twice), Dream Well (Irish Derby, Prix du Jockey-Club) and High Chaparral (p238).
1515684

Below: Three Andre Fabre trained fillies fight out the finish of the Prix Vermeille and **INTREPIDITY** (Thierry Jarnet) beats Wemyss Bight (Pat Eddery) and Bright Moon.

1936393

BOB'S RETURN (IRE)

Brown colt, foaled 5 March 1990
By Bob Back (USA) out of Quality of Life (IRE) by Auction Ring (USA)
Bred by Baronrath Stud Limited, Straffan, Co. Kildare
Owned by Mrs G.A.E. Smith
Trained by Mark H. Tompkins at Cottage Stables, Newmarket, Suffolk.

2422494

Racing Record

Year	Timeform Annual Rating	Starts	Wins	2nd	3rd	4th	Prize Money
1992	99	4	2	-	-	1	£ 12,025
1993	123	5	3	-	-	-	£ 275,271
1994	123	6	-	2	-	1	£ 99,134

Principal Performances

1992   Won Zetland Stakes (Listed Race) (2yo) Newmarket (10f)
1993   Won Derby Trial Stakes (G3) (3yo) Lingfield (11.5f)
       Won Great Voltigeur Stakes (G2) (3yo colts & geldings) York (11.9f)
       Won St Leger Stakes (G1) (3yo colts & fillies) Doncaster (14.6f)
1994   4th Prix Ganay (G1) Longchamp (10.5f)
       2nd Hardwicke Stakes (G2) Royal Ascot (12f)
       2nd Eclipse Stakes (G1) Sandown (10f)

*****

*T*he essay on Bob's Return in Timeform's annual publication 'Racehorses of 1993' discussed the issue of opening the St Leger to horses above the age of three. This has been a recurring theme in these annuals for some years and one that I am strongly opposed to, whilst acknowledging that a change is desirable if the St Leger is to regain its importance in the racing calendar. The French equivalent of the St Leger, the Prix Royal-Oak (p391), was opened to older horses in 1979 and the Irish St Leger (p392) followed suit in 1983. The Irish version never attracted the very best three-year-olds

and opening up the race has made it more competitive. The same is not true of the Prix Royal-Oak which has shown a gradual decline in the quality of winners and has reached such an all-time low in the last few years that the race no longer justifies its Group 1 status. The same fate awaits the St Leger if it is opened to older horses. Racing's decision makers do very occasionally come up with a good idea and the French did so when they decreased the distance of their Derby, the Prix du Jockey-Club, from twelve to ten furlongs. If we were to do the same in England it would have the immediate effect of tempting more 2000 Guineas horses to run in the Derby. The French destroyed their Triple Crown when they opened up the Prix Royal-Oak, but ours is still in place and would be more attractive to owners and trainers were we to reduce the distance of the St Leger to twelve furlongs. Then running the Derby at the intermediate distance between the 2000 Guineas and the St Leger would give an ideal two furlong increase in distance between the races. More horses would attempt the Triple Crown and racing receive a much needed shot in the arm. If we do nothing then the St Leger will lose further credibility because the fact must be faced that fourteen furlongs is no longer a distance over which connections of the very best horses want to race them. It is commercial suicide nowadays to run a prospective stallion over further than twelve furlongs and many recent St Leger winners such as Milan, Scorpion and Brian Boru have started their stud careers covering National Hunt mares. A twelve furlong St Leger would see more of its winners and placed horses contest the Prix de l'Arc de Triomphe, the Champion Stakes and other autumn championship races. Potential Triple Crown winners Nashwan and Sea The Stars both would probably have run in a twelve furlong St Leger but instead Nashwan ran next day in the Prix Niel and Sea The Stars in the Irish Champion Stakes. Bob's Return was retired to Southcourt Stud at Linslade in Bedfordshire but relocated to Kilbarry Lodge Stud in Waterford, where he died in 2008. His best runners were Joncol (G1 Hennessy Gold Cup, Leopardstown & £310,315), Oneway (7 races & £147,146), Bob Lingo (Galway Plate Chase & £199,542), Ground Ball (9 races & £190,187) and Across The Bay (G2 Rendlesham Hurdle & £142,642 to date).

0436193

Above: **BOB'S RETURN** (Philip Robinson) wins the St Leger beating Armiger (right). It was the jockey's second English classic victory following Pebbles (p46). Top left: **MARK TOMPKINS** with Bob's Return after the St Leger. This has been the trainer's only English classic winner to date, although his Even Top came close in 1996 when beaten by a short-head in the 2000 Guineas by Mark of Esteem (p166).

LAS MENINAS (IRE)

Bay filly, foaled 1 April 1991
By Glenstal (USA) out of Spanish Habit (IRE) by Habitat (USA)
Bred by Swettenham Stud and Partners
Owned by Robert E. Sangster
Trained by Tommy Stack at Thomastown, Golden, Co. Tipperary.

0814594

Racing Record

Year	Timeform Annual Rating	Starts	Wins	2nd	3rd	4th	Prize Money
1993	110	2	1	1	-	-	£ 40,674
1994	115	6	1	1	-	-	£ 140,181

Principal Performances

1993   Won Silver Flash E.B.F. Stakes (Listed Race) (2yo fillies) Leopardstown (6f)
     2nd Phoenix Stakes (G1) (2yo colts & fillies) Leopardstown (6f)
1994   Won 1000 Guineas Stakes (G1) (3yo fillies) Newmarket (8f)
     2nd Irish 1000 Guineas Stakes (G1) (3yo fillies) Curragh (8f)

*****

*A*ccording to ratings published by Timeform in their annual 'Racehorses', Las Meninas is one of the
least talented winners of the 1000 Guineas in the period 1950-2015 (see p385-6); only Night Off
(1965) and Special Duty (p320) are rated below her. Had the photo-finish gone in favour of Balanchine
instead, then she would be remembered as a double English classic winner and Las Meninas as just
another very smart handicapper that managed to run into a place in a classic race. Las Meninas comes
from a fairly undistinguished family. Her dam was unraced and apart from her classic winning
daughter, produced only minor winners. Grandam Donna Cressida won a Group 2 stakes in Ireland
and is out of Cresca (1963, by Saint Crespin), an unraced half-sister to Irish 1000 Guineas winner
Wenduyne (1966, by Moutiers). As a broodmare Las Meninas' record has been disappointing. Her first
foal Stanley Wigfield (1996, by Woodman), was a poor maiden, including when tried over hurdles,

142

Swinging Trio (1997, by Woodman) won a minor race and Greek Revival (2000, by Royal Academy) won three minor races in 2002.

1414494

Above: In such a tight finish that it took the judge more than fifteen minutes to announce the result, **LAS MENINAS** (John Reid) beat subsequent Oaks winner Balanchine (blue cap)(p150) by a short-head with Coup de Genie (left) a close third. This was a third English classic victory for Reid and his second in the 1000 Guineas following On The House (p26).

1614594   3733192   3214494

Above left: **TOMMY STACK** trained his only English classic winner to date with Las Meninas. Stack is better known as the rider of Red Rum when that horse won his historic third Grand National Steeple Chase in 1977. He was champion National Hunt jockey in Britain during 1974/75 and 1976/77.

Above centre: Born in Banbridge, County Down on 5 August 1955, **JOHN REID** was apprenticed to Leslie Crawford in Ireland before transferring his indentures to Verley Bewicke at Downs House, Chilton in Berkshire in the early 1970's. His first big race victory was on Ile De Bourbon in the King George VI and Queen Elizabeth Stakes at Ascot in 1978, a race he won again on Swain for Godolphin in 1997. English classic victories came with On The House, Dr Devious (p126), Las Meninas and finally Nedawi (p196). Reid also won the Prix de l'Arc de Triomphe in 1988 on Tony Bin. He retired in 1991 having ridden 1,937 winners in Britain and 48 Group 1 winners worldwide. John Reid was made an M.B.E. in 1997 for services to horse-racing.

Above right: The 1000 Guineas victory of Las Meninas must have surely given **ROBERT SANGSTER** one of his most satisfying days in racing. Sangster had sold his home-bred Balanchine to Godolphin during the previous winter and now watched her beaten in a classic by a filly he had retained. Las Meninas was his last English classic winner following The Minstrel (1977) and Golden Fleece (p30) in the Derby and Lomond (p40), El Gran Senor (p48) and Rodrigo de Triano (p124) in the 2000 Guineas. Robert Sangster died on 7 April 2004, aged 67.

MISTER BAILEYS (GB)

Bay colt, foaled 14 February 1991
By Robellino (USA) out of Thimblerigger (GB) by Sharpen Up (GB)
Bred by Ranston (Bloodstock) Limited
Owned by G.R. Bailey Limited
Trained by Mark S. Johnston at Kingsley House Stables, Middleham, Yorkshire.

3004194

Racing Record

Year	Timeform Annual Rating	Starts	Wins	2nd	3rd	4th	Prize Money
1993	112	5	3	-	1	-	£ 87,443
1994	123	4	1	-	1	1	£ 184,084

Principal Performances

1993   Won Vintage Stakes (G3) (2yo) Goodwood (7f)
　　　　Won Royal Lodge Stakes (G2) (2yo colts & geldings) Ascot (8f)
1994   Won 2000 Guineas Stakes (G1) (3yo colts & fillies) Newmarket (8f)
　　　　3rd Dante Stakes (G2) (3yo) York (10.4f)
　　　　4th Derby Stakes (G1) (3yo colts & fillies) Epsom (12f)

*****

M *ister Baileys was shrewdly bought as a foal by Paul Venner for only 10,000 guineas and went on to become the first English classic winner trained in the north of England since Mrs McArdy won the 1000 Guineas in 1977. Despite doubts about his ability to stay further than one mile due to his headstrong tendencies, Mister Baileys was given his chance in the Derby and swept around Tattenham Corner in a six-length lead only to fade with a furlong to run and finish fourth. After disappointing back over one mile at Goodwood, the colt was retired to the National Stud at Newmarket but suffered a life-threatening attack of grass sickness which caused ongoing health and fertility problems. In 2003, by now completely infertile, Mister Baileys was retired from stud duties and he died in 2009. His dam was moderate on the racecourse but was out of Oaks third Tender Annie, a half-sister to Aiming High*

144

(1958, by Djebe – Coronation S), grandam of Miss Petard (1970, by Petingo – G2 Ribblesdale S). This is also the family of Oath (p206) and Pelder (p207). Good winners by Mister Baileys included Bahia Breeze (LR Bosra Sham S, Pipalong S), Gee Dee Nen (9 races on the flat, over hurdles and fences), Parkview Love (9 races, LR Woodcote S), Mister Arjay (13 races on the flat & over hurdles) and Kahlua Kiss (4 races).

3004394

Above: **MISTER BAILEYS** (Jason Weaver) and Grand Lodge (Frankie Dettori) fight out a tremendous finish to the 2000 Guineas with the former prevailing by a short-head.

3004694

Right: **PAUL VENNER** managing director of G.R. Bailey Limited, with Jason Weaver and Mister Baileys in the winner's circle after the 2000 Guineas.

Below centre: The Royal Lodge Stakes winner **ROBELLINO** stood at Littleton Stud in Hampshire. Mister Baileys was his only English classic winner but he was also the sire of Royal Rebel (Ascot Gold Cup twice) and Classic Park (Irish 1000 Guineas). Below left: Mister Baileys was **MARK JOHNSTON**'s first English classic winner. He has since trained a second with Attraction (p256) in the 1000 Guineas of 2004. Below right: **JASON WEAVER** won his only English classic on Mister Baileys. Other big race victories included the Ascot Gold Cup on Double Trigger and the St James's Palace Stakes on Bijou d'Inde, both horses trained by Mark Johnston. Weaver was champion apprentice in Britain in 1993 and retired in 2002. He now works in racing media.

3137392

1317780

3138594

145

USER FRIENDLY (GB) : Bay 1989

Slip Anchor (GB) B. 1982	Shirley Heights (GB) Br. 1975	Mill Reef (USA)
		Hardiemma (GB)
	Sayonara (GER) B. 1965	Birkhahn (GER)
		Suleika (GER)
Rostova (GB) Br. 1981	Blakeney (GB) B. 1966	Hethersett (GB)
		Windmill Girl (GB)
	Poppy Day (GB) B. 1968	Soleil (FR)
		Red Poppy (GB)

SAYYEDATI (GB) : Bay 1990

Shadeed (USA) B. 1982	Nijinsky (CAN) B. 1967	Northern Dancer (CAN)
		Flaming Page (CAN)
	Continual (USA) B/br. 1976	Damascus (USA)
		Continuation (USA)
Dubian (GB) B. 1982	High Line (GB) Ch. 1966	High Hat (GB)
		Time Call (GB)
	Melodina (GB) Br. 1968	Tudor Melody (GB)
		Rose of Medina (GB)

ZAFONIC (USA) : Bay 1990

Gone West (USA) B/br. 1984	Mr Prospector (USA) B. 1970	Raise A Native (USA)
		Gold Gigger (USA)
	Secrettame (USA) Ch. 1978	Secretariat (USA)
		Tamerett (USA)
Zaizafon (USA) Ch. 1982	The Minstrel (CAN) Ch. 1974	Northern Dancer (CAN)
		Fleur (CAN)
	Mofida (GB) Ch. 1974	Right Tack (GB)
		Wold Lass (GB)

COMMANDER IN CHIEF (GB) : Bay/brown 1990

Dancing Brave (USA) B. 1983	Lyphard (USA) B. 1969	Northern Dancer (CAN)
		Goofed (USA)
	Navajo Princess (USA) B. 1974	Drone (USA)
		Olmec (USA)
Slightly Dangerous (USA) B. 1979	Roberto (USA) B. 1969	Hail To Reason (USA)
		Bramalea (USA)
	Where You Lead (USA) Ch. 1970	Raise A Native (USA)
		Noblesse (FR)

INTREPIDITY (GB) : Bay 1990

Sadler's Wells (USA) B. 1981	Northern Dancer (CAN) B. 1961	Nearctic (CAN)
		Natalma (USA)
	Fairy Bridge (USA) B. 1975	Bold Reason (USA)
		Special (USA)
Intrepid Lady (USA) B/br. 1970	Bold Ruler (USA) B. 1954	Nasrullah (GB)
		Miss Disco (USA)
	Stepping Stone (USA) B. 1950	Princequillo (IRE)
		Step Across (USA)

BOB'S RETURN (IRE) : Brown 1990

Bob Back (USA) Br. 1981	Roberto (USA) B. 1969	Hail To Reason (USA)
		Bramalea (USA)
	Toter Back (USA) Ch. 1967	Carry Back (USA)
		Romantic Miss (USA)
Quality of Life (IRE) B. 1985	Auction Ring (USA) B. 1972	Bold Bidder (USA)
		Hooplah (USA)
	Flirting Countess (GB) Ch. 1975	Ridan (USA)
		Narrow Escape (GB)

LAS MENINAS (IRE) : Bay 1991

Glenstal (USA) B. 1980	Northern Dancer (CAN) B. 1961	Nearctic (CAN)
		Natalma (USA)
	Cloonlara (USA) B. 1974	Sir Ivor (USA)
		Fish-Bar (IRE)
Spanish Habit (GB) B. 1979	Habitat (USA) B. 1966	Sir Gaylord (USA)
		Little Hut (USA)
	Donna Cressida (GB) Br. 1972	Don (ITY)
		Cresca (GB)

MISTER BAILEYS (GB) : Bay 1991

Robellino (USA) B. 1978	Roberto (USA) B. 1969	Hail To Reason (USA)
		Bramalea (USA)
	Isobelline (USA) B. 1971	Pronto (ARG)
		Isobella (USA)
Thimblerigger (GB) Ch. 1976	Sharpen Up (GB) Ch. 1969	Atan (USA)
		Rocchetta (GB)
	Tender Annie (GB) Br. 1959	Tenerani (ITY)
		Annie Oakley (GB)

ERHAAB (USA)

Black colt, foaled 24 May 1991
By Chief's Crown (USA) out of Histoire (FR) by Riverman (USA)
Bred by Shadwell Farm Inc. & Shadwell Estate Co. Ltd.
Owned by Sheikh Hamdan Al-Maktoum
Trained by John L. Dunlop at Castle Stables, Arundel, Sussex.

1726994

Racing Record

Year	Timeform Annual Rating	Starts	Wins	2nd	3rd	4th	Prize Money
1993	102	6	2	1	1	-	£ 13,834
1994	127	5	2	1	1	-	£ 582,828

Principal Performances

1993   3rd Horris Hill Stakes (G3) (2yo colts & geldings) Newbury (7.3f)
1994   2nd Feilden Stakes (Listed Race) (3yo) Newmarket (9f)
          Won Dante Stakes (G2) (3yo) York (10.4f)
          Won Derby Stakes (G1) (3yo colts & fillies) Epsom (12f)
          3rd Eclipse Stakes (G1) (3yo & upwards) Sandown (10f)

*****

In common with the majority of Derby winners of the 1990's Erhaab was rated under 130 by Timeform and he cannot be regarded as anything but a below average winner. After disappointing performances at Sandown and Ascot, the colt was found to have sustained damage to the suspensory ligaments behind both knees and his sale to Japan for a reported £3.5m was announced in October 1994. Chief's Crown won eight Grade 1 races and was placed in all three legs of the U.S. Triple Crown. Histoire, a minor winner in France, was an expensive purchase for Sheikh Hamdan, in foal to Nureyev, at Keeneland in 1988. That foal, named Oumaldaaya, won the G2 Premio Lydia Tesio. Erhaab's grandam Helvetie bred numerous winners including Hamanda (G3 Prix de la Porte Maillot). Further back this is the family of two fillies which both finished third in the 1000 Guineas Stakes, Solar Myth (1946, by Hyperion) and Keystone (1938, by Umidwar – Cheveley Park S). Erhaab stood at the

Agricultural Association East Stud in Hokkaido but was unpopular with Japanese breeders, siring less than 300 foals in his five years there before the stallion was brought back to the west during 1999. There were no graded stakes winners in Japan and Erhaab has done no better at Shadwell Farm in Kentucky, Beech House Stud, Newmarket, Wood Farm Stud in Shropshire or at Batsford Stud at Moreton-in-Marsh in Gloucestershire. His best offspring is Sohraab, the winner of £107, 152, seven races and runner-up twice in Listed Races.

2719694

Above: **ERHAAB** (Willie Carson) wins the Derby beating King's Theatre and Colonel Collins with 2000 Guineas winner Mister Baileys (p144) (rail) in fourth place. It was Carson's fourth Derby and his last English classic winner (for more details of Willie Carson's career, see p11).

1342492

Above: **H.H. SHEIKH HAMDAN AL-MAKTOUM, WILLIE CARSON** and **JOHN DUNLOP** won four English classics together with Salsabil (p102), Shadayid (p112) and Erhaab. The trio were also associated with many other top-class winners including Aqaarid (Fillies Mile), Ashayer (Prix Marcel Boussac), Marju (St James's Palace S), Mehthaaf (Irish 1000 Guineas), Bahri and Lahib (both winners of the Queen Elizabeth II S).

BALANCHINE (USA)

Chesnut filly, foaled 16 April 1991
By Storm Bird (CAN) out of Morning Devotion (USA) by Affirmed (USA)
Bred by Swettenham Stud
1993: Owned by Robert E. Sangster and trained by Peter W. Chapple-Hyam
at Manton, Marlborough, Wiltshire.
1994-95: Owned by Sheikh Maktoum Al-Maktoum & Godolphin
1994: Trained by Hilal Ibrahim in Dubai, United Arab Emirates.
1995: Trained by Saeed bin Suroor at Moulton Paddocks, Newmarket.

3537495

Racing Record

Year	Timeform Annual Rating	Starts	Wins	2nd	3rd	4th	Prize Money
1993	93	2	2	-	-	-	£ 11,699
1994	131	3	2	1	-	-	£ 520,624
1995	119	3	-	1	-	-	£ 9,581

Principal Performances

1994   2nd 1000 Guineas Stakes (G1) (3yo fillies) Newmarket (8f)
        Won Oaks Stakes (G1) (3yo fillies) Epsom (12f)
        Won Irish Derby Stakes (G1) (3yo colts & fillies) Curragh (12f)
1995   2nd Prix Foy (G3) Longchamp (12f)

*****

*B*alanchine *was the first English classic winner ever to be trained outside Europe but her classic season was cut short by a serious bout of colic weeks after the Irish Derby. Kept in training in 1995, the filly was unable to reproduce her best. Her sire Storm Bird won the Dewhurst Stakes and was syndicated to stand in the U.S. for $30m. Morning Devotion was a stakes placed winner and also bred Derby third Romanov (1994, by Nureyev – G2 Jockey Club S) and Red Slippers (1989, by Nureyev – G2 Sun Chariot S), herself dam of West Wind (2004, by Machiavellian – G1 Prix de Diane). Grandam Morning Has Broken was a half-sister to It's In The Air (1976, by Mr Prospector), a multiple Grade 1 winner in the U.S. Balanchine's record as a broodmare has been generally disappointing; Gulf News (1999, by Woodman) won twice and was second in the G2 Prix Niel. Ibtecar (2000, by Seeking The*

150

Gold) and Oberlin (2005, by Gone West) were minor winners. Balsamine (2012, by Street Cry) won twice in France during 2014.

2220294

Above: The umbrellas are up at Epsom and the Oaks runners cross to the stand-side rail searching for better ground; **BALANCHINE** (Frankie Dettori) defeats Wind In Her Hair and Hawajiss (rail). This was a first English classic victory for Dettori who was also champion jockey for the first time in 1994. Below left: Godolphin's first trainer **HILAL IBRAHIM**, who disappeared from the European racing scene after 1994. Below right: Balanchine in the winner's circle after the Oaks with owner Sheikh Maktoum.

0924094

0406594

Below left: **MAKTOUM AL-MAKTOUM** owned seven English classic winners; Touching Wood (see p34), Ma Biche (p36), Shadeed (p60), Hatoof (p122), Jet Ski Lady (p118), Moonshell (p158) and Balanchine. He suffered a fatal heart attack in Australia on 4 January 2006. Below centre: **BALANCHINE** wins the Irish Derby thrashing King's Theatre and Colonel Collins, both placed in the Derby at Epsom. Below right: **FRANKIE DETTORI** looks worried on Balanchine waiting to hear the result of the 1000 Guineas; fifteen minutes later the judge called Las Meninas as the short-head winner.

0422190

3024294

2914494

151

MOONAX (IRE)

Chesnut colt, foaled 22 March 1991
By Caerleon (USA) out of Moonsilk (IRE) by Solinus (GB)
Bred by Liscannor Stud Limited
1993-94: Owned by Sheikh Mohammed Al-Maktoum
1995-97: Owned by Godolphin
Trained by Barry W. Hills at Faringdon Place, Lambourn, Berkshire.

3236895

Racing Record

Year	Timeform Annual Rating	Starts	Wins	2nd	3rd	4th	Prize Money
1993	-	1	-	-	-	-	-
1994	121	8	4	1	1	-	£ 218,190
1995	122	4	1	3	-	-	£ 146,672
1996	120	4	1	2	1	-	£ 56,249
1996/7	106h N.H.	3	-	1	1	-	£ 1,196
1997	103	2	-	-	1	-	£ 5,294

Principal Performances

1994   2nd Chester Vase (G3) (3yo) Chester (12.3f)
       Won St Leger Stakes (G1) (3yo colts & fillies) Doncaster (14.6f)
       Won Prix Royal-Oak (G1) (3yo & upwards) Longchamp (15.5f)
1995   Won Yorkshire Cup (G2) York (13.9f)
       2nd Gold Cup (G1) Royal Ascot (20f)
       2nd Irish St Leger Stakes (G1) Curragh (14f)
       2nd Prix du Cadran (G1) Longchamp (20f)
1996   2nd Prix du Cadran (G1) Longchamp (20f)
       2nd Prix Royal-Oak (G1) Longchamp (15.5f)
1997   3rd Ormonde Stakes (G3) Chester (13.4f)

*T*he mercurial and occasionally downright dangerous Moonax went best for the sympathetic hands of Pat Eddery, but the jockey never lost his respect for the horse's space and when asked to pose for photographs with Moonax after winning the Prix Royal-Oak, Eddery replied 'I'm not getting anywhere near that so and so'. Or words to that effect! At the end of the 1996 flat racing season it was decided to try Moonax over hurdles. After two placed efforts, Moonax showed his dislike for jumping by behaving in an unruly manner before finishing unplaced at Ludlow. With that experiment abandoned, Moonax returned to the flat but his temper was by now thoroughly unpredictable and the stableman leading him up at Chester wore body armour for protection in case the horse attacked him. His dam Moonsilk was a half-sister to the 1000 Guineas winner, Nocturnal Spree (1972, by Supreme Sovereign) and Tootens (1978, by Northfields – G1 Prix Saint-Alary). Grandam Night Attire showed little sign of ability in three races but came from the same family as Erhaab (p148). Moonax retired to Clongeel Stud at Mallow in County Cork but sired no runners of any real consequence and died in May 2004. Moonax was the first English classic winner to be sent jumping since Aurelius (1958, by Aureole), the infertile 1961 St Leger winner.

1032894

Above: **MOONAX** (Pat Eddery) wins the St Leger beating Broadway Flyer (ridden and trained by two of Barry Hills' sons) and Double Trigger. This was Eddery's third win in this classic after Moon Madness (see p70) and Toulon (p120), a first for Barry Hills and second for Sheikh Mohammed following Oh So Sharp (p58).

2032894

2739294

Above left: **BARRY HILLS** looks slightly apprehensive as he congratulates MOONAX after the St Leger.

Above right: On his best days **MOONAX** was not averse to a good battle; here, he defeats Always Earnest in a closely-fought finish to the Prix Royal-Oak at Longchamp in Paris. The following year Moonax took the fight a little too literally and attempted to bite Always Earnest inside the final furlong of the Prix du Cadran. Perhaps he was outraged at being beaten?

PENNEKAMP (USA)
Bay colt, foaled 26 March 1992
By Bering (GB) out of Coral Dance (FR) by Green Dancer (USA)
Bred by Mrs Magdalen O. Bryant
Owned by Sheikh Mohammed Al-Maktoum
Trained by Andre Fabre at Chantilly, Oise, France.

1410194

Racing Record

Year	Timeform Annual Rating	Starts	Wins	2nd	3rd	4th	Prize Money
1994	123	4	4	-	-	-	£ 165,235
1995	130	3	2	-	-	-	£ 134,678

Principal Performances

1994 Won Prix du Haras de la Huderie (Listed Race) (2yo) Deauville (7f)
      Won Prix de la Salamandre (G1) (2yo colts & fillies) Longchamp (7f)
      Won Dewhurst Stakes (G1) (2yo colts & fillies) Newmarket (7f)
1995 Won Prix Djebel (Listed Race) (3yo colts) Evry (6.5f)
      Won 2000 Guineas Stakes (G1) (3yo colts & fillies) Newmarket (8f)

*****

*P*ennekamp went to Epsom for the Derby unbeaten in six races which included a thrilling victory in
the 2000 Guineas and came away with an injury forcing his retirement. One of those six wins
came in the Prix de la Salamandre, which was first run in 1872. Pennekamp was the last English classic
winner to win la Salamandre before the race was scrapped in 2000, apparently because it was too
successful and taking the kudos from the Grand Criterium, traditionally France's juvenile
championship event. Evidently it didn't occur to the French decision makers that dropping la
Salamandre to Group 2 would have done the job rather better than creating an entirely new Group 1,
run in late-autumn at Saint-Cloud, invariably on heavy ground. After six years at Kildangan Stud at
Monasterevin in County Kildare, followed by spells at stud in France and Sweden in 2002-2004,
Pennekamp was sold to Brachlyn Stud, Mullingar, Ireland in 2005. Pennekamp has had some success
as a National Hunt stallion getting the Triumph Hurdle winner Penzance. Alexander Three D (G3 Park
Hill S, LR Galtres S), Topkamp (LR Cecil Frail S) and Historian (LR Prix Rose de Mai) have been

154

Pennekamp's best winners on the flat. His daughter Pennegale is the dam of Mubtaahij (2012, by Dubawi - G2 UAE Derby). The group-placed winner Coral Dance had previously bred Nasr El Arab (1985, by Al Nasr), the winner of four G1 graded stakes in the U.S. Grandam Carvinia won twice in France and was a half-sister to the high-class French horse Carvin (1962, by Marino – Criterium de St-Cloud, 3rd Prix du Jockey-Club).

2616395

Above: **PENNEKAMP** (Thierry Jarnet) beats odds-on favourite Celtic Swing (rail) and Bahri in a very good renewal of the 2000 Guineas. Below: **ANDRE FABRE** and **SHEIKH MOHAMMED** pose with their winner. This was a first 2000 Guineas for the owner and second for Fabre following Zafonic (p134). Below centre: **THIERRY JARNET** rode his only English classic winner to date on Pennekamp.

2716495

0420294

1520986

Above right: Prix du Jockey-Club winner **BERING**, the sire of Pennekamp, at Chantilly in 1986. Bering was a successful stallion his progeny including Peter Davies (G1 Racing Post Trophy), American Post (G1 Racing Post Trophy, Grand Criterium, Poule d'Essai des Poulains), Matiara (G1 Poule d'Essai des Pouliches), Miss Berbere (G2 Prix d'Astarte), Moiava and Signe Divin (G2 Criterium de Maisons-Laffitte) and Serrant (G2 GP d'Evry, Prix Maurice de Nieul).

Left: Success for **PENNEKAMP** in Britain's two-year-old championship race, the Dewhurst Stakes, beating Green Perfume and Eltish (pink cap).

1137794

HARAYIR (USA)

Bay filly, foaled 22 March 1992
By Gulch (USA) out of Saffaanh (USA) by Shareef Dancer (USA)
Bred by Shadwell Farm Incorporated
Owned by Sheikh Hamdan Al-Maktoum
Trained by Major W.R. Hern at Kingwood House Stables, Lambourn.

2616795

Racing Record

Year	Timeform Annual Rating	Starts	Wins	2nd	3rd	4th	Prize Money
1994	108	4	2	1	1	-	£ 67,543
1995	119	9	4	1	2	1	£ 241,553

Principal Performances

1994   Won Lowther Stakes (G2) (2yo fillies) York (6f)
        3rd Cheveley Park Stakes (G1) (2yo fillies) Newmarket (6f)
1995   Won 1000 Guineas Stakes (G1) (3yo fillies) Newmarket (8f)
        3rd Coronation Stakes (G1) (3yo fillies) Royal Ascot (8f)
        3rd Falmouth Stakes (G2) (Fillies & mares) Newmarket (8f)
        Won Hungerford Stakes (G3) (3yo & upwards) Newbury (7f)
        Won Celebration Mile (G2) (3yo & upwards) Goodwood (8f)
        Won Challenge Stakes (G2) (3yo & upwards) Newmarket (7f)

*****

*H*arayir was sound, tough and genuine and went through a busy classic season without missing a cue until sustaining an injury when exercising at Belmont Park before what was scheduled to be her last race in the Breeders' Cup Mile. Retained by her owner for stud, Harayir foaled several winners including Moonjaz (1997, by Nashwan), Izdiham (1999, by Nashwan – LR Gala S) Azizi (2007, by Haafhd) and Enfijaar (2010, by Invincible Spirit). Harayir descends from a very successful family developed at the Moller's White Lodge Stud, which includes Teenoso (p42) and Favoletta (1968, by Baldric – Irish 1000 Guineas). Her dam Saffaanh, a listed-placed winner, was out of Give Thanks (G1

Irish Oaks, G3 Musidora S, G3 Lancashire Oaks) and traces back in the tail-female line to the famous White Lodge foundation mare Horama (1943, by Panorama).

2016695

Above: **HARAYIR** and Richard Hills win the first ever English classic to be run on a Sunday. Willie Carson, having chosen to ride the wrong filly, finishes second on Aqaarid (left) carrying the owner's first colours, with subsequent Oaks heroine, Moonshell (p158) in third place. Below right: **RICHARD HILLS** (below left) returns to unsaddle his first English classic winner. Among the many well-known faces waiting to welcome him is Major Dick Hern (seated), greeting his last classic winner in a training career which started at Major Lionel Holliday's Lagrange Stables at Newmarket in 1958.

0517300

3516795

3716695

Right: **MAJOR DICK HERN** with his trophy after Harayir's 1000 Guineas. He had won sixteen English classics beginning with Hethersett in the St Leger of 1962. Five more St Leger winners followed in Provoke (1965), Bustino (1974), Dunfermline (1977), Cut Above (see p24) and Sun Princess (p44). Troy (1979), Henbit (p8) and Nashwan (p96) won the Derby, Dunfermline, Bireme (p10) and Sun Princess, the Oaks, and Highclere a first 1000 Guineas for Hern and The Queen in 1974. Nashwan also won the 2000 Guineas. The best horse Major Hern ever had was Brigadier Gerard, winner of seventeen of his eighteen races, including the 2000 Guineas (1971). Other top horses trained by Hern include Buoy (Coronation Cup), Ela-Mana-Mou (King George VI & Queen Elizabeth S, Eclipse S), Elmaamul (Eclipse S), Relkino (Lockinge S), Little Wolf & Longboat (Ascot Gold Cup), Sallust (Sussex S), Galivanter (July Cup), Homing (Queen Elizabeth II S) and brilliant sprinter Dayjur (Nunthorpe S, King's Stand S). Four times champion trainer in Britain, Major Hern died on 22 May 2002, aged 81.

MOONSHELL (IRE)

Bay filly, foaled 20 February 1992
By Sadler's Wells (USA) out of Moon Cactus (GB) by Kris (GB)
Bred by Sheikh Mohammed bin Rashid Al-Maktoum
1994: Owned by Sheikh Mohammed Al-Maktoum
Trained by Henry R.A. Cecil at Warren Place, Newmarket
1995: Owned by Sheikh Maktoum Al-Maktoum & Godolphin
Trained by Saeed bin Suroor at Moulton Paddocks, Newmarket.

0916695

Racing Record

Year	Timeform Annual Rating	Starts	Wins	2nd	3rd	4th	Prize Money
1994	90	1	1	-	-	-	£ 4,481
1995	117	2	1	-	1	-	£ 167,435
1996	-	2	-	-	1	-	£ 1,579

Principal Performances

1995   3rd 1000 Guineas Stakes (G1) (3yo fillies) Newmarket (8f)
      Won Oaks Stakes (G1) (3yo fillies) Epsom (12f)

*****

*M*oonshell was one of the first horses removed by Sheikh Mohammed Al-Maktoum from the care of Henry Cecil, the 'Trainer of Genius' and others of equal standing and sent to be trained under the Godolphin banner in Dubai and Newmarket. It is the prerogative of any owner of racehorses to do as he wishes with his property, but no entirely satisfactory reason has ever been put forward for taking horses away from the best trainers in Europe. It is possible that the Maktoum family might have enjoyed even greater success if the Godolphin idea had been left on the back burner. Moonshell was injured after winning the Oaks and unable to run again that year. Brought back to the track in 1996, she could not recapture her best form. As a broodmare, Moonshell produced a few minor winners including Alunissage (1998, by Rainbow Quest) and Moonsprite (2000, by Seeking The Gold), but her best foal proved to be the unraced Forest Pearl (1999, by Woodman), who bred the multiple Australian G1 winner, Miss Finland (2003, by Redoute's Choice). Moonshell died on 21 January 2006 at

Woodpark Stud in County Meath whilst foaling a colt by Pivotal which was named Hatta Diamond and won a small race for trainer Mark Johnston in 2009.

2421295

Above: **MOONSHELL** wins the Oaks beating Dance A Dream giving jockey Frankie Dettori his second victory in this classic following Balanchine (p150) and Saeed bin Suroor his first.

2522293

1522290

Above left: **SHEIKH MOHAMMED AL-MAKTOUM**, who with his elder brother, **SHEIKH MAKTOUM AL-MAKTOUM** (right) seen leading in his third Oaks winner Moonshell, was the driving force behind the foundation of the Godolphin enterprise.

Above right: **MOON CACTUS** was a very useful filly, racing for Sheikh Mohammed, winning the Sweet Solera Stakes, Prestige Stakes and finishing second in the G1 Prix de Diane. Moon Cactus also bred Doyen (G1 King George VI & Queen Elizabeth S, G2 Prix Niel, Hardwicke S). Her grandam, Moonlight Night (1972, by Levmoss - G3 Musidora S), was third in the Oaks and comes from a highly successful family developed at the Joel's Childwick Bury Stud which includes Light Cavalry (p12) and Fairy Footsteps (p14). Crocket (1960, by King of the Tudors – Coventry S, Gimcrack S, Middle Park S, Craven S, St James's Palace S), a champion

British juvenile, also descends from this family. Moonshell's grandam Lady Moon was bought by Sheikh Mohammed for 600,000 guineas, carrying Moon Cactus, at the 1986 Joel dispersal sale at Tattersalls.
2921395

159

LAMMTARRA (USA)

Chesnut colt, foaled 2 February 1992
By Nijinsky (CAN) out of Snow Bride (USA) by Blushing Groom (FR)
Bred by Gainsborough Farm Incorporated
Owned by Saeed Maktoum Al-Maktoum
1994: Trained by Alex A. Scott at Gainsborough Stables, Newmarket
1995: Trained by Saeed bin Suroor at Moulton Paddocks, Newmarket.

2427295

Racing Record

Year	Timeform Annual Rating	Starts	Wins	2nd	3rd	4th	Prize Money
1994	93	1	1	-	-	-	£ 8,773
1995	134	3	3	-	-	-	£ 1,298,061

Principal Performances

1995   Won Derby Stakes (G1) (3yo colts & fillies) Epsom (12f)
        Won King George VI and Queen Elizabeth Stakes (G1) Ascot (12f)
        Won Prix de l'Arc de Triomphe (G1) Longchamp (12f)

*****

*L*ammtarra was the first colt to win the Derby on his seasonal debut since Grand Parade in 1919 and only two winners since 1900, Bois Roussel (1938) and Morston (1973), had succeeded having raced only once before in their lives. The 1995 Derby, the first run on a Saturday since Coronation Year 1953, saw the long-standing time record for the race, set by Mahmoud in 1936, beaten by a second and a half, also expunging the record time for the course and distance set by Bustino in the Coronation Cup 1975. Lammtarra was the first Derby winner produced from a mating between Derby and Oaks winners. Snow Bride was a grand-daughter of Royal Statute (1969, by Northern Dancer), the dam of Akureyri (1978, by Buckpasser – G1 Fountain of Youth S). Lammtarra was retired to Dalham Hall Stud in Newmarket, but after only one season there an offer of $30m was accepted and Lammtarra was fired off to Arrow Stud in Japan, where he was a dismal failure, siring only three graded stakes winners, all at G3 level. In Europe, his best progeny were Simeon (G3 Classic Trial S, 3rd Prix du Jockey-Club) and Melikah (LR Pretty Polly S, 2nd Irish Oaks, 3rd Oaks S). During August 2006 it was *reported that Sheikh Mohammed Al-Maktoum had brought Lammtarra back from Japan to spend his retirement at Dalham Hall Stud, where he died on 6 July 2014.*

© Clare Bancroft

Above: An image taken by a good friend and colleague, Clare Bancroft, who was tragically killed in a motor accident in Spain in 2007. **LAMMTARRA** (Walter Swinburn) winning the Derby beating Tamure (second right) and Presenting (white colours), giving trainer Saeed bin Suroor his only Derby success to date.

1427395

3237595

Above left: **LAMMTARRA** (Frankie Dettori) winning the King George VI and Queen Elizabeth Stakes beating Pentire and Strategic Choice. Above right: **FRANKIE DETTORI** celebrates in typical ebullient fashion after victory in the Prix de l'Arc de Triomphe in Paris. Below left: Trainer **ALEX SCOTT** was shot and killed by his stud-groom on 30 September 1994. Below centre: **SAEED MAKTOUM AL-MAKTOUM** also won the Oaks with Lammtarra's dam, Snow Bride (p98). Below right: Sheikh Mohammed and Saeed bin Suroor (left) lead in **WALTER SWINBURN** on his third Derby winner.

2737293

2927395

0921795

161

CLASSIC CLICHE (IRE)

Bay colt, foaled 13 March 1992
By Salse (USA) out of Pato (GB) by High Top (GB)
Bred by Lord Victor Matthews
1994: Owned by Ivan Allan, trained by
Henry R.A. Cecil at Warren Place, Newmarket, Suffolk
1995-97: Owned by Godolphin, trained by
Saeed bin Suroor at Moulton Paddocks, Newmarket, Suffolk.

3024295

Racing Record

Year	Timeform Annual Rating	Starts	Wins	2nd	3rd	4th	Prize Money
1994	91	2	1	1	-	-	£ 7,370
1995	120	5	2	1	-	1	£ 302,259
1996	128	4	2	1	-	-	£ 280,954
1997	126	5	1	2	-	-	£ 90,776

Principal Performances

1995   Won Dante Stakes (G2) (3yo) York (10.4f)
       4th Prix du Jockey-Club (G1) (3yo colts & fillies) Chantilly (12f)
       2nd King Edward VII Stakes (G2) (3yo colts & geldings) Royal Ascot (12f)
       Won St Leger Stakes (G1) (3yo colts & fillies) Doncaster (14.6f)
1996   Won Yorkshire Cup (G2) (4yo & upwards) York (13.9f)
       Won Gold Cup (G1) (4yo & upwards) Royal Ascot (20f)
       2nd King George VI & Queen Elizabeth Stakes (G1) (4yo & upwards) Ascot (12f)
1997   2nd Gold Cup (G1) (4yo & upwards) Royal Ascot (20f)
       2nd Goodwood Cup (G2) (3yo & upwards) Goodwood (16f)
       Won Prix Kergorlay (G2) (3yo & upwards) Deauville (15f)

*****

A fter being awarded a rating by Timeform at the end of his classic season that suggested he was the worst winner of the St Leger since Timeform ratings began in the 1940's, Classic Cliché improved considerably as a four-year-old and further belied his miler's pedigree by winning the Gold

162

Cup at Royal Ascot. This most genuine and consistent racehorse also finished second in the top British all-aged twelve furlong race, the King George VI & Queen Elizabeth Stakes. Classic Cliché comes from a fairly ordinary family, the best of which formerly rarely aspired to racing above top handicap level; his dam, just a useful handicapper, was a sister to Stewards' Cup winner, Crews Hill, a gelding group placed in England and a minor stakes winner in the U.S. After the St Leger winner, Pato bred another top winner in My Emma (1993, by Marju – G1 Prix Vermeille) and through her daughter Lust (1994, by Pursuit of Love) was fourth dam of Lightening Pearl (2009, by Marju – G1 Cheveley Park S). Classic Cliché was originally retired to Wood Farm Stud at Ellerdine in Shropshire but was moved to Kilbarry Lodge Stud in County Waterford where he still stands. His best progeny to date have been Macadamia (G2 Falmouth Stakes, Royal Hunt Cup H) and Colloquial (6 races, £73,746). Under National Hunt rules Roulez Cool (LR Prix James Hennessy Steeple Chase, Auteuil), Stagecoach Pearl (9 races, £100,870) and Preacher Boy (2 races, £73,748, 3rd G3 Hennessy Gold Cup Handicap Steeple Chase) have done well for Classic Cliché.

2634195

Above: **FRANKIE DETTORI** rides his first St Leger and second English classic winner following Balanchine (p150) on Classic Cliché beating Minds Music (rail) and Istidaad (blue sleeves). It was also the first victory in this race for trainer **SAEED BIN SUROOR** (below right) and his third English classic following Moonshell (p158) and Lammtarra (p160).

2221396

2008185

0405197

Above left: **CLASSIC CLICHE** (Mick Kinane) becomes the first English classic winner to win the Gold Cup at Royal Ascot since Ocean Swell in 1945. There had been a few high-profile Gold Cup failures in the intervening years, notably Black Tarquin (St Leger 1948) second in 1949, Alcide (St Leger 1958), beaten a short-head in 1959 and Blakeney (Derby 1969), second behind Precipice Wood in 1970. Above centre: **IVAN ALLAN**, who owned the 1984 St Leger winner Commanche Run (p54), sold Classic Cliché to Godolphin after his two-year-old season.

ERHAAB (USA) : Brown 1991

	Chief's Crown (USA) B. 1982	Danzig (USA) B. 1977	Northern Dancer (CAN)
			Pas De Nom (USA)
		Six Crowns (USA) Ch. 1976	Secretariat (USA)
			Chris Evert (USA)
	Histoire (FR) B/br. 1979	Riverman (USA) B. 1969	Never Bend (USA)
			River Lady (USA)
		Helvetie (GB) B. 1965	Klairon (FR)
			Heiress (GB)

BALANCHINE (USA) : Chesnut 1991

	Storm Bird (CAN) B. 1978	Northern Dancer (CAN) B. 1961	Nearctic (CAN)
			Natalma (USA)
		South Ocean (CAN) B. 1967	New Providence (CAN)
			Shining Sun (CAN)
	Morning Devotion (USA) Ch. 1982	Affirmed (USA) Ch. 1975	Exclusive Native (USA)
			Won't Tell You (USA)
		Morning Has Broken (USA) Ch. 1974	Prince John (USA)
			A Wind Is Rising (USA)

MOONAX (IRE) : Chesnut 1991

	Caerleon (USA) B. 1980	Nijinsky (CAN) B. 1967	Northern Dancer (CAN)
			Flaming Page (CAN)
		Foreseer (USA) B/br. 1969	Round Table (USA)
			Regal Gleam (USA)
	Moonsilk (IRE) B. 1980	Solinus (GB) B. 1975	Comedy Star (USA)
			Cawston's Pride (GB)
		Night Attire (GB) Ch. 1966	Shantung (FR)
			Twilight Hour (GB)

PENNEKAMP (USA) : Bay 1992

	Bering (GB) Ch. 1983	Arctic Tern (USA) Ch. 1973	Sea-Bird (FR)
			Bubbling Beauty (USA)
		Beaune (FR) Ch. 1974	Lyphard (USA)
			Barbra (FR)
	Coral Dance (FR) B. 1978	Green Dancer (USA) B. 1972	Nijinsky (CAN)
			Green Valley (FR)
		Carvinia (FR) Br. 1970	Diatome (GB)
			Coraline (FR)

HARAYIR (USA) : Bay 1992

Gulch (USA) B. 1984	Mr Prospector (USA) B. 1970	Raise A Native (USA)
		Gold Digger (USA)
	Jameela (USA) B/br. 1976	Rambunctious (USA)
		Asbury Mary (USA)
Saffaanh (USA) B. 1986	Shareef Dancer (USA) B. 1980	Northern Dancer (CAN)
		Sweet Alliance (USA)
	Give Thanks (GB) B. 1980	Relko (FR)
		Parthica (GB)

MOONSHELL (IRE) : Bay 1992

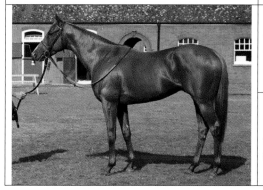

Sadler's Wells (USA) B. 1981	Northern Dancer (CAN) B. 1961	Nearctic (CAN)
		Natalma (USA)
	Fairy Bridge (USA) B. 1975	Bold Reason (USA)
		Special (USA)
Moon Cactus (GB) B. 1987	Kris (GB) Ch. 1976	Sharpen Up (GB)
		Doubly Sure (GB)
	Lady Moon (GB) B. 1980	Mill Reef (USA)
		Moonlight Night (FR)

LAMMTARRA (USA) : Chestnut 1992

Nijinsky (CAN) B. 1967	Northern Dancer (CAN) B. 1961	Nearctic (CAN)
		Natalma (USA)
	Flaming Page (CAN) B. 1959	Bull Page (USA)
		Flaring Top (USA)
Snow Bride (USA) Ch. 1986	Blushing Groom (FR) Ch. 1974	Red God (USA)
		Runaway Bride (GB)
	Awaasif (CAN) B. 1979	Snow Knight (GB)
		Royal Statute (CAN)

CLASSIC CLICHE (IRE) : Bay 1992

Salse (USA) B. 1985	Topsider (USA) B. 1974	Northern Dancer (CAN)
		Drumtop (USA)
	Carnival Princess (USA) Ch. 1974	Prince John (USA)
		Carnival Queen (USA)
Pato (GB) B. 1982	High Top (GB) Br. 1969	Derring-do (GB)
		Camenae (GB)
	Patosky (GB) B. 1969	Skymaster (GB)
		Los Patos (GB)

MARK OF ESTEEM (IRE)

Bay colt, foaled 26 March 1993
By Darshaan (GB) out of Homage (GB) by Ajdal (USA)
Bred by Sheikh Mohammed bin Rashid Al-Maktoum
1995: Owned by Sheikh Mohammed Al-Maktoum and
trained by Henry Cecil at Warren Place, Newmarket, Suffolk
1996: Owned by Godolphin and trained by Saeed bin Suroor
at Moulton Paddocks, Newmarket, Suffolk.

3530896

Racing Record

Year	Timeform Annual Rating	Starts	Wins	2nd	3rd	4th	Prize Money
1995	105	2	1	1	-	-	£ 8,687
1996	137	5	3	-	-	-	£ 356,452

Principal Performances

1996   Won 2000 Guineas Stakes (G1) (3yo colts & fillies) Newmarket (8f)
       Won Celebration Mile (G2) (3yo & upwards) Goodwood (8f)
       Won Queen Elizabeth II Stakes (G1) (3yo & upwards) Ascot (8f)

*****

*F*rankie Dettori's trademark 'flying dismount' has become something expected of him after every big-race victory, but his premature dismount while still on the track and embrace with the Godolphin travelling head-lad (opposite centre) might have cost him his first 2000 Guineas winner had the rules of racing been strictly enforced or if the connections of any other runner had decided to object. Mark of Esteem had to miss the Derby but came back in the autumn with two more top-class performances. The colt was retired to Dalham Hall Stud at Newmarket and became a fairly successful stallion siring classic winners Ameerat (p224) and Sir Percy (p282), Reverence (G1 Sprint Cup, Nunthorpe S), High Accolade (G2 King Edward VII S, G3 Cumberland Lodge S), Bribon (G1 Metropolitan H), Redback (G3 Greenham S, Solario S, 3rd G1 2000 Guineas) and Ordnance Row (G3 Supreme S, Sovereign S). Mark of Esteem's daughter Puggy is the dam of Avenir Certain (G1 Poule d'Essai des Pouliches, G1 Prix de Diane). Mark of Esteem was retired from stud duties due to declining fertility in 2007 and was put down at Dalham Hall Stud in May 2014 after a short illness. His unraced *dam Homage was a half-sister to Local Suitor (1982, by Blushing Groom - G2 Mill Reef S) and Local Talent (1986, by Northern Dancer – G1 Prix Jean Prat). Grandam Home Love (1976, by Vaguely Noble), was also unraced, but a half-sister to Folk Art (1982, by Nijinsky – G1 Oak Leaf S) and Mashaallah (1988, by Nijinsky), the winner of three Group 1 events including the Irish St Leger. This is the family of Northern Baby (p101), tracing back in the tail-female line to Flambette (1918, by Durbar – CCA Oaks).*

2314896

Above: **MARK OF ESTEEM** (Frankie Dettori) wins the 2000 Guineas beating Even Top (off shot) and Bijou d'Inde (left). Below right: Godolphin's private trainer, **SAEED BIN SUROOR**, trained his fourth successive English classic winner with Mark of Esteem.

1714996

1914996

2514996

Above: In a rare clash between contemporary Guineas winners, the very good colt beats the very good filly as **FRANKIE DETTORI** (on his way to a unique seven-timer) and Mark of Esteem beat Pat Eddery riding Bosra Sham in the Queen Elizabeth II Stakes at Ascot.

3430696

BOSRA SHAM (USA)

Chesnut filly, foaled 28 February 1993
By Woodman (USA) out of Korveya (USA) by Riverman (USA)
Bred by Gerald W. Leigh
Owned by Wafic Said
Trained by Henry R.A. Cecil at Warren Place, Newmarket, Suffolk.

1908197

Racing Record

Year	Timeform Annual Rating	Starts	Wins	2nd	3rd	4th	Prize Money
1995	115	2	2	-	-	-	£ 94,511
1996	132	4	3	1	-	-	£ 369,029
1997	130	4	2	-	1	1	£ 124,943

Principal Performances

1995   Won Fillies' Mile (G1) (2yo fillies) Ascot (8f)
1996   Won Fred Darling Stakes (G3) (3yo fillies) Newbury (7f)
        Won 1000 Guineas Stakes (G1) (3yo fillies) Newmarket (8f)
        2nd Queen Elizabeth II Stakes (G1) (3yo & upwards) Ascot (8f)
        Won Champion Stakes (G1) (3yo & upwards) Newmarket (10f)
1997   Won Brigadier Gerard Stakes (G3) Sandown (10f)
        Won Prince of Wales's Stakes (G2) Royal Ascot (10f)
        3rd Eclipse Stakes (G1) Sandown (10f)
        4th International Stakes (G1) York (10.4f)

*****

B osra Sham's pedigree, she was a full-sister to the French classic winner Hector Protector (1988),
and half-sister to another in Shanghai (1989, by Procida – G1 Poule d'Essai des Poulains), made
*her the most sought after yearling at the 1994 Tattersalls Houghton Sales in Newmarket. At 530,000
guineas she was the highest priced yearling sold in Europe that year. Bosra Sham went on to win three
Group 1 races and was rated by Timeform the best winner of the 1000 Guineas since Hula Dancer in
1963 (p385-6). As a broodmare Bosra Sham has been very disappointing, producing only one stakes
winner Rosberg (2003, by A P Indy – CANG3 Premier's S) and the minor winners Shami (1999, by
Rainbow Quest) and Bosra's Valentine (2000, by Sadler's Wells). Korveya (G3 Prix Chloe) was out of*

168

Konafa (2nd 1000 Guineas), the dam of Proskona (1981, by Mr Prospector – G2 Premio Umbra). This is the family of Snow Bride (p98), Lammtarra (p160) and Brief Truce (1989, by Irish River – G1 St James's Palace S).

1435995

Above: **BOSRA SHAM** (Pat Eddery) wins the Fillies' Mile beating Bint Shadayid (grey) and Matiya.

Below: A different race but almost the same result as **BOSRA SHAM** and Pat Eddery lead home Matiya (pink cap) and Bint Shadayid in the 1000 Guineas. This was a fourth victory in this classic for Henry Cecil and the only occasion that Eddery won it.

0815396

1041487

2912696

0832785

Above left: **GERALD LEIGH** was a successful owner and breeder who also bred Brocade (Prix de la Foret), Barathea (Irish 2000 Guineas) and Gossamer (Irish 1000 Guineas) at his Eydon Hall Stud in Northamptonshire. Gerald Leigh died in 2002, aged seventy-one. Above centre: **WAFIC SAID**, the Syrian businessman and philanthropist, for whom Bosra Sham was a first English classic winner. Above right: **WOODMAN** stood at Coolmore's Ashford Stud in Kentucky and sired a number of top-class horses before his death on 19 July 2007. These included Hector Protector (Poule d'Essai des Poulains, Prix Jacques Le Marois), Hansel (Preakness and Belmont Stakes), Timber Country (Preakness Stakes) and Hawk Wing (Eclipse Stakes).

LADY CARLA (GB)

Bay filly, foaled 8 March 1993
By Caerleon (USA) out of Shirley Superstar (GB) by Shirley Heights (GB)
Bred by Meon Valley Stud, Bishop's Waltham, Hampshire
Owned by Wafic Said
Trained by Henry R.A. Cecil at Warren Place, Newmarket, Suffolk.

0816096

Racing Record

Year	Timeform Annual Rating	Starts	Wins	2nd	3rd	4th	Prize Money
1995	90	1	1	-	-	-	£ 4,402
1996	122	3	2	-	-	1	£ 220,973
1997	-	2	-	-	-	-	-

Principal Performances

1996   Won Oaks Trial Stakes (Listed Race) (3yo fillies) Lingfield (11.5f)
      Won Oaks Stakes (G1) (3yo fillies) Epsom (12f)
      4th Irish Oaks Stakes (G1) (3yo fillies) Curragh (12f)

*****

*L*ady Carla was a 220,000 guineas yearling purchase by Tim Bulwer-Long for Wafic Said at Tattersalls Houghton Sales, on the day before they purchased Bosra Sham (p168). To buy both the same year's 1000 Guineas and Oaks winners is without precedent. Lady Carla went on to more than justify her price-tag with a nine-length victory in the Oaks. Amid unsubstantiated rumours, first aired on Channel 4's 'The Morning Line', that Lady Carla had a serious wind problem, the filly next ran in the Irish Oaks, but could finish only fourth of the six runners. After disappointing twice the following season, Lady Carla was retired. She descended from a family that flourished during the 1960's through the offspring of Zanzara (1951, by Fairey Fulmar), her fourth dam. This famous mare bred fourteen winners including Showdown (1961, by Infatuation – Middle Park S), a champion sire in Australia, Farfalla (1967, by Crocket – Queen Mary S) and Matatina (1960, by Grey Sovereign – Nunthorpe S). In December 2009 Lady Carla was returned to Tattersalls as part of the dispersal of her owner's bloodstock and was bought by Irish breeder Timmy Hyde, for 1,05m guineas. She has proved a poor investment, the best of her offspring being Avalon (2002, by Kingmambo – winner & 3rd G2 Great Voltigeur S), High Ruler (2008, by Mr Greeley – winner & 4th Irish 2000 Guineas) and Indigo Magic (1999, by Gone West), a successful stallion in South Africa.

0519296

Above: **LADY CARLA** (Pat Eddery) wins the Oaks Stakes beating Pricket (blue cap). This was a fourth success in this classic for trainer, Henry Cecil.

2719196

0118794

Above left: **WAFIC SAID** leading in his second and last English classic winner, Lady Carla. The owner quit horse-racing in 2009 and his bloodstock was dispersed at that year's Tattersalls December Sales.

Above right: **PATRICK EDDERY** was born at Newbridge, County Kildare on 18 March 1952. Pat rode his first winner on Alvaro at Epsom in April 1969 and went on to a total of 4,632 winners in Great Britain and was champion jockey eleven times, plus once in Ireland, before he retired at the end of 2003. His fourteen English classic winners were Polygamy (1974), Scintillate (1979) and Lady Carla in the Oaks; Grundy (1975), Golden Fleece (p30) and Quest for Fame (p106)(Derby); Lomond (p40), El Gran Senor (p48) and Zafonic (p134)(2000 Guineas); Bosra Sham (p168)(1000 Guineas); Moon Madness (p70), Toulon (p120), Moonax (p152) and Silver Patriarch (p186) in the St Leger. As well as these classic winners, Pat also won big races on Erimo Hawk and Celeric (Ascot Gold Cup), Vitiges and Pebbles (Champion S), Crow (Coronation Cup), Sadler's Wells (Eclipse S), Record Token and Danehill (Haydock Sprint Cup), Assert and Caerleon (Benson & Hedges Gold Cup), Grundy (King George VI & Queen Elizabeth S, Irish Derby), Sharpo (July Cup & Nunthorpe S twice), Sheikh Albadou (Nunthorpe S and Breeder's Cup Sprint), Posse, Kings Lake, Distant View and Reel Buddy (Sussex S), May Hill, Busaca and Ramruma (Yorkshire Oaks), Warning (Queen Elizabeth II S), Caerleon and Sanglamore (Prix du Jockey-Club) and Detroit, Rainbow Quest and Trempolino (Prix de l'Arc de Triomphe). The best horse Eddery rode was Dancing Brave (p66), on which he won the King George VI and Queen Elizabeth Stakes and the Prix de l'Arc de Triomphe in 1986.

SHAAMIT (IRE)

Bay colt, foaled 11 February 1993
By Mtoto (GB) out of Shomoose (IRE) by Habitat (USA)
Bred by Khalifa Abdullah Dasmal
Owned by Khalifa Dasmal
Trained by William J. Haggas at Somerville Lodge, Newmarket, Suffolk.

0919696

Racing Record

Year	Timeform Annual Rating	Starts	Wins	2nd	3rd	4th	Prize Money
1995	90	2	1	-	-	1	£ 4,574
1996	127	4	1	-	1	1	£ 580,000

Principal Performances

1996   Won Derby Stakes (G1) (3yo colts & fillies) Epsom (12f)
    3rd King George VI and Queen Elizabeth Stakes (G1) Ascot (12f)
    4th Irish Champion Stakes (G1) Leopardstown (10f)

*****

*T*he tall, unfurnished Shaamit won the Derby on only his third outing and looked set to progress into a very good horse. But a minor injury prevented the colt running in the Irish Derby and when he did return at Ascot in late-July was beaten fairly and squarely by the four-year-olds Pentire and Classic Cliché (p162). Two more defeats in Ireland and France further undermined Shaamit's reputation. A tendon injury incurred at Longchamp meant that plans to keep him in training for another year were abandoned and he was retired to the National Stud at Newmarket. In 1998, Shaamit became the first European horse to shuttle to South Africa, covering there during the southern hemisphere breeding season. He was subsequently moved to Scarvagh House Stud in County Down where the stallion died of a ruptured stomach on 7 April 2001. Shaamit left only five crops of foals born in Europe and by far the best of those proved to be the St Leger winner Bollin Eric (p240). The unraced Shomoose was a daughter of the stakes placed winner Epithet. One has to go back to Mi Carina (1956, by Ocarina – Prix Vermeille) before encountering another classic winner in this family.

172

1619796

Above: The Derby Stakes; **SHAAMIT** and Michael Hills hold the late runs of the unlucky in running second and third placed horses, Dushyantor (pink cap) and Shantou (p174).

1726187

2319696

Above left: **MTOTO**, sire of Shaamit, winning the Eclipse Stakes in 1987 beating Reference Point (p78) and Triptych. Above right: **MICHAEL HILLS, KHALIFA DASMAL** and **WILLIAM HAGGAS** (below left) with their Derby trophies. This was a first English classic victory for all three.

Right: **MICHAEL HILLS** never rode another English classic winner but he did win many other Group 1 races including on Arcadian Heights (Ascot Gold Cup), Royal Applause and Red Clubs (Haydock Sprint Cup), Pentire (King George VI and Queen Elizabeth S), Storming Home (Champion S), First Island (Sussex S), Nicer and Hula Angel (Irish 1000 Guineas), Nicolotte (Queen Anne S) and La Cucaracha and Handsome Sailor (Nunthorpe S). Hills retired at the end of the 2012 season.

173

SHANTOU (USA)

Bay colt, foaled 30 April 1993
By Alleged (USA) out of Shaima (USA) by Shareef Dancer (USA)
Bred by Darley Stud Management Inc.
Owned by Sheikh Mohammed Al-Maktoum
Trained by John H.M. Gosden at Stanley House Stables, Newmarket.

2512396

Racing Record

Year	Timeform Annual Rating	Starts	Wins	2nd	3rd	4th	Prize Money
1995	-	0	-	-	-	-	-
1996	124	10	4	2	3	1	£ 532,779
1997	125	4	2	-	1	-	£ 291,470

Principal Performances

1996   3rd Derby Stakes (G1) (3yo colts & fillies) Epsom (12f)
        3rd King Edward VII Stakes (G2) (3yo colts & geldings) Ascot (12f)
        Won St Leger Stakes (G1) (3yo colts & fillies) Doncaster (14.6f)
        Won Gran Premio del Jockey-Club (G1) San Siro (12f)
        4th Breeders' Cup Turf (G1) Woodbine, Canada (12f)
1997   Won Gran Premio di Milano (G1) San Siro (12f)
        Won Princess of Wales's Stakes (G2) Newmarket (12f)
        3rd Geoffrey Freer Stakes (G2) Newbury (13.3f)

*****

*S*hantou had a reputation for being difficult in training and went to Doncaster for the St Leger with his honesty questioned by Timeform, but returned home to Newmarket having won the race in courageous style. With his reputation restored, Shantou was subsequently victorious in Italy and ran very well at the Breeders' Cup. The colt was kept in training at four and won another Group 1 before retiring to stud in Italy. Shaima was a stakes winner in both England and the U.S. and was followed by Rosefinch (1989, by Blushing Groom – G1 Prix Saint-Alary) as the second foal of Oh So Sharp (p58) to excel on the racecourse. Shantou's great grandam, Oh So Fair (1967, by Graustark) is also the dam of Roussalka (1972, by Habitat – Coronation S, Nassau S) and Our Home (1977, by Habitat – 2nd 1000

Guineas). Moved to Burgage Stud in County Carlow, Shantou's best runners have been Sweet Stream (G1 Prix Vermeille, G2 Park Hill S), Papetti (7 races, 3rd G1 Derby Italiano), Basaltico (LR GP de Nantes), Toe The Line (LR Loughbrown S), Briar Hill (G1 Cheltenham Champion Bumper, G1 Navan Novice H), Toe The Line (LR Loughbrown S), Ballynagour (G3 Byrne Group Chase), De Valira (G2 hurdles winner), Polly Peachum (Listed hurdles winner) and Wounded Warrior (G2 chase winner).

1630096

Above: **SHANTOU** and Frankie Dettori provide trainer John Gosden with his first English classic victory. In a hard-fought St Leger they beat Dushyantor (right) and Samraan (star on cap).

1339092   3331592   3330096

Above right: **FRANKIE DETTORI** startles the sponsor's girls with his flying dismount from Shantou after the St Leger. This was the second successive victory in this classic for Dettori (above, centre) following Classic Cliché (p162). Above left: **SHEIKH MOHAMMED AL-MAKTOUM** owned his first winner in Britain in 1977 and became a leading figure in British horse-racing during the mid-1980's. He was the driving force in establishing Dubai as an international thoroughbred racing country. Since 1994 most of the Sheikh's horses have raced under the Godolphin banner, but previously he was a very successful owner in his own right winning ten English classic races between 1985 and 1996. Oh So Sharp and Musical Bliss (p94) won the 1000 Guineas; Pennekamp (p154) the 2000 Guineas; Oh So Sharp, Unite (p80), Diminuendo (p88) and Intrepidity (p138), the Oaks and Oh So Sharp and Moonax (p152), the St Leger. Shantou was the last English classic winner to date to race in Sheikh Mohammed's maroon and white colours. Other top-class horses to race for him include Singspiel (Coronation Cup, Japan Cup, Dubai World Cup), Swain (King George VI & Queen Elizabeth S twice, Coronation Cup), Old Vic (Prix du Jockey-Club, Irish Derby), Pebbles (p46), Indian Skimmer (Prix de Diane, Champion S, Prix d'Ispahan), Tel Quel (Champion S), Opera House (Eclipse S, King George VI & Queen Elizabeth S), Belmez and King's Theatre (King George VI & Queen Elizabeth S), In The Wings (Coronation Cup, Grand Prix de Saint-Cloud, Breeder's Cup Turf), Winged Love (Irish Derby) and Carnegie (Prix de l'Arc de Triomphe, Grand Prix de Saint-Cloud). Sheikh Mohammed is the current Prime Minister of the United Arab Emirates and ruler of Dubai.

ENTREPRENEUR (GB)

Bay colt, foaled 7 March 1994
By Sadler's Wells (USA) out of Exclusive Order (USA) by Exclusive Native (USA)
Bred by Cheveley Park Stud Limited
Owned by Michael Tabor and Mrs John Magnier
Trained by Michael R. Stoute at Freemason Lodge, Newmarket, Suffolk.

2514097

Racing Record

Year	Timeform Annual Rating	Starts	Wins	2nd	3rd	4th	Prize Money
1996	106	3	2	-	-	1	£ 9,106
1997	123	3	1	-	-	1	£ 180,719

Principal Performances

1997 Won 2000 Guineas Stakes (G1) (3yo colts & fillies) Newmarket (8f)
     4th Derby Stakes (G1) (3yo colts & fillies) Epsom (12f)

*****

*E*ntrepreneur was bought on behalf of a Coolmore partnership for 600,000 guineas at Tattersalls Houghton Sales, the joint highest priced yearling of 1995. Following rave reports about his work at Newmarket and a private gallop at Sandown on 26 April, which became even more private when his trainer moved the time forward to avoid the prying cameras of Channel 4 (much to their fury!), Entrepreneur became the 'talking horse' for the 2000 Guineas. With that classic safely tucked away the colt was hailed by sections of the media as the new wonder horse and considered unbeatable in the Derby. Returning injured from that defeat, Entrepreneur ran only once more before being retired to Coolmore Stud at Fethard in County Tipperary and also shuttled to The Oaks Stud at Cambridge in New Zealand during the southern hemisphere breeding season. His progeny were in the main disappointing and the stallion was moved in 2002 to Suwa Farm in Japan. Three years later Entrepreneur was sold on again, this time to obscurity at Russia's Voskhod Stud. The best of Entrepreneur's runners during his time at Coolmore were Vintage Tipple (G1 Irish Oaks) and Damson (G1 Phoenix Stakes). His daughter Marie Vision is the dam of The Grey Gatsby (2011, by Mastercraftsman - G1 Prix du Jockey-Club, G1 Irish Champion S).

1114097

Above & opposite: **ENTREPRENEUR** (Mick Kinane) wins the 2000 Guineas beating Revoque (left) by three-quarters of a length, with Poteen (no.8), Starborough (white cap) and Zamindar next to finish.

0617897

1913997

Above left: The 6/4 on favourite **ENTREPRENEUR** and Mick Kinane cantering to the start for the Derby. Only thirty horses in all the previous runnings of this classic had started at odds-on and Entrepreneur became the fourteenth odds-on loser. Above right: **MICHAEL TABOR** with the 2000 Guineas trophy; this was Tabor's first English classic winner.

1619082

Right: **EXCLUSIVE ORDER** was a talented racehorse in France winning the G1 Prix Maurice de Gheest, G3 Prix du Calvados and G3 Prix de la Porte Maillot. Purchased for $825,000 at Keeneland for Cheveley Park Stud at the end of her racing days, she proved an even better broodmare foaling several good winners including Mizaaya (1989, by Riverman), Sadler's Image (1991, by Sadler's Wells – LR Godolphin S, 3rd G3 Chester Vase), Dance A Dream (1992, by Sadler's Wells - LR Cheshire Oaks, 2nd G1 Oaks S), Exclusive (1995, by Polar Falcon – G1 Coronation S, 3rd G1 1000 Guineas S) as well as Entrepreneur. This is the family of the celebrated mare Selene (1919, by Chaucer), from which the 17th Earl of Derby bred Sickle (1924, by Phalaris – 2nd 2000 Guineas), Pharamond (1925, by Phalaris – Middle Park S), Hyperion (1930, by Gainsborough), winner of the Derby and St Leger, and All Moonshine (1941, by Bobsleigh), dam of champion sire Mossborough. This image of Exclusive Order and Maurice Philipperon was taken at Newmarket in 1982 when the filly ran one of her few disappointing races in the 1000 Guineas.

177

SLEEPYTIME (IRE)

Bay filly, foaled 20 February 1994
By Royal Academy (USA) out of Alidiva (GB) by Chief Singer (IRE)
Bred by Charles H. Wacker III
Owned by Greenbay Stables Limited
Trained by Henry R.A. Cecil at Warren Place, Newmarket, Suffolk.

3211997

Racing Record

Year	Timeform Annual Rating	Starts	Wins	2nd	3rd	4th	Prize Money
1996	108	2	1	-	1	-	£ 20,402
1997	121	3	1	-	1	1	£ 128,042
1998	-	1	-	-	-	-	-

Principal Performances

1996   3rd Fillies' Mile (G1) (2yo fillies) Ascot (8f)
1997   Won 1000 Guineas Stakes (G1) (3yo fillies) Newmarket (8f)
　　　　3rd Coronation Stakes (G1) (3yo fillies) Royal Ascot (8f)

*****

*S*leepytime *raced in the colours of her breeder's Greenbay Stables, as did her dam and half-brother Ali-Royal, also trained by Henry Cecil. Unlucky in running in both the Fillies' Mile and the Fred Darling Stakes, Sleepytime finally got the good pace she needed and the room to race on the day it mattered most and won the 1000 Guineas from a representative field of the best fillies around at the time. Given an uninspired ride in a slowly-run Coronation Stakes, where she could never reach the leaders, Sleepytime then bowed out for the rest of the season before returning in April 1998, finishing tailed-off and was retired to stud. Winners bred from Sleepytime include Gentleman's Deal (2001, by Danehill – 9 races, G3 Winter Derby & £143,109), Spanish Harlem (2004, by Danehill – 2nd G3 Gallinule S), Dame Ellen (2006, by Elusive Quality – LR Perfect Sting S), Lashyn (2009, by Mr Greeley), Oh Star (2011, by Tale of the Cat) and Hathal (2012, by Speightstown), a listed race winner in 2015.*

1714397

Above: **SLEEPYTIME** wins the 1000 Guineas running right away from Oh Nellie (left) and Dazzle (rail) eventually scoring by four lengths. This was a first English classic winner for **KIEREN FALLON** (below centre) and fifth victory in this race for Henry Cecil.

1414197

Right: **CHARLES WACKER III** with Sleepytime in the winner's circle after the 1000 Guineas.

Below left: **CHIEF SINGER** (1981, by Ballad Rock), pictured here with Ray Cochrane at Royal Ascot winning the St James's Palace Stakes, also won the July Cup and Sussex Stakes and was second in the 2000 Guineas behind El Gran Senor (p48).

Below right: **ALIDIVA** (Steve Cauthen) was a useful filly winning the Oak Tree Stakes at Goodwood in 1990. She was an even better broodmare, all her first three foals winning at the top level. Taipan (1992, by Last Tycoon – G1 Europa-Preis, Premio Roma, G2 Grand Prix de Deauville), Ali-Royal (1993, by Royal Academy – G1 Sussex S, G3 Earl of Sefton S) and Sleepytime. Alidiva's winning dam Alligatrix was third in the Fillies Mile. Alligatrix was also the dam of the top-class colt Croco Rouge (1985, by Rainbow Quest - G1 Prix Lupin, Prix d'Ispahan, 2nd G1 Prix du Jockey-Club, 3rd Prix de l'Arc de Triomphe. This is the family of Polonia (1984, by Danzig – G1 Prix de l'Abbaye), a half-sister to the top-class U.S. runners Canal (1961, by Round Table) and Cabildo (1963), the last two named being full brothers to Sleepytime's great-grandam, Shore (1964).

2518584

1824696

1134690

179

REAMS OF VERSE (USA)

Chestnut filly, foaled 23 April 1994
By Nureyev (USA) out of Modena (USA) by Roberto (USA)
Bred by Juddmonte Farms
Owned by Khalid Abdullah
Trained by Henry R.A. Cecil at Warren Place, Newmarket, Suffolk.

0606197

Racing Record

Year	Timeform Annual Rating	Starts	Wins	2nd	3rd	4th	Prize Money
1996	108	4	3	1	-	-	£ 113,481
1997	121	5	2	-	1	1	£ 221,955

Principal Performances

1996 Won May Hill Stakes (G3) (2yo fillies) Doncaster (8f)
      Won Fillies' Mile (G1) (2yo fillies) Ascot (8f)
1997 Won Musidora Stakes (G3) (3yo fillies) York (10.4f)
      Won Oaks Stakes (G1) (3yo fillies) Epsom (12f)
      4th Yorkshire Oaks (G1) (3yo fillies) York (11.9f)
      3rd Sun Chariot Stakes (G2) (Fillies & mares) Newmarket (10f)

*****

A fter an eleven lengths victory at York, Reams of Verse started as 6/5 on favourite to be the first odds-on winner of the Oaks since Noblesse in 1963. Her hard-fought victory at Epsom seemed to leave its mark on Reams of Verse and she didn't win again, being retired to her owner's stud in the U.S.A. Reams of Verse was a reasonably good broodmare for Juddmonte Farms producing several winners, the best of which were Many Volumes (2004, by Chester House – LR Gala S), Eagle Poise (2006, by Empire Maker - G3 Valedictory S) and World Domination (2008, by Empire Maker – winner and 4th G2 Dante S). Her daughter, the minor winner, Ithaca (2001, by Distant View) is the dam of Zacinto (2006, by Dansili, G2 Celebration Mile). Reams of Verse descended from a highly successful family for Mr Abdullah. Her unraced dam was an $85,000 purchase for Juddmonte at Keeneland carrying Elmaamul (1987, by Diesis - G1 Eclipse S), a colt which finished third in the Derby behind his owner's Quest For Fame (p106). Modernise (1989, by Known Fact), a U.S. stakes winner, Modesta

(2001, by Sadler's Wells – LR Lady Godiva S) and Manifest (2006, by Rainbow Quest – G2 Yorkshire Cup) were other good runners out of Modena. Midsummer (2000, by Kingmambo), another daughter of Modena, was the dam of Midday (2006, by Oasis Dream – G1 Nassau S x 3, G1 Yorkshire Oaks, G1 Prix Vermeille, 2ⁿᵈ G1 Oaks S) and Hot Snap (2010, by Pivotal – G3 Nell Gwyn S). Zaizafon (1982, by The Minstrel – G3 Seaton Delaval S), a half-sister to Modena, is dam of the brothers Zafonic (p134) and Zamindar (1994, by Gone West).

0606397

Above: **REAMS OF VERSE** and Kieren Fallon storm through to win the Oaks Stakes beating French challenger Gazelle Royale (no.7) and Crown Of Light (right). This was a first Oaks victory for both the jockey and owner and a fifth for Henry Cecil. Khalid Abdullah had previously owned three Oaks runners-up before this success.

1017697

1611680

Above left: **HENRY** and **NATALIE CECIL** with Khalid Abdullah (left) and Grant Pritchard-Gordon (2ⁿᵈ right) talking with Kieren Fallon in the winner's circle after the Oaks Stakes. This was the second consecutive year that Cecil had trained the winners of both fillies' classics. Above right: The brilliantly successful stallion **NUREYEV** and Philippe Paquet cantering to the start at Newmarket before the 1980 2000 Guineas. Nureyev sired 135 stakes winners including European classic winners Miesque (p72), Reams of Verse, Sonic Lady (Irish 1000 Guineas, Sussex S), Soviet Star (Poule d'Essai des Poulains, Sussex S, July Cup, Prix du Moulin), Mehthaaf (Irish 1000 Guineas), Peintre Celebre (Prix du Jockey-Club, Prix de l'Arc de Triomphe, GP de Paris) and Spinning World (Irish 2000 Guineas, Prix Jacques Le Marois twice, Prix du Moulin, Breeders' Cup Mile). Other G1 winners by Nureyev include Black Hawk and Heart Lake (both Yasuda Kinen), Skimming (Pacific Classic), Stravinsky (July Cup, Nunthorpe S) and Zilzal (Sussex S, Queen Elizabeth II S). Nureyev died on 29 October 2001 and is buried at Walmac Farm.

MARK OF ESTEEM (IRE) :
Bay 1993

Darshaan (GB) Br. 1981	Shirley Heights (GB) B. 1975	Mill Reef (USA)
		Hardiemma (GB)
	Delsy (FR) Br. 1972	Abdos (FR)
		Kelty (FR)
Homage (GB) B. 1989	Ajdal (USA) B. 1984	Northern Dancer (CAN)
		Native Partner (USA)
	Home Love (USA) B. 1976	Vaguely Noble (IRE)
		Homespun (USA)

BOSRA SHAM (USA) : Chesnut 1993

Woodman (USA) Ch. 1983	Mr Prospector (USA) B. 1970	Raise A Native (USA)
		Gold Digger (USA)
	Playmate (USA) Ch. 1975	Buckpasser (USA)
		Intriguing (USA)
Korveya (USA) Ch. 1982	Riverman (USA) B. 1969	Never Bend (USA)
		River Lady (USA)
	Konafa (CAN) B. 1973	Damascus (USA)
		Royal Statute (CAN)

LADY CARLA (GB) : Bay 1993

Caerleon (USA) B. 1980	Nijinsky (CAN) B. 1967	Northern Dancer (CAN)
		Flaming Page (CAN)
	Foreseer (USA) B/br. 1969	Round Table (USA)
		Regal Gleam (USA)
Shirley Superstar (GB) B. 1985	Shirley Heights (GB) B. 1975	Mill Reef (USA)
		Hardiemma (GB)
	Odeon (IRE) B. 1976	Royal And Regal (USA)
		Cammina (GB)

SHAAMIT (IRE) : Bay 1993

Mtoto (GB) B. 1983	Busted (GB) B. 1963	Crepello (GB)
		Sans Le Sou (IRE)
	Amazer (FR) B. 1967	Mincio (FR)
		Alzara (GB)
Shomoose (IRE) B. 1985	Habitat (USA) B. 1966	Sir Gaylord (USA)
		Little Hut (USA)
	Epithet (GB) B. 1979	Mill Reef (USA)
		Namecaller (USA)

SHANTOU (USA) : Bay 1993

		Hoist The Flag (USA) B. 1968	Tom Rolfe (GB)
Alleged (USA) B. 1974			Wavy Navy (USA)
		Princess Pout (USA) B. 1966	Prince John (USA)
			Determined Lady (USA)
Shaima (USA) B. 1988		Shareef Dancer (USA) B. 1980	Northern Dancer (CAN)
			Sweet Alliance (USA)
		Oh So Sharp (GB) Ch. 1982	Kris (GB)
			Oh So Fair (USA)

ENTREPRENEUR (GB) : Bay 1994

		Northern Dancer (CAN) B. 1961	Nearctic (CAN)
Sadler's Wells (USA) B. 1981			Natalma (USA)
		Fairy Bridge (USA) B. 1975	Bold Reason (USA)
			Special (USA)
Exclusive Order (USA) Ch. 1979		Exclusive Native (USA) Ch. 1965	Raise A Native (USA)
			Exclusive (USA)
		Bonavista (USA) B. 1964	Dead Ahead (USA)
			Ribotina (ITY)

SLEEPYTIME (IRE) : Bay 1994

		Nijinsky (CAN) B. 1967	Northern Dancer (CAN)
Royal Academy (USA) B. 1987			Flaming Page (CAN)
		Crimson Saint (USA) Ch. 1969	Crimson Satan (USA)
			Bolero Rose (USA)
Alidiva (IRE) B. 1987		Chief Singer (IRE) Bl. 1981	Ballad Rock (IRE)
			Principia (FR)
		Alligatrix (USA) Br. 1980	Alleged (USA)
			Shore (USA)

REAMS OF VERSE (USA) : Chesnut 1994

		Northern Dancer (CAN) B. 1961	Nearctic (CAN)
Nureyev (USA) B. 1977			Natalma (USA)
		Special (USA) B. 1969	Forli (ARG)
			Thong (USA)
Modena (USA) B. 1983		Roberto (USA) B. 1969	Hail To Reason (USA)
			Bramalea (USA)
		Mofida (GB) Ch. 1974	Right Tack (GB)
			Wold Lass (GB)

BENNY THE DIP (USA)

Bay or brown colt, foaled 25 March 1994
By Silver Hawk (USA) out of Rascal Rascal (USA) by Ack Ack (USA)
Owned & bred by Charles Landon Knight II
Trained by John H.M. Gosden at Stanley House, Newmarket, Suffolk.

1405197

Racing Record

Year	Timeform Annual Rating	Starts	Wins	2nd	3rd	4th	Prize Money
1996	112	5	3	1	1	-	£ 97,319
1997	127	6	2	2	1	-	£ 778,948

Principal Performances

1996 Won Royal Lodge Stakes (G2) (2yo colts & geldings) Ascot (8f)
       3rd Racing Post Trophy (G1) (2yo) Doncaster (8f)
1997 Won Dante Stakes (G2) (3yo) York (10.4f)
       Won Derby Stakes (G1) (3yo colts & fillies) Epsom (12f)
       2nd Eclipse Stakes (G1) (3yo & upwards) Sandown (10f)
       3rd International Stakes (G1) (3yo & upwards) York (10.4f)

*****

Considered by his trainer as unlikely to stay the Derby distance, Benny the Dip was given a superb ride by Willie Ryan, who kicked clear of his field early in the straight and the colt held on bravely by a short-head. Before the result of the extremely close photo-finish had even been announced a television interviewer greeted Ryan with the obviously carefully considered question 'How do you feel?' The jockey's laconic response of 'I don't know yet' was understandable. These intrusive and banal interviews should be stopped immediately; a jockey's first duty should be to make his report to his employers, the owner and trainer, and to weigh-in, before giving media interviews. Benny the Dip never won again after Epsom but ran well in defeat at both Sandown and York. The colt was retired to Claiborne Farm in Kentucky but produced nothing of much note and after covering at Cheveley Park Stud in Newmarket during 2002 was sold to Rathbarry Stud in County Cork. Benny the Dip fractured a knee in his exercise paddock only two weeks after arriving in Ireland and had to be put down. His best runners were Charley Bates (winner, 2ⁿᵈ G2 Goodwood Cup) and Senor Benny (10 victories including LR Abergwaun S three times). Rascal Rascal, a winner in the U.S., was bought by Charles Landon Knight at the Spendthrift Farm dispersal at Keeneland in November 1986. The mare also bred Beggarman Thief (1990, by Arctic Tern – G3 Horris Hill S) and Cryptic Rascal (1995, by Cryptoclearance), a multiple stakes winner in the U.S. Benny the Dip's grandam Savage Bunny was a three-parts sister to U.S. stakes winner Distinctive (1966, by Never Bend).

1417997

Above: Having been at least five lengths ahead two furlongs out, **BENNY THE DIP** and Willie Ryan just hold off the challenge of Silver Patriarch (p186) and Pat Eddery to win the 1997 Derby, the first to carry a total prize money of over a million pounds. Romanov (spotted cap) is third and odd-on Entrepreneur (p176) (rails) only fourth.

Below centre: **WILLIE RYAN** (below right) returns to the winner's circle on his only English classic winner. The jockey had first sat on the horse in a gallop only three days before and remarked to **JOHN GOSDEN** (below left) that Benny the Dip was 'the laziest and most moronic horse I've ever ridden'.

3317897   2817697   1247192

185

SILVER PATRIARCH (IRE)

Grey colt, foaled 8 May 1994
By Saddlers' Hall (IRE) out of Early Rising (USA) by Grey Dawn (USA)
Owned & bred by Peter S. Winfield
Trained by John L. Dunlop at Castle Stables, Arundel, Sussex.

0314399

Racing Record

Year	Timeform Annual Rating	Starts	Wins	2nd	3rd	4th	Prize Money
1996	98	4	2	-	-	1	£ 13,985
1997	125	6	2	2	1	-	£ 467,482
1998	125	7	2	3	-	1	£ 262,989
1999	125	7	2	1	1	2	£ 155,488

Principal Performances

1996   Won Zetland Stakes (Listed Race) (2yo) Newmarket (10f)
1997   Won Derby Trial Stakes (G3) (3yo) Lingfield (11.5f)
      2nd Derby Stakes (G1) (3yo colts & fillies) Epsom (12f)
      2nd Great Voltigeur Stakes (G2) (3yo) York (11.9f)
      Won St Leger Stakes (G1) (3yo colts & fillies) Doncaster (14.6f)
1998   Won Coronation Cup (G1) Epsom (12f)
      4th Grand Prix de Saint-Cloud (G1) Saint-Cloud (12f)
      2nd Irish St Leger Stakes (G1) Curragh (14f)
      Won Gran Premio del Jockey-Club (G1) San Siro (12f)
1999   Won Jockey Club Stakes (G2) Newmarket (12f)
      4th Coronation Cup (G1) Epsom (12f)
      4th King George VI and Queen Elizabeth Stakes (G1) Ascot (12f)
      Won Geoffrey Freer Stakes (G2) Newbury (13.3f)
      3rd Irish St Leger Stakes (G1) Curragh (14f)
      2nd Gran Premio del Jockey-Club (G1) San Siro (12f)

*S*ilver Patriarch was a genuine, consistent racehorse and unlucky not to win the Derby. Last entering the home straight, Pat Eddery found a dream run up the inside rail but was still four or five lengths behind Benny The Dip entering the last furlong. Silver Patriarch staged a dramatic late charge and had his nose in front just after the post, but not where it mattered most. Retired to the National Stud at Newmarket after four seasons of honest endeavour on the racecourse, the best runners sired by Silver Patriarch before his death in October 2009 were Party Boss (8 wins & £140,476 including two Listed Races), Silver By Nature (G3 Grand National Trial Handicap Chase & £174,459) and Carrickboy (G3 Byrne Group Plate). Peter Winfield had bought Early Rising for $160,000 at Keeneland in 1988 from her breeder, Paul Mellon. Her grandam, Key Bridge (1959, by Princequillo), was an outstanding broodmare for Mellon, producing Fort Marcy (1964, by Amerigo), three times U.S. champion grass horse, Key To The Mint (1969, by Graustark), a multiple G1 winner, Key To The Kingdom (1970, by Bold Ruler), the sire of Ma Biche (p36), and Key To Content (1977, by Forli – G1 United Nations H). For Winfield, Early Rising had bred My Patriarch (1990, by Be My Guest – G3 Henry II S). Silver Patriarch's sire Saddlers' Hall, won the Coronation Cup and was a half-brother to Sun Princess (p44).

1828297

1028397

Above left: **SILVER PATRIARCH** wins the St Leger beating Vertical Speed and giving jockey Pat Eddery his 4,000th winner in Britain. Above right: **PETER WINFIELD** with his homebred classic winner after the St Leger. Winfield died in 1999 and left a half-share in Silver Patriarch to the National Stud.

Below: Victory in the Coronation Cup for **SILVER PATRIARCH** and Pat Eddery; small compensation for a narrow defeat in the Derby.

1417498

KING OF KINGS (IRE)

Bay colt, foaled 27 February 1995
By Sadler's Wells (USA) out of Zummerudd (IRE) by Habitat (USA)
Bred by J.T. Jones and Ron Con Limited
Owned by Mrs John Magnier and Michael Tabor
Trained by Aidan P. O'Brien at Ballydoyle, Cashel, Co. Tipperary.

1020297

Racing Record

Year	Timeform Annual Rating	Starts	Wins	2nd	3rd	4th	Prize Money
1997	115	5	4	1	-	-	£ 152,470
1998	125	2	1	-	-	-	£ 171,800

Principal Performances

1997   Won Railway Stakes (G3) (2yo) Curragh (6f)
       Won Tyros Stakes (Listed Race) (2yo) Curragh (7f)
       Won National Stakes (G1) (2yo colts & fillies) Curragh (8f)
1998   Won 2000 Guineas Stakes (G1) (3yo colts & fillies) Newmarket (8f)

*****

*K*ing of Kings was bought on behalf of a Coolmore partnership for 250,000 guineas at Tattersalls Houghton Yearling Sales in Newmarket. The colt became the first English classic winner trained by Aidan O'Brien after succeeding Vincent O'Brien (no relation) at Ballydoyle. He was also the first of many horses to be described in glowing terms by his trainer. According to Aidan O'Brien, King of Kings was 'brilliant...he had all the ability...he was unbelievable'. After aggravating a knee injury during the Derby at Epsom, King of Kings was retired to Ashford Stud in Kentucky and to Coolmore Australia for the southern hemisphere breeding season. In Europe he sired only one good winner in Geminiani (G3 Prestige S, 2nd G3 Musidora S), but in Australia he got Group 1 winners Ike's Dream, King's Chapel and Reigning To Win. King of Kings was sold to Gestut Sohrenhof in Switzerland in November 2004. The stallion was subsequently moved on again to Somerset Stud in South Africa and in 2014 transferred to The Fort Stud, also in Natal, where he died in late-February 2015. King of Kings descends from a family noted for speed and precocity – few of the best of them stay beyond six furlongs. Zummerudd only ran twice and failed to win but was a full-sister to Ancestral (1980 – G3 Railway S) and Steel Habit (1979), the dam of Batshoof (1986, by Sadler's Wells – G2 Prince of Wales's S) and Sound Print*

(1988, by Be My Guest), a champion miler in Hong Kong. Before King of Kings she bred the minor stakes winner, Furajet (1988, by The Minstrel) and General Monash (1992, by Thorn Dance – G2 Prix Robert Papin) and subsequently the listed winner Amethyst (1997, by Sadler's Wells – 2ⁿᵈ G1 Irish 1000 Guineas). King of Kings' grandam Ampulla (G3 Cherry Hinton S) was a half-sister to Steel Heart (1972, by Habitat – G1 Middle Park S, G2 Gimcrack S) and Chili Girl (1971, by Skymaster), the dam of Chilibang (1984, by Formidable – G2 King's Stand S).

1913298

Above: **KING OF KINGS** and Mick Kinane winning the 2000 Guineas beating Lend A Hand (no.12). This was the second successive 2000 Guineas won by a son of the outstanding Coolmore Stud stallion Sadler's Wells, following Entrepreneur (p176).

3619201

3021396

3617299

Above left: **SUSAN MAGNIER** enjoyed the first of many English classic victories with King of Kings.

Above centre: **MICHAEL J. KINANE** rode his third 2000 Guineas winner on King of Kings following Tirol (p104) and Entrepreneur. The best was yet to come; Sea The Stars (p310).

Above right: **AIDAN O'BRIEN** was appointed as private trainer to Coolmore's Ballydoyle stables at the age of twenty-six in 1996 after making his name as an outstanding trainer of National Hunt horses. His first English classic success with King of Kings was soon followed by another with Shahtoush (p192), and from the turn of the century the trickle became a torrent as twenty more classic winners came across the Irish Sea from O'Brien's County Tipperary stables. Perennial champion trainer in Ireland, O'Brien has dominated the Irish classics with six victories in the 1000 Guineas, ten in the 2000 Guineas, four in the Oaks and eleven in the Derby, all since 1997. O'Brien's dominance of the Irish Derby in particular, with Ballydoyle-trained horses commonly filling most of the first four places, has often caused that classic to be distinctly uncompetitive.

CAPE VERDI (IRE)

Bay filly, foaled 3 February 1995
By Caerleon (USA) out of Afrique Bleu Azur (USA) by Sagace (FR)
Bred by Swettenham Stud
1997: Owned by Robert E. Sangster and trained by
Peter W. Chapple-Hyam at Manton, Marlborough, Wiltshire
1998-1999: Owned by Godolphin and trained by Saeed bin Suroor
at Moulton Paddocks, Newmarket, Suffolk.

1613598

Racing Record

Year	Timeform Annual Rating	Starts	Wins	2nd	3rd	4th	Prize Money
1997	110	4	2	1	-	1	£ 61,885
1998	126	2	1	-	-	-	£ 128,800
1999	116	2	-	-	1	-	£ 6,100

Principal Performances

1997   Won Lowther Stakes (G2) (2yo fillies) York (6f)
       4th Cheveley Park Stakes (G1) (2yo fillies) Newmarket (6f)
1998   Won 1000 Guineas Stakes (G1) (3yo fillies) Newmarket (8f)
1999   3rd Falmouth Stakes (G2) (Fillies & mares) Newmarket (8f)

*****

C ape Verdi was only the sixth filly to run in the Derby since 1918 and the first to start favourite
since the legendary Sceptre failed to win at odds of even money in 1902. Sceptre had won both the
1000 and 2000 Guineas and went on to victory in the Oaks and St Leger. Either racehorses were made
of sterner stuff in those days or their connections were considerably more enterprising; or perhaps
both! Cape Verdi fractured a hind pastern in training during July and on her return to the track in
1999 was unable to reproduce her best form. Afrique Bleu Azur was a minor winner in France, a sister
to Arcangues (1988 – G1 Prix d'Ispahan, Breeders Cup Classic) and half-sister to Agathe (1991, by
Manila – G3 Prix de Psyche), placed in two French fillies' classics and dam of Aquarelliste (1998, by
Danehill – G1 Prix de Diane, Prix Vermeille, Prix Ganay). This was a very successful family for

190

owner/breeder Daniel Wildenstein which also included Acoma (1973, by Rheffic – G3 Prix Minerve) and Ashmore (1971, by Luthier - G2 GP de Deauville). Cape Verdi has foaled several winners including Benandonner (2003, by Giants Causeway – 13 races, £148,883), Salsa Verdi (2004, by Giants Causeway), Paracel (2005, by Gone West), Nabucco (2009, by Dansili – LR James Seymour S, LR Godolphin S) and Thouwra (2010, by Pivotal).

2613598

Above: **CAPE VERDI** and Frankie Dettori win the 1000 Guineas Stakes by five lengths beating the subsequent Oaks winner Shahtoush (green cap) (see p192) and Exclusive (rail).

2513698

Left: **FRANKIE DETTORI** rewards Cape Verdi with a kiss in the winner's circle after the 1000 Guineas as Sheikh Mohammed Al-Maktoum and Saeed bin Suroor (left) look on.

Below: **SAGACE** and Yves Saint-Martin won the Prix de l'Arc de Triomphe in 1984. He was the sire of Arcangues (see opposite page) and Saganeca (G2 Prix de Royallieu), dam of Sagamix (1995, by Linamix – G1 Prix de l'Arc de Triomphe). Sagace died in 1989 after only three seasons at stud.

15T2883

2615885

Above left: **CAERLEON** won the Prix du Jockey-Club, ridden by Pat Eddery, in 1983. He was a very successful stallion siring five English classic winners; Generous (p116), Moonax (p152), Lady Carla (p170), Cape Verdi and Mutafaweq (p208). Marienbard (Prix de l'Arc de Triomphe), Grape Tree Road (Grand Prix de Paris), Kostroma (G1 Beverly D. S), Only Royale (G1 Yorkshire Oaks twice), Warrsan (G1 Coronation Cup) and Shake The Yoke (G1 Coronation S) were other top-class horses by Caerleon. The stallion died at Coolmore Stud on 2 February 1998.

SHAHTOUSH (IRE)

Bay filly, foaled 29 April 1995
By Alzao (USA) out of Formulate (GB) by Reform (IRE)
Bred by Barronstown Stud and Ron Con Limited
Owned by Mrs David Nagle and Mrs John Magnier
Trained by Aidan P. O'Brien at Ballydoyle, Cashel, Co. Tipperary.

0227998

Racing Record

Year	Timeform Annual Rating	Starts	Wins	2nd	3rd	4th	Prize Money
1997	-	5	1	1	1	1	£ 19,359
1998	120	6	2	1	-	-	£ 234,663

Principal Performances

1997 3rd Moyglare Stud Stakes (G1) (2yo fillies) Curragh (7f)
1998 2nd 1000 Guineas Stakes (G1) (3yo fillies) Newmarket (8f)
 Won Oaks Stakes (G1) (3yo fillies) Epsom (12f)

*****

S hahtoush was a relatively cheap yearling buy at IR60,000 guineas on behalf of a Coolmore partnership. After an undistinguished two-year-old season when her form did not merit inclusion in Timeform's 1997 Racehorses annual, the filly won a first Oaks for trainer Aidan O'Brien with his first ever runner at Epsom. Retired after two poor efforts at York and Leopardstown, Shahtoush produced nothing at stud remotely approaching her own ability, the best being the minor winner, Satine (2000, by Danehill). Of her other foals, Sea Of Moyle (2002, by Giant's Causeway) was useless, Custody (2006, by Fusaichi Pegasus) failed to win in nine attempts, finishing second on four occasions and the unraced Sweet Dreams Baby (2007, by Montjeu) is the dam of the useful winner Roxy Star (2012, by Fastnet Rock). Shahtoush comes from a very successful family developed at the Wernher's Someries Stud in Newmarket. Her grandam Tabulator was a sister to Double Zero (1964), a filly virtually useless on the racecourse and sold for 2,400 guineas at Tattersalls 1967 December Sales, but dam of Twice A Prince

192

(1970, by Prince John – 2nd Belmont S) and Play The Red (1973, by Crimson Satan – 2nd Preakness S). Further back, this line traces to Doubleton (1938, by Bahram), ancestress of Sagacity (1958, by Le Sage – Oxfordshire S, Yorkshire Cup, Goodwood Cup), Dual (1958, by Chanteur – Solario S), Duplation (1960, by Vimy – Lingfield Derby Trial S) and best of all, Meld (1952, by Alycidon), winner of the 1000 Guineas, Oaks and St Leger and dam of Charlottown (1963, by Charlottesville – Derby S, Coronation Cup).

2917498

Above: **SHAHTOUSH** and Mick Kinane winning the Oaks Stakes beating Bahr (Frankie Dettori). This was a fifth English classic for Kinane and his first victory in the Oaks.

3417498

2110479

Above left: **DAVID NAGLE** (centre) of Barronstown Stud and **JOHN MAGNIER** of Coolmore (right) receiving the Oaks trophy on behalf of their wives. Above right: **FORMULATE** was one of the best two-year-old fillies of 1978 winning three group races including the Fillies' Mile at Ascot. She is pictured here in training with Henry Cecil at Warren Place, with work rider Billy Aldridge in the saddle. At stud Formulate produced at least fourteen live foals, the best of which were Shahtoush and Game Plan (1987, by Darshaan), winner of the G2 Pretty Polly Stakes at the Curragh and runner-up in the Oaks behind Salsabil (p102).

HIGH-RISE (IRE)

Bay colt, foaled 3 May 1995
By High Estate (GB) out of High Tern (GB) by High Line (GB)
Bred by Sheikh Mohammed Obaid Al-Maktoum
1997-98: Owned by Sheikh Mohammed Obaid Al-Maktoum and trained by Luca M. Cumani at
Bedford House Stables, Newmarket, Suffolk
1999-2000: Owned by Godolphin and trained by Saeed bin Suroor
in Dubai and at Moulton Paddocks Stables, Newmarket, Suffolk.

0623898

Racing Record

Year	Timeform Annual Rating	Starts	Wins	2nd	3rd	4th	Prize Money
1997	84	1	1	-	-	-	£ 3,494
1998	130	5	3	1	-	-	£ 767,666
1999	122	4	-	1	1	-	£ 281,732
2000	120	3	1	-	1	-	£ 156,923

Principal Performances

1998   Won Derby Trial Stakes (G3) (3yo) Lingfield (11.5f)
      Won Derby Stakes (G1) (3yo colts & fillies) Epsom (12f)
      2nd King George VI and Queen Elizabeth Stakes (G1) Ascot (12f)
1999   3rd Japan Cup (G1) Tokyo, Japan (12f turf)
2000   Won Dubai City of Gold (Listed Race) Nad Al Sheba, Dubai (12f turf)

*****

*I*t cannot be denied that the promising racing career of High-Rise was done no favours by his transfer from Luca Cumani to join the Godolphin operation based in Dubai and Newmarket. His form deteriorated by ten pounds according to Timeform ratings and he won only once in two seasons for new trainer, Saeed bin Suroor. High-Rise was a decent Derby winner and looked unlucky when denied a clear run in the Prix de l'Arc de Triomphe, ultimately beaten only three lengths by the winner. High-Rise fractured a sesamoid in his last race at Belmont Park and was retired to Lex Company Stud

194

at Shizunai in Japan. The stallion was returned to Europe in 2004 to stand at Park House Stud in County Carlow as a National Hunt stallion. High-Rise has sired a few winners on the flat and over jumps but none worth mentioning by name. High Estate was a top two-year-old but never recovered his best form after splitting a pastern when winning the Group 2 Royal Lodge Stakes and was exported to Japan in 1996. High Tern was bought at Tattersalls 1996 December Sales for only 6,500 guineas and has bred numerous other winners for Sheikh Obaid, but none of stakes winning class. Her dam Sunbittern also bred High Hawk (1980, by Shirley Heights – G2 Ribblesdale S, Park Hill S), the dam of the top class colt In The Wings (1986, by Sadler's Wells - G1 Coronation Cup, Prix Ganay, Grand Prix de Saint-Cloud). This is also the family of Zomaradah (1995, by Deploy – G1 Oaks d'Italia).

1817898

Above: **HIGH-RISE** provides his owner with his first English classic success, beating City Honours (white cap), Border Arrow (left) and Sunshine Street (right) in the Derby Stakes.

Below left: **OLIVIER PESLIER** celebrates his first English classic winner by 'doing a Dettori' flying dismount from High-Rise. It must be said that Dettori usually achieves greater elevation, but a good effort nonetheless! Sheikh Mohammed (right) congratulates Sheikh Obaid lower right of picture. Below right: **SHEIKH OBAID AL-MAKTOUM** and **LUCA CUMANI** with their Derby trophies. For Cumani, it was a second victory in this classic following Kahyasi (see p86).

2217998

2317998

195

NEDAWI (GB)

Chesnut colt, foaled 9 April 1995
By Rainbow Quest (USA) out of Wajd (USA) by Northern Dancer (CAN)
Bred by Sheikh Mohammed bin Rashid Al-Maktoum
Owned by Godolphin
Trained by Saeed bin Suroor in Dubai and at Moulton Paddocks Stables, Newmarket, Suffolk.

0630698

Racing Record

Year	Timeform Annual Rating	Starts	Wins	2nd	3rd	4th	Prize Money
1997	-	0	-	-	-	-	-
1998	124	4	3	-	1	-	£ 223,605
1999	126	3	-	2	-	-	£ 202,951

Principal Performances

1998　Won (dead-heat) Gordon Stakes (G3) (3yo) Goodwood (12f)
　　　Won St Leger Stakes (G1) (3yo colts & fillies) Doncaster (14.6f)
1999　2nd King George VI and Queen Elizabeth Stakes (G1) Ascot (12f)

*****

A less memorable winner of the St Leger than Nedawi would be hard to find. He appeared gifted the race by injuries to Derby second and third City Honours and Border Arrow, and the late decision to re-route his highly regarded stable-mate Sea Wave to Longchamp for the Prix Niel (where he refused to race and unseated Frankie Dettori after leaving the stalls). Derby winner High-Rise also missed the St Leger to go for the Arc. Nedawi, having only his fourth race, beat a substandard field at Doncaster. Unlike many St Leger winners, he was given a chance over long distances as a four-year-old, but failed to stay the distance of the Gold Cup at Royal Ascot. Nedawi was sold as a stallion to Brazil where his most notable offspring has been Mr Nedawi, winner of Grade 1 races in Brazil, Argentina and Uruguay. Wajd was bought as a yearling for $1.3m at the Nelson Bunker Hunt Dispersal Sale and won the G2 Grand Prix d'Evry. Before Nedawi she had bred Wall Street (1993, by Mr Prospector – G3 Cumberland Lodge S), probably best remembered as the first leg of Dettori's unique seven-timer at Ascot on 28 September 1996. Nedawi's grandam Dahlia was one of the greatest

196

mares in living memory, winning eleven G1 races in France, England, Ireland, Canada and the U.S. and was dam of Dahar (1981, by Lyphard - G1 Prix Lupin), dollar millionaire Rivlia (1982, by Riverman) and U.S. Grade 1 winners Delegant (1984, by Grey Dawn) and Dahlia's Dreamer (1989, by Theatrical).

1330898

Above: **NEDAWI** wins the St Leger beating High And Low (centre) and Sunshine Street (red cap). Below left: **SHEIKH MOHAMMED** and **SAEED BIN SUROOR** (left) in the winner's circle with Nedawi after the St Leger. Below right: **JOHN REID** demonstrates a rather poor imitation of Frankie Dettori's 'flying dismount'; it was Reid's fourth and last English classic victory and his first in the St Leger.

3130698

3030898

Right: 1985 Prix de l'Arc de Triomphe and Coronation Cup winner **RAINBOW QUEST** and Pat Eddery at Longchamp. Rainbow Quest was a successful stallion siring over one hundred stakes winners and three English classic winners, Quest For Fame (see p106), Nedawi and Millenary (p220). His progeny also included the G1 winners, Saumarez (Prix de l'Arc de Triomphe), Raintrap (Prix Royal-Oak), Sunshack (Coronation Cup), Fiji (Gamely S), Spectrum (Irish 2000 Guineas, Champion S), Croco Rouge (Prix Lupin), Colour Vision (Ascot Gold Cup), High And Low (Yorkshire Oaks), Urgent Request (Santa Anita H) and Edabiya (Moyglare Stud S). Rainbow Quest was put down following surgery for a severe bout of colic on 7 July 2007. He had been at Juddmonte's Banstead Manor Stud at Cheveley near Newmarket, throughout his stud career.

T122085

ISLAND SANDS (IRE)

Bay or brown colt, foaled 27 January 1996
By Turtle Island (IRE) out of Tiavanita (USA) by J O Tobin (USA)
Bred by Mrs. T.V. Ryan
1998: Owned by Mrs Michael Meredith and
trained by David R.C. Elsworth at Whitsbury, Hampshire
1999-2000: Owned by Godolphin and trained by Saeed bin Suroor
at Moulton Paddocks, Newmarket, Suffolk
2001: Owned by Maktoum Al-Maktoum and trained by David R. Loder
at Sefton Lodge Stables, Newmarket, Suffolk.

2217299

Racing Record

Year	Timeform Annual Rating	Starts	Wins	2nd	3rd	4th	Prize Money
1998	106	2	2	-	-	-	£ 8,410
1999	122	2	1	-	-	-	£ 175,300
2000	109	1	-	1	-	-	£ 7,685
2001	115	4	1	1	1	-	£ 21,532

Principal Performances

1999   Won 2000 Guineas Stakes (G1) (3yo colts & fillies) Newmarket (8f)
2000   2nd Prix Quincey (G3) Deauville (8f)
2001   2nd Prix Edmond Blanc (G3) Saint-Cloud (8f)
         3rd Sandown Mile (G2) Sandown Park (8f)

*****

*A*t the end of his classic season Island Sands was the second lowest rated winner of the 2000 Guineas in the history of Timeform's Racehorses annuals, above only Rockavon (p386-7) at 120. Island Sands' subsequent racing career was blighted by injury and his reputation tarnished by five defeats and only one victory in a Haydock minor event after his classic triumph. His dam Tiavanita was a useless racehorse, finishing unplaced in all her twelve starts, but she was a half-sister to Corrupt

198

(1988, by Lear Fan – G2 Great Voltigeur S, G3 Lingfield Derby Trial S). Her unraced dam Nirvanita was a half-sister to Nadjar (1976, by Zeddaan – G1 Prix d'Ispahan, Prix Jacques Le Marois). This is a family that had previously done well in Germany; third dam Nuclea (1961, by Orsini), was a top two-year-old there and a half-sister to Neckar (1948, by Ticino – Deutsches Derby), six times leading sire in Germany, and Naxos (1950, by Ticino - Preis der Diana). However, his immediate pedigree was unfashionable and with his record of unsoundness no stud in Europe, America or Australasia wanted Island Sands and he was exported to China as a stallion.

2514699

Above: Run on the Newmarket July course for the first time since the 1945 race won by Court Martial because of development work on the Rowley Mile, **ISLAND SANDS** (Frankie Dettori) wins the 2000 Guineas beating Enrique (white cap) and Mujahid (striped cap). This was a second victory in this classic for Dettori, Saeed bin Suroor and Godolphin following Mark of Esteem (p166).

3538294

3333592

3713793

Above right: **TURTLE ISLAND** (G1 Irish 2000 Guineas, Phoenix S, G2 Gimcrack S, G3 Norfolk & Greenham S), pictured winning at Newbury ridden by John Reid, was a disappointing stallion at Coolmore Stud and was exported to Italy. **DAVID LODER** (left) was the last trainer to handle Island Sands and **DAVID ELSWORTH** (centre), the first. Godolphin purchased the then unbeaten colt out of Elworth's yard at the end of the 1998 season.

199

BENNY THE DIP (USA) : Black 1994

Silver Hawk (USA) B. 1979	Roberto (USA) B. 1969	Hail To Reason (USA)
		Bramalea (USA)
	Gris Vitesse (USA) Gr. 1966	Amerigo (GB)
		Matchiche (FR)
Rascal Rascal (USA) B/br. 1981	Ack Ack (USA) B. 1966	Battle Joined (USA)
		Fast Turn (USA)
	Savage Bunny (USA) B/br. 1974	Never Bend (USA)
		Tudor Jet (USA)

SILVER PATRIARCH (IRE) : Grey 1994

Saddlers' Hall (IRE) B. 1988	Sadler's Wells (USA) B. 1981	Northern Dancer (CAN)
		Fairy Bridge (USA)
	Sunny Valley (IRE) B. 1972	Val De Loir (FR)
		Sunland (GB)
Early Rising (USA) Gr. 1980	Grey Dawn (FR) Gr. 1962	Herbager (FR)
		Polamia (USA)
	Gliding By (USA) B. 1975	Tom Rolfe (USA)
		Key Bridge (USA)

KING OF KINGS (IRE) : Bay 1995

Sadler's Wells (USA) B. 1981	Northern Dancer (CAN) B. 1961	Nearctic (CAN)
		Natalma (USA)
	Fairy Bridge (USA) B. 1975	Bold Reason (USA)
		Special (USA)
Zummerud (IRE) B. 1981	Habitat (USA) B. 1966	Sir Gaylord (USA)
		Little Hut (USA)
	Ampulla (IRE) B. 1974	Crowned Prince (USA)
		A.1. (GB)

CAPE VERDI (IRE) : Bay 1995

Caerleon (USA) B. 1980	Nijinsky (CAN) B. 1967	Northern Dancer (CAN)
		Flaming Page (CAN)
	Foreseer (USA) B/br. 1969	Round Table (USA)
		Regal Gleam (USA)
Afrique Bleu Azur (USA) B/br. 1987	Sagace (FR) B. 1980	Luthier (FR)
		Seneca (FR)
	Albertine (FR) B. 1981	Irish River (FR)
		Almyre (FR)

SHAHTOUSH (IRE) : Bay 1995

Alzao (USA) B. 1980	Lyphard (USA) B. 1969	Northern Dancer (CAN)
		Goofed (USA)
	Lady Rebecca (GB) B. 1971	Sir Ivor (USA)
		Pocahontas (USA)
Formulate (GB) Ch. 1976	Reform (GB) B. 1964	Pall Mall (IRE)
		Country House (GB)
	Tabulator (GB) Ch. 1963	Never Say Die (USA)
		Two Fold (GB)

HIGH-RISE (IRE) : Bay 1995

High Estate (IRE) B. 1986	Shirley Heights (GB) B. 1975	Mill Reef (USA)
		Hardiemma (GB)
	Regal Beauty (USA) B/br. 1981	Princely Native (USA)
		Dennis Belle (USA)
High Tern (IRE) Gr. 1982	High Line (GB) Ch. 1966	High Hat (GB)
		Time Call (GB)
	Sunbittern (GB) Gr. 1970	Sea Hawk (FR)
		Pantoufle (GB)

NEDAWI (GB) : Chesnut 1995

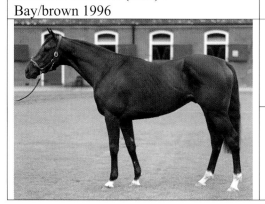

Rainbow Quest (USA) B. 1981	Blushing Groom (FR) Ch. 1974	Red God (USA)
		Runaway Bride (GB)
	I Will Follow (USA) B. 1975	Herbager (FR)
		Where You Lead (USA)
Wajd (USA) Ch. 1987	Northern Dancer (CAN) B. 1961	Nearctic (CAN)
		Natalma (USA)
	Dahlia (USA) Ch. 1970	Vaguely Noble (IRE)
		Charming Alibi (USA)

ISLAND SANDS (IRE) : Bay/brown 1996

Turtle Island (IRE) B. 1991	Fairy King (USA) B. 1982	Northern Dancer (CAN)
		Fairy Bridge (USA)
	Sisania (GB) B. 1983	High Top (GB)
		Targo's Delight (GB)
Tiavanita (USA) B/br. 1986	J O Tobin (USA) B/br. 1974	Never Bend (USA)
		Hill Shade (USA)
	Nirvanita (FR) B. 1971	Right Royal (FR)
		Nuclea (GER)

WINCE (GB)

Bay filly, foaled 26 April 1996
By Selkirk (USA) out of Flit (USA) by Lyphard (USA)
Bred by Juddmonte Farms
Owned by Khalid Abdullah
Trained by Henry R.A. Cecil at Warren Place, Newmarket, Suffolk.

1017499

Racing Record

Year	Timeform Annual Rating	Starts	Wins	2nd	3rd	4th	Prize Money
1998	94	6	2	1	1	-	£ 14,179
1999	117	3	2	-	-	-	£ 153,300

Principal Performances

1999   Won Fred Darling Stakes (G3) (3yo fillies) Newbury (7f)
        Won 1000 Guineas Stakes (G1) (3yo fillies) Newmarket (8f)

*****

*W*ince hardly performed like a potential classic winner as a two-year-old and won only two small races in six outings. With the Rowley Mile course under renovation, both Guineas classics were run on the Newmarket July Course for the first time since 1945. The tall, attractive Wince had made dramatic improvement over the winter and was made favourite on the day having been available at 33/1 less than one month earlier. Following her narrow victory at Newmarket, Wince was hot favourite to follow up in the Irish 1000 Guineas but finished unplaced. The filly never ran again, problems with a hind joint forcing her retirement in mid-August. Wince has bred several winners for her owner's Juddmonte Farms; the best by far being Quiff (2001, by Sadler's Wells - G1 Yorkshire Oaks, 2nd G1 St Leger). Flit, a minor winner, was a full-sister to Skimble (1989), a multiple stakes winner in the U.S., and half-sister to Contredance (1982, by Danzig – G1 Lassie S). Nimble Feet (1985), a sister to Contredance, was the dam of Eltish (1992, by Cox's Ridge – G2 Royal Lodge S, 3rd G1 Dewhurst S) and Forest Gazelle (1991, by Green Forest – G3 Los Angeles H).*

0815199

Above: **WINCE** (Kieren Fallon) wins the 1000 Guineas beating Wannabe Grand (left) and Valentine Waltz (green cap) by half-a-length and a short-head.

Below left: **KIEREN FALLON** and Wince in the winner's circle. This was Fallon's second 1000 Guineas success following Sleepytime (see p178) and third English classic. For owner **KHALID ABDULLAH** (below centre) it was a first victory in this classic, his eighth overall and completed the notable feat of having won all five English classics.

2414999   2109194   3212599

Above right: **SIR HENRY RICHARD AMHURST CECIL** was born on 11 January 1943 near Aberdeen. His father had been killed in action with the Parachute Regiment in North Africa only two weeks earlier. Henry's mother, Rohays, later married Captain Sir Cecil Boyd-Rochfort, five times champion trainer in Britain. After school, Henry and his twin brother, David, worked at various studs and stables around the world until Henry returned to Newmarket in 1964 to assist Boyd-Rochfort. He started to train on his own account from Marriott Stables on Racecourse Side, Newmarket in 1969. 1975 brought his first English classic winner, Bolkonski in the 2000 Guineas. Wollow followed up in the same race in 1976 and Cecil was champion trainer for the first time. When his father-in-law Sir Noel Murless retired in 1976, Henry and his first wife Julie moved into Warren Place on the Bury St Edmunds side of Newmarket. He was champion on nine more occasions and trained twenty-five English classic winners; One In A Million (1979), Fairy Footsteps (p14), Oh So Sharp (p58), Bosra Sham (p168), Sleepytime and Wince in the 1000 Guineas. Slip Anchor (p62), Reference Point (p78), Commander in Chief (p136) and Oath (p206) won the Derby and Light Cavalry (p12), Oh So Sharp, Reference Point and Michelozzo (p100), the St Leger. Cecil's eight Oaks winners testify to his skill with fillies, Oh So Sharp, Diminuendo (p88), Snow Bride (p98), Lady Carla (p170), Reams of Verse (p180), Ramruma (p204), Love Divine (p214) and Light Shift (p292) all won the Epsom classic. To the afore-mentioned Bolkonski and Wollow was added another 2000 Guineas winner and the best horse that Cecil ever trained, the brilliant Frankel (p330). Henry Cecil was knighted for services to horse-racing in the Queen's Birthday Honours 2011 and died on 11 June 2013 after a long illness.

RAMRUMA (USA)

Chesnut filly, foaled 17 February 1996
By Diesis (GB) out of Princess Of Man (IRE) by Green God (IRE)
Bred by Newgate Stud Company
Owned by H.R.H. Prince Fahd Salman
Trained by Henry R.A. Cecil at Warren Place, Newmarket, Suffolk.

2525399

Racing Record

Year	Timeform Annual Rating	Starts	Wins	2nd	3rd	4th	Prize Money
1998	78	2	-	1	1	-	£ 1,478
1999	123	6	5	1	-	-	£ 496,910
2000	116	3	-	-	2	-	£ 27,800

Principal Performances

1999   Won Oaks Trial Stakes (Listed Race) (3yo fillies) Lingfield (11.5f)
       Won Oaks Stakes (G1) (3yo fillies) Epsom (12f)
       Won Irish Oaks Stakes (G1) (3yo fillies) Curragh (12f)
       Won Yorkshire Oaks (G1) (Fillies & mares) York (11.9f)
       2nd St Leger Stakes (G1) (3yo colts & fillies) Doncaster (14.6f)
2000   3rd Yorkshire Oaks (G1) (Fillies & mares) York (11.9f)

*****

*A*fter an undistinguished two-year-old season, Ramruma improved markedly racing over twelve
furlongs in 1999, winning three G1 Oaks races in succession. The filly was retired after
disappointing at Ascot in October 2000. Ramruma's dam won the Musidora Stakes and bred numerous
winners, the best of them was Ausherra (1988, by Diesis - LR Lingfield Oaks Trial S), but this was a
formerly moderate family raised to new heights by the exploits of Ramruma. The triple Oaks winner
was sent to the 2003 Tattersalls December Sales as part of the dispersal of Fahd Salman's bloodstock
after his death in 2001 and purchased by John Magnier of Coolmore Stud for 2.1m guineas.
Ramruma's best foal has been Flying Cross (2007, by Sadler's Wells – winner & 3rd G1 Irish St Leger).

1819399

Above: **RAMRUMA** (Kieren Fallon) wins the Oaks beating Noushkey and Zahrat Dubai. This was a sixth Oaks victory for Henry Cecil and a second and last English classic winner for owner Fahd Salman, following Generous (p116). Below left: The owner's brother Ahmed Salman leading in Ramruma. It was Fallon's second Oaks success after Reams of Verse (see p180) and his fourth in an English classic.

Below right: **RAMRUMA** and Fallon win their second European classic, the Irish Oaks at the Curragh.

3019499

2125499

2125205

2430399

Above right: After a falling out with Henry Cecil, **KIEREN FALLON** (above left) was replaced by Pat Eddery when **RAMRUMA** completed her Oaks treble at York beating Ela Athena and Silver Rhapsody.

OATH (IRE)

Bay colt, foaled 22 April 1996
By Fairy King (USA) out of Sheer Audacity (IRE) by Troy (IRE)
Bred by Mrs Max Morris
Owned by The Thoroughbred Corporation
1998: Trained by Roger Charlton at Beckhampton, Marlborough, Wilts.
September 1998-1999: Trained by Henry R.A. Cecil at Warren Place, Newmarket.

1726699

Racing Record

Year	Timeform Annual Rating	Starts	Wins	2nd	3rd	4th	Prize Money
1998	89	3	1	-	1	-	£ 4,314
1999	125	4	2	1	-	-	£ 641,345

Principal Performances

1999 Won Dee Stakes (Listed Race) (3yo colts & geldings) Chester (10.3f)
      Won Derby Stakes (G1) (3yo colts & fillies) Epsom (12f)

*****

*O*ath was bought for IR450,000 at Goffs yearling sales in County Kildare on behalf of The
Thoroughbred Corporation, a syndicate headed by Saudi prince, Ahmed bin Salman. Originally
put into training with Roger Charlton, the colt was moved to Henry Cecil after his first race. Oath's
three outings during 1998 suggested the colt was well below classic winning standard, but he showed
dramatic improvement as a three-year-old, winning the Derby decisively. After disappointing at Ascot,
Oath was found to have broken a bone in his knee and in October the news came that the colt had been
sold to stand at Yushun Farm in Hokkaido, Japan for a reported $8m. That Oath was not a success at
stud in Japan can be seen from his sale back to Ireland during 2006, the intention being that he would
stand at Coolagown Stud in County Cork. The welcome home reception from Irish breeders must have
been decidedly lukewarm because Oath was eventually put up for auction at Goresbridge Sales in
County Kilkenny. There he was bought for €205,000 by an agent acting on behalf of the Maharajah of
Idar to stand in India at the Pratap Stud in Gujarat. Sheer Audacity never won but had previously bred
Pelder (1990, by Be My Guest – G1 Premio Parioli, Prix Ganay) and Napoleon's Sister (1995, by Alzao -

206

LR Lupe S). She was a three parts sister to Miss Petard (1990, by Petingo – G2 Ribblesdale S), the dam of Rejuvenate (1983, by Ile De Bourbon – G2 Park Hill S, G3 Musidora S). This is also the family of 2000 Guineas winner, Mister Baileys (p144).

2719799

Above: **OATH** gives Kieren Fallon his first Derby victory, beating Daliapour (Gerald Mosse). For Henry Cecil, it was his fourth and last Derby success. Below left: **PRINCE AHMED SALMAN** leads Oath and Kieren Fallon into the winner's circle at Epsom.

3219799

0810678

Above right: Epsom Derby winner **TROY** also won the Irish Derby, King George VI and Queen Elizabeth Stakes and the Benson & Hedges Gold Cup. Troy sired only four crops of foals before dying of acute peritonitis during May 1983 at Highclere Stud near Newbury in Berkshire, where he had been syndicated to stand for £7.2m. The best winners sired by Troy were the European classic winners, Helen Street (Irish Oaks) and Walensee (Prix Vermeille). He was also a successful sire of brood-mares. Helen Street was dam of Street Cry (1998, by Machiavellian - G1 Dubai World Cup) and through her listed placed daughter Helsinki (1993, by Machiavellian), grandam of Shamardal (2002, by Giant's Causeway – G1 Dewhurst S, Poule d'Essai des Poulains, Prix du Jockey Club). Walensee produced Westerner (1999, by Danehill - G1 Ascot Gold Cup). Troy's daughter, Cocotte, is the dam of Pilsudski (1992, by Polish Precedent - G1 Eclipse & Champion S).

MUTAFAWEQ (USA)

Bay colt, foaled 21 February 1996
By Silver Hawk (USA) out of The Caretaker (IRE) by Caerleon (USA)
Bred by Muirfield Ventures and Jayeff B Stables
Owned by Godolphin
Trained by Saeed bin Suroor in Dubai and at Moulton Paddocks Stables, Newmarket, Suffolk.

2522299

Racing Record

Year	Timeform Annual Rating	Starts	Wins	2nd	3rd	4th	Prize Money
1998	99	2	1	1	-	-	£ 8,736
1999	129	5	3	-	-	1	£ 308,253
2000	123	6	2	-	2	-	£ 701,256
2001	120	6	1	-	1	-	£ 165,525

Principal Performances

1999   Won King Edward VII Stakes (G2) (3yo colts & geldings) Ascot (12f)
      4th Great Voltigeur Stakes (G2) (3yo colts & geldings) York (11.9f)
      Won St Leger Stakes (G1) (3yo colts & fillies) Doncaster (14.6f)
2000   3rd Tattersalls Gold Cup (G1) Curragh (10.5f)
      Won Deutschland Preis (G1) Dusseldorf (12f)
      3rd Irish St Leger Stakes (G1) Curragh (14f)
      Won Canadian International Stakes (G1) Woodbine, Canada (12f turf)
2001   Won Coronation Cup (G1) Epsom (12f)
      3rd Hardwicke Stakes (G2) Royal Ascot (12f)

*****

*M*utafaweq was hardly a model of consistency but he won four Group 1 races and on his day was very courageous and hard to beat. He retired in 2002 to stand at the Breeders Stallion Station in Japan and moved to Big Red Farm in 2003. For 2007, Mutafaweq was transferred to Takahashi Meiji Farm in Hokkaido where he still stands. His best winner is Meiner Falke, placed at G1 level in Japan and Cosmo Lavandin was a top Japanese jump performer. Mutafaweq was purchased at Keeneland as a yearling for $310,000 and is the first foal of his dam, a dual Listed Race winner of over

$855,000 in the U.S. and Ireland and fourth in the Irish 1000 Guineas. This is a fairly ordinary American family, seemingly upgraded by the use of top stallions Caerleon and Silver Hawk.

0634399

Above: With Frankie Dettori in Ireland to ride Daylami in the Irish Champion Stakes, Richard Hills takes the St Leger ride on **MUTAFAWEQ** and beats Ramruma (see p204) in a gruelling battle. Below left: **RICHARD HILLS** with his jockey cap trophy. This was his only St Leger winner, but he also won the 1000 Guineas three times on Harayir (p156), Lahan (p212) and Ghanaati (p312), the 2000 Guineas on Haafhd (p252) and the Oaks on Eswarah (p268). Richard Hills retired on 31 March 2012.

1834399

1016501

Above right: **MUTAFAWEQ**'s final victory; he and Frankie Dettori get the better of a duel with Wellbeing over the last two furlongs at Epsom for the Coronation Cup.

Right: **SILVER HAWK**, seen here with the late Tony Murray at Newmarket in April 1982, won the Solario and Craven Stakes, was third in the Derby and second in the Irish Derby. He was the sire of many top-class runners including Mubtaker (G2 Geoffrey Freer S & £704,819), Benny The Dip (p184), Hawkster (3xG1 & $1,409,477), Silver Wisp (G2 Jockey Club S, 3rd G1 Derby S), Memories of Silver (G1 Beverly D. S & $1,448,715), Albarahin (G2 Prix Dollar), Magnificent Star (G1 Yorkshire Oaks) and Red Bishop (10 races & $958,907).

2219682

KING'S BEST (USA)

Bay colt, foaled 24 January 1997
By Kingmambo (USA) out of Allegretta (GB) by Lombard (GER)
Bred by M3 Elevage
Owned by Saeed Suhail
Trained by Sir Michael Stoute at Freemason Lodge, Newmarket, Suffolk.

0512500

Racing Record

Year	Timeform Annual Rating	Starts	Wins	2nd	3rd	4th	Prize Money
1999	112	3	2	-	-	-	£ 28,648
2000	132	3	1	1	-	-	£ 181,700

Principal Performances

1999   Won Acomb Stakes (Listed Race) (2yo) York (7f)
2000   2nd Craven Stakes (G3) (3yo colts & geldings) Newmarket (8f)
        Won 2000 Guineas Stakes (G1) (3yo colts & fillies) Newmarket (8f)

*****

*K*ing's Best was purchased at Deauville for FF2.3m as a yearling. The American jockey Gary *Stevens* had allowed the colt to stride along in front for his first two victories and when Kieren Fallon attempted to restrain King's Best in the Dewhurst Stakes, he refused to settle and finished last. After another defeat on his seasonal debut in 2000, painstaking efforts were made to channel King's Best's nervous energy in the right direction. Before the 2000 Guineas Fallon rode him in all his work and visits to the parade ring at Newmarket were arranged to familiarise the colt with his big-race surroundings. On the day, a strong pace and a big field enabled Fallon to drop King's Best to the back and get him covered-up. Despite experiencing some trouble obtaining a clear run, King's Best sprinted clear of the excellent Giant's Causeway (who was to win five Group 1 races during the season) and won by three and a half lengths. A muscle problem caused King's Best to miss the Epsom Derby and during the Irish Derby he was pulled-up after racing five furlongs when fracturing the cannon bone of his off-foreleg. A successful operation saved King's Best for stud and he was retired to Kildangan Stud at Monasterevin in County Kildare. As a sire, King's Best has been successful despite never staying in one *place for very long. He shuttled for three southern hemisphere breeding seasons to Australia and later to Argentina. In 2009 he was moved to France and then to Darley Japan in 2013. His best winners have been Workforce (p324), Proclamation (G1 Sussex S), Creachadoir (G1 Lockinge S), Eishin Flash (G1 Tokyo Yushun-Japanese Derby), Sajjhaa (G1 Dubai Duty Free & G1 Jebel Hatta), King's Apostle (G1 Prix Maurice de Gheest), Royal Diamond (G1 Irish St Leger) and Dubai Surprise (G1 Premio Lydia Tesio). Other group winners have included Allybar (G3 in Dubai), Best Name (G3 Prix du Prince D'Orange), Best Alibi (G2 York S), Kesampour (G2 Prix Greffulhe), Not Just Swing (G3 Prix d'Hedouville), Notability (G2 Oettingen-Rennen), Simon De Montfort (G3 Prix La Force), Meleagros (G3 Prix d'Hedouville) and Calming Influence (G2 Godolphin Mile).*

1813700

Above: **KING'S BEST** wins the 2000 Guineas beating Giant's Causeway and Barathea Guest (left). Below: **SIR MICHAEL STOUTE, SAEED SUHAIL** and **KIEREN FALLON** with their winner. This was a fourth victory in this classic for Stoute and first for Fallon. Saeed Suhail went on to win the Derby with Kris Kin (p248).

2313800

(Left) **ALLEGRETTA** was useful at her best but failed to train on and was tailed-off in her last two races in England. Sold for only 24,000 guineas at Tattersalls 1981 December Sales, she has been a phenomenally successful broodmare, establishing a classic dynasty principally through her daughter Urban Sea (1989, by Miswaki), winner of the Prix de l'Arc de Triomphe and dam of the Derby winners, Galileo (p228) and Sea The Stars (p310). Another daughter, Allez Les Trois (1991, by Riverman - G3 Prix de Flore) bred Prix du Jockey-Club winner Anabaa Blue (1998, by Anabaa) and is grandam of Tamayuz (2005, by Nayef – G1 Prix Jean Prat, Prix Jacques Le Marois).

0510381

211

LAHAN (GB)

Bay filly, foaled 22 January 1997
By Unfuwain (USA) out of Amanah (USA) by Mr Prospector (USA)
Bred by Shadwell Estate Company Limited
Owned by Sheikh Hamdan Al-Maktoum
1999: Trained by John H.M. Gosden at Stanley House, Newmarket, Suffolk and during 2000 at
Manton, Marlborough, Wiltshire.

1414100

Racing Record

Year	Timeform Annual Rating	Starts	Wins	2nd	3rd	4th	Prize Money
1999	104	2	2	-	-	-	£ 26,143
2000	117	2	1	-	-	1	£ 146,925

Principal Performances

1999   Won Rockfel Stakes (G2) (2yo fillies) Newmarket (7f)
2000   Won 1000 Guineas Stakes (G1) (3yo fillies) Newmarket (8f)

*****

T *he very wet spring of 2000 hampered John Gosden's efforts to prepare Lahan for the 1000
Guineas. Snow and twelve inches of rain during March led to the cancellation of four days work
on the Manton gallops. In an effort to keep the filly warm, Lahan was moved to the box nearest the
boiler room. Still not forward enough to do herself justice on her seasonal debut at Newbury, Lahan
stripped much fitter at Newmarket and won in good style, bursting through to lead over a furlong out
and staying on strongly. Unfortunately Lahan was cast in her box, injured herself, and was retired
without racing again. Lahan was the first foal of her dam, a daughter of Cheval Volant (1987, by Kris S
– G1 Hollywood Starlet S), who has since bred another winner in Wajaha (2006, by Haafhd). Cheval
Volant was bought by Sheikh Hamdan, carrying Amanah, at Keeneland for $1.4m but had been sold to
Japan for only $110,000 before Lahan was foaled. This family traces back to Flaring Top (1947, by
Menow), the grandam of Nijinsky (p61). Lahan has to date proved a disappointment as a broodmare
foaling only minor winners Almanshood (2002, by Bahri), Ejeed (2005, by Rahy) and Agiaal (2008, by
Sakhee).*

212

1814300

Above: **LAHAN** (Richard Hills) wins the 1000 Guineas beating 66/1 outsider Princess Ellen (left).

Below left: **RICHARD HILLS** in the winner's circle with his second winner of the 1000 Guineas after Harayir (see p156). For owner **SHEIKH HAMDAN** (right), Lahan was his fourth winner of this classic since 1990 following Salsabil (p102), Shadayid (p112) and Harayir. Below right: **JOHN GOSDEN** was winning his third English classic having previously won the St Leger with Shantou (p174) and the Derby with Benny the Dip (p184).

1114400

0317995

Right: **UNFUWAIN**, a half-brother to Nashwan (p96) and Nayef (1998, by Gulch – G1 Champion S, Dubai Sheema Classic, International S, Prince of Wales's S), was a top-class racehorse winning four group races and placing in the King George VI and Queen Elizabeth Stakes and Prix de l'Arc de Triomphe. Retired to Sheikh Hamdan's Nunnery Stud in Norfolk, he sired the European classic winners, Lailani, Bolas and Petrushka (all Irish Oaks), Eswarah (p268) and Lahan. Other good winners by Unfuwain include Zahrat Dubai (G1 Nassau S), Vadawina (G1 Prix Saint-Alary) and Alhaarth (G1 Dewhurst S). Unfuwain died at Nunnery Stud during January 2002.

0125288

LOVE DIVINE (GB)

Bay filly, foaled 12 February 1997
By Diesis (GB) out of La Sky (IRE) by Law Society (USA)
Bred by Trevor Harris
Owned by Lordship Stud
Trained by Henry R.A. Cecil at Warren Place, Newmarket, Suffolk.

1430600

Racing Record

Year	Timeform Annual Rating	Starts	Wins	2nd	3rd	4th	Prize Money
1999	80	1	-	1	-	-	£ 1,010
2000	120	5	2	1	-	2	£ 286,985

Principal Performances

2000 Won Lupe Stakes (Listed Race) (3yo fillies) Goodwood (9.9f)
Won Oaks Stakes (G1) (3yo fillies) Epsom (12f)
2nd Yorkshire Oaks (G1) (Fillies & mares) York (11.9f)
4th Prix Vermeille (G1) (3yo fillies) Longchamp (12f)
4th Champion Stakes (G1) Newmarket (10f)

*****

A virus causing respiratory problems struck Henry Cecil's Warren Place stables in 2000. Love Divine was finally fit enough to race at Goodwood in May and an impressive success there saw the filly start favourite for the Oaks at Epsom. After her classic victory Love Divine was aimed at the Irish and Yorkshire Oaks, but following a disappointing gallop, missed the Curragh race, which was won by the Oaks fourth, Petrushka. Love Divine met her York engagement, but was beaten by Petrushka and two further defeats at Longchamp and Newmarket saw Love Divine retired without winning again. She descends in the tail female line from the legendary Pretty Polly (1901, by Gallinule), winner of the 1000 Guineas, Oaks and St Leger, and fifth-dam of the great Brigadier Gerard (see p13). Stakes placed La Sky was a three-quarters sister to Legal Case (1986, by Alleged – G1 Champion S). This is the family of Swain (1992, by Nashwan – G1 Coronation Cup, King George VI & Queen Elizabeth

214

S twice) and Dan Excel (SIN-G1 International Cup). Love Divine has proved a good broodmare producing the winners Kissing (2004, by Grand Lodge), Native Ruler (2006, by Cape Cross - 2ⁿᵈ G2 Jockey Club S), Hamelin (2010, by Cape Cross), Arabian Oasis (2012, by Oasis Dream) and best of all, the St Leger winner Sixties Icon (p284). Love Divine was in-foal to Dansili and expected to visit Dubawi in 2015.

2418000

Above: **LOVE DIVINE** (Richard Quinn) wins the Oaks beating Kalypso Katie (grey), Melikah and Petrushka (black cap). This was Quinn's first Oaks and second English classic victory following Snurge (p108) in the 1990 St Leger.

Below left: **TREVOR HARRIS** of Lordship Stud with his homebred Oaks winner in the winner's circle at Epsom.

2918100

11T01282

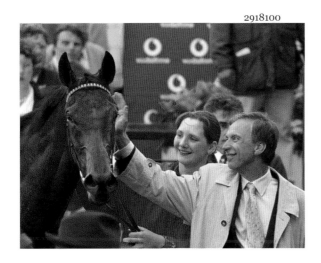

Above: **DIESIS** was the last colt to win both the Middle Park and Dewhurst Stakes before the misguided decision was taken to run both races on the same day as part of the unnecessary 'Future Champions Day'. Thankfully the mistake was realised and the time gap between two of the most important races for juvenile colts restored for 2015. Diesis proved highly successful at stud, siring the Oaks winners, Diminuendo (p88), Ramruma (p204) and Love Divine. Top-class colts by Diesis include the Eclipse Stakes winners Halling and Elmaamul. Diesis was put down on November 18, 2006 at Mill Ridge Farm, Lexington after fracturing a hip. Lordship Stud bought **LA SKY** (left) in foal to Diesis at Keeneland's 1995 November Sale for $290,000.

0636091

SINNDAR (IRE)

Bay colt, foaled 27 February 1997
By Grand Lodge (USA) out of Sinntara (IRE) by Lashkari (GB)
Owned and bred by H.H. Aga Khan
Trained by John M. Oxx at Currabeg, The Curragh, Co. Kildare.

3230700

Racing Record

Year	Timeform Annual Rating	Starts	Wins	2nd	3rd	4th	Prize Money
1999	105	2	2	-	-	-	£ 108,728
2000	134	6	5	1	-	-	£ 1,642,114

Principal Performances

1999   Won National Stakes (G1) (2yo colts) Curragh (8f)
2000   Won Derrinstown Stud Derby Trial (G3) (3yo) Leopardstown (10f)
       Won Derby Stakes (G1) (3yo colts & fillies) Epsom (12f)
       Won Irish Derby Stakes (G1) (3yo colts & fillies) Curragh (12f)
       Won Prix Niel (G2) (3yo) Longchamp (12f)
       Won Prix de l'Arc de Triomphe (G1) Longchamp (12f)
                                        *****

S inndar was the first horse ever to win the Derby, Irish Derby and Prix de l'Arc de Triomphe. The colt descends from a family developed by Marcel Boussac and acquired by the Aga Khan when he bought the Boussac bloodstock in a 'lock, stock and barrel' deal in 1978. Sinntara was talented but slow, winning the listed Giolla Mear Stakes and the Irish Cesarewitch. Sinndar was retired to his owner's Gilltown Stud at Kilcullen in County Kildare, moving to Haras de Bonneval in France during 2005. He has proved a successful stallion siring the Group 1 winners Shawanda (Irish Oaks, Prix Vermeille, dam of Enke (p348), Youmzain (Grand Prix de Saint-Cloud, 2nd Prix de l'Arc de Triomphe three times), Rosanara (Prix Marcel Boussac) and Shareta (Yorkshire Oaks, Prix Vermeille). Other group winners by Sinndar include Visindar (G2 Prix Greffulhe), Four Sins (G2 Blandford S), Gertrude Bell (G2 Lancashire Oaks), Aqaleem (G3 Lingfield Derby Trial S), Pictavia (G3 Select S) and Kaldera (G3 Deutsches St Leger).

216

1718300

Above: **SINNDAR** wins the Derby after a good battle with Sakhee to become the first Irish-trained winner since Secreto (p50) sixteen years earlier. Two streakers are tailed-off, but beating Kingsclere. This was the fourth victory in this classic for the **AGA KHAN** (below centre), following Shergar (p18), Shahrastani (p68) and Kahyasi (p86).

3621300

0207100

Above left: **SINNDAR** and John Murtagh win a second Derby at the Curragh beating Glyndebourne and Ciro (centre). Above right: **JOHN OXX** and **JOHN MURTAGH**; Sinndar was Oxx's first runner in the Derby and his first English classic winner, as it was for Murtagh.

2434400

1633099

1815394

Above left: John Murtagh salutes **SINNDAR**, European champion, after the Prix de l'Arc de Triomphe. Above right: Sinndar was by far the best horse sired by Lord Howard de Walden's **GRAND LODGE** (G1 Dewhurst S, St James's Palace S, 2nd G1 2000 Guineas, Champion S, 3rd G1 Sussex S, Irish Champion S).

WINCE (GB) : Bay 1996

	Selkirk (USA) Ch. 1988	Sharpen Up (GB) Ch. 1969	Atan (USA)
			Rocchetta (GB)
		Annie Edge (IRE) Ch. 1980	Nebbiolo (GB)
			Friendly Court (IRE)
	Flit (USA) B. 1988	Lyphard (USA) B. 1969	Northern Dancer (CAN)
			Goofed (USA)
		Nimble Folly (USA) Ch. 1977	Cyane (USA)
			Instant Sin (USA)

RAMRUMA (USA) : Chesnut 1996

	Diesis (GB) Ch. 1980	Sharpen Up (GB) Ch. 1969	Atan (USA)
			Rocchetta (GB)
		Doubly Sure (GB) B. 1971	Reliance (FR)
			Soft Angels (GB)
	Princess of Man (IRE) Ch. 1975	Green God (IRE) Ch. 1968	Red God (USA)
			Thetis (GB)
		White Legs (GB) Ch. 1957	Preciptic (GB)
			Caspian Sea (GB)

OATH (IRE) : Bay 1996

	Fairy King (USA) B. 1982	Northern Dancer (CAN) B. 1961	Nearctic (CAN)
			Natalma (USA)
		Fairy Bridge (USA) B. 1975	Bold Reason (USA)
			Special (USA)
	Sheer Audacity (IRE) B. 1984	Troy (GB) B. 1976	Petingo (GB)
			La Milo (GB)
		Miss Upward (GB) B. 1964	Alcide (GB)
			Aiming High (GB)

MUTAFAWEQ (USA) : Bay 1996

	Silver Hawk (USA) B. 1979	Roberto (USA) B. 1969	Hail To Reason (USA)
			Bramalea (USA)
		Gris Vitesse (USA) Gr. 1966	Amerigo (GB)
			Matchiche (FR)
	The Caretaker (IRE) B. 1987	Caerleon (USA) B. 1980	Nijinsky (CAN)
			Foreseer (USA)
		Go Feather Go (USA) B. 1972	Go Marching (USA)
			Feather Bed (USA)

KING'S BEST (USA) : Bay 1997

			Raise A Native (USA)
Kingmambo (USA) B. 1990		Mr Prospector (USA) B. 1970	Gold Digger (USA)
		Miesque (USA) B. 1984	Nureyev (USA)
			Pasadoble (USA)
Allegretta (GB) Ch. 1978		Lombard (GER) Ch. 1967	Agio (GER)
			Promised Lady (GB)
		Anatevka (GER) Ch. 1969	Espresso (GB)
			Almyra (GER)

LAHAN (GB) : Bay 1997

			Nearctic (CAN)
Unfuwain (USA) B. 1985		Northern Dancer (CAN) B. 1961	Natalma (USA)
		Height Of Fashion (FR) B. 1979	Bustino (GB)
			Highclere (GB)
Amanah (USA) Ch. 1992		Mr Prospector (USA) B. 1970	Raise A Native (USA)
			Gold Digger (USA)
		Cheval Volant (USA) Ch. 1987	Kris S (USA)
			Flight (USA)

LOVE DIVINE (GB) : Bay 1997

			Atan (USA)
Diesis (GB) Ch. 1980		Sharpen Up (GB) Ch. 1969	Rochetta (GB)
		Doubly Sure (GB) B. 1971	Reliance (GB)
			Soft Angels (GB)
La Sky (IRE) B. 1988		Law Society (USA) Br. 1972	Alleged (USA)
			Bold Bikini (USA)
		Maryinsky (USA) Ch. 1977	Northern Dancer (CAN)
			Extra Place (USA)

SINNDAR (IRE) : Bay 1997

			Danzig (USA)
Grand Lodge (USA) Ch. 1991		Chief's Crown (USA) B. 1982	Six Crowns (USA)
		La Papagena (GB) Br. 1983	Habitat (USA)
			Magic Flute (GB)
Sinntara (IRE) B. 1989		Lashkari (GB) B. 1981	Mill Reef (USA)
			Larannda (FR)
		Sidama (FR) B. 1982	Top Ville (IRE)
			Stoyana (FR)

MILLENARY (GB)

Bay colt, foaled 21 April 1997
By Rainbow Quest (USA) out of Ballerina (IRE) by Dancing Brave (USA)
Bred by Abergwaun Farms
Owned by L. Neil Jones
Trained by John L. Dunlop at Castle Stables, Arundel, Sussex.

1830200

Racing Record

Year	Timeform Annual Rating	Starts	Wins	2nd	3rd	4th	Prize Money
1999	87	2	-	-	1	-	£ 2,053
2000	122	5	4	-	-	-	£ 292,200
2001	124	5	1	2	1	-	£ 130,339
2002	121	6	1	1	2	-	£ 100,060
2003	121	6	1	3	-	1	£ 108,280
2004	121	5	3	-	2	-	£ 174,000
2005	123	6	2	-	2	1	£ 151,500

Principal Performances

2000   Won Chester Vase (G3) (3yo) Chester (12.3f)
       Won Gordon Stakes (G3) (3yo) Goodwood (12f)
       Won St Leger Stakes (G1) (3yo colts & fillies) Doncaster (14.6f)
2001   Won Jockey Club Stakes (G2) Newmarket (12f)
       3rd Coronation Cup (G1) Epsom (12f)
       2nd Irish St Leger Stakes (G1) Curragh (14f)
2002   Won Princess of Wales's Stakes (G2) Newmarket (12f)
       3rd Cologne Pokal (G1) Cologne, Germany (12f)
2003   Won Princess of Wales's Stakes (G2) Newmarket (12f)
2004   Won Yorkshire Cup (G2) York (13.9f)
       Won (dead-heat) Doncaster Cup (G2) Doncaster (18f)
       Won Jockey Club Cup (G3) Newmarket (16f)

2005   Won Lonsdale Cup (G3) York (15.9f)
       Won Doncaster Cup (G2) Doncaster (18f)

*****

*M*illenary was remarkably tough and sound, retaining his ability over six seasons racing and still as good at eight-years-old as he had been in his classic year. He was retired to Knockhouse Stud at Kilmacow, County Kilkenny and if ever a horse earned honourable retirement it was Millenary. As a National Hunt sire he is in the early stages of his career, but Millenary has already had a few winners, the best to date being Brother Brian, a hurdles winner at Newbury and Cheltenham. The battle-hardened old warrior descends from a classic family developed at Ballymacoll Stud, ironically the breeders of Air Marshall, runner-up in Millenary's St Leger. The minor winner Ballerina was bought by Neil Jones at the 1994 Tattersalls December Sales for 130,000 guineas. Her dam Dancing Shadow was stakes placed and a half-sister to Sun Princess (p44) and Saddlers' Hall. Dancing Shadow did well at stud for Ballymacoll, breeding Dancing Bloom (1990, by Sadler's Wells – G3 Princess Royal Stakes, 2nd G1 Yorkshire Oaks twice) and River Dancer (1983, by Irish River – 2nd G1 Prix Morny, 3rd G1 Poule d'Essai des Pouliches), the dam of Spectrum (p44) and Ballet Shoes (1990, by Ela-Mana-Mou), herself only a minor winner, but dam of Petrushka (1997, by Unfuwain – G1 Irish Oaks, Yorkshire Oaks, Prix de l'Opera, 3rd G1 1000 Guineas, 4th G1 Oaks). Another daughter of River Dancer, the unraced Well Head (1989, by Sadler's Wells), was the dam of Conduit (p306) and grandam of Glass Harmonium (2006, by Verglas – Aus G1 Mackinnon S). Since Millenary, Ballerina has bred for Neil Jones, his full-sister Head In The Clouds (1998 – G3 Princess Royal S) and Let The Lion Roar (2001, by Sadler's Wells – 3rd G1 Derby). There are more details about this excellent family on pages 44-5.

2830400

Above & below: **MILLENARY** and Richard Quinn win the St Leger beating Air Marshall (John Reid). This was the jockey's second success in this classic following Snurge (p108) in 1990. Below centre: **RICHARD QUINN** and **JOHN DUNLOP** in the winner's circle with Millenary. Dunlop had previously won the St Leger with Moon Madness (p70) and Silver Patriarch (p186) in 1986 and 1997. Below right: **NEIL JONES** with the St Leger trophy after his first English classic victory.

1030500   1630500   2730200

221

GOLAN (IRE)

Bay colt, foaled 24 February 1998
By Spectrum (IRE) out of Highland Gift (IRE) by Generous (IRE)
Bred by Ballymacoll Stud Farm Limited
2000-2001: Owned by Lord Weinstock
2002: Owned by Exors of the late Lord Weinstock
Trained by Sir Michael Stoute at Beech Hurst Stables, Newmarket.

0719201

Racing Record

Year	Timeform Annual Rating	Starts	Wins	2nd	3rd	4th	Prize Money
2000	102	1	1	-	-	-	£ 3,877
2001	125	6	2	1	1	1	£ 674,124
2002	129	4	1	1	-	-	£ 534,000

Principal Performances

2001　Won 2000 Guineas Stakes (G1) (3yo colts & fillies) Newmarket (8f)
　　　2nd Derby Stakes (G1) (3yo colts & fillies) Epsom (12f)
　　　3rd Irish Derby Stakes (G1) (3yo colts & fillies) Curragh (12f)
　　　Won Prix Niel (G2) (3yo) Longchamp (12f)
　　　4th Prix de l'Arc de Triomphe (G1) Longchamp (12f)
2002　Won King George VI and Queen Elizabeth Stakes (G1) Ascot (12f)
　　　2nd International Stakes (G1) York (10.4f)

*****

G olan won the 2000 Guineas on only his second racecourse appearance and went on to show high-class form at both ten and twelve furlongs before retiring to Coolmore Stud at Fethard in County Tipperary. He also covered at Windsor Park Stud at Cambridge in New Zealand during the southern hemisphere breeding season. However, Golan was not well supported by breeders and was moved to Coolmore's Grange Stud at Fermoy in County Cork in 2007 where he is standing as a National Hunt stallion. The best of his offspring on the flat have been Beauty Flash (G1 Hong Kong Mile), Kibbutz (G1

222

Victoria Derby), Regime (G3 Classic Trial S, G3 Mooresbridge S) and Misunited (G3 Lillie Langtry S, LR Oyster S, LR Saval Beg S, 3rd G1 Ascot Gold Cup). Golan descends from a family that was present at Ballymacoll when the stud was owned by Dorothy Paget. Way back in his tail female line will be found Carpet Slipper (1930, by Phalaris), the dam of Godiva (1937, by Hyperion – 1000 Guineas, Oaks S) and Windsor Slipper (1939, by Windsor Lad – Irish Triple Crown). This great broodmare was also grandam of Silken Glider (1954, by Airborne – Irish Oaks, 2nd Oaks S) and great-grandam of Valoris (1963, by Tiziano – Irish 1000 Guineas, Oaks S) and Country House (1955, by Vieux Manoir), the dam of Reform (1964, by Pall Mall – see below).This is the family of Derby winner North Light (p260). Highland Gift died in April 2015 after foaling her twelfth foal, a colt by Arcano, which survived.

0313101

Above: Kieren Fallon wins his second and Sir Michael Stoute his fifth 2000 Guineas as **GOLAN** beats Tamburlaine (red cap) and Frenchmans Bay (left).   Below: Two brave horses battle out the finish of the King George VI and Queen Elizabeth Stakes. Golan and Fallon beat Nayef and Richard Hills by a head.

0925202

Right: **LORD WEINSTOCK** entered horse-racing in 1958 in partnership with Sir Michael Sobell. They had immediate success when their first horse, London Cry, won the Cambridgeshire Handicap. In 1960, Weinstock and Sobell purchased Ballymacoll Stud in County Meath from the estate of Dorothy Paget and the best horse they bred there was Troy (p207). Other top-class winners have included Reform (St James's Palace, Sussex & Champion S), Spectrum (Irish 2000 Guineas, Champion S), Sallust (Sussex S, Prix du Moulin) Sun Princess (p44), Hellenic (Yorkshire Oaks), Pilsudski (Eclipse & Champion S) and Tartan Bearer (2005, G2 Dante S, G3 Gordon Richards S, 2nd G1 Derby S, Prince of Wales's S, King George VI & Queen Elizabeth S, 3rd Irish Derby S), a full-brother to Golan. Arnold Weinstock died on 23 July 2002, four days before Golan won at Ascot.

1327001

AMEERAT (GB)

Bay filly, foaled 4 April 1998
By Mark of Esteem (IRE) out of Walimu (IRE) by Top Ville (IRE)
Bred and owned by Sheikh Ahmed bin Rashid Al-Maktoum
Trained by Michael A. Jarvis at Kremlin House, Newmarket, Suffolk.

1829800

Racing Record

Year	Timeform Annual Rating	Starts	Wins	2nd	3rd	4th	Prize Money
2000	102	3	1	1	-	-	£ 20,870
2001	116	4	1	-	-	-	£ 180,750

Principal Performances

2000   2nd May Hill Stakes (G3) (2yo fillies) Doncaster (8f)
2001   Won 1000 Guineas Stakes (G1) (3yo fillies) Newmarket (8f)

*****

*A*meerat was never as good again as she was on the day she won the 1000 Guineas. A reasonable run at Royal Ascot was followed by two poor ones at Goodwood and Newmarket and she was retired to stud as one of the lowest rated English classic winners in Timeform history. Ameerat was the fifth consecutive winner of the 1000 Guineas that failed to win again after their Newmarket victory. Her first foal, Own Boss (2004, by Seeking The Gold) was a minor winner for Michael Jarvis' stable in 2007. Her second, Sowaylm (2007, by Tobougg) also won, as did Kawssaj (2008, by Dubawi) and Oojooba (2009, by Monsun). Saadatt (2010, by New Approach) and Ebn Naas (2011, by Monsun) are to date unraced and in 2012, Ameerat foaled a filly by New Approach. Ameerat was from the first crop of Mark of Esteem (see p166); her dam won three minor races and is out of Summer Impressions, a moderate filly originally trained at Newmarket by Henry Cecil, that had to go to Cagnes-sur-Mer to win a race, an event for amateur riders. A half-sister to Oh So Sharp (p58), great grandam Roussalka (1972, by Habitat – G2 Coronation S, Nassau S twice) was a good broodmare producing Gayane (1984, by Nureyev – LR Oak Tree S, 2nd G1 July Cup) and Ristna (1988, by Kris – G2 Sun Chariot S). This family is discussed further on pages 58-59 and 174.

224

2213701

Above: **AMEERAT** (Philip Robinson) wins the 1000 Guineas beating Muwakleh (right) and Toroca (left).
Below: Enthusiastic applause greets Michael Jarvis' long-overdue first English classic winner.

1613501

1732193

0533404

0606297

Above: **SHEIKH AHMED AL-MAKTOUM**; Ameerat has been his only English classic winner to date. He also owned Mtoto, winner of the Eclipse and King George VI & Queen Elizabeth Stakes. **PHILIP ROBINSON** (centre) rode his third and last English classic winner on Ameerat. He had previously won the 1000 Guineas with Pebbles (see p46) and the St Leger on Bob's Return (p140). **MICHAEL JARVIS** (right) had held a trainer's license for over thirty-three years before winning his first English classic with Ameerat.

225

IMAGINE (IRE)

Bay filly, foaled 20 February 1998
By Sadler's Wells (USA) out of Doff The Derby (USA) by Master Derby (USA)
Bred by Barronstown Stud and Orpendale
Owned by Mrs John Magnier and Mrs David Nagle
Trained by Aidan P. O'Brien at Ballydoyle, Cashel, Co. Tipperary.

0316701

Racing Record

Year	Timeform Annual Rating	Starts	Wins	2nd	3rd	4th	Prize Money
2000	108	6	2	1	1	1	£ 58,780
2001	119	4	2	1	1	-	£ 323,252

Principal Performances

2000   4th Fillies' Mile (G1) (2yo fillies) Ascot (8f)
         Won Park Stakes (G3) (2yo fillies) Curragh (7f)
         2nd Rockfel Stakes (G2) (2yo fillies) Newmarket (7f)
2001   Won Irish 1000 Guineas Stakes (G1) (3yo fillies) Curragh (8f)
         Won Oaks Stakes (G1) (3yo fillies) Epsom (12f)

*****

A relatively undistinguished two-year-old season saw Imagine achieve a rating more than a stone below average classic winning standard for a filly, but she improved enough in her classic season to win weak renewals of the Irish 1000 Guineas and the Oaks. Her final Timeform rating still put her nearly four pounds below the average rating achieved by Oaks winners since 1950 (see p387-8). Imagine bruised a foot in early-July preparing for the Irish Oaks and it was found impossible to get her race-fit again, forcing her retirement. At stud, Imagine has been a successful broodmare. Her first foal Horatio Nelson (2003, by Danehill) won three group races including the G1 Grand Criterium. Red Rock Canyon (2004, by Rock Of Gibraltar) was a minor winner and G1 placed, Kitty Matcham (2005, by Rock Of Gibraltar) won the G2 Rockfel Stakes and Viscount Nelson (2007, by Giant's Causeway) was successful at G2 level in Dubai. Point Piper (2010), Adeste Fideles (2011) and Assagher (2012), all three by Giant's Causeway, were minor winners in Europe. Imagine's latest offspring to race, General

226

Macarthur (2013, by War Front) won at Dundalk for Aidan O'Brien's stable during early- September 2015. Doff The Derby, who died in 1999, was a goldmine for her owners, her foals consistently making high prices at auction, one, Padua's Pride (1997, by Caerleon) was sold for 2.5m guineas, the highest price then achieved for a foal. Doff The Derby was a half-sister to Trillion (1974, by Hail To Reason – G1 Prix Ganay), the dam of Triptych (1982, by Riverman), the winner of nine Group 1 races in France and England. The dual Prix de l'Arc de Triomphe winner Treve (2010, by Motivator), has Trillion as her fourth dam.

0716601

Above: **IMAGINE** and Mick Kinane winning the Oaks beating the unlucky Flight Of Fancy (left) and Relish The Thought (rail). The race represented a notable result for Sadler's Wells, sire of the first three finishers, a feat not achieved in a English classic since the Derby winner Hermit (1864, by Newminster) did so in the 1882 1000 Guineas. Imagine's dam Doff The Derby, her 1988 colt by Caerleon, Generous (see p116) having won the Derby, thus became the first mare to produce two English classic winners since Glass Slipper with Light Cavalry (p12) and Fairy Footsteps (p14) in 1980-81.

1516601

0818201

Above left: **SUSAN MAGNIER** in the winner's circle at Epsom with Imagine and Mick Kinane. The other part-owner, Diane Nagle is standing with her back to camera lower left. They had previously co-owned another Oaks winner, Shahtoush (p192). Above right: **AIDAN O'BRIEN** and **MICK KINANE** at Royal Ascot in June 2001. Imagine was a second Oaks winner for both men following Shahtoush. For O'Brien this was a third English classic victory, having trained the 2000 Guineas winner King Of Kings (p188), also ridden by Kinane. Mick Kinane had also won the 2000 Guineas on Tirol (p104) and Entrepreneur (p176) and the Derby on Commander in Chief (p136).

GALILEO (IRE)

Bay colt, foaled 30 March 1998
By Sadler's Wells (USA) out of Urban Sea (USA) by Miswaki (USA)
Bred by David Tsui and Orpendale
Owned by Mrs John Magnier and Michael Tabor
Trained by Aidan P. O'Brien at Ballydoyle, Cashel, Co. Tipperary.

1520701

Racing Record

Year	Timeform Annual Rating	Starts	Wins	2nd	3rd	4th	Prize Money
2000	107	1	1	-	-	-	£ 8,840
2001	134	7	5	1	-	-	£ 1,612,270

Principal Performances

2001   Won Derby Trial Stakes (G3) (3yo) Leopardstown (10f)
      Won Derby Stakes (G1) (3yo colts & fillies) Epsom (12f)
      Won Irish Derby Stakes (G1) (3yo colts & fillies) Curragh (12f)
      Won King George VI and Queen Elizabeth Stakes (G1) Ascot (12f)
      2nd Irish Champion Stakes (G1) Leopardstown (10f)

*****

*G*alileo went to Epsom unbeaten and posted the most impressive Derby victory since Generous (see *p116). The spin concerning the colt's ability and his supposed best distance started immediately. Aidan O'Brien was quoted as saying 'This is a serious horse....capable of producing the unbelievable ...(with)... the speed of a sprinter and the strength of a miler....explosive and very special.' The plan, as revealed by O'Brien, was to drop Galileo back to ten furlongs for the Eclipse Stakes and then to eight furlongs for Ascot's Queen Elizabeth II Stakes. The young trainer was however overruled by the more experienced heads involved and the horse was kept to twelve furlongs for his next two races. As soon as Galileo was brought back to ten furlongs he was beaten twice and there cannot be much doubt that twelve furlongs was his optimum distance. Retired to Coolmore Stud at Fethard in County Tipperary, Galileo has been a great success as a sire and looks the natural successor to the phenomenon that was Sadler's Wells. The best of his Group 1 winners include the European classic winners, Sixties Icon (p284), Soldier Of Fortune (Irish Derby), Cima De Triomphe (Derby Italiano), New Approach (p304),*

228

Cape Blanco (Irish Derby), Frankel (p330), Golden Lilac (Prix de Diane), Misty For Me (Irish 1000 Guineas), Roderic O'Connor (Irish 2000 Guineas), Marvellous (Irish 1000 Guineas), Treasure Beach (Irish Derby), Great Heavens (Irish Oaks), Was (p346), Intello (Prix du Jockey-Club), Magician (Irish 2000 Guineas), Ruler Of The World (p356), Australia (p368) and Gleneagles (p372). Other top-level winners have included Red Rocks (Breeders' Cup Turf), Teofilo (Dewhurst S), Lush Lashes and Tapestry (both Yorkshire Oaks), Rip Van Winkle (Sussex S), Galikova (Prix Vermeille), Nathaniel (Eclipse & King George VI & Queen Elizabeth S), Noble Mission (Tattersalls Gold Cup, Grand Prix de Saint-Cloud, Champion S), Adelaide (Secretariat S, Cox Plate) and Found (Prix Marcel Boussac).

Above: **GALILEO** (Mick Kinane) wins the Derby beating Golan (p222) and Tobougg (2nd left). This was a second Derby victory for Kinane following Commander in Chief (p136) and first for Aidan O'Brien.   2816901

Left: GALILEO and Kinane complete a Derby double at the Curragh in Ireland beating Derby Italiano winner Morshdi and Golan (left).
0619301

Below left and opposite: GALILEO wins a hard-fought battle with Fantastic Light (Frankie Dettori) in the King George VI and Queen Elizabeth Stakes.

Below right: **MICK KINANE, SUSAN MAGNIER** (centre) and **MICHAEL TABOR** (left) in the much missed old winner's circle at Ascot before the 'improvements' to the racecourse were made during 2005.

0720601

3120701

MILAN (GB)

Bay colt, foaled 8 March 1998
By Sadler's Wells (USA) out of Kithanga (IRE) by Darshaan (GB)
Bred by Fittocks Stud, Upend, Newmarket
Owned by Michael Tabor and Mrs John Magnier
Trained by Aidan P. O'Brien at Ballydoyle, Cashel, Co. Tipperary.

3216001

Racing Record

Year	Timeform Annual Rating	Starts	Wins	2nd	3rd	4th	Prize Money
2000	100	1	1	-	-	-	£ 7,800
2001	129	8	2	2	1	1	£ 666,083
2002	-	1	-	-	-	-	-

Principal Performances

2001   3rd Prix Lupin (G1) (3yo colts & fillies) Longchamp (10.5f)
Won Great Voltigeur Stakes (G2) (3yo colts & geldings) York (11.9f)
Won St Leger Stakes (G1) (3yo colts & fillies) Doncaster (14.6f)
2nd Breeders' Cup Turf (G1) Belmont Park, U.S.A. (12f)

*****

*M*ilan was bred at Luca Cumani's Fittocks Stud at Cheveley near Newmarket and sold at the Houghton Yearling Sales to a Coolmore partnership for 650,000 guineas. Cumani thus became the first person to train (Commanche Run, see p54) and breed a St Leger winner since William l'Anson in 1864. Milan was a good winner of the classic by the standards of the ten preceding years, there not having been a winner higher rated by Timeform since Snurge (p108). After the St Leger, Milan ran well, without having the run of the race, in both the Prix de l'Arc de Triomphe and Breeders' Cup Turf. He was retired after fracturing his off-fore cannon bone at the Curragh in May 2002. Standing at Grange Stud at Fermoy in County Cork, Milan has done well as a National Hunt sire, getting the G1 winners, Jezki (Champion Hurdle, Hattons Grace Hurdle, Aintree Hurdle), Darlan (Christmas Hurdle, Kempton), Beat That (Sefton Novices Hurdle), Apache Stronghold (Flogas Novice Chase), Martello Tower (Spa Novices Hurdle) and Sizing Granite (Maghull Novices Chase), as well as Raya Star (G2 Scottish Champion Hurdle) and Lambro (G2 Coolmore Novice Hurdle, Fairyhouse).

230

2823087

1126601

Above right: **MILAN** wins Mick Kinane and Aidan O'Brien their third English classic of the year, easily beating Demophilos and Mr Combustible (rails) in the St Leger. Until Galileo (p228) gave Sadler's Wells his first English Derby winner, which was soon followed by this first St Leger, some blinkered members of the racing media were still clinging obstinately to the belief that the progeny of the great stallion did not truly stay twelve furlongs. They conveniently chose to ignore his four Oaks winners, three of the Prix du Jockey-Club, four Irish Derbys, two Irish Oaks and three winners of the King George VI and Queen Elizabeth Stakes, all run over twelve furlongs, preferring to point to his failure to sire a Derby winner. The English classic results of 2001 finally put this absurd theory to bed once and for all. Above left: Milan was bred at **LUCA** and **SARA CUMANI**'s Fittocks Stud near Newmarket.

2932793

0720184

Above left: **KITHANGA** was a good winner for Luca Cumani, her victories including the G3 St Simon Stakes at Newbury and the listed Galtres Stakes at York (photo above). Her dam Kalata was sold by the Aga Khan at Tattersalls 1987 December Sales, bought by Cumani for 38,000 guineas. Kadissya (1979, by Blushing Groom), a half-sister to Kalata, is the dam of Kahyasi (p86). At the 1995 December Sales, Kalata was sold again for 60,000 guineas, not having bred another winner since Kithanga. This is also the family of Key Change (1993, by Darshaan – G1 Yorkshire Oaks) and German classic winner Karpino (2012, by Cape Cross – G2 Mehl-Mullens Rennen). Above right: The sire and maternal grandsire of Milan met twice on the racecourse. Here **DARSHAAN** and Yves Saint-Martin beat Pat Eddery on **SADLER'S WELLS** in the Prix du Jockey Club at Chantilly 1984; Rainbow Quest finishes third. The following month Sadler's Wells finished second to Teenoso (p43) in the King George VI and Queen Elizabeth Stakes at Ascot with Darshaan unplaced.

ROCK OF GIBRALTAR (IRE)

Bay colt, foaled 8 March 1999
By Danehill (USA) out of Offshore Boom (IRE) by Be My Guest (USA)
Bred by Joe Crowley and Mr & Mrs A.P. O'Brien
Owned by Sir Alex Ferguson and Mrs John Magnier
Trained by Aidan P. O'Brien at Ballydoyle, Cashel, Co. Tipperary.

0123301

Racing Record

Year	Timeform Annual Rating	Starts	Wins	2nd	3rd	4th	Prize Money
2001	118	7	5	1	-	-	£ 372,581
2002	133	6	5	1	-	-	£ 897,223

Principal Performances

2001   Won Railway Stakes (G3) (2yo) Curragh (6f)
      Won Gimcrack Stakes (G2) (2yo colts & geldings) York (6f)
      Won Grand Criterium (G1) (2yo colts & fillies) Longchamp (7f)
      Won Dewhurst Stakes (G1) (2yo) Newmarket (7f)
2002   Won 2000 Guineas Stakes (G1) (3yo colts & fillies) Newmarket (8f)
      Won Irish 2000 Guineas Stakes (G1) (3yo colts & fillies) Curragh (8f)
      Won St James's Palace Stakes (G1) (3yo colts) Royal Ascot (8f)
      Won Sussex Stakes (G1) (3yo & upwards) Goodwood (8f)
      Won Prix du Moulin de Longchamp (G1) (3yo & upwards) Longchamp (8f)
      2nd Breeders' Cup Mile (G1) (3yo & upwards) Arlington Park, U.S.A. (8f turf)

*****

R ock Of Gibraltar had an outstanding racing career during which he became the first horse to win seven consecutive Group 1 races beating the record of six by the 1971 Derby winner, Mill Reef. Retired to Coolmore Stud at Fethard in County Tipperary, Rock Of Gibraltar has been a fairly successful stallion siring Society Rock (G1 Golden Jubilee S, G1 Sprint Cup), Eagle Mountain (G1 Hong Kong Cup), Varenar (G1 Prix de la Foret), Mount Nelson (G1 Eclipse S), Samitar (G1 Irish 1000

Guineas), Prince Gibraltar (G1 Criterium de Saint-Cloud, G2 Prix Greffulhe), Alboran Sea (G1 winner in South Africa) and Ajaxana (G2 German 1000 Guineas). Offshore Boom, a minor winner and placed in listed company in Ireland, was purchased by her current owners for IR11,000 guineas in 1997. Her dam Push A Button also won in Ireland and was a half-sister to the high-class racehorse and very successful stallion Riverman (1969, by Never Bend – G1 Poule d'Essai des Poulains, Prix d'Ispahan, G2 Prix Jean Prat). Push A Button bred five winners in all, the best being Winning Venture (1997, by Owington – 3rd G1 Gran Criterium, G2 Champagne S).

3413202

1513302

Above: Three views of the 2000 Guineas finish; (left) **ROCK OF GIBRALTAR** (John Murtagh) leads home third-placed Redback (rail), while out in the centre of the track (right) Hawk Wing's spectacular late run just fails by a neck to catch his stablemate. The big screen in the background illustrates how far apart the two horses were racing. A similarly unsatisfactory finish to a 2000 Guineas occurred in 2014 when all first three placed horses raced wide apart across the width of the course and this will continue to happen until the management stop placing the starting stalls in the middle of the track.

2513102

3230601

Above left: **SIR ALEX FERGUSON** and **JOHN MURTAGH** with Rock Of Gibraltar after the 2000 Guineas. This was the jockey's second English classic victory following Sinndar (p216).

Above right: **JOHN MAGNIER** of Coolmore Stud; he and Sir Alex became embroiled in a dispute over the terms of the ownership of Rock Of Gibraltar after the horse retired to stud. This was eventually settled out of court.

KAZZIA (GER)

Bay filly, foaled 12 April 1999
By Zinaad (GB) out of Khoruna (GER) by Lagunas (GB)
Bred by Mrs R. Grunewald
2001: Owned by Rennstall Wohler and trained by Andreas Wohler at Bremen in Germany
2002: Owned by Godolphin and trained by Saeed bin Suroor at Moulton Paddocks, Newmarket,
Suffolk.

2013402

Racing Record

Year	Timeform Annual Rating	Starts	Wins	2nd	3rd	4th	Prize Money
2001	105	2	2	-	-	-	£ 55,611
2002	121	5	3	-	-	1	£ 697,719

Principal Performances

2001   Won Premio Dormello (G3) (2yo fillies) San Siro, Milan (8f)
2002   Won 1000 Guineas Stakes (G1) (3yo fillies) Newmarket (8f)
       Won Oaks Stakes (G1) (3yo fillies) Epsom (12f)
       Won Flower Bowl Invitational Stakes (G1) Belmont, U.S.A. (10f turf)

*****

K *azzia was bought privately for Godolphin on the judgement of Sheikh Mohammed and became the first German-bred horse to win a Group 1 race in Britain. Zinaad (1989, by Shirley Heights) was a son of Time Charter (see p32) and not a success at stud even in the relatively calm waters of German racing. Kazzia's dam Khoruna was moderate, but came from a good German family which includes Kamiros (1982, by Star Appeal – G1 Europa Preis), a son of Kazzia's third-dam Kandia (1972, by Luciano – G1 Aral-Pokal). At stud, Kazzia produced the winners Eastern Anthem (2004, by Singspiel - G1 Dubai Sheema Classic), Zeitoper (2007, by Singspiel - G3 Prix de Conde), Kailani (2009, by Monsun – LR Pretty Polly S) and Kazziana (2012, by Shamardal). Moonsail (2008, by Monsun) and King's Land (2011, by New Approach) both failed to win. Kazzia died on 11 March 2013 after giving birth to a filly foal by Dubawi, which survived, at Dalham Hall Stud in Newmarket.*

234

2113602

Above: **KAZZIA** wins the 1000 Guineas beating Snowfire (blinkers), Alasha (noseband) and Dolores (right) with Quarter Moon (left) staying-on in fifth place. It was Frankie Dettori, Saeed bin Suroor and Godolphin's second victory in this classic following Cape Verdi (p190). Below left: **FRANKIE DETTORI**'s crowd-pleasing 'flying dismount' and (below right) he congratulates **SHEIKH MOHAMMED AL-MAKTOUM**, whose decision it was to run Kazzia in the 1000 Guineas.

3313402

3713402

Below: Dettori and **KAZZIA** win their second English classic, beating Quarter Moon in the Oaks. This was a third Oaks victory for Dettori and Godolphin after Balanchine (p150) and Moonshell (p158) and second for Saeed bin Suroor, who trained Moonshell.

1218102

MILLENARY (GB) : Bay 1997

Rainbow Quest (USA) B. 1981	Blushing Groom (FR) Ch. 1974	Red God (USA)
		Runaway Bride (GB)
	I Will Follow (USA) B. 1975	Herbager (FR)
		Where You Lead (USA)
Ballerina (IRE) B. 1991	Dancing Brave (USA) B. 1983	Lyphard (USA)
		Navajo Princess (USA)
	Dancing Shadow (IRE) B. 1977	Dancer's Image (USA)
		Sunny Valley (IRE)

GOLAN (IRE) : Bay 1998

Spectrum (IRE) B. 1992	Rainbow Quest (USA) B. 1981	Blushing Groom (FR)
		I Will Follow (USA)
	River Dancer (IRE) B. 1983	Irish River (FR)
		Dancing Shadow (IRE)
Highland Gift (IRE) B. 1993	Generous (IRE) Ch. 1988	Caerleon (USA)
		Doff The Derby (USA)
	Scots Lass (GB) B. 1982	Shirley Heights (GB)
		Edinburgh (GB)

AMEERAT (GB) : Bay 1998

Mark of Esteem (IRE) B. 1993	Darshaan (GB) Br. 1981	Shirley Heights (GB)
		Delsy (FR)
	Homage (GB) B. 1989	Ajdal (USA)
		Home Love (USA)
Walimu (IRE) B. 1989	Top Ville (IRE) B. 1976	High Top (GB)
		Sega Ville (FR)
	Summer Impressions (USA) Ch. 1980	Lyphard (USA)
		Roussalka (GB)

IMAGINE (IRE) : Bay 1998

Sadler's Wells (USA) B. 1981	Northern Dancer (CAN) B. 1961	Nearctic (CAN)
		Natalma (USA)
	Fairy Bridge (USA) B. 1975	Bold Reason (USA)
		Special (USA)
Doff The Derby (USA) B. 1981	Master Derby (USA) Ch. 1972	Dust Commander (USA)
		Madam Jerry (USA)
	Margarethen (USA) B. 1962	Tulyar (IRE)
		Russ-Marie (USA)

GALILEO (IRE) : Bay 1998

Sadler's Wells (USA) B. 1981	Northern Dancer (CAN) B. 1961	Nearctic (CAN)
		Natalma (USA)
	Fairy Bridge (USA) B. 1975	Bold Reason(USA)
		Special (USA)
Urban Sea (USA) Ch. 1989	Miswaki (USA) Ch. 1978	Mr Prospector (USA)
		Hopespringseternal (USA)
	Allegretta (GB) Ch. 1978	Lombard (GER)
		Anatevka (GER)

MILAN (GB) : Bay 1998

Sadler's Wells (USA) B. 1981	Northern Dancer (CAN) B. 1961	Nearctic (CAN)
		Natalma (USA)
	Fairy Bridge (USA) B. 1975	Bold Reason(USA)
		Special (USA)
Kithanga (IRE) B. 1990	Darshaan (GB) Br. 1981	Shirley Heights (GB)
		Delsy (FR)
	Kalata (IRE) B. 1984	Assert (IRE)
		Kalkeen (IRE)

ROCK OF GIBRALTAR (IRE) : Bay 1999

Danehill (USA) B. 1986	Danzig (USA) B. 1977	Northern Dancer (CAN)
		Pas De Nom (USA)
	Razyana (USA) B. 1981	His Majesty (USA)
		Spring Adieu (CAN)
Offshore Boom (IRE) Ch. 1985	Be My Guest (USA) Ch. 1974	Northern Dancer (CAN)
		What A Treat (USA)
	Push A Button (IRE) B. 1980	Bold Lad (IRE)
		River Lady (USA)

KAZZIA (GER) : Bay 1999

Zinaad (GB) B/br. 1989	Shirley Heights (GB) B. 1975	Mill Reef (USA)
		Hardiemma (GB)
	Time Charter (IRE) B. 1979	Saritamer (USA)
		Centrocon (GB)
Khoruna (GER) B. 1991	Lagunas (GB) B. 1981	Ile De Bourbon (USA)
		Liranga (GER)
	Khora (GER) B. 1984	Corvaro (USA)
		Kandia (GER)

HIGH CHAPARRAL (IRE)

Bay colt, foaled 1 March 1999
By Sadler's Wells (USA) out of Kasora (IRE) by Darshaan (GB)
Bred by Sean Coughlan
Owned by Michael Tabor and Mrs John Magnier
Trained by Aidan P. O'Brien at Ballydoyle, Cashel, Co. Tipperary.

0521902

Racing Record

Year	Timeform Annual Rating	Starts	Wins	2nd	3rd	4th	Prize Money
2001	115	3	2	1	-	-	£ 123,597
2002	130	6	5	-	1	-	£ 2,293,781
2002	132	4	3	-	1	-	£ 1,028,933

Principal Performances

2001   Won Racing Post Trophy (G1) (2yo) Doncaster (8f)
2002   Won Derby Trial Stakes (G3) (3yo) Leopardstown (10f)
       Won Derby Stakes (G1) (3yo colts & fillies) Epsom (12f)
       Won Irish Derby Stakes (G1) (3yo colts & fillies) Curragh (12f)
       3rd Prix de l'Arc de Triomphe (G1) Longchamp (12f)
       Won Breeders' Cup Turf (G1) Belmont, U.S.A. (12f)
2003   Won Royal Whip Stakes (G2) Curragh (10f)
       Won Irish Champion Stakes (G1) Leopardstown (10f)
       3rd Prix de l'Arc de Triomphe (G1) Longchamp (12f)
       Won (dead-heat) Breeders' Cup Turf (G1) Santa Anita, U.S.A. (12f)

*****

*H*igh Chaparral was bought on behalf of a Coolmore partnership for 270,000 guineas at Tattersalls Houghton Yearling Sales. The colt went on to become the third successive Derby winner to be trained in Ireland. Kept off the track after June by a bout of coughing, High Chaparral

238

returned in October and became the first Epsom Derby winner to win at the Breeders' Cup in America. High Chaparral's reappearance in 2003 was delayed by a shoulder injury, but he came back at least as good as ever in early-August and was the first horse to win the Breeders' Cup Turf twice. Retired to Coolmore Stud at Fethard in County Tipperary and shuttled to Windsor Park Stud in New Zealand for the southern hemisphere breeding seasons, High Chaparral has had great success in Australia, siring So You Think (G1 Cox Plate twice), Monaco Consul (G1 Victoria Derby), Shoot Out and Dundeel (both G1 Australian Derby), Descarado (G1 Caulfield Cup), Contributor (G1 Chipping Norton S, Ranvet S) and Fenway (G1 Vinery Stud S). Other Group/Grade 1 winners include Toronado (Sussex S, Queen Anne S), Wrote (Breeders' Cup Juvenile Turf) and Wigmore Hall (Northern Dancer S twice), while So You Think enhanced his reputation further when shipped to Europe winning five more Group 1 races including the Eclipse and Prince of Wales's Stakes. German classic winner Lucky Lion (G1 Grosser Dalmayr-Preis, G2 Mehl Mullens-Rennen), Western Hymn (G2 Prix Eugene Adam), High Jinx (G1 Prix du Cadran) and Free Eagle (G1 Prince of Wales's S) are also by High Chaparral. The unraced Kasora was bred by the Aga Khan out of Kozana (G2 Prix de Malleret), a half-sister to Karkour (1978, by Relko – G1 Prix du Cadran). The third dam Koblenza (1966, by Hugh Lupus – Poule d'Essai des Pouliches), descended from a family developed by Francois Dupre at his Haras d'Ouilly, whose bloodstock was bought by the Aga Khan in 1977. On 21 December 2014 Coolmore released the news that High Chaparral had been euthanized due to a perforated intestine discovered during exploratory surgery for colic.

2718402

2521802

Above left: Jockey John Murtagh benefits from Mick Kinane's decision to ride Hawk Wing and wins his second Epsom Derby on **HIGH CHAPARRAL**, with Hawk Wing (left) finishing second. Above right: Kinane chooses correctly this time as HIGH CHAPARRAL wins the Irish Derby with Ballydoyle trained horses filling the first three places.

Right: Was this the moment when a young boy first had a dream? Nine-year-old **JOSEPH O'BRIEN**, son of trainer Aidan, in the winner's circle at the Curragh with High Chaparral after the Irish Derby. Ten years later, Joseph rode Camelot (see p340) to victory in two English classics and the Irish Derby.

1521902

BOLLIN ERIC (GB)

Bay colt, foaled 18 February 1999
By Shaamit (IRE) out of Bollin Zola (IRE) by Alzao (USA)
Bred by Sir Neil and Lady Westbrook
Owned by Sir Neil Westbrook
Trained by Tim D. Easterby at Habton Grange, Great Habton, Yorkshire.

2431202

Racing Record

Year	Timeform Annual Rating	Starts	Wins	2nd	3rd	4th	Prize Money
2001	95	4	2	1	1	-	£ 24,631
2002	125	6	1	2	3	-	£ 324,029
2003	123	8	1	1	1	4	£ 157,634

Principal Performances

2002 2nd Dante Stakes (G2) (3yo) York (10.4f)
       2nd King Edward VII Stakes (G2) (3yo colts & geldings) Ascot (12f)
       3rd Great Voltigeur Stakes (G2) (3yo colts & geldings) York (11.9f)
       Won St Leger Stakes (G1) (3yo colts & fillies) Doncaster (14.6f)
2003 3rd Yorkshire Cup (G2) York (13.9f)
       2nd Hardwicke Stakes (G2) Royal Ascot (12f)
       4th King George VI and Queen Elizabeth Stakes (G1) Ascot (12f)
       Won Lonsdale Stakes (G3) York (15.9f)
       4th Irish St Leger Stakes (G1) Curragh (14f)

*****

*S*omewhat surprisingly, given his lack of success at twelve furlongs, Bollin Eric was only tried once over two miles as a four-year-old, ending 2003 with that race as his only victory and once again chasing horses too fast for him in the Prix de l'Arc de Triomphe. Bollin Eric began his stallion career at the National Stud at Newmarket, but predictably received little support from flat racing breeders and was moved to Wood Farm Stud in Shropshire and then in 2012 to Colmer Stud at Bridport in Dorset where he covers primarily National Hunt mares. He has sired no runners of any particular note either *on the flat or over jumps to date, although his daughter Ericarrow has bred the German stakes winner Eric (2011, by Tertullian – G3 Furstenberg-Rennen). Bollin Zola, an IR6,500 yearling purchase for Sir Neil and Lady Westbrook, was a fairly useful handicapper and bred three winners before Bollin Eric, including Bollin Joanne (1993, by Damister – G3 Duke of York S). The St Leger winner's great grandam, Crestia (1977, by Prince Tenderfoot) was a half-sister to the top-class French stayer El Badr (1975, by Weavers Hall – G1 Prix du Cadran twice).*

2431302

Above: **BOLLIN ERIC** becomes the first St Leger winner trained in the north of England since Peleid in 1973. It was the only English classic victory for his owner/breeders, Sir Neil and Lady Westbrook, who prefixed all their horse's names with Bollin after a river which ran through their farm in Cheshire. The St Leger second, Highest, became the fourth runner-up in the final classic for trainer Sir Michael Stoute, who at that time had still to saddle the winner.

2811197

© Keith Robinson

2939094

Above left: **TIM EASTERBY** enjoyed his first and to date only English classic success with Bollin Eric. He took over Habton Grange from his legendary father Peter in 1996.

Above centre: **SIR NEIL** and **LADY WESTBROOK** in the winner's circle at Doncaster after their St Leger victory with Bollin Eric.

Above right: **KEVIN DARLEY** rode his first English classic winner on Bollin Eric. He had been champion apprentice in Britain during 1978 and was overall champion in 2000. Darley also won the 1994 Racing Post Trophy and 1995 Prix du Jockey-Club on Celtic Swing, the Deutsches Derby on Belenus in 1999, the 1000 Guineas on Attraction (p256) and retired in 2007.

REFUSE TO BEND (IRE)

Bay colt, foaled 17 March 2000
By Sadler's Wells (USA) out of Market Slide (USA) by Gulch (USA)
Bred by Moyglare Stud Farm Limited
2002-2003: Owned by Moyglare Stud Farm and trained
by Dermot K. Weld at Rosewell House, The Curragh, Co. Kildare
2004: Owned by Godolphin and trained by Saeed bin Suroor in Dubai and at Moulton Paddocks
Stables, Newmarket, Suffolk.

0914003

Racing Record

Year	Timeform Annual Rating	Starts	Wins	2nd	3rd	4th	Prize Money
2002	110	2	2	-	-	-	£ 124,656
2003	124	6	3	-	-	-	£ 236,249
2004	128	7	2	-	1	-	£ 418,990

Principal Performances

2002 Won National Stakes (G1) (2yo colts & fillies) Curragh (7f)
2003 Won 2000 Guineas Trial Stakes (Listed) (3yo colts) Leopardstown (8f)
      Won 2000 Guineas Stakes (G1) (3yo colts & fillies) Newmarket (8f)
      Won Desmond Stakes (G3) Leopardstown (8f)
2004 Won Queen Anne Stakes (G1) Royal Ascot (8f)
      Won Eclipse Stakes (G1) Sandown Park (10f)
      3rd Queen Elizabeth II Stakes (G1) Ascot (8f)

*****

*A*fter winning a sub-standard 2000 Guineas, Refuse To Bend was sent off as favourite for the Derby but ran too freely and finished unplaced. Returned to a mile, he won at Leopardstown after a ten-week break but disappointed at Longchamp and shortly after was purchased privately by Sheikh Mohammed Al-Maktoum for his Godolphin stable. Refuse To Bend won two more Group 1 races *in 2004 before retiring to Kildangan Stud on The Curragh in County Kildare. The stallion was also shuttled to Australia for the southern hemisphere breeding season and later transferred to Whitsbury Manor Stud in Hampshire. Refuse To Bend suffered a fatal heart attack at Haras du Logis in Normandy during February 2012 before covering a mare at his new location. His best progeny have been Sarafina (G1 Prix de Diane, Grand Prix de Saint-Cloud), Wavering (G1 Prix Saint-Alary) Glencadam Gold (Aus-G1 Metropolitan H), Refuse To Bobbin (G1 Premio Presidente della Repubblica), Frisson (G1 winner in Brazil), Falest (G3 Premio Tudini) and Without Fear (multiple stakes winner in Scandinavia). Market Slide, U.S. stakes placed, was also the dam of Media Puzzle (1997, by Theatrical – G1 Melbourne Cup) and was out of Grenzen, a multiple stakes winner in the U.S. and dam of Twilight Agenda (1986, by Devil's Bag – G1 Meadowlands Cup, 2nd Breeders Cup Classic) and the grandam of Go And Go (1987, by Be My Guest – G1 Belmont S).*

2314003

Above: **REFUSE TO BEND** wins the 2000 Guineas beating the unlucky in-running Zafeen (white cap) and Norse Dancer (near-side). This is the only English classic victory to date for the six-time champion jockey in Ireland, **PAT SMULLEN** (below right) and the first for **DERMOT WELD** (below left) since Blue Wind (p22). Below centre: **WALTER HAEFNER**, the owner of Moyglare Stud which he purchased in 1962. Notable horses bred there include Assert (Prix du Jockey-Club, Irish Derby), Bikala (Prix du Jockey-Club), Dance Design (Irish Oaks), Go And Go and Media Puzzle (see above).

1517796

3717996

1420102

RUSSIAN RHYTHM (USA)

Chesnut filly, foaled 12 February 2000
By Kingmambo (USA) ex Balistroika (USA) by Nijinsky (CAN)
Bred by Brushwood Stables
Owned by Cheveley Park Stud
Trained by Sir Michael Stoute at Freemason Lodge, Newmarket, Suffolk.

1328902

Racing Record

Year	Timeform Annual Rating	Starts	Wins	2nd	3rd	4th	Prize Money
2002	113	4	3	1	-	-	£ 114,420
2003	123	5	3	1	-	-	£ 539,700
2004	122	1	1	-	-	-	£ 116,000

Principal Performances

2002   Won Princess Margaret Stakes (G3) (2yo fillies) Ascot (6f)
       Won Lowther Stakes (G2) (2yo fillies) York (6f)
       2nd Cheveley Park Stakes (G1) (2yo fillies) Newmarket (6f)
2003   Won 1000 Guineas Stakes (G1) (3yo fillies) Newmarket (8f)
       Won Coronation Stakes (G1) (3yo fillies) Royal Ascot (8f)
       Won Nassau Stakes (G1) (3yo & upwards) (Fillies & mares) Goodwood (9.9f)
       2nd Queen Elizabeth II Stakes (G1) Ascot (8f)
2004   Won Lockinge Stakes (G1) (4yo & upwards) Newbury (8f)

*****

*I*n her classic season Russian Rhythm completed a treble of victories last achieved by Happy Laughter (1950, by Royal Charger). Very genuine and consistent with an excellent turn of finishing speed, Russian Rhythm strained a suspensory ligament after making a successful reappearance in

2004 and was retired to her owner's stud at Newmarket. Her first foal Barynya (2006, by Pivotal) was placed on all her three starts. Safina (2007, by Pivotal) was a minor winner and fourth in the G3 Nell Gwyn Stakes. Russian Realm (2010, by Dansili) has won three races to date and Russian Heroine (2012, by Invincible Spirit) was a winner for Sir Michael Stoute's stable in 2015. Russian Rhythm was put down on 20 August 2014 after suffering a severe attack of colic and her sixth and last foal was named Russian Finale (2013, by Dansili). The unraced Balistroika was a half-sister to Desirable (1981, by Lord Gayle – G1 Cheveley Park S), the dam of Shadayid (p112), and another winner of the Cheveley Park Stakes in Park Appeal (1982, by Ahonoora), the dam of Cape Cross (see p259) and grandam of Diktat (1995, by Warning – G1 Haydock Sprint Cup) and Alydaress (1986, by Alydar – G1 Irish Oaks). Novitiate (1959, by Fair Trial), Russian Rhythm's fourth dam was a half-sister to Red Velvet (1967, by Red God – Princess Margaret S), Lord David (1968, by Tesco Boy – 3rd Champion S) and Miss Melody (1970, by Tudor Melody), the dam of Masarika (1981, by Thatch – G1 Prix Robert Papin, Poule d'Essai des Pouliches). This is the family of top-class sprinter Welsh Abbot (1955, by Abernant). With such illustrious relations it is no surprise that it took a bid of $370,000 to pinhook Russian Rhythm as a foal at Keeneland and a bid of 440,000 guineas to secure her for Cheveley Park Stud when resold as a yearling at Tattersalls in Newmarket.

2914203

Above: **RUSSIAN RHYTHM** (Kieren Fallon) wins the 1000 Guineas from the unlucky Six Perfections (left) and Intercontinental (pink cap). This was the first English classic winner for David and Patricia Thompson, the owners of Cheveley Park Stud.

Below left: **KIEREN FALLON, MICHAEL STOUTE** and **PATRICIA THOMPSON** in the winner's circle after the 1000 Guineas. It was Fallon's third victory in this classic following Sleepytime (p178) and Wince (p202) and second for Stoute after Musical Bliss (p94). Below right: **RUSSIAN RHYTHM** and Fallon win the Coronation Stakes beating Soviet Song.

0914303

2719403

CASUAL LOOK (USA)

Bay filly, foaled 10 May 2000
By Red Ransom (USA) out of Style Setter (USA) by Manila (USA)
Owned and bred by William S. Farish III
2002: Trained by Ian A. Balding
2003: Trained by Andrew M. Balding both at Park House, Kingsclere, Hampshire.

0632802

Racing Record

Year	Timeform Annual Rating	Starts	Wins	2nd	3rd	4th	Prize Money
2002	107	5	1	2	1	1	£ 62,682
2003	114	7	1	-	2	-	£ 300,906

Principal Performances

2002 2nd Fillies' Mile (G1) (2yo) Ascot (8f)
      2nd Rockfel Stakes (G2) (2yo fillies) Newmarket (7f)
2003 Won Oaks Stakes (G1) (3yo fillies) Epsom (12f)
      3rd Irish Oaks Stakes (G1) (3yo fillies) Curragh (12f)
      3rd Queen Elizabeth II Challenge Cup (G1) Keeneland, U.S.A. (9f)

*****

C *asual Look was rated by Timeform as the worst winner of the Oaks since Long Look was assessed at 112 in 1965. The next eight fillies finished within five lengths of the winner and only two of those managed to win a race afterwards. Runner-up Yesterday was repeatedly denied an opening and finished very fast. Casual Look failed to build on her classic victory and was beaten in all her subsequent races. At stud she has bred the minor winners Hidden Glance (2005, by Kingmambo) and Mushreq (2007, by Distorted Humor) and also Casual Smile (2011, by Sea The Stars – G3 Matchmaker S, Monmouth Park). Style Setter was a winner in the U.S. and had previously foaled Shabby Chic (1996, by Red Ransom – LR Prix de Liancourt, 3rd G1 Yellow Ribbon S) and American Style (1999, by Quiet American – 3rd G1 Dwyer S). The grandam of Casual Look, Charleston Rag (G1 Frizette S) was out of*

246

Music Ville (1972, by Charlottesville), a stakes placed three-quarters sister to Meadow Court (1962, by Court Harwell – Irish Derby, King George VI & Queen Elizabeth S, 2nd Derby S, St Leger S).

0717503

Above: **CASUAL LOOK** and Martin Dwyer hold off the fast finishing Yesterday (blaze) to win the Oaks by a neck, with Summitville (stars) in third place. This was a first English classic victory for William Farish III, the owner of Lane's End Farm in Kentucky.

2730696

2939199

1219402

Above left: **IAN BALDING** trained Casual Look in 2002 before retiring at the end of the season and handing over the licence to his son, **ANDREW** (centre). Ian is probably best remembered as the trainer of the brilliant Mill Reef, the 1971 Derby winner, but also saddled the European classic winners, Mrs Penny (Prix de Diane, Prix Vermeille), Forest Flower (Irish 1000 Guineas) and Glint of Gold (Derby Italiano). Other Group 1 winners trained by Balding included Diamond Shoal (Grand Prix de St-Cloud), Silly Season (Dewhurst & Champion S), Gold and Ivory (Preis von Europa), Berkeley Springs (Cheveley Park S), Selkirk (Queen Elizabeth II S), Dashing Blade (Dewhurst S), Tagula (Prix Morny), Lochangel (Nunthorpe S), Silver Fling (Prix de l'Abbaye) and champion sprinter Lochsong (Prix de l'Abbaye twice, Nunthorpe S, King's Stand S).

Above right: **MARTIN DWYER** rode his first English classic winner on Casual Look. Three years later he had his greatest moment in racing when winning the Derby on Sir Percy (see p282). Dwyer has also won G1 races on Phoenix Reach (Canadian International, Hong Kong Vase, Dubai Sheema Classic), Sir Percy (Dewhurst S) and Nayarra (Gran Criterium).

KRIS KIN (USA)

Chesnut colt, foaled 5 March 2000
By Kris S (USA) out of Angel In My Heart (FR) by Rainbow Quest (USA)
Bred by Flaxman Holdings Limited
Owned by Saeed Suhail
Trained by Sir Michael Stoute at Freemason Lodge, Newmarket, Suffolk.

1217803

Racing Record

Year	Timeform Annual Rating	Starts	Wins	2nd	3rd	4th	Prize Money
2002	81	2	1	-	-	-	£ 5,379
2003	126	5	2	-	2	-	£ 986,000

Principal Performances

2003 Won Dee Stakes (G3) (3yo colts & geldings) Chester (10.3f)
       Won Derby Stakes (G1) (3yo colts & fillies) Epsom (12f)
       3rd King George VI and Queen Elizabeth Stakes (G1) Ascot (12f)
       3rd Prix Niel (G2) (3yo colts & fillies) Longchamp (12f)

*****

*K*ris Kin was bought as a yearling at Keeneland by Charles Gordon-Watson, acting on behalf of Saeed Suhail, for $275,000 at a sale that was postponed for twenty-four hours due to the 11 September terrorist attacks on New York. Written-off by Raceform's race-reader as having no chance in the Derby after winning at Chester, Kris Kin nevertheless became the first supplementary entry to win the classic, beating the subsequent Irish Derby and King George VI and Queen Elizabeth Stakes winner, Alamshar in the process. However, on his overall form Kris Kin has to be rated as a below average Derby winner. He was retired to Derrinstown Stud at Maynooth in County Kildare and was moved to Morristown Lattin Stud at Naas in County Kildare for 2006. Kris Kin was not popular with Irish breeders and was sold to Allevamento I Mandorli in Italy during November 2010. The stallion failed to sire a stakes winner in Europe and was sold on again, this time to obscurity in Libya. In August 2012, Kris Kin was killed instantly after breaking his neck trying to jump a gate at the Al Shaab

Stud near Tripoli. Angel In My Heart won the Group 3 Prix de Psyche and was placed at Group 1 level in France and the U.S. She has also bred Cause Of Causes (2008, by Dynaformer), twice a winner at listed level over jumps. Kris Kin's grandam Sweetly was the dam of Common Grounds (1985, by Kris - G1 Prix de la Salamandre) and Lightning Fire (1986, by Kris – LR Prix Imprudence).

0617803

Above and opposite: **KRIS KIN** and Kieren Fallon win the Derby beating The Great Gatsby (rail) and Alamshar (no.1). It was Fallon's second Derby victory following Oath (see p206).

1517803

3613700

Above right: **SAEED SUHAIL** had previously won the 2000 Guineas with King's Best (p210) and above, parades his Derby winner past the stands. Sadly this traditional old number board has been demolished, presumably in the name of progress and to save the few pounds they were paying the casual labour to operate it!

Right: **SIR MICHAEL STOUTE** (black top hat) greets his third Derby winner. His previous victories were with the Aga Khan owned colts Shergar (p18) and Shahrastani (p68). To the right of picture (bare-headed) is Charles Gordon-Watson, who bought Kris Kin at the Keeneland Sales in Kentucky.

2217803

BRIAN BORU (GB)

Bay colt, foaled 16 March 2000
By Sadler's Wells (USA) out of Eva Luna (USA) by Alleged (USA)
Bred by Juddmonte Farms
Owned by Mrs John Magnier
Trained by Aidan P. O'Brien at Ballydoyle, Cashel, Co. Tipperary.

0230903

Racing Record

Year	Timeform Annual Rating	Starts	Wins	2nd	3rd	4th	Prize Money
2002	117	3	2	1	-	-	£ 136,718
2003	124	6	1	1	2	1	£ 374,321
2004	120	9	1	2	1	-	£ 166,632

Principal Performances

2002   2nd Beresford Stakes (G3) (2yo) Curragh (8f)
       Won Racing Post Trophy (G1) (2yo colts & fillies) Doncaster (8f)
2003   3rd Derby Trial Stakes (G2) (3yo) Leopardstown (10f)
       4th Irish Derby Stakes (G1) (3yo colts & fillies) Curragh (12f)
       2nd Great Voltigeur Stakes (G2) (3yo colts & geldings) York (11.9f)
       Won St Leger Stakes (G1) (3yo colts & fillies) Doncaster (14.6f)
       3rd Canadian International Stakes (G1) Woodbine, Canada (12f)
2004   Won Alleged Stakes (Listed Race) Leopardstown (10f)
       2nd Prix Kergorlay (G2) Deauville (15f)
       2nd Irish St Leger Stakes (G1) Curragh (14f)
       3rd Canadian International Stakes (G1) Woodbine, Canada (12f)

*****

B rian Boru was the product of a foal-sharing scheme between Coolmore and Khalid Abdullah's Juddmonte Farms, involving Sadler's Wells. Juddmonte sent a number of mares to the champion stallion and the progeny were shared between the two organisations. The colt was the second winner of the Racing Post Trophy to be run on the straight mile at Doncaster. In 2001 the race had been switched because of bad ground and problems with the starting stalls, but in 2002 it was by design. Doncaster lamely justified the decision to keep to the straight mile by claiming it was more likely that the race would be run on 'a consistent surface'. When inaugurated as the Timeform Gold Cup in 1961, it was run on the round course for the convenience of spectators and for the education of the prospective staying horses taking part, which would have to race around bends as three-year-olds. In common with many racecourses since the millennium, Doncaster seem to have abandoned any idea of pleasing ordinary racegoers, being more concerned with providing corporate facilities and bowing to the wishes of television producers and bookmakers. Unlike the majority of St Leger winners, Brian Boru was given his chance over longer distances as a four-year-old but failed to show the same level of form as in his classic season. He was retired to The Beeches Stud at Glencairn in County Wexford as a National Hunt stallion, moved to Dunraven Stud near Bridgend for two seasons and to Longford House Stud at Templemore in County Tipperary in 2015. The best horses sired by Brian Boru to date are Bold Sir Brian and Sub Lieutenant, Grade 2 winning hurdlers, Fox Appeal, a winner at the same level over fences and Next Sensation (G3 Grand Annual Challenge Cup Chase). Eva Luna won the G2 Park Hill Stakes and Brian Boru was her second foal following Moon Search (1999, by Rainbow Quest - G2 Prix de Royallieu). Eva Luna also bred Kitty O'Shea (2002, by Sadler's Wells – LR Park Express S) and Sea Moon (2008, by Beat Hollow – G2 Great Voltigeur S, Hardwicke S). The grandam, Media Luna (2nd G1 Oaks S), bred Rougeur (1989, by Blushing Groom), stakes placed in the U.S. and the dam of Flute (1998, by Seattle Slew – G1 Kentucky Oaks, Alabama S).

1430903

Above: **BRIAN BORU** (J.P.Spencer) wins the St Leger beating High Accolade (yellow cap) and Phoenix Reach (partially hidden on the rail).

Left: **JAMIE SPENCER** displays his jockey cap trophy for winning the St Leger on Brian Boru. It was a first English classic for the twenty-three year old, who had to endure the disappointment of defeat on both hot-favourites in the 1000 and 2000 Guineas of 2002. Following this classic success, Spencer was appointed stable-jockey at Ballydoyle for 2004, succeeding Mick Kinane. Spencer was champion jockey in Ireland in 2004 and in Britain for the 2005 and 2007 seasons. His other top-level winners include Tarascon, Gossamer and Just The Judge (Irish 1000 Guineas), Kyllachy (Nunthorpe S), Powerscourt (Tattersalls Gold Cup), Ad Valorem (Middle Park S), Goodricke (Haydock Sprint Cup), David Junior (Champion & Eclipse S), Excellent Art (St James's Palace S), Red Evie (Lockinge S), Sariska (p314), Fame And Glory (Ascot Gold Cup) and Excelebration (Queen Elizabeth II S).

3630903

HAAFHD (GB)

Chesnut colt, foaled 18 February 2001
By Alhaarth (IRE) out of Al Bahathri (USA) by Blushing Groom (FR)
Bred by Shadwell Estate Company Limited
Owned by Sheikh Hamdan Al-Maktoum
Trained by Barry W. Hills at Faringdon Place, Lambourn, Berkshire.

0436103

Racing Record

Year	Timeform Annual Rating	Starts	Wins	2nd	3rd	4th	Prize Money
2003	115	4	2	-	2	-	£ 61,414
2004	129	5	3	-	-	1	£ 430,874

Principal Performances

2003 Won Washington Singer Stakes (Listed Race) (2yo) Newbury (7f)
      3rd Champagne Stakes (G2) (2yo colts & geldings) Doncaster (7f)
      3rd Dewhurst Stakes (G1) (2yo colts & fillies) Newmarket (7f)
2004 Won Craven Stakes (G3) (3yo colts & geldings) Newmarket (8f)
      Won 2000 Guineas Stakes (G1) (3yo colts & fillies) Newmarket (8f)
      Won Champion Stakes (G1) (3yo & upwards) Newmarket (10f)

*****

*H*aafhd won a good renewal of the 2000 Guineas beating four colts subsequently successful at
Group 1 level. After running disappointingly at Royal Ascot and Goodwood, Haafhd came back
to form to prove himself the best British colt of his generation when winning the all-aged Champion
Stakes. The colt was retired to his owner's Nunnery Stud at Thetford, described by racing manager
Angus Gold, as 'a very important cog in his ..(Hamdan Al-Maktoum's).. breeding operation'. Despite
this, Haafhd has been a disappointing sire, his best runners on the flat to date being Silver Grecian (G2
Superlative S), Junoob (AUS-G2 Neville Sellwood S, Ascend Sales Hill S) and Noble Protector (AUS-G2
Sunline S, LR Aphrodite S). Under National Hunt rules, Countrywide Flame (G1 Triumph Hurdle,
Fighting Fifth Hurdle) and Carlito Brigante (G3 Coral Cup H) have been his best winners.

252

2013704

Above: **HAAFHD** wins the 2000 Guineas beating Snow Ridge (left), Azamour (green colours) and Grey Swallow (grey). It was the only victory in this race for jockey Richard Hills and his fourth English classic. Richard's father Barry was also registering his fourth English classic success and second 2000 Guineas following Tap On Wood in 1979. Hamdan Al-Maktoum had previously won the 2000 Guineas with Nashwan (p96).

0912985

0114996

Above left: **AL BAHATHRI and** Tony Murray, leading the parade before the 1985 1000 Guineas in which she finished second to Oh So Sharp (p58), was a high-class racemare winning the Irish 1000 Guineas and Coronation Stakes. She was an equally good broodmare producing listed winner Hasbah (1987, by Kris) and Munir (1998, by Indian Ridge - G2 Challenge Stakes), as well as Haafhd. Her dam Chain Store, a full-sister to multiple U.S. graded stakes winner Double Discount (1973), had previously bred Geraldine's Store (1979, by Exclusive Native – G2 Diana H). This is the family of Commissary (1966, by To Market – Del Mar Oaks), General Holme (1979, by Noholme - G3 Prix du Prince d'Orange), Lahib (1988, by Riverman – G1 Queen Elizabeth II S, Queen Anne S), Lord Shanakill (2006, by Speightstown – G1 Prix Jean Prat) and Red Cadeaux (2006, by Cadeaux Genereux – G1 Hong Kong Vase & £4,998,408). Above right: **ALHAARTH** was best as a two-year-old, going unbeaten through five races including the Dewhurst Stakes. Apart from Haafhd, his best progeny have been Phoenix Reach (G1 Dubai Sheema Classic), Mourayan (G1 Sydney Cup), Bandari (G2 Hardwicke S) and Awzaan (G1 Middle Park S). Below: **HAAFHD** returns to his best and wins the Champion Stakes beating Chorist (blue cap) and Azamour.

0535404

253

HIGH CHAPARRAL (IRE) :
Bay 1999

	Sadler's Wells (USA) B. 1981	Northern Dancer (CAN) B. 1961	Nearctic (CAN)
			Natalma (USA)
		Fairy Bridge (USA) B. 1975	Bold Reason(USA)
			Special (USA)
	Kasora (IRE) B. 1993	Darshaan (GB) Br. 1981	Shirley Heights (GB)
			Delsy (FR)
		Kozana (GB) Br. 1982	Kris (GB)
			Koblenza (FR)

BOLLIN ERIC (GB) : Bay 1999

	Shaamit (IRE) B. 1993	Mtoto (GB) B. 1983	Busted (GB)
			Amazer (FR)
		Shomoose (IRE) B. 1985	Habitat (USA)
			Epithet (GB)
	Bollin Zola (GB) B. 1986	Alzao (USA) B. 1980	Lyphard (USA)
			Lady Rebecca (GB)
		Sauntry (IRE) Br. 1982	Ballad Rock (IRE)
			Crestia (IRE)

REFUSE TO BEND (IRE) : Bay 2000

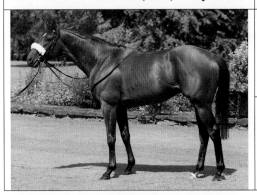

	Sadler's Wells (USA) B. 1981	Northern Dancer (CAN) B. 1961	Nearctic (CAN)
			Natalma (USA)
		Fairy Bridge (USA) B. 1975	Bold Reason(USA)
			Special (USA)
	Market Slide (USA) Ch. 1991	Gulch (USA) B. 1984	Mr Prospector (USA)
			Jameela (USA)
		Grenzen (USA) Ch. 1975	Grenfall (USA)
			My Poly (USA)

RUSSIAN RHYTHM (USA) :
Chesnut 2000

	Kingmambo (USA) B. 1990	Mr Prospector (USA) B. 1970	Raise A Native (USA)
			Gold Digger (USA)
		Miesque (USA) B. 1984	Nureyev (USA)
			Pasadoble (USA)
	Balistroika (USA) Ch. 1988	Nijinsky (CAN) B. 1967	Northern Dancer (CAN)
			Flaming Page (CAN)
		Balidaress (IRE) Gr. 1973	Balidar (GB)
			Innocence (GB)

CASUAL LOOK (USA) : Bay 2000

		Roberto (USA) B. 1969	Hail To Reason (USA)
Red Ransom (USA) B. 1987			Bramalea (USA)
		Arabia (USA) B. 1977	Damascus (USA)
			Christmas Wind (CAN)
Style Setter (USA) Ch. 1990		Manila (USA) B. 1983	Lyphard (USA)
			Dona Ysidra (USA)
		Charleston Rag (IRE) Ch. 1982	General Assembly (USA)
			Music Ville (IRE)

KRIS KIN (USA) : Chesnut 2000

		Roberto (USA) B. 1969	Hail To Reason (USA)
Kris S (USA) B. 1977			Bramalea (USA)
		Sharp Queen (USA) B. 1965	Princequillo (IRE)
			Bridgework (USA)
Angel In My Heart (FR) Ch. 1992		Rainbow Quest (USA) B. 1981	Blushing Groom (FR)
			I Will Follow (USA)
		Sweetly (FR) B. 1975	Lyphard (USA)
			Sweet And Lovely (FR)

BRIAN BORU (GB) : Bay 2000

		Northern Dancer (CAN) B. 1961	Nearctic (CAN)
Sadler's Wells (USA) B. 1981			Natalma (USA)
		Fairy Bridge (USA) B. 1975	Bold Reason(USA)
			Special (USA)
Eva Luna (USA) B. 1992		Alleged (USA) B. 1974	Hoist The Flag (USA)
			Princess Pout (USA)
		Media Luna (GB) B. 1981	Star Appeal (IRE)
			Sounion (GB)

HAAFHD (GB) : Chesnut 2001

		Unfuwain (USA) B. 1985	Northern Dancer (CAN)
Alhaarth (IRE) B. 1993			Height of Fashion (FR)
		Irish Valley (USA) Ch. 1982	Irish River (FR)
			Green Valley (FR)
Al Bahathri (USA) Ch. 1982		Blushing Groom (FR) Ch. 1974	Red God (USA)
			Runaway Bride (GB)
		Chain Store (USA) B. 1972	Nodouble (USA)
			General Store (USA)

ATTRACTION (GB)

Bay filly, foaled 19 February 2001
By Efisio (GB) ex Flirtation (GB) by Pursuit of Love (GB)
Bred by Floors Farming, Kelso, Roxburghshire
Owned by the Duke of Roxburghe
Trained by Mark S. Johnston at Kingsley House, Middleham, Yorkshire.

3021604

Racing Record

Year	Timeform Annual Rating	Starts	Wins	2nd	3rd	4th	Prize Money
2003	118	5	5	-	-	-	£ 101,450
2004	125	7	4	2	-	-	£ 680,399
2005	119	3	1	-	-	1	£ 117,748

Principal Performances

2003 Won Hilary Needler Trophy (Listed Race) (2yo fillies) Beverley (5f)
      Won Queen Mary Stakes (G3) (2yo fillies) Royal Ascot (5f)
      Won Cherry Hinton Stakes (G2) (2yo fillies) Newmarket (6f)
2004 Won 1000 Guineas Stakes (G1) (3yo fillies) Newmarket (8f)
      Won Irish 1000 Guineas Stakes (G1) (3yo fillies) Curragh (8f)
      Won Coronation Stakes (G1) (3yo fillies) Royal Ascot (8f)
      2nd Falmouth Stakes (G1) (Fillies & mares) Newmarket (8f)
      2nd Matron Stakes (G1) (Fillies & mares) Leopardstown (8f)
      Won Sun Chariot Stakes (G1) (Fillies & mares) Newmarket (8f)
2005 Won Matron Stakes (G1) (Fillies & mares) Leopardstown (8f)

*****

*A*ttraction was apparently such an unattractive proposition as a yearling that her owner decided not to send her to the sales and put her into training with no greater ambition than hoping to win a race with the filly. From such modest beginnings, Attraction developed into the outstanding filly of her generation at both two and three and the first ever to win both the English and Irish 1000 Guineas. Her four-year-old season was restricted by injury, but Attraction came back to win the Matron Stakes in September. Retired to her owner's Floors Stud, Attraction started very well with the winners Elation (2007, by Cape Cross), Devastation (2008, by Montjeu), Cushion (2010, by Galileo) and Fountain of

Youth (2011, by Oasis Dream - G3 Sapphire S) from her first five foals. The mare is due to Frankel (p330) in 2015 and then is booked to visit Dubawi (p319). Timeform's 'Racehorses of 2003' annual describes Attraction as 'hardly bred in the purple' and certainly her sire Efisio was never the height of fashion despite getting several high class performers. However, her once-raced dam descends in the tail-female line from Verdict (1920, by Shogun – Coronation Cup), a mare designated as 'half-bred' and a family not admitted to the English General Stud Book until the weight of success of her descendants, principally So Blessed (1965, by Princely Gift – July Cup, Nunthorpe S) and Lucasland (1962, by Lucero – July Cup), forced a reappraisal in 1969. Lucasland is Attraction's fourth dam and other top-class winners tracing back to her include Lord Of Men (1993, by Groom Dancer – G1 Prix de la Salamandre) and Sonic Lady (1983, by Nureyev – G1 Irish 1000 Guineas, Sussex S, Prix du Moulin).

0205204

Above: **ATTRACTION** and Kevin Darley win the 1000 Guineas beating Sundrop (off shot), Hathrah (left) and Red Bloom (blue cap). It was a first win in this classic for owner, trainer and jockey. Darley had previously won the St Leger on Bollin Eric (see p240) and Mark Johnston, the 2000 Guineas with Mister Baileys (p144). Below left: The **DUKE OF ROXBURGHE**, who bred and raced Attraction.

2221704

0521704

Above right: **ATTRACTION** and Kevin Darley follow up their victories in the English and Irish 1000 Guineas with a third successive Group 1 win in the Coronation Stakes at Royal Ascot beating Majestic Desert and Red Bloom (rail). It was the first time that these three races had been won by the same filly.

OUIJA BOARD (GB)

Bay filly, foaled 6 March 2001
By Cape Cross (IRE) out of Selection Board (GB) by Welsh Pageant (GB)
Bred by Stanley Estate and Stud Company
Owned by Lord Derby
Trained by Edward A.L. Dunlop at Gainsborough Stables, Newmarket.

3315206

Racing Record

Year	Timeform Annual Rating	Starts	Wins	2nd	3rd	4th	Prize Money
2003	98	3	1	-	2	-	£ 7,039
2004	125	5	4	-	1	-	£ 925,840
2005	121	5	2	1	-	-	£ 796,888
2006	125	9	3	2	2	1	£ 1,780,915

Principal Performances

2004 Won Pretty Polly Stakes (Listed Race) (3yo fillies) Newmarket (10f)
Won Oaks Stakes (G1) (3yo fillies) Epsom (12f)
Won Irish Oaks Stakes (G1) (3yo fillies) Curragh (12f)
3rd Prix de l'Arc de Triomphe (G1) Longchamp (12f)
Won Breeders' Cup Filly & Mare Turf (G1) Lone Star Park, U.S.A. (11f)

2005 Won Princess Royal Stakes (G3) (Fillies & mares) Newmarket (12f)
2nd Breeders' Cup Filly & Mare Turf (G1) Belmont Park, U.S.A. (10f)
Won Hong Kong Vase (G1) Sha Tin, Hong Kong (12f)

2006 3rd Queen Elizabeth II Cup (G1) Sha Tin, Hong King (10f)
2nd Coronation Cup (G1) Epsom (12f)
Won Prince of Wales's Stakes (G1) Royal Ascot (10f)
Won Nassau Stakes (G1) (Fillies & mares) Goodwood (9.9f)
2nd Irish Champion Stakes (G1) Leopardstown (10f)
Won Breeders' Cup Filly & Mare Turf (G1) Churchill Downs, U.S.A. (11f)
3rd Japan Cup (G1) Tokyo, Japan (12f)

O *uija Board was tough and game, maintaining a high level of performance over three years. She raced in seven countries on three continents and won G1 races in each except Dubai and Japan. Hyped-up as one of the great racehorses by sections of the media, she was certainly not that in terms of ability, but Ouija Board's worldwide achievements, resilience and consistency will take some matching. Retired to Lord Derby's Stanley Stud, Ouija Board has produced the winners Voodoo Prince (2008, by Kingmambo – G3 Easter Cup, Caulfield), Aegaeus (2009, by Monsun) and Filia Regina (2010 by Galileo). Her best performer to date is Australia (2011, by Galileo - p368). Ouija Board's 2013 colt by Dubawi was purchased privately for Godolphin in 2014. Unfortunately Ouija Board slipped her colt foal by Galileo in 2014, but visited the stallion again in 2015. Selection Board was a full-sister to Teleprompter (1980), a much-travelled gelding and the winner of eleven races including the G1 Arlington Million. Their dam Ouija was out of the 18th Earl of Derby's blind mare Samanda (1956, by Alycidon), immortalised in Caroline Silver's 1973 book Classic Lives. This is the family of Kingston Town (1976, by Bletchingly), the winner of fourteen G1 races in Australia, Ibn Bey (1984, by Mill Reef – G1 Irish St Leger, G1 Europa Preis), Roseate Tern (1986, by Blakeney – G1 Yorkshire Oaks, 2nd Oaks S, 3rd St Leger S) and Owington (1991, by Green Desert – G1 July Cup).*

0317004

Above: **OUIJA BOARD** and Kieren Fallon turn the Oaks into a procession, beating All Too Beautiful by seven lengths with Punctilious and Necklace third and fourth. It was a third win in this classic for Fallon following Reams of Verse (p180) and Ramruma (p204).

1317204

2122703

Above left: **LORD DERBY** (left) leads in Ouija Board and Kieren Fallon at Epsom. This Oaks victory gave the 19th Earl of Derby his first classic win and the first in the famous black and white colours since Sun Stream in the Oaks of 1945. It was also a first English classic success for trainer, **ED DUNLOP** (right).

Above right: **CAPE CROSS** was a top miler winning the Lockinge and Queen Anne Stakes. As a stallion he has exceeded all expectations siring several Group 1 winners including Sea The Stars (p310), Able One (Champions Mile, Hong Kong), Behkabad (Grand Prix de Paris), Seachange (in New Zealand), Golden Horn (p378) and Ouija Board. Cape Cross stands at Kildangan Stud at Monasterevin in County Kildare.

259

NORTH LIGHT (IRE)

Bay colt, foaled 1 March 2001
By Danehill (USA) out of Sought Out (IRE) by Rainbow Quest (USA)
Bred by Ballymacoll Stud Farm Limited
2003: Owned by The Exors of the late Lord Weinstock
2004: Owned by Ballymacoll Stud
Trained by Sir Michael Stoute at Freemason Lodge, Newmarket, Suffolk.

0722904

Racing Record

Year	Timeform Annual Rating	Starts	Wins	2nd	3rd	4th	Prize Money
2003	95	2	1	1	-	-	£ 4,900
2004	126	4	2	1	-	-	£ 1,081,376
2005	123	1	-	1	-	-	£ 11,000

Principal Performances

2004 Won Dante Stakes (G2) (3yo) York (10.4f)
      Won Derby Stakes (G1) (3yo colts & fillies) Epsom (12f)
      2nd Irish Derby Stakes (G1) (3yo colts & fillies) Curragh (12f)
2005 2nd Brigadier Gerard Stakes (G3) Sandown Park (10f)

*****

N orth Light was an ordinary Derby winner but won decisively at Epsom beating two other classic winners. The colt returned home lame and sore after the Irish Derby and could not run again until finishing a creditable fifth in the Arc. Unusually for a Derby winner, North Light was kept in training at four, but suffered a career ending pelvic injury in late-June. He was retired to Adena Springs at Paris in Kentucky and transferred to Adena Springs North at Aurora in Ontario, Canada for 2011. North Light moved back to Britain to stand at Lanwades Stud at Newmarket in 2014, returning to Adena Springs for 2015. His best offspring are the St Leger winner Arctic Cosmos (see p328), Celtic New Year (G2 Del Mar H), Chips All In (G3 San Simeon S, Eddie D S), Go Forth North (G3 Harold Ramser S) and Gol Tricolor (G2 in Brazil). Sought Out won the Group 1 Prix du Cadran and traces to

260

Coventry Belle (1938, by Hyperion), one of the foundation mares of Ballymacoll Stud. North Light's half-brother Cover Up (1997, by Machiavellian), won the Group 3 Jockey Club Cup and Sagaro Stakes. For more about this family see Golan (p222).

1817404

Above: A second Derby in succession for Sir Michael Stoute and jockey Kieren Fallon as **NORTH LIGHT** beats Rule of Law (p262) and Let The Lion Roar (left). It was Fallon's third victory in this classic following Oath (p206) and Kris Kin (p248) and fourth for trainer Michael Stoute (p325).

0216689

Right: **DANEHILL**, pictured here with Pat Eddery, was a top-class sprinter, winning the Sprint Cup at Haydock and Royal Ascot's Cork and Orrery Stakes. He was sold by Khalid Abdulla to a partnership of Coolmore and Arrowfield Stud in New South Wales. Danehill was very successful in Australia where he was champion sire on nine occasions. This prompted Coolmore to buy the horse outright in an AUS$24m deal which made Danehill the most valuable thoroughbred in Australian history. In Europe, G1 winners by him include Rock of Gibraltar (p232), Desert King (Irish 2000 Guineas & Derby), Dylan Thomas (Irish Derby, King George VI and Queen Elizabeth S, Prix de l'Arc de Triomphe), Aquarelliste (Prix de Diane, Prix Vermeille), Banks Hill (Prix Jacques Le Marois, Coronation S, Breeders' Cup Filly & Mare Turf), Duke of Marmalade (Prix Ganay, Prince of Wales's S, King George VI and Queen Elizabeth S) and George Washington (p276). Danehill Dancer (p279), Dansili (p365) and Redoute's Choice are all top-class stallions by Danehill. Danehill was put down after fracturing a hip in a paddock accident at Coolmore on 13 May 2003.

RULE OF LAW (USA)

Bay colt, foaled 6 March 2001
By Kingmambo (USA) out of Crystal Crossing (IRE) by Royal Academy (USA)
Bred by Robert E. Sangster and Ben Sangster
2003: Owned by Sheikh Mohammed Al-Maktoum and
trained by David R. Loder at Godolphin Stables, Newmarket, Suffolk
2004: Owned by Godolphin and
trained by Saeed bin Suroor at Moulton Paddocks, Newmarket, Suffolk.

0731004

Racing Record

Year	Timeform Annual Rating	Starts	Wins	2nd	3rd	4th	Prize Money
2003	109	4	2	-	2	-	£ 41,729
2004	125	5	2	2	-	1	£ 679,532

Principal Performances

2003   Won Acomb Stakes (Listed Race) (2yo) York (7f)
      3rd Royal Lodge Stakes (G2) (2yo colts & geldings) Ascot (8f)
2004   2nd Dante Stakes (G2) (3yo) York (10.4f)
      2nd Derby Stakes (G1) (3yo colts & fillies) Epsom (12f)
      4th Irish Derby Stakes (G1) (3yo colts & fillies) Curragh (12f)
      Won Great Voltigeur Stakes (G2) (3yo colts & geldings) York (11.9f)
      Won St Leger Stakes (G1) (3yo colts & fillies) Doncaster (14.6f)

*****

*R*ule of Law was a useful two-year-old without really giving any indication of being up to classic standard. Transferred to Godolphin, the colt improved into a classy, consistent and genuine performer in 2004 placing in two classics before winning the St Leger in brave style. Rule of Law was injured training in Dubai during the winter of 2004/5 and although kept in training for a further two years was unable to race again. He was retired to stand at the Darley Japan Stallion Complex at Hidaka Cho, Hokkaido and was there for five breeding seasons 2007-11, until returning to Europe to Kedrah House Stud in County Tipperary for 2012. The best winner sired by Rule of Law in Japan was

Am Ball Bleiben (G3 Keihan Hai). Crystal Crossing, a listed race winner in England, was a grand-daughter of Favoletta (1968, by Baldric – Irish 1000 Guineas) and a half-sister to Furioso (1971, by Ballymoss – 2ⁿᵈ Oaks S), the dam of Teenoso (p42) and Topsy (1976, by Habitat – G2 Sun Chariot S). Rule of Law is a half-brother to two pattern-placed winners in Totally Devoted (2006, by Seeking The Gold) and Dame Marie (2009, by Smart Strike). Other top-class runners from this successful family include Give Thanks (1980, by Relko – G1 Irish Oaks), Lacquer (1964, by Shantung – Irish 1000 Guineas), Sovereign (1965, by Pardao – Coronation S), Harayir (p156) and Sir Percy (p282). All of these winners descend from the Moller's White Lodge Stud matron Urshalim (1951, by Nasrullah).

1731004

Above: **RULE OF LAW** (Kerrin McEvoy) wins the St Leger beating Quiff, the fifth runner-up in this classic for Sir Michael Stoute. It was a fourth St Leger victory for Godolphin following Classic Cliché (see p162), Nedawi (p196) and Mutafaweq (p208).

2119006   1919391   1720505

Above left: Rule of Law was also a fourth St Leger winner for **SAEED BIN SUROOR**, Godolphin's private trainer. He had been previously successful with Classic Cliché, Nedawi and Mutafaweq.

Above centre: **BEN SANGSTER**, co-breeder with his father of Rule of Law.

Above right: **KERRIN McEVOY** was recording his only English classic victory and became the first Australian to ride a St Leger winner since Ron Hutchinson won on Intermezzo for Gerald Oldham and Harry Wragg in 1969.

FOOTSTEPSINTHESAND (GB)

Bay colt, foaled 15 February 2002
By Giant's Causeway (USA) out of Glatisant (GB) by Rainbow Quest (USA)
Bred by Hascombe and Valiant Studs
Owned by Michael Tabor and Mrs John Magnier
Trained by Aidan P. O'Brien at Ballydoyle, Cashel, Co. Tipperary.

0612405

Racing Record

Year	Timeform Annual Rating	Starts	Wins	2nd	3rd	4th	Prize Money
2004	114	2	2	-	-	-	£ 40,851
2005	120	1	1	-	-	-	£ 185,600

Principal Performances

2004   Won Kilavullan Stakes (G3) (2yo) Leopardstown (7f)
2005   Won 2000 Guineas Stakes (G1) (3yo colts & fillies) Newmarket (8f)

*****

A 170,000 guinea yearling purchase, Footstepsinthesand was the first 2000 Guineas winner since World War II never to race again and therefore must be judged on his victory at Newmarket over two 100/1 outsiders. As one of those failed to reach a place in seven subsequent starts, the 2005 running has to be rated a poor renewal of the classic. Following earlier statements delaying the colt's return to the racecourse, the announcement came in late-June that Footstepsinthesand had been retired due to a recurring foot injury, originally sustained at Newmarket. It was a very disappointing end to the brief racing career of a good-looking, unbeaten colt. Due to his early retirement, Footstepsinthesand was able to commence his stud career for the 2005 southern hemisphere breeding season at Coolmore Australia in New South Wales before shipping back to Coolmore Stud at Fethard in County Tipperary for 2006. In 2007, the stallion was sent to Argentina to stand at Haras La Mission for a season. His best winners to date have been Pure Champion (formerly Steinbeck - G1 Windsor Park

Plate, G3 Solonaway S), Chachamaidee (G1 Matron S, G2 Lennox S), Shamalgan (G1 Premio Vittorio di Capua, G2 Oettingen-Rennen), Barefoot Lady (G2 Canadian S, G3 Nell Gwyn S), Giant Sandman (G2 Goldene Peitsche), Minakshi (G2 Canadian S), Infiltrada (multiple stakes winner including G1 in Argentina), Formosina (G2 Railway S), J Wonder (G3 Fred Darling S, G3 Oak Tree S) Sandy's Charm (G3 Prix de Lieurey), Arnold Lane (G3 Silberne Peitsche), Sand Puce (multiple G2 & G3 stakes winner in Argentina), King Kon (G2 in Argentina), Sandiva (G3 Nell Gwyn S), Living The Life (G2 Presque Downs Masters S), Onenightidreamed (G3 Amethyst S), Rosso Corsa (G3 Prix du Palais-Royal) and Kaspersky (G2 Premio Carlo Vittadini). Glatisant (G3 Prestige S) also bred Pedro The Great (2010, by Henrythenavigator – G1 Phoenix S) and was out of Dancing Rocks (G2 Nassau S). Third dam, Croda Rossa (1967, by Grey Sovereign – Premio Lydia Tesio), was a half-sister to Cerreto (1970, by Claude – G1 Derby Italiano) and Croda Alta (1975, by Caro - G2 Premio Chiusura).

2112405

Above: **FOOTSTEPSINTHESAND** wins the 2000 Guineas beating Rebel Rebel (right). It was jockey Kieren Fallon's third victory in this race following King's Best (see p210) and Golan (p222).

3012405

Above: **MICHAEL** and **DOREEN TABOR** in the winner's circle after the 2000 Guineas, with **KIEREN FALLON**, **AIDAN O'BRIEN** (second right) and **JOHN MAGNIER** (right). This was O'Brien's third 2000 Guineas win following King of Kings (p188) and Rock of Gibraltar (p232) and his ninth English classic. Tabor had previously owned shares in 2000 Guineas winners Entrepreneur (p176) and King of Kings.

VIRGINIA WATERS (USA)

Bay filly, foaled 15 February 2002
By Kingmambo (USA) ex Legend Maker (IRE) by Sadler's Wells (USA)
Bred by Barnett Enterprises
Owned by Mrs John Magnier and Michael Tabor
Trained by Aidan P. O'Brien at Ballydoyle, Cashel, Co. Tipperary.

1923405

Racing Record

Year	Timeform Annual Rating	Starts	Wins	2nd	3rd	4th	Prize Money
2004	-	4	1	1	1	-	£ 33,553
2005	116	8	2	-	1	1	£ 278,193

Principal Performances

2004   3rd CL Weld Park Stakes (G3) (2yo fillies) Curragh (7f)
　　　 2nd Flame of Tara E.B.F. Stakes (Listed Race) (2yo fillies) Curragh (6f)
2005   Won 1000 Guineas Trial Stakes (G3) (3yo fillies) Leopardstown (7f)
　　　 Won 1000 Guineas Stakes (G1) (3yo fillies) Newmarket (8f)
　　　 4th Oaks Stakes (G1) (3yo fillies) Epsom (12f)
　　　 3rd Matron Stakes (G1) (Fillies & mares) Leopardstown (8f)

*****

*V*irginia Waters only twice showed form worthy of a classic winner in twelve races. Excuses concerning the soft ground were made for some of her subsequent defeats, but by the end of 2005 it was apparent that her 1000 Guineas had been contested by a below standard field. Virginia Waters' first foal, Emperor Claudius (2007, by Giant's Causeway), won four races for Aidan O'Brien including a Listed Race at the Curragh and was second in the Chesham Stakes at Royal Ascot. Ballroom (2008, by Storm Cat), Where (2010) and Dove Mountain (2011), both by Danehill Dancer, all failed to win and Visalia (2009, by Dansili) only ran once. Virginia Waters' dam Legend Maker won the G3 Prix de Royaumont and also bred Alexander Of Hales (2004, by Danehill – G3 Gallinule S, 2nd G1 Irish Derby) and the minor winner Chevalier (2000, by Danehill – 2nd G1 Criterium International). The grandam High Spirited was a full-sister to High Hawk (1980 – G2 Ribblesdale S, G2 Park Hill S, G3 Prix de*

Royallieu), the dam of In The Wings (1986, by Sadler's Wells – G1 Prix Ganay, Coronation Cup, Grand Prix de Saint-Cloud. This is the family of Infamy (1984, by Shirley Heights – G1 Rothmans International), High-Rise (see p194) and Zomaradah (1995, by Deploy – G1 Oaks d'Italia), the dam of the top-class runner and leading stallion Dubawi (p319).

2612605

Above: **VIRGINIA WATERS** (Kieren Fallon) decisively wins the 1000 Guineas beating Maids Causeway (centre). Third-placed Vista Bella is off-shot; Karen's Caper (left) finished fourth.

0512705

Above: The scene in the Newmarket winner's circle from the previous day is almost exactly repeated as **KIEREN FALLON** poses with Virginia Waters. To the right of picture is **JOHN MAGNIER** and to the left **TOM MAGNIER**. Behind Fallon is **PAUL SHANAHAN** of Coolmore and **DOREEN TABOR**, while to the right **MICHAEL TABOR** congratulates **AIDAN O'BRIEN** on a Guineas victory double last achieved in 1967 by Noel Murless and George Moore with Royal Palace and Fleet . The last time an identical owner, trainer, jockey combination had won both Guineas races at Newmarket had been on the July Course in 1942, when King George VI, Fred Darling and Gordon Richards won with Sun Chariot and Big Game. This was a first success in this classic for O'Brien and fourth for Fallon, following Sleepytime (p178), Wince (p202) and Russian Rhythm (p244).

267

ESWARAH (GB)

Bay filly, foaled 21 April 2002
By Unfuwain (USA) out of Midway Lady (USA) by Alleged (USA)
Bred by Shadwell Estate Company Limited
Owned by Hamdan Al-Maktoum
2004: Trained by Ben Hanbury at Diomed Stables, Newmarket
2005: Trained by Michael A. Jarvis at Kremlin House Stables, Newmarket, Suffolk.

2113905

Racing Record

Year	Timeform Annual Rating	Starts	Wins	2nd	3rd	4th	Prize Money
2004	-	0	-	-	-	-	-
2005	117	5	3	-	-	1	£ 258,395

Principal Performances

2005 Won Fillies' Trial Stakes (Listed Race) (3yo) Newbury (10f)
      Won Oaks Stakes (G1) (3yo fillies) Epsom (12f)
      4th Yorkshire Oaks (G1) (Fillies & mares) York (11.9f)

*****

*T*he classic fillies of 2005 were generally a below average bunch but it was very disappointing that Eswarah, a good winner of the Oaks on only her third outing, did not manage to show any improvement afterwards. Out of her depth in the King George VI & Queen Elizabeth Stakes, she was found to have a chip in her off-fore knee after running at York and was retired to her owner's stud. Eswarah's first foal, Sheklaan (2007, by Kingmambo) was useless and temperamental, but her third, Firdaws (2009, by Mr Greeley) won and was third in the G1 Fillies' Mile. Qawaafy (2010, by Street Cry) was a minor winner for Roger Varian. In 2015 Eswarah was due to visit the champion sprinter Oasis Dream at Banstead Manor Stud. Eswarah was the best of Midway Lady's (see p64) twelve foals up to 2005. Grandam Smooth Bore was a minor stakes winner in the U.S. Until the fifth dam of Eswarah, Marche Lorraine (1949, by Blue Moon – Prix Cleopatre), was exported to the U.S., this was a

268

French family tracing in the tail-female line to classic winner Sauge Pourpree (1905, by Perth – Poule d'Essai des Pouliches, Prix du Cadran).

1414105

Above and opposite: **ESWARAH** provides jockey Richard Hills with his fifth English classic and first in the Oaks, beating Something Exciting and the Irish trained trio Pictavia (rail), 1000 Guineas winner Virginia Waters (p266) and Silk And Scarlet (pink colours). Eswarah's dam Midway Lady became the ninth Oaks winner to breed an Oaks winner, but the first since Musa (successful in 1899) bred the 1912 winner, Mirska.

Below left: **SHEIKH HAMDAN AL-MAKTOUM** leads in his second Oaks winner following Salsabil (p102). This was the Dubai sheikh's tenth English classic victory.

3713805

1017700

Above right: **MICHAEL JARVIS** won his second and last English classic with Eswarah. Jarvis worked his way up from the bottom rung of racing's ladder and looked after Charlottown, the 1966 Derby winner, during his time with Gordon Smyth at Heath House in his home town of Lewes in Sussex. Jarvis first held a licence as one of the private trainers employed by David Robinson and won his first big race with Tudor Music in the 1969 Sprint Cup at Haydock. He was to win this Group 1 race twice more with Green God and Petong. Other top-class winners trained by Jarvis include Prorutori and Morshdi (both Derby Italiano), Holding Court (Prix du Jockey-Club), Carroll House (Irish Champion S, Prix de l'Arc de Triomphe), Beldale Flutter (Futurity S, Benson & Hedges Gold Cup), Rakti (Prince of Wales's S, Champion S, Queen Elizabeth II S, Lockinge S) and Ameerat (p224). Jarvis retired due to ill-health in February 2011 and his long-time assistant Roger Varian, took over the Kremlin House Stables in Fordham Road, Newmarket. Michael Jarvis died on 20 September 2011, aged seventy-three.

MOTIVATOR (GB)

Bay colt, foaled 22 February 2002
By Montjeu (IRE) out of Out West (USA) by Gone West (USA)
Bred by Deerfield Farm
Owned by The Royal Ascot Racing Club
Trained by Michael L.W. Bell at Fitzroy Stables, Newmarket, Suffolk.

1413305

Racing Record

Year	Timeform Annual Rating	Starts	Wins	2nd	3rd	4th	Prize Money
2004	122	2	2	-	-	-	£ 124,803
2005	131	5	2	2	-	-	£ 1,067,654

Principal Performances

2004 Won Racing Post Trophy (G1) (2yo) Doncaster (8f)
2005 Won Dante Stakes (G2) (3yo) York (10.4f) (photo above)
      Won Derby Stakes (G1) (3yo colts & fillies) Epsom (12f)
      2nd Eclipse Stakes (G1) Sandown Park (3yo & upwards) (10f)
      2nd Irish Champion Stakes (G1) (3yo & upwards) Leopardstown (10f)

*****

*M*otivator was a bargain 75,000 guineas yearling purchase by John Warren at Tattersalls
October Sales. Described as 'looking like a Kenyan athlete' as a yearling, he was still 'on the
weak side' according to Timeform as a two-year-old, when the colt won his only two starts, including
the Racing Post Trophy. This race was then in its fifth year of being run on the straight mile at
Doncaster and that racecourse's decision-makers seem determined to ignore part of the original
concept of this race, which was to provide a better education for prospective stayers. Ten years later,
the Racing Post Trophy of 2014 was still run on the straight mile and further ill-considered and
unnecessary changes to the autumn racing program in 2011 now mean that there is not a single Group
1 race for two-year-olds run around a bend anywhere in Britain and only one Group 2. Motivator's
easy Dante win and five-length Derby victory prompted a surge of enthusiasm for the then unbeaten
colt from the racing media that ultimately proved misplaced. Motivator was a good Derby winner, but
a champion he was not, as three defeats after Epsom proved, although the decision to bring the colt

270

back to ten furlongs was surely a factor in two of those reverses. Motivator was syndicated at £120,000 per share at a total valuation of £6m to stand at the Royal Studs at Sandringham in Norfolk. Motivator missed the entire 2010 breeding season through injury and was transferred to Haras du Quesnay in Normandy for 2013 after a slow start to his stallion career. However, Motivator came good the same year siring Treve, the best horse in Europe, winner of the Prix de Diane, Prix Vermeille and Prix de l'Arc de Triomphe twice. Other group winners have included Ridasiyna (G1 Prix de l'Opera), Sky Hunter (G2 Dubai City of Gold, G3 St Simon S, 3rd G1 Prix du Jockey-Club), Clinical (G3 Princess Elizabeth S), Ferevia (G3 Prix Penelope), Felician (G3 Badener Meile), Pallasator (G2 Doncaster Cup), Robin Hoods Bay (G3 Winter Derby), Skia (G3 Prix Fille de l'Air), Daytona Bay (G3 Hamburger Stuten-Preis), Cocktail Queen (G2 Prix Gontaut-Biron, G2 Grand Prix de Deauville), Shahah (G3 Prix d'Aumale) and Pollenator (G2 May Hill S). A listed winner in England, Out West also bred Macarthur (2004 – G2 Hardwicke S, G3 Ormonde S, 3rd G1 Coronation Cup), a full-brother to Motivator. Grandam Chellingoua was out of Uncommitted (1974, by Buckpasser), a half-sister to Wavering Monarch (1979, by Majestic Light – G1 San Fernando S). This is the family of Posse (1977, by Forli – Sussex S), Zilzal (1986, by Nureyev – Sussex S, Queen Elizabeth II S) and Polish Precedent (1986, by Danzig – Prix Jacques Le Marois).

2214305

Above: John Murtagh celebrates his third Derby victory on **MOTIVATOR** beating Walk In The Park (left) and Dubawi (right). Murtagh had won the race on Sinndar (see p216) and High Chaparral (p238).

0735604

2213305

Above left: **MOTIVATOR** (Kieren Fallon) wins the Racing Post Trophy beating Albert Hall (left). Above right: Trainer **MICHAEL BELL** with Motivator, his first English classic winner, after the Dante Stakes at York.

271

ATTRACTION (GB) : Bay 2001

	Efisio (GB) B. 1982	Formidable (USA) B. 1975	Forli (ARG)
			Native Partner (USA)
		Eldoret (IRE) B. 1976	High Top (GB)
			Bamburi (GB)
	Flirtation (GB) B. 1994	Pursuit of Love (GB) B. 1989	Groom Dancer (USA)
			Dance Quest (FR)
		Eastern Shore (GB) Ch. 1979	Sun Prince (GB)
			Land Ho (GB)

OUIJA BOARD (GB) : Bay 2001

	Cape Cross (IRE) B/br. 1994	Green Desert (USA) B. 1983	Danzig (USA)
			Foreign Courier (USA)
		Park Appeal (IRE) Br. 1982	Ahonoora (GB)
			Balidaress (IRE)
	Selection Board (GB) B. 1982	Welsh Pageant (FR) B. 1966	Tudor Melody (GB)
			Picture Light (FR)
		Ouija (GB) B. 1971	Silly Season (USA)
			Samanda (GB)

NORTH LIGHT (IRE) : Bay 2001

	Danehill (USA) B. 1986	Danzig (USA) B. 1977	Northern Dancer (CAN)
			Pas de Nom (USA)
		Razyana (USA) B. 1981	His Majesty (USA)
			Spring Adieu (CAN)
	Sought Out (IRE) B. 1988	Rainbow Quest (USA) B. 1981	Blushing Groom (FR)
			I Will Follow (USA)
		Edinburgh (GB) B. 1974	Charlottown (GB)
			Queen's Castle (IRE)

RULE OF LAW (USA) : Bay 2001

	Kingmambo (USA) B. 1990	Mr Prospector (USA) B. 1970	Raise A Native (USA)
			Gold Digger (USA)
		Miesque (USA) B. 1984	Nureyev (USA)
			Pasadoble (USA)
	Crystal Crossing (IRE) B. 1994	Royal Academy (USA) B. 1987	Nijinsky (CAN)
			Crimson Saint (USA)
		Never So Fair (GB) B. 1987	Never So Bold (IRE)
			Favoletta (GB)

FOOTSTEPSINTHESAND (GB) :
Bay 2002

		Storm Cat (USA) B/br. 1983	Storm Bird (CAN)
	Giant's Causeway (USA) Ch. 1997		Terlingua (USA)
		Mariah's Storm (USA) B. 1991	Rahy (USA)
			Immense (USA)
	Glatisant (GB) B. 1991	Rainbow Quest (USA) B. 1981	Blushing Groom (FR)
			I Will Follow (USA)
		Dancing Rocks (GB) B. 1979	Green Dancer (USA)
			Croda Rossa (ITY)

VIRGINIA WATERS (USA) :
Bay 2002

		Mr Prospector (USA) B. 1970	Raise A Native (USA)
	Kingmambo (USA) B. 1990		Gold Digger (USA)
		Miesque (USA) B. 1984	Nureyev (USA)
			Pasadoble (USA)
	Legend Maker (IRE) B. 1994	Sadler's Wells (USA) B. 1981	Northern Dancer (CAN)
			Fairy Bridge (USA)
		High Spirited (GB) B. 1987	Shirley Heights (GB)
			Sunbittern (GB)

ESWARAH (GB) : Bay 2002

		Northern Dancer (CAN) B. 1961	Nearctic (CAN)
	Unfuwain (USA) B. 1985		Natalma (USA)
		Height of Fashion (FR) B. 1979	Bustino (GB)
			Highclere (GB)
	Midway Lady (USA) B. 1983	Alleged (USA) B. 1974	Hoist The Flag (USA)
			Princess Pout (USA)
		Smooth Bore (USA) Ch. 1976	His Majesty (USA)
			French Leave (USA)

MOTIVATOR (GB) : Bay 2002

		Sadler's Wells (USA) B. 1981	Northern Dancer (CAN)
	Montjeu (IRE) B. 1996		Fairy Bridge (USA)
		Floripedes (FR) B. 1985	Top Ville (IRE)
			Toute Cy (FR)
	Out West (USA) Br. 1994	Gone West (USA) B. 1984	Mr Prospector (USA)
			Secrettame (USA)
		Chellingoua (USA) B. 1983	Sharpen Up (GB)
			Uncommitted (USA)

SCORPION (IRE)

Bay colt, foaled 5 February 2002
By Montjeu (IRE) out of Ardmelody (GB) by Law Society (USA)
Bred by Grangemore Stud, Pollardstown, Co. Kildare
Owned by Mrs John Magnier and Michael Tabor
Trained by Aidan P. O'Brien at Ballydoyle, Cashel, Co. Tipperary.

0717107

Racing Record

Year	Timeform Annual Rating	Starts	Wins	2nd	3rd	4th	Prize Money
2004	-	0	-	-	-	-	-
2005	126	7	3	2	-	-	£ 659,897
2006	111	3	-	1	-	-	£ 50,850
2007	125	5	1	3	-	-	£ 247,312

Principal Performances

2005   2nd Gallinule Stakes (G3) (3yo) Curragh (10f)
        2nd Irish Derby Stakes (G1) (3yo colts & fillies) Curragh (12f)
        Won Grand Prix de Paris (G1) (3yo colts & fillies) Longchamp (12f)
        Won St Leger Stakes (G1) (3yo colts & fillies) Doncaster (14.6f)
2006   2nd Finale Stakes (Listed Race) Curragh (12f)
2007   2nd Ormonde Stakes (G3) Chester (13.4f)
        Won Coronation Cup (G1) Epsom (12f)
        2nd Hardwicke Stakes (G2) Royal Ascot (12f)
        2nd Irish St Leger Stakes (G1) Curragh (14f)

*****

S corpion fractured a hind pastern and was side-lined for a year before making a return to the racetrack in October 2006 when running well below his best. His victory at Epsom as a five-year-old, beating two other English classic winners, gave Scorpion his third G1 success. He was retired to Coolmore's Castle Hyde Stud in County Cork as a National Hunt stallion and currently stands at a fee of €4,000. Scorpion's unraced dam also bred Danish Rhapsody (1993 – LR Foundation S) and Garuda

(1994 – LR Magnolia S), both by Danehill, and Memories (1991, by Don't Forget Me – LR Solonaway S). Grandam Thistlewood was also unraced, but a half-sister to champion stayer Ardross (1975, by Run The Gantlet – G1 Ascot Gold Cup twice, Prix Royal-Oak). Thistlewood's half-sister Gesedeh (1983, by Ela-Mana-Mou – G3 Prix de Flore) was the grandam of Electrocutionist (2001, by Red Ransom – G1 International S, Dubai World Cup). Le Melody (1971, by Levmoss), third dam of Scorpion, was a minor winner in Ireland out of Arctic Melody (1962, by Arctic Slave – Musidora S).

2521805

Above: Frankie Dettori wins the St Leger on **SCORPION**; The Geezer, bought to join Godolphin at the end of the season, finishes second. It was **AIDAN O'BRIEN**'s (below centre) third win in this classic in five years after Milan (p230) and Brian Boru (p250). Below left: **FRANKIE DETTORI** celebrates his tenth English classic victory and his third St Leger following Classic Cliché (p162) and Shantou (p174). The jockey's decision to ride Scorpion for their rival Coolmore was said to have upset his retaining Godolphin stable and left a 'sour taste' in the mouth of Sheikh Mohammed Al-Maktoum. Below right: SCORPION (Kieren Fallon) wins the Grand Prix de Paris at Longchamp. It was the first time this historic race, first run in 1863, had been contested over twelve furlongs.

1422105

1407205

Below left: **SCORPION** (Mick Kinane) returns to his best and wins the Coronation Cup beating stable companion Septimus and Maraahel (left). Below right: Scorpion gave part-owner **MICHAEL TABOR** his second St Leger.

2013507

1713196

GEORGE WASHINGTON (IRE)

Bay colt, foaled 1 March 2003
By Danehill (USA) out of Bordighera (USA) by Alysheba (USA)
Bred by Lael Stables
Owned by Mrs John Magnier, Michael Tabor and Derrick Smith
Trained by Aidan P. O'Brien at Ballydoyle, Cashel, Co. Tipperary.

1022006

Racing Record

Year	Timeform Annual Rating	Starts	Wins	2nd	3rd	4th	Prize Money
2005	118	5	4	-	1	-	£ 317,350
2006	133	5	2	1	1	-	£ 392,853
2007	124	4	-	-	2	1	£ 95,775

Principal Performances

2005   Won Railway Stakes (G2) (2yo) Curragh (6f)
      Won Phoenix Stakes (G1) (2yo colts & fillies) Curragh (6f)
      Won National Stakes (G1) (2yo colts & fillies) Curragh (7f)
2006   Won 2000 Guineas Stakes (G1) (3yo colts & fillies) Newmarket (8f)
      2nd Irish 2000 Guineas Stakes (G1) (3yo colts & fillies) Curragh (8f)
      3rd Celebration Mile (G2) Goodwood (8f)
      Won Queen Elizabeth II Stakes (G1) Ascot (8f)
2007   4th Queen Anne Stakes (G1) Royal Ascot (8f)
      3rd Eclipse Stakes (G1) Sandown Park (10f)
      3rd Prix du Moulin de Longchamp (G1) Longchamp (8f)

*****

*G*eorge Washington was bought for 1.15m guineas at Tattersalls October Yearling Sales in Newmarket, the highest priced yearling of his year, and proved worth every penny. A top-class two-year-old, he trained on into the best colt of his generation and is rated a very good 2000 Guineas winner. George Washington was retired at the end of 2006 to Coolmore Stud at Fethard, County Tipperary but was returned to training after proving almost totally infertile. His only foal, a filly named Date With Destiny, was sold for 320,000 guineas as a yearling and was a minor winner for

Richard Hannon's stable. Sadly, George Washington broke his off-fore leg at Monmouth Park in November 2007 and had to be put down. Bordighera, a minor winner and stakes placed in France, was out of Blue Tip (G3 Prix Penelope), and before George Washington had foaled Grandera (1998, by Grand Lodge – G1 Prince of Wales's S, Irish Champion S).

0412006

Above: **GEORGE WASHINGTON** (Kieren Fallon) hangs badly right inside the final furlong but wins the 2000 Guineas comfortably from subsequent Derby winner, Sir Percy (right).

Left: **AIDAN O'BRIEN** with his difficult charge George Washington (Mick Kinane) at Goodwood before the Celebration Mile. After the horse's apparent reluctance to go through with his effort in this race, Timeform came close to describing George Washington as 'unreliable, for temperamental or other reasons'. The colt had refused to leave the winner's circle after one of his races as a two-year-old and refused to enter it at Newmarket after the 2000 Guineas. O'Brien described George Washington's temperamental quirks as being caused by 'brilliance and arrogance often coming together'. Horse psychologist Kelly Marks, speaking on BBC television, called O'Brien's remarks 'spin' and added that 'arrogance is a purely human trait'.

0120206

0322006

Above and opposite: **GEORGE WASHINGTON** (Mick Kinane) on his best behaviour, wins the Queen Elizabeth II Stakes beating Araafa, Court Masterpiece (right) and Killybegs (rail).

SPECIOSA (IRE)

Bay filly, foaled 28 April 2003
By Danehill Dancer (IRE) out of Specifically (USA) by Sky Classic (CAN)
Bred by K. and Mrs Cullen
Owned by Michael Sly, Pamela Sly and Dr. Thomas Davies
Trained by Pamela Sly at Singlecote, Thorney, Peterborough.

0121006

Racing Record

Year	Timeform Annual Rating	Starts	Wins	2nd	3rd	4th	Prize Money
2005	104	6	2	1	2	-	£ 57,256
2006	115	5	2	-	-	1	£ 240,817
2007	115	6	-	2	-	-	£ 45,555

Principal Performances

2005　3rd May Hill Stakes (G3) (2yo fillies) Doncaster (8f)
　　　　Won Rockfel Stakes (G2) (2yo fillies) Newmarket (7f)
2006　Won Nell Gwyn Stakes (G3) (3yo fillies) Newmarket (7f)
　　　　Won 1000 Guineas Stakes (G1) (3yo fillies) Newmarket (8f)
　　　　4th Oaks Stakes (G1) (3yo fillies) Epsom (12f)
2007　2nd Earl of Sefton Stakes (G3) Newmarket (9f)
　　　　2nd Pretty Polly Stakes (G1) (Fillies & mares) Curragh (10f)

*****

*S*peciosa was a 30,000 guineas purchase at the April 2005 Doncaster Breeze-Up Sale. After the filly had won the Rockfel Stakes in October, at least two large offers were made for her during the winter of 2005/6; one of £1m being turned down by the other two owners after Pamela Sly recommended it was accepted. They decided to 'live the dream', as they put it. On Guineas day, Speciosa made all the running on her favoured soft ground and won decisively from a field of fillies which were poor by classic standards, although second-placed Confidential Lady did go on to show slightly better form when winning the classic Prix de Diane at Chantilly. Speciosa did not win again but

278

was twice able to reproduce her best form as a four-year-old. Retained by her owners as a broodmare, of Speciosa's first four foals, Vermuyden (2009, by Oasis Dream), Specialty (2010, by Oasis Dream), Asteroidea (2011, by Sea The Stars) and Sperrin (2012, by Dubawi), Specialty and Asteroidea are minor winners. Her 2013 filly by Teofilo is in training with Pamela Sly and was followed by a 2014 colt by Dutch Art. Speciosa was due to foal to Dark Angel in May 2015, after which she will be rested for a year. Specifically, a minor winner in the U.S., was purchased by Newsells Park Stud for 1.85m guineas, in foal to Danehill Dancer, at the Tattersalls 2005 December Sales, a far cry from the $17,000 she made at Keeneland in 2000. She and her half-sister Pride (2000, by Peintre Celebre – G1 Grand Prix de Saint-Cloud, Champion S) are out of Specificity (LR George Stubbs S), a half-sister to Touching Wood (p34) out of Mandera (1970, by Vaguely Noble – G3 Princess Royal S). This is the family of the outstanding racehorse and sire Bold Ruler (1954, by Nasrullah).

0912206

Above: **SPECIOSA** wins a first classic for her connections, beating Confidential Lady and Nasheej (left) in the 1000 Guineas on a rain-soaked day at Newmarket.

1839194

2714796

Above left: Irish-born jockey **MICHAEL FENTON** was winning his second European classic; he had previously won the Oaks d'Italia on Zanzibar for Newmarket trainer, Michael Bell. Above right: **DANEHILL DANCER** (1993, by Danehill), pictured here with Mick Kinane in the saddle, was best as a two-year-old winning the G1 Phoenix and National Stakes. He has been a very successful sire with his G1 winners including Where Or When (Queen Elizabeth II S), Planteur (Prix Ganay), Again (Moyglare Stud S, Irish 1000 Guineas), Choisir (Golden Jubilee S), Lillie Langtry (Coronation S, Matron S), Mastercraftsman (National S, Irish 2000 Guineas, St James's Palace S), Dancing Rain (p334) and Legatissimo (p374). The stallion was retired due to declining fertility in 2014. Left: **PAMELA SLY** was the first British woman to officially train an English classic winner. She described herself as 'only a Fenland farmer' and Speciosa as 'a witch'. The filly was on a magnesium supplement as a two-year-old in an effort to calm her down.
1510606

ALEXANDROVA (IRE)

Bay filly, foaled 23 April 2003
By Sadler's Wells (USA) out of Shouk (GB) by Shirley Heights (GB)
Bred by Quay Bloodstock
Owned by Mrs John Magnier, Michael Tabor and Derrick Smith
Trained by Aidan P. O'Brien at Ballydoyle, Cashel, Co. Tipperary.

3114006

Racing Record

Year	Timeform Annual Rating	Starts	Wins	2nd	3rd	4th	Prize Money
2005	114	4	1	1	1	-	£ 47,011
2006	123	5	3	1	1	-	£ 605,253

Principal Performances

2005 2nd Fillies' Mile (G1) (2yo fillies) Newmarket (8f)
2006 2nd Musidora Stakes (G3) (3yo fillies) York (10.4f)
       Won Oaks Stakes (G1) (3yo fillies) Epsom (12f)
       Won Irish Oaks Stakes (G1) (3yo fillies) Curragh (12f)
       Won Yorkshire Oaks (G1) (Fillies & mares) York (12f)
       3rd Prix de l'Opera (G1) (Fillies & mares) Longchamp (10f)

*****

A lexandrova, a 420,000 guineas yearling purchase at Tattersalls October Sales at Newmarket, was far superior to rest of the middle-distance fillies of her classic year. She easily won three successive Oaks races at Epsom, the Curragh and York but the quality of the opposition was not sufficient to establish Alexandrova as anything better than an average winner of the Oaks. As a broodmare she has so far been slightly disappointing with Alex My Boy (2011, by Dalakhani – G2 Prix Kergorlay; G3 Prix de Barbeville) the only winner from her first three foals; Drops (2009, by Kingmambo) and Bella Qatara (2010, by Dansili) both being retired as maidens. Shouk, a minor winner in 1997, had previously produced Magical Romance (2002, by Barathea – G1 Cheveley Park S), sold at Tattersalls 2006 December Sales, in foal to Pivotal, for 4.6m guineas, then a world record price for a broodmare. Akexandrova is a full-sister to Masterofthehorse (2006 – 3rd G1 Derby S, 4th Irish Derby). This is the family of Pongee (2000, by Barathea – G2 Lancashire Oaks). Far back in the tail

280

female line can be found the name of Lost Soul (1931, by Solario), one of the foundation mares for Major Lionel Holliday's successful Cleaboy Stud, ancestress of English classic winners Neasham Belle and Hethersett (see p85).

2514006

Above and opposite: **ALEXANDROVA** (Kieren Fallon) powers to a six-lengths victory in the Oaks beating Rising Cross (striped sleeves), Short Skirt (left) and 1000 Guineas winner Speciosa (pink cap). This was a third Oaks victory for Aidan O'Brien and Fallon's fourth.

Left: **KIEREN FALLON** was born in Crusheen, County Clare on 22 February 1965. In a controversial riding career he has ridden over 2,550 winners in Great Britain and been champion jockey on six occasions. The low points have included a six-month ban for pulling colleague Stewart Webster off his horse after a race at Beverley in 1994, losing lucrative retainers with top trainers Henry Cecil and Michael Stoute, alcohol and drug problems; for the latter Fallon was banned from riding for a total of two years. He was acquitted from charges of race fixing in a high-profile trial at The Old Bailey in 2007. Fallon has sixteen English classic winners; 1000 Guineas: Sleepytime (p178), Wince (p202), Russian Rhythm (p244) and Virginia Waters (p266); 2000 Guineas: King's Best (p210), Golan (p222), Footstepsinthesand (p264), George Washington (p276) and Night Of Thunder (p360); Derby: Oath (p206), Kris Kin (p248) and North Light (p260); Oaks: Reams of Verse (p180), Ramruma (p204), Ouija Board (p258) and Alexandrova. Other top-class winners have included Oratorio (Eclipse S), Yeats (Ascot Gold Cup, Coronation Cup), Golan (King George VI & Queen Elizabeth S), Hurricane Run (Irish Derby, Prix de l'Arc de Triomphe) and Dylan Thomas (Irish Derby, Prix de l'Arc de Triomphe).

© Healy Racing

3519806

Above left: **ALEXANDROVA** wins the Irish Oaks beating Scottish Stage and Rising Cross (right) and (above right) completes her Oaks treble at York, ridden by Mick Kinane, deputising for the suspended Kieren Fallon.

SIR PERCY (GB)

Bay colt, foaled 27 January 2003
By Mark of Esteem (IRE) out of Percy's Lass (GB) by Blakeney (GB)
Bred by The Old Suffolk Stud, Hundon, Suffolk.
Owned by Anthony E. Pakenham
Trained by Marcus P. Tregoning at Kingwood House Stables, Lambourn.

1223706

Racing Record

Year	Timeform Annual Rating	Starts	Wins	2nd	3rd	4th	Prize Money
2005	122	4	4	-	-	-	£ 201,326
2006	129	3	1	1	-	-	£ 811,117
2007	122	3	-	-	-	1	£ 135,948

Principal Performances

2005   Won Vintage Stakes (G2) (2yo) Goodwood (7f)
       Won Dewhurst Stakes (G1) (2yo colts & fillies) Newmarket (7f)
2006   2nd 2000 Guineas Stakes (G1) (3yo colts & fillies) Newmarket (8f)
       Won Derby Stakes (G1) (3yo colts & fillies) Epsom (12f)
2007   4th Dubai Sheema Classic (G1) Nad Al Sheba, Dubai (12f turf)

*****

*S*ir Percy, a bargain-buy 16,000 guineas Tattersalls yearling, was a top-class two-year-old, training-on to become a classic winner at three. The colt returned stiff and jarred-up from Epsom and the exceptionally hot and dry summer forced his trainer to wait until the autumn before resuming any serious training. Sir Percy was unable to produce his best in four races after the Derby and his retirement to Lanwades Stud at Moulton, Newmarket was announced in August 2007. The stallion has also been shuttling to Rich Hill Stud in New Zealand for the southern hemisphere breeding season. Sir Percy has made a sound start at stud, siring Sir Andrew (G2 in N.Z.), Alla Speranza (G3 Kilternan S), Wake Forest (G3 Hamburg Trophy), Coquet (LR Montrose S), Sound Hearts (LR Pride S), Indigo Lady

(LR Silver S), Lady Pimpernel (G3 Robert J Frankel S), Nafaqa (LR Flying Scotsman S), Lady Tiana (G2 Lancashire Oaks) and Newsletter (LR Kilvington S). Percy's Lass, who died in 2003, won the G3 September Stakes and was a half-sister to Braiswick (1986, by King of Spain – G1 EP Taylor & G2 Sun Chariot S). More details of this excellent White Lodge Stud family can be found on page 263.

0214506

Above: Not since the dramatic Derby of 1913 had there been a four-horse finish to rival that won by **SIR PERCY**. In a move reminiscent of Ernie Johnson when he won the 1969 Derby on Sir Percy's maternal grandsire Blakeney, Martin Dwyer brings the colt up the rail to defeat Dragon Dancer (noseband) by a short-head with Dylan Thomas (pink cap) a head away in third and Hala Bek (left) a further short-head back in fourth place. This was a first Derby victory for all the winner's connections and second English classic for Dwyer, previously successful in the Oaks on Casual Look (see p246).

2124305

Above: **SIR PERCY** goes through his two-year-old season unbeaten and confirms himself a high-class colt by beating Horatio Nelson (right) and Opera Cape (left) in the Dewhurst Stakes.

1030799

Left: **MARCUS TREGONING** had his only English classic victory to date with Sir Percy. Right: 1969 Derby winner Blakeney at The National Stud during December 1986. **BLAKENEY** was a successful sire, his winners including Juliette Marny (Oaks S), Julio Mariner (St Leger S), Tyrnavos (Irish Derby), Mountain Lodge (Irish St Leger) and Roseate Tern (Yorkshire Oaks). Blakeney died in 1992 and is buried at The National Stud.

2135286

SIXTIES ICON (GB)

Bay colt, foaled 14 February 2003
By Galileo (IRE) out of Love Divine (GB) by Diesis (GB)
Bred by Lordship Stud, Newmarket, Suffolk
Owned by Mrs Susan Roy
Trained by Jeremy Noseda at Shalfleet Stables, Newmarket, Suffolk.

2020806

Racing Record

Year	Timeform Annual Rating	Starts	Wins	2nd	3rd	4th	Prize Money
2005	-	0	-	-	-	-	-
2006	125	7	3	-	1	-	£ 325,197
2007	125	3	1	-	-	-	£ 51,102
2008	120	8	4	1	-	-	£ 157,037

Principal Performances

2006 3rd King Edward VII Stakes (G2) (3yo colts & geldings) Ascot (12f)
       Won Gordon Stakes (G3) (3yo) Goodwood (12f)
       Won St Leger Stakes (G1) (3yo colts & fillies) York (13.9f)
2007 Won Jockey Club Stakes (G2) Newmarket (12f)
2008 2nd Jockey Club Stakes (G2) Newmarket (12f)
       Won Festival Stakes (Listed Race) Goodwood (9.9f)
       Won Glorious Stakes (G3) Goodwood (12f)
       Won Geoffrey Freer Stakes (G2) Newbury (13.3f)
       Won Cumberland Lodge Stakes (G3) Ascot (12f)

*****

S ixties Icon, a 230,000 guineas yearling purchase, improved steadily through his classic season *and won a sub-standard St Leger. Operated on for a wind infirmity after a mostly disappointing 2007, Sixties Icon came back as a five-year-old and added three more group race victories to his record. Retired to Norman Court Stud at West Tytherley near Salisbury in Wiltshire, Sixties Icon was advertised at a covering fee of £6,000 for 2015. With only four crops of racing age, early results for the stallion have been encouraging, his winners including Chilworth Icon (G3 Premio Primi Passi), Cruck*

*Realta (LR Ballymacoll Stud S), Audacia (LR Pipalong S) and Epsom Icon (LR Washington Singer S).
The family of Sixties Icon is covered in detail in the essay about his dam, the Oaks winner Love Divine
(p214). It remains to add that his fifth dam, Rich Relation (1952, by Midas), was a full-sister to Sybil's
Nephew (1948 – Dee S, 2nd Derby S) and a half-sister to Sybil's Niece (1951, by Admiral's Walk – Queen
Mary S), the dam of dual British champion sire (1975, 1981), Great Nephew (1962, by Honeyway – Prix
du Moulin, 2nd 2000 Guineas), the sire of Grundy (p11), Shergar (p18), Mrs Penny (1977 – G1 Cheveley
Park S, Prix de Diane, Prix Vermeille), Tolmi (1978 – G1 Coronation S) and Canadian champion
Carotene (1983, G1 Yellow Ribbon S, G1 Pan American H).*

1821006

Above: Due to reconstruction work at Doncaster, the St Leger was run at York for the first time since 1945.
SIXTIES ICON led home a 1-2-3 for first-crop stallion Galileo, whose own sire Sadler's Wells had achieved the
same feat in the Oaks of 2001 (p227). This was a fourth St Leger victory for winning jockey Frankie Dettori,
following Classic Cliché (p162), Shantou (p174) and Scorpion (p274). Before leaving York it should be mentioned
they are one of the worst offenders for the non-stop, mainly useless waffle, spewing out from most racecourse's
public address from midday onwards. Racecourse management seem to have forgotten that silence is golden.

2021006

1710314

Above left: **SUSAN ROY** with Sixties Icon in the winner's circle after the St Leger. Above right: **JEREMY
NOSEDA**; Sixties Icon is his only English classic winner to date. Noseda also trained Araafa (G1 Irish 2000
Guineas), Proclamation (G1 Sussex S) and Simply Perfect (G1 Fillies' Mile).

COCKNEY REBEL (IRE)

Bay colt, foaled 16 March 2004
By Val Royal (FR) out of Factice (USA) by Known Fact (USA)
Bred by Oak Lodge Bloodstock, Naas, Co. Kildare
Owned by Phil Cunningham
Trained by Geoffrey A. Huffer at Grange House, Newmarket, Suffolk.

1912107

Racing Record

Year	Timeform Annual Rating	Starts	Wins	2nd	3rd	4th	Prize Money
2006	108	3	1	1	1	-	£ 78,955
2007	127	3	2	-	-	-	£ 363,041

Principal Performances

2006 3rd Champagne Stakes (G2) (2yo colts & geldings) York (7f)
2007 Won 2000 Guineas Stakes (G1) (3yo colts & fillies) Newmarket (8f)
      Won Irish 2000 Guineas Stakes (G1) (3yo colts & fillies) Curragh (8f)

*****

A 30,000 guineas bargain-buy at the Doncaster St Leger yearling sale, Cockney Rebel was a *surprise winner of the 2000 Guineas but another classic victory in Ireland confirmed Newmarket was no fluke. A stress fracture of the pelvis sustained at Royal Ascot kept Cockney Rebel off the track during the summer but he was back in training and an intended runner in the Queen Elizabeth II Stakes when he injured his near-foreleg at exercise. Another three months rest was required and the decision was taken to retire the colt to The National Stud at Newmarket. Cockney Rebel was unpopular with British breeders and moved to Haras de Saint-Arnoult in Normandy during 2013. His best runners to date have been Redstart (G3 Fred Darling S), Cockney Sparrow (G2 Scottish Champion H), Groovejet (2nd G2 Park Hill S) and Street Buzz (NOR-LR Emirates Derby Mile). Cockney Rebel descends from a former top U.S. family, that of Golden Fleece (p30), which has underachieved in recent times. His great grandam Cornish Princess (1970, by Cornish Prince), was stakes placed and out of Rare*

Exchange (1960, by Swaps), a stakes placed half-sister to Jaipur (1959, by Nasrullah – Belmont S) and Rare Treat (1952, by Stymie), the grandam of U.S. champion What A Treat (1962, by Tudor Minstrel), herself the dam of Be My Guest (1974, by Northern Dancer – G2 Goodwood Mile), champion sire in Britain 1982.

Above: 25/1 shot **COCKNEY REBEL** wins the 2000 Guineas beating 33/1 outsider Vital Equine. The Tote Exacta Forecast (first two in the correct order) paid £1831.20. Not since Roland Gardens won at odds of 28/1 in 1978 had a 2000 Guineas winner been so neglected by the betting public.

Above left: **GEOFF HUFFER** won his only English classic with Cockney Rebel. Huffer was in his second spell with a training licence after a thirteen-year break, some of which had been spent in prison for VAT and duty fraud. Huffer's best horse prior to Cockney Rebel was Persian Heights, winner of the St James's Palace Stakes in 1988 and unluckily disqualified after winning the International Stakes at York on merit. Above centre: Owner **PHIL CUNNINGHAM** won his first classic with Cockney Rebel. Above right: Thirty-four year old **OLIVIER PESLIER** was winning his second English classic following High-Rise (see p194). Four times champion jockey in his native France, Peslier has ridden many big-race winners including Peintre Celebre (Prix du Jockey-Club, Grand Prix de Paris, Prix de l'Arc de Triomphe), Helissio (Grand Prix de Saint-Cloud, Prix de l'Arc de Triomphe, Prix Ganay), Falco (Poule d'Essai des Poulains), Golden Lilac and Torrestrella (both Poule d'Essai des Pouliches), Sagamix and Solemia (both Prix de l'Arc de Triomphe), Westerner (Prix du Cadran, Ascot Gold Cup), Goldikova (Prix de la Foret, Prix d'Ispahan twice, Prix Jacques Le Marois, Prix du Moulin, Queen Anne S, Breeders' Cup Mile three times), Intello (Prix du Jockey-Club), Queen Maud and Galikova (both Prix Vermeille) and Banks Hill (Prix Jacques Le Marois, Coronation S, Breeders' Cup Filly & Mare Turf). Other G1 winners for Peslier around the world include Jungle Pocket and Zenno Rob Roy (both Japan Cup), Winged Love (Irish Derby), Desert Prince, Saffron Walden and Cockney Rebel (all Irish 2000 Guineas), Doctor Dino (Man O'War S), Harbinger (King George VI & Queen Elizabeth S), Ouija Board and Vision d'Etat (both Prince of Wales's S), Keltos (Lockinge S), Air Express (Queen Elizabeth II S), Xaar (Prix de la Salamandre, Dewhurst S) and Borgia (Deutsches Derby). Once described by John McCririck during television coverage of the Breeders' Cup as weak in a finish, Peslier has proved the stupidity of that statement time and time again.

FINSCEAL BEO (IRE)

Chesnut filly, foaled 19 February 2004
By Mr Greeley (USA) ex Musical Treat (IRE) by Royal Academy (USA)
Bred by Rathbarry Stud, Fermoy, County Cork
Owned by Michael A. Ryan
Trained by James S. Bolger at Glebe House, Coolcullen, County Carlow.

3412307

Racing Record

Year	Timeform Annual Rating	Starts	Wins	2nd	3rd	4th	Prize Money
2006	118	5	3	1	-	-	£ 178,422
2007	123	6	2	1	-	-	£ 423,115
2008	120	6	-	1	2	-	£ 150,652

Principal Performances

2006   Won Prix Marcel Boussac (G1) (2yo fillies) Longchamp (8f)
         Won Rockfel Stakes (G2) (2yo fillies) Newmarket (7f)
2007   Won 1000 Guineas Stakes (G1) (3yo fillies) Newmarket (8f)
         2nd Poule d'Essai des Pouliches (G1) (3yo fillies) Longchamp (8f)
         Won Irish 1000 Guineas Stakes (G1) (3yo fillies) Curragh (8f)
2008   2nd Tattersalls Gold Cup (G1) Curragh (10.5f)
         3rd Queen Anne Stakes (G1) Royal Ascot (8f)

*****

*F*insceal Beo put up excellent performances when winning the English and Irish 1000 Guineas and *came very close to landing an ambitious classic treble never achieved before in the Poule d'Essai des Pouliches. Those three hard races within a month seemed to finish her and Finsceal Beo was never quite the same again, although she did show glimpses of her best form as a four-year-old. Finsceal Beo's first foal, Finsceal Fior (2010, by Galileo) was unraced due to injury; her second, Too The Stars*

288

(2011, by Sea The Stars) was a minor winner in 2014. Ol' Man River (2012, by Montjeu), her third foal, was bought at Goffs Orby Sales for €2.85m on behalf of a Coolmore partnership and won the G2 Beresford Stakes. Finsceal Beo's filly (2014, by Frankel), set an Irish record for a foal at auction when purchased for €1.8m at Goffs. Finsceal Beo herself was purchased at the Goffs Million Sale as a yearling for €340,000 and is the third foal of the stakes placed winner Musical Treat. The grandam, Mountain Ash (G3 Premio Royal Mares), was out of Red Berry (1971, by Great Nephew – 2nd Cheveley Park S), a daughter of 1000 Guineas runner-up Big Berry (1951, by Big Game). Big Berry's half-brother, Pipe of Peace (1954, by Supreme Court – Middle Park, Greenham & Gordon S) was third in both the 2000 Guineas and Derby. Their dam, Red Briar (1944, by Owen Tudor) was a three-parts sister to Red Ray (1947, by Hyperion), the great grandam of the brilliant racehorse and sire Mill Reef (p85).

2612307

Above and opposite: **FINSCEAL BEO** (Kevin Manning) wins the 1000 Guineas, beating Arch Swing (red cap) and Simply Perfect (grey) in impressive style. This was a second English classic victory for **JAMES BOLGER** (below left), who had won the Oaks sixteen years earlier with Jet Ski Lady (p118).

1305107   0333904   0227390

Above centre: Forty-year-old **KEVIN MANNING** won his first English classic on Finsceal Beo. Manning had previously won the Irish Oaks on Margarula and top races in Britain and France including the Dewhurst Stakes (Teofilo) and the Prix de l'Opera (Alexander Goldrun).

Above right: **ROYAL ACADEMY** is probably best remembered as the horse on which Lester Piggott made his remarkable comeback to the saddle at the age of fifty-five in 1990. Apart from that Breeders' Cup Mile victory, Royal Academy also won the July Cup and is the sire of Sleepytime (p178), Bullish Luck (G1 Champions Mile, Sha Tin twice), Oscar Schindler (G1 Irish St Leger twice), Bel Esprit (2xG1 in Australia), Zalaiyka (G1 Poule d'Essai des Pouliches), Ali-Royal (G1 Sussex S), Tamburlaine (2nd 2000 Guineas) and Val Royal (G1 Breeders' Cup Mile), the sire of Cockney Rebel (p286). Royal Academy was retired from stud duty in 2010 and died at Coolmore Australia on 22 February 2012.

SCORPION (IRE) : Bay 2002

	Montjeu (IRE) B. 1996	Sadler's Wells (USA) B. 1981	Northern Dancer (CAN)
			Fairy Bridge (USA)
		Floripedes (FR) B. 1985	Top Ville (IRE)
			Toute Cy (FR)
	Ardmelody (IRE) B. 1987	Law Society (USA) Br. 1982	Alleged (USA)
			Bold Bikini (USA)
		Thistlewood (IRE) Gr. 1979	Kalamoun (GB)
			Le Melody (IRE)

GEORGE WASHINGTON (IRE) : Bay 2003

	Danehill (USA) B. 1986	Danzig (USA) B. 1977	Northern Dancer (CAN)
			Pas De Nom (USA)
		Razyana (USA) B. 1981	His Majesty (USA)
			Spring Adieu (CAN)
	Bordighera (USA) Ch. 1992	Alysheba (USA) B. 1984	Alydar (USA)
			Bel Sheba (USA)
		Blue Tip (FR) B. 1982	Tip Moss (FR)
			As Blue (GB)

SPECIOSA (IRE) : Bay 2003

	Danehill Dancer (IRE) B. 1993	Danehill (USA) B. 1986	Danzig (USA)
			Razyana (USA)
		Mira Adonde (USA) B/br. 1986	Sharpen Up (GB)
			Lettre d'Amour (USA)
	Specifically (USA) B. 1994	Sky Classic (USA) Ch. 1987	Nijinsky (CAN)
			No Class (CAN)
		Specificity (USA) B. 1988	Alleged (USA)
			Mandera (USA)

ALEXANDROVA (IRE) : Bay 2003

	Sadler's Wells (USA) B. 1981	Northern Dancer (CAN) B. 1961	Nearctic (CAN)
			Natalma (USA)
		Fairy Bridge (USA) B. 1975	Bold Reason(USA)
			Special (USA)
	Shouk (GB) B. 1994	Shirley Heights (GB) B. 1975	Mill Reef (USA)
			Hardiemma (GB)
		Souk (IRE) B. 1988	Ahonoora (GB)
			Soumana (FR)

SIR PERCY (GB) : Bay 2003

		Darshaan (GB) Br. 1981	Shirley Heights (GB)
Mark of Esteem (IRE) B. 1993			Delsy (FR)
		Homage (GB) B. 1989	Ajdal (USA)
			Home Love (USA)
Percy's Lass (GB) B/br. 1984		Blakeney (GB) B. 1966	Hethersett (GB)
			Windmill Girl (GB)
		Laughing Girl (GB) B. 1973	Sassafras (FR)
			Violetta (ITY)

SIXTIES ICON (GB) : Bay 2003

		Sadler's Wells (USA) B. 1981	Northern Dancer (CAN)
Galileo (IRE) B. 1998			Fairy Bridge (USA)
		Urban Sea (USA) Ch. 1989	Miswaki (USA)
			Allegretta (GB)
Love Divine (GB) B. 1997		Diesis (GB) Ch. 1980	Sharpen Up (GB)
			Doubly Sure (GB)
		La Sky (IRE) B. 1988	Law Society (USA)
			Maryinsky (USA)

COCKNEY REBEL (IRE) : Bay 2004

		Royal Academy (USA) B. 1987	Nijinsky (CAN)
Val Royal (FR) B. 1996			Crimson Saint (USA)
		Vadlava (FR) Br. 1984	Bikala (IRE)
			Vadsa (USA)
Factice (USA) Ch. 1993		Known Fact (USA) Bl. 1977	In Reality (USA)
			Tamerett (USA)
		Wacky Princess (USA) Ch. 1986	Miswaki (USA)
			Cornish Princess (USA)

FINSCEAL BEO (IRE) : Chesnut 2004

		Gone West (USA) B. 1984	Mr Prospector (USA)
Mr Greeley (USA) Ch. 1992			Secrettame (USA)
		Long Legend (USA) Ch. 1978	Reviewer (USA)
			Lianga (USA)
Musical Treat (IRE) Ch. 1996		Royal Academy (USA) B. 1987	Nijinsky (CAN)
			Crimson Saint (USA)
		Mountain Ash (GB) B. 1989	Dominion (GB)
			Red Berry (GB)

LIGHT SHIFT (USA)

Bay filly, foaled 22 March 2004
By Kingmambo (USA) out of Lingerie (GB) by Shirley Heights (GB)
Bred by Flaxman Holdings Limited
Owned by Niarchos Family
Trained by Henry R.A. Cecil at Warren Place, Newmarket, Suffolk.

1517607

Racing Record

Year	Timeform Annual Rating	Starts	Wins	2nd	3rd	4th	Prize Money
2006	93	3	1	1	1	-	£ 8,500
2007	121	6	3	1	1	-	£ 338,608

Principal Performances

2007 Won Cheshire Oaks (Listed Race) (3yo fillies) Chester (11.4f)
Won Oaks Stakes (G1) (3yo fillies) Epsom (12f)
2nd Irish Oaks Stakes (G1) (3yo fillies) Curragh (12f)
3rd Nassau Stakes (G1) (Fillies & mares) Goodwood (9.9f)

*****

Light Shift was a slightly fortunate winner of the Oaks as the runner-up Peeping Fawn suffered a rough passage through the race and beat Light Shift twice afterwards at the Curragh and Goodwood. Light Shift was retained by the Niarchos family as a broodmare. Her first foal, Dr Yes (2009, by Dansili) won two minor races in 2012 for Sir Henry Cecil's stable. In both 2010 and 2011, the mare was barren to Galileo, but Light Shift successfully foaled a bay filly by Oasis Dream in 2012. The Oaks winner's dam Lingerie was retired still a maiden after twelve attempts in France but has made up for that at stud. Her first two foals, Limnos (1994, by Hector Protector – G2 Prix Jean de Chaudenay, G3 Prix Foy) and Shiva (1995, by Hector Protector – G1 Tattersalls Gold Cup, G3 Brigadier Gerard & Earl of Sefton S), were both bred in Japan. Grandam Northern Trick was a top-class runner, also racing in the Niarchos colours, as did all those previously mentioned, winning the French classics, Prix de Diane and Prix Vermeille and finishing second in the Prix de l'Arc de Triomphe. Smoking Sun (2009, by Smart Strike – G2 Prix d'Harcourt) descends from this family, as does Main Sequence (2009, by Aldebaran, G1 United Nations S, Turf Classic, Breeders Cup Turf, 2nd G1 Derby S), with Lingerie's daughter Burning Sunset (1997, by Caerleon) as respectively their dam and grandam.

292

3313507

Above: **LIGHT SHIFT** and Ted Durcan end a seven year classic drought for Henry Cecil, winning the Oaks beating the Aidan O'Brien trained duo, Peeping Fawn (left) and All My Loving (right). It was a twenty-fourth English classic victory for Cecil and eighth in the Oaks. The record for Oaks victories by a trainer is held by Robert Robson, who recorded thirteen wins between 1802 and 1825.

2913007

0113106

Above left: The fortunes of **HENRY CECIL**'s Warren Place stables at Newmarket had been in decline since Love Divine (see p214) won the Oaks in 2000. There had not been a classic winner since and the size of Cecil's string had gone from a full house of over two hundred to around sixty horses. There were signs of an upturn during 2006 which culminated in Passage of Time winning the Criterium de Saint-Cloud, the first Group 1 victory since Beat Hollow had won the Grand Prix de Paris in July 2000. The traditional Cecil standard flew over Warren Place again after the success of Light Shift. The flag depicting the Horn of Leys, which is said to have been given to one of Cecil's ancestors by King Robert the Bruce of Scotland, was raised at Warren Place after every Group 1 victory. Above right: Irishman **TED DURCAN** rode his first English classic winner on Light Shift.

AUTHORIZED (IRE)

Bay colt, foaled 14 February 2004
By Montjeu (IRE) out of Funsie (FR) by Saumarez (GB)
Bred by Marengo Investments, Knighton House Ltd and M. Kinane
Owned by Saleh Al Homaizi and Imad Al Sagar
Trained by Peter W. Chapple-Hyam at St. Gatien, Newmarket, Suffolk.

2218307

Racing Record

Year	Timeform Annual Rating	Starts	Wins	2nd	3rd	4th	Prize Money
2006	118	2	1	-	1	-	£ 95,366
2007	133	5	3	1	-	-	£ 1,191,296

Principal Performances

2006 Won Racing Post Trophy (G1) (2yo colts & fillies) Newbury (8f)
2007 Won Dante Stakes (G2) (3yo) York (10.4f)
      Won Derby Stakes (G1) (3yo colts & fillies) Epsom (12f)
      2nd Eclipse Stakes (G1) Sandown Park (10f)
      Won International Stakes (G1) York (10.4f)

*****

*A*uthorized was bought as a foal for 95,000 guineas on behalf of his Kuwaiti owners. Sent up to Tattersalls Sales again as a yearling, the colt was knocked down to Peter Chapple-Hyam for 400,000 guineas but remained in the same ownership. Easy 2007 victories at York and Epsom were followed by a tactically disastrous defeat at Sandown, where the winner raced alone up the stand's side rail. A good victory over top four-year-old Dylan Thomas in the International Stakes preceded a lamentable final performance in the Prix de l'Arc de Triomphe. Authorized was retired to Dalham Hall Stud in Newmarket having been acquired by Darley as a future stallion after the Derby. He was transferred to Haras du Logis at Louviere-en-Auge, Normandy for 2014. Authorized has made a good start at stud with the winners Ambivalent (G1 Pretty Polly S, G2 Middleton S), Complacent (G1 winner in Australia), Seal Of Approval (G1 British Champions Fillies & Mares S), Rehn's Nest (G3 Park Express S, 2nd G1 Irish 1000 Guineas), Sugar Boy (G3 Classic Trial S), Daksha (G3 Prix Allez France), Tiger

Roll (G1 Triumph Hurdle), Hartnell (AUS-G1 The BMW, G3 Bahrain Trophy, LR Queen's Vase), Honor Bound and Toujours L'Amour (LR Lingfield Oaks Trial S), Battalion (LR Foundation S) and Nichols Canyon (LR Noel Murless S, Prix Denisy), also a Grade 1 winner over hurdles. The unraced Funsie descends from the same family as Solemia (2008, by Poliglote – G1 Prix de l'Arc de Triomphe).

2913907

Above: **AUTHORIZED** wins the Derby beating Eagle Mountain (centre), Aqaleem (striped cap) and future St Leger winner Lucarno (right). Aidan O'Brien saddled eight runners, a record for this race, but only Eagle Mountain finished in the first four.

3314007
1818307

Above left: **FRANKIE DETTORI** celebrates his first Derby victory after fourteen losing rides. It was his twelfth English classic success and a second Derby for Peter Chapple-Hyam after Dr Devious (p126). Above right: **AUTHORIZED** and Dettori avenge their Eclipse Stakes defeat by Notnowcato (right) in the International Stakes, with Dylan Thomas splitting them.

Right: **MONTJEU**, pictured here at Ascot in 2000 with Mick Kinane, was a racehorse bordering on greatness with wins in the Prix du Jockey-Club, Irish Derby, Prix de l'Arc de Triomphe and King George VI and Queen Elizabeth Stakes. Before his death on 29 March 2012, Montjeu was the sire of many classic winners including Motivator (p270), Pour Moi (p336), Camelot (p340), Hurricane Run (Irish Derby, Prix de l'Arc de Triomphe, King George VI and Queen Elizabeth S), Fame And Glory (Criterium de Saint-Cloud, Irish Derby, Ascot Gold Cup, Tattersalls Gold Cup, Coronation Cup), Scorpion (p274), Masked Marvel (p338), and Leading Light (p358).

0524600

LUCARNO (USA)

Bay colt, foaled 10 February 2004
By Dynaformer (USA) out of Vignette (USA) by Diesis (GB)
Bred by Augustin Stable
Owned by George W. Strawbridge, Jr
Trained by John H. Gosden at Clarehaven Stables, Newmarket, Suffolk.

1418207

Racing Record

Year	Timeform Annual Rating	Starts	Wins	2nd	3rd	4th	Prize Money
2006	-	0	-	-	-	-	-
2007	121	8	4	2	-	2	£ 516,904
2008	121	6	1	-	-	-	£ 56,770

Principal Performances

2007   Won Fairway Stakes (Listed Race) (3yo) Newmarket (10f)
      4th Derby Stakes (G1) (3yo colts & fillies) Epsom (12f)
      2nd King Edward VII Stakes (G2) (3yo colts & geldings) Ascot (12f)
      4th Princess of Wales's Stakes (G2) Newmarket (12f)
      Won Great Voltigeur Stakes (G2) (3yo colts & geldings) York (12f)
      Won St Leger Stakes (G1) (3yo colts & fillies) Doncaster (14.6f)
2008   Won Princess of Wales's Stakes (G2) Newmarket (12f)

*****

*L*ucarno was below the very top-class of his generation and won a poor renewal of the St Leger to earn from Timeform one of the lowest ratings ever given to a winner of that classic (p390-1). *Lucarno was generally very disappointing as a four-year-old and was retired to Wood Farm Stud at Ellerdine in Shropshire. After relocating to France for 2012-13, Lucarno was brought to Shade Oak Stud at Ellesmere as a National Hunt stallion, his big, strong physique, soundness and excellent conformation making him eminently suitable for that role. It is early days for Lucarno as a jumps stallion, but on the flat he has sired Powder Hound, winner of two races and £32,744. The St Leger* *winner's dam won at listed level in the U.S. and Lucarno is her third live foal and second winner. The grandam Be Exclusive (G3 Prix Chloe) bred numerous winners, but none better than listed class. Felidia (1985, by Golden Fleece), a half-sister to Be Exclusive, produced Lexicon (1995, by Conquistador Cielo), a multiple stakes winner in California. This is a fairly ordinary branch of a powerful U.S. family – one has to go back in the tail-female line as far as The Apple (1886, by Hermit), imported from England in 1893, to find a mare of any significance.*

2819607

Above: **LUCARNO** (Jimmy Fortune) stays on well to win the St Leger beating Mahler (Mick Kinane).

1737992

3433204

2233204

Above left: **GEORGE STRAWBRIDGE** has enjoyed great success with his mostly home-bred horses in Britain, France and America. His winners include Selkirk (Queen Elizabeth II S), Silver Fling (Prix de l'Abbaye), Tikkanen (Breeders' Cup Turf), Turgeon (Prix Royal-Oak, Irish St Leger), Moonlight Cloud (six G1 races, including Prix Jacques Le Marois) and With Anticipation (Man O'War S twice).

Above centre: A native of Co. Wexford, thirty-five year old **JIMMY FORTUNE** won his first English classic on Lucarno. His other big-race winners include Raven's Pass (Queen Elizabeth II S), Oasis Dream (Middle Park S), Dar Re Mi (Yorkshire Oaks), Mount Abu (Prix de la Foret), and Virtual (Lockinge S).

Above right: **JOHN GOSDEN** was in his second year at Clarehaven Stables in Newmarket, having moved there from Manton after the end of the 2005 season. Lucarno was his fourth English classic victory following Shantou (see p174), Benny The Dip (p184) and Lahan (p212).

HENRYTHENAVIGATOR (USA)

Bay or brown colt, foaled 28 February 2005
By Kingmambo (USA) out of Sequoyah (IRE) by Sadler's Wells (USA)
Bred by Westrn Bloodstock
Owned by Mrs John Magnier
Trained by Aidan P. O'Brien at Ballydoyle, Cashel, Co. Tipperary.

3713508

Racing Record

Year	Timeform Annual Rating	Starts	Wins	2nd	3rd	4th	Prize Money
2007	115	4	2	1	1	-	£ 99,881
2008	131	7	4	2	-	1	£ 1,284,716

Principal Performances

2007   Won Coventry Stakes (G2) (2yo) Royal Ascot (6f)
      2nd Phoenix Stakes (G1) (2yo colts & fillies) Curragh (6f)
2008   Won 2000 Guineas Stakes (G1) (3yo colts & fillies) Newmarket (8f)
      Won Irish 2000 Guineas Stakes (G1) (3yo colts & fillies) Curragh (8f)
      Won St James's Palace Stakes (G1) (3yo colts) Royal Ascot (8f) (photo above)
      Won Sussex Stakes (G1) Goodwood (8f)
      2nd Queen Elizabeth II Stakes (G1) Ascot (8f)
      2nd Breeders' Cup Classic (G1) Santa Anita, USA (10f aw)

*****

*T*he highlight of the 2008 flat racing season was the rivalry between Raven's Pass and Henrythenavigator. The latter won the first three of their encounters, including the 200th running of the 2000 Guineas, but the more progressive Raven's Pass beat his arch-rival at both Ascot in September and Santa Anita in October to tip the Timeform ratings in his favour by two pounds. Henrythenavigator was retired to Coolmore's Ashford Stud in Kentucky at an initial fee of $65,000 but was later transferred to Coolmore Stud at Fethard in County Tipperary where he is currently priced at €15,000. His first crop were three-year-olds in 2013 and included George Vancouver (G1 Breeders' Cup Juvenile Turf) and Pedro The Great (G1 Phoenix S). The pick of Henrythenavigator's second crop has so far been Sudirman (G1 Phoenix S). Sequoyah (1998) and her full-sister Listen (2005) were also trained by Aidan O'Brien and won the Group 1 Moyglare Stud Stakes and Fillies' Mile respectively. Their dam Brigid won in France and was a sister to Or Vision (1983 – LR Prix Imprudence), the dam of Dolphin

298

Street (1990, by Bluebird – G1 Prix de la Foret), Insight (1995, by Sadler's Wells – G1 E.P. Taylor S) and Saffron Walden (1996, by Sadler's Wells – G1 Irish 2000 Guineas). Sequoyah has also bred Queen Cleopatra (2003, by Kingmambo – G3 1000 Guineas Trial S, 3rd G1 Irish 1000 Guineas, Prix de Diane). This is the family of U.S. champion two-year-old Silent Screen (1967, by Prince John).

3311808

Above: **HENRYTHENAVIGATOR** (John Murtagh) wins the 2000 Guineas beating subsequent Derby winner New Approach (see p304) by a nose, the first time this was given as the winning distance in an English classic.

1612008

2715608

Above left: **JOHN MURTAGH** celebrates after winning the 2000 Guineas on Henrythenavigator. It was Murtagh's fifth English classic victory and second in this race following Rock of Gibraltar (p232).

Above right: The third of five clashes between **HENRYTHENAVIGATOR** and Raven's Pass and the last time that the former finished in front. There is a head between the two colts in the Sussex Stakes.

Right: **KINGMAMBO** was a top-class miler winning the Poule d'Essai des Poulains, St James's Palace Stakes and Prix du Moulin. He excelled as a stallion siring many top level winners including Lemon Drop Kid (Belmont S), King's Best (p210), Campanologist (4 G1 wins in Europe), Russian Rhythm (p244), Rule Of Law (p262), Virginia Waters (p266), Light Shift (p292), El Condor Pasa (Japan Cup, Grand Prix de Saint-Cloud), King Kamehameha (Tokyo Yushun), Encke (p348), Alkaased (Grand Prix de Saint-Cloud, Japan Cup) and Divine Proportions (Poule d'Essai des Pouliches, Prix de Diane). Kingmambo was retired from stud duties in September 2010.

0834193

NATAGORA (FR)

Grey filly, foaled 18 February 2005
By Divine Light (JPN) out of Reinamixa (FR) by Linamix (FR)
Bred by Bertrand Gouin and Georges Duca
Owned by Stefan Friborg
Trained by Pascal Bary at Chantilly, Oise, France.

0106108

Racing Record

Year	Timeform Annual Rating	Starts	Wins	2nd	3rd	4th	Prize Money
2007	116	7	5	2	-	-	£ 265,649
2008	116	8	2	2	2	-	£ 531,473

Principal Performances

2007   Won Prix La Fleche (Listed Race) (2yo) Longchamp (5f)
        Won Prix du Bois (G3) (2yo) Maisons-Laffitte (5f)
        Won Prix Robert Papin (G2) (2yo colts & fillies) Maisons-Laffitte (5.5f)
        2nd Prix Morny (G1) (2yo colts & fillies) Deauville (6f)
        Won Cheveley Park Stakes (G1) (2yo fillies) Newmarket (6f)
2008   Won Prix Imprudence (Listed Race) (3yo fillies) Maisons-Laffitte (7f)
        Won 1000 Guineas Stakes (G1) (3yo fillies) Newmarket (8f)
        3rd Prix du Jockey-Club (G1) (3yo colts & fillies) Chantilly (10.5f)
        3rd Prix Rothschild (ex Prix d'Astarte) (G1) Deauville (8f)
        2nd Prix Jacques Le Marois (G1) Deauville (8f)
        2nd Prix de la Foret (G1) Longchamp (7f)

*****

N atagora was purchased for only €30,000 at Deauville Yearling Sales and was by a stallion bred and raced in Japan which stood at Haras de Lonray in Colombiers, France for just four seasons (2004-7) before being exported to Turkey. Divine Light's sire was Sunday Silence, by some distance the most influential stallion to have stood in Japan in the history of the sport, being champion sire there every year from 1995 to 2007. Natagora is now owned by Sheikh Hamdan Al-Maktoum and her first foal Rayaheen (2010, by Nayef) won a maiden race during 2012; her second Mumtaza (2011, by Nayef), proved to be little better than useless in 2013-14, but Raaqy (2013, by Dubawi) was a winner in 2015. Natagora was due to visit Frankel (p330) in 2015. Reinamixa won a French claimer and was a half-sister to listed winner Reinstate (1987, by Kaldoun), out of Reine Margie, a winning juvenile. Reine Margie was half-sister to the dam of Resless Kara (1985, by Akarad – G1 Prix de Diane), out of Reine Des Sables (1966, by Mincio), a group placed winner in France, and a daughter of Begrolles (1956, by Fairey Fulmar - Prix d'Astarte).

3311908

Above: **NATAGORA** (Christophe Lemaire) wins the 1000 Guineas beating Spacious. This was the first French-trained winner of this classic since Hatoof (see p122) in 1992. Below left: Lemaire celebrates his first English classic victory. Below right: **LESTER PIGGOTT** (centre) presented the trophies for the 1000 Guineas to **CHRISTOPHE LEMAIRE** and **PASCAL BARY**.

0112108

2212208

Left: Natagora is to date the only English classic winner for **PASCAL BARY**.

Right: **NATAGORA** wins the Cheveley Park Stakes beating Fleeting Spirit. This was Pascal Bary's first winner in Britain.

0812105

3220607

301

LOOK HERE (GB)

Bay filly, foaled 28 February 2005
By Hernando (FR) out of Last Look (GB) by Rainbow Quest (USA)
Bred by Lawn Stud, Potterspury, Northamptonshire
Owned by Julian Richmond-Watson
Trained by Ralph Beckett at Whitsbury Racing Stables, Fordingbridge.

1914409

Racing Record

Year	Timeform Annual Rating	Starts	Wins	2nd	3rd	4th	Prize Money
2007	84	1	1	-	-	-	£ 4,534
2008	123	3	1	1	1	-	£ 271,653
2009	119	5	-	1	2	-	£ 73,518

Principal Performances

2008 2nd Oaks Trial Stakes (Listed Race) (3yo fillies) Lingfield (11.5f)
      Won Oaks Stakes (G1) (3yo fillies) Epsom (12f)
      3rd St Leger Stakes (G1) (3yo colts & fillies) Doncaster (14.6f)
2009 3rd Coronation Cup (G1) Epsom (12f)
      3rd Pretty Polly Stakes (G1) (Fillies & mares) Curragh (10f)
      2nd Arc Trial Stakes (G3) Newbury (11f)

*****

*L*ook Here was bred and raced by the-then senior steward of The Jockey Club, Julian Richmond-Watson, at his small stud which housed only five broodmares. After the Oaks the filly was sidelined by a problem the nature of which her connections were reluctant to disclose. This enraged sections of the racing media who seemed to think they had an automatic 'right to know'. The owner of a racehorse pays the trainer to train it and the jockey to ride it. They keep the whole racing show on the road and the only 'right to know' belongs to them, not to the media, the betting public or to bookmakers. Look Here was kept in training at four but her form declined slightly and she was unable to win again. Her first foal Sea Here (2011, by Sea The Stars) failed to win in Britain and was exported to Qatar. Hereawi (2013, by Dubawi) is also in training with Ralph Beckett. Last Look was unraced and died in 2007 after producing a dead foal by Royal Applause. Look Here was by some distance the *best of her dam's seven previous foals, which all won. Grandam Derniere Danse failed to win but was a three-parts sister to Noblequest (1982, by Gay Mecene - G1 Prix de la Salamandre). Third-dam Dance Quest (1981, by Green Dancer), also bred Divine Danse (1988, by Kris – G2 Prix du Gros-Chene, 2nd G1 Prix Morny) and Pursuit of Love (1989, by Groom Dancer – G2 Prix Maurice de Gheest, 2nd G1 July Cup, 3rd 2000 Guineas). The fourth dam of Look Here was the good sprinter, Polyponder (1974, by Barbizon – G3 Prix du Gros-Chene).*

0213108

Above: **LOOK HERE** (Seb Sanders) wins the Oaks beating Moonstone (pink colours) and Katiyra (rail). At 33/1 she was the longest priced Oaks winner since Jet Ski Lady (see p118) started at 50/1 in 1991. Below: Look Here was a first English classic winner for **JULIAN RICHMOND-WATSON** (left), **RALPH BECKETT** and **SEB SANDERS** (right).

0410114   2009114   2227604

Left: **HERNANDO** (1990, by Niniski), won the Prix du Jockey-Club and the Prix Lupin in 1993. He proved a successful stallion for Lanwades Stud at Moulton near Newmarket siring Holding Court (Prix du Jockey-Club), Sulamani (6 G1 victories incl. Prix du Jockey-Club, International S, Arlington Million, Turf Classic S, Canadian International), Gitano Hernando (G1 Goodwood S), Casual Conquest (G1 Tattersalls Gold Cup), Foreign Affairs (12 races & £377,594), Alianthus (7 stakes races & £340,440), Rainbow Peak (G1 Gran Premio del Jockey Club) and Look Here. Hernando died during 2013.

0140193

303

NEW APPROACH (IRE)

Chestnut colt, foaled 18 February 2005
By Galileo (IRE) out of Park Express (IRE) by Ahonoora (GB)
Bred by Lodge Park Stud, Freshford, Co. Kilkenny
2007: Owned by Mrs James S. Bolger
2008: Owned by H.R.H. Princess Haya of Jordan
Trained by James S. Bolger at Glebe House, Coolcullen, Co. Carlow.

0917708

Racing Record

Year	Timeform Annual Rating	Starts	Wins	2nd	3rd	4th	Prize Money
2007	127	5	5	-	-	-	£ 357,322
2008	132	6	3	2	1	-	£ 1,634,746

Principal Performances

2007 Won Tyros Stakes (G3) (2yo) Leopardstown (7f)
      Won E.B.F. Futurity Stakes (G2) (2yo) Curragh (7f)
      Won National Stakes (G1) (2yo colts & fillies) Curragh (7f)
      Won Dewhurst Stakes (G1) (2yo colts & fillies) Newmarket (7f)
2008 2nd 2000 Guineas Stakes (G1) (3yo colts & fillies) Newmarket (8f)
      2nd Irish 2000 Guineas Stakes (G1) (3yo colts & fillies) Curragh (8f)
      Won Derby Stakes (G1) (3yo colts & fillies) Epsom (12f)
      3rd International Stakes (G1) Newmarket (10f)
      Won Irish Champion Stakes (G1) Leopardstown (10f)
      Won Champion Stakes (G1) Newmarket (10f)

*****

*N*ew Approach was a €430,000 yearling purchase at Goffs, his breeder Seamus Burns immediately buying back half of the colt. Burns' reinvestment bore fruit when Sheikh Mohammed's Darley Stud Management purchased his share in early-September 2007, though New Approach continued to race in Mrs Jackie Bolger's colours for the remainder of the year. Darley purchased the Bolger-owned half of the colt in November and ownership for the rest of his racing career passed to Sheikh Mohammed's wife, Princess Haya. In April 2008, twelve days before the 2000

Guineas, James Bolger announced that New Approach was unlikely to run in the Epsom Derby and the colt was taken out of the ante-post betting on the race. After the Irish 2000 Guineas, Bolger changed his mind and New Approach was declared at the five-day stage for the Derby amid press accusations of showing 'total contempt for punters'. Some cynics might speculate that a good many of these 'punters' might have been members of the racing media themselves and their various associates. New Approach was retired to Dalham Hall Stud at Newmarket at an initial fee of £30,000 and made a sensational start with his first three-year-olds in 2013. They included two English classic winners, Dawn Approach (p350) and Talent (p354), and Libertarian (G2 Dante S, 2nd Derby S). More good victories followed with May's Dream (G1 Australasian Oaks), Sultanina (G3 Pinnacle S, G1 Nassau S), Ceisteach (G3 Robert G Dick Memorial S), Elliptique (G3 Grand Prix de Vichy), Herald The Dawn (G2 Futurity S) and Tha'ir (LR Gala S). Park Express (1983 – G1 Irish Champion S) died in 2006 and had previously bred Shinko Forest (1993, by Green Desert), a top-level winner in Japan, and Dazzling Park (1996, by Warning – G3 Matron S, 3rd Irish 1000 Guineas). Third dam Lachine (1960, by Grey Sovereign) won the Ebbisham Stakes. This is the family of European stakes winners Waky Nao (1993, by Alzao – G1 Premio Vittorio di Capua) and Bandari (1999, by Alhaarth – G2 Hardwicke & Great Voltigeur S).

1913308

Above: **NEW APPROACH** (Kevin Manning) wins the Derby beating Tartan Bearer, despite engaging in a sustained fight with his jockey for over half the race.

2713308

1810108

Above left: **PRINCESS HAYA** (above centre) and Sheikh Mohammed lead in New Approach after the Derby. It was a first victory in this classic for all the winner's connections. Above right and opposite: **NEW APPROACH** and Kevin Manning win the Champion Stakes; the first Derby winner to triumph in this race since Sir Ivor in 1968.

CONDUIT (IRE)

Chesnut colt, foaled 23 March 2005
By Dalakhani (IRE) out of Well Head (IRE) by Sadler's Wells (USA)
Bred by Ballymacoll Stud Farm Ltd.
Owned by Ballymacoll Stud
Trained by Sir Michael Stoute at Freemason Lodge, Newmarket, Suffolk.

1614309

Racing Record

Year	Timeform Annual Rating	Starts	Wins	2nd	3rd	4th	Prize Money
2007	86	3	1	-	1	-	£ 4,368
2008	130	6	4	1	1	-	£ 1,273,625
2009	130	6	2	1	1	2	£ 2,273,854

Principal Performances

2008 2nd King Edward VII Stakes (G2) (3yo colts & geldings) Ascot (12f)
   Won Gordon Stakes (G3) (3yo) Goodwood (12f)
   Won St Leger Stakes (G1) (3yo colts & fillies) Doncaster (14.6f)
   Won Breeders' Cup Turf (G1) Santa Anita, U.S.A. (12f)
2009 3rd Eclipse Stakes (G1) Sandown (10f)
   Won King George VI and Queen Elizabeth Stakes (G1) Ascot (12f)
   4th Prix de l'Arc de Triomphe (G1) Longchamp (12f)
   Won Breeders' Cup Turf (G1) Santa Anita, U.S.A. (12f)
   4th Japan Cup (G1) Tokyo, Japan (12f turf)

*****

C onduit improved out of all recognition as a three-year-old and ended 2008 as the joint highest Timeform rated winner of the St Leger since Reference Point (see p78). The colt was able to confirm this rating in 2009, winning a second Breeders' Cup Turf and the first to do so outright - High

Chaparral (p238) had dead-heated when completing his double in that race. Conduit was retired to stand at Shigeyuki Okada's Big Red Farm, Hokkaido in Japan but proved unpopular with Japanese breeders and during the summer of 2015 was sold to Tullyraine House Stud at Banbridge in County Down to replace the Irish Derby winner, Winged Love (1992, by In The Wings), who had died in May 2015. Apart from Conduit, Well Head bred six other winners, the best of the rest was Hard Top (2002, by Darshaan – G2 Great Voltigeur S). Minor winner Spring Symphony (1998), a sister to Hard Top, is the dam of Arab Spring (2010, by Monsun – G3 John Porter S). Well Head sadly died after foaling Conduit and the colt had to be fostered. There are more details about this successful Ballymacoll family in the pages covering Sun Princess (p44-5) and Millenary (p220-1).

2516308

Above: After saddling twenty-five losers, including five runners-up, since his first attempt on the race in 1974, Sir Michael Stoute finally wins the St Leger with **CONDUIT** (Frankie Dettori) beating Unsung Heroine (right) and Oaks winner Look Here (p302). This was a fifth St Leger victory for Dettori and his thirteenth English classic.

2714309

Above: **CONDUIT** (Ryan Moore) wins the King George VI and Queen Elizabeth Stakes beating Tartan Bearer, a full-brother to Golan (p222), and Ask. For the first time in the relatively short history of this race (it was inaugurated in 1951, being run in its first year as the King George VI and Queen Elizabeth Festival of Britain Stakes), all the first three were trained at the same stable. In addition, the first two finishers were owned and bred by Ballymacoll Stud.

LIGHT SHIFT (USA) : Bay 2004

		Mr Prospector (USA) B. 1970	Raise A Native (USA)
	Kingmambo (USA) B. 1990		Gold Digger (USA)
		Miesque (USA) B. 1984	Nureyev (USA)
			Pasadoble (USA)
		Shirley Heights (GB) B. 1975	Mill Reef (USA)
	Lingerie (GB) B. 1988		Hardiemma (GB)
		Northern Trick (USA) Ch. 1981	Northern Dancer (CAN)
			Trick Chick (USA)

AUTHORIZED (IRE) : Bay 2004

		Sadler's Wells (USA) B. 1981	Northern Dancer (CAN)
	Montjeu (IRE) B. 1996		Fairy Bridge (USA)
		Floripedes (FR) B. 1985	Top Ville (IRE)
			Toute Cy (FR)
		Saumarez (GB) B/br. 1987	Rainbow Quest (USA)
	Funsie (FR) B. 1999		Fiesta Fun (GB)
		Vallee Dansante (USA) B. 1981	Lyphard (USA)
			Green Valley (FR)

LUCARNO (USA) : Bay 2004

		Roberto (USA) B. 1969	Hail To Reason (USA)
	Dynaformer (USA) B/br. 1985		Bramalea (USA)
		Andover Way (USA) B/br. 1978	His Majesty (USA)
			On The Trail (USA)
		Diesis (GB) Ch. 1980	Sharpen Up (GB)
	Vignette (USA) B. 1995		Doubly Sure (GB)
		Be Exclusive (IRE) B. 1986	Be My Guest (USA)
			Exclusive Fable (USA)

HENRYTHENAVIGATOR (USA) : Bay 2005

		Mr Prospector (USA) B. 1970	Raise A Native (USA)
	Kingmambo (USA) B. 1990		Gold Digger (USA)
		Miesque (USA) B. 1984	Nureyev (USA)
			Pasadoble (USA)
		Sadler's Wells (USA) B. 1981	Northern Dancer (CAN)
	Sequoyah (IRE) B. 1998		Fairy Bridge (USA)
		Brigid (USA) Ch. 1991	Irish River (FR)
			Luv Luvin' (USA)

NATAGORA (FR) : Grey 2005

Divine Light (JPN) B/br. 1995	Sunday Silence (USA) B/br. 1986	Halo (USA)
		Wishing Well (USA)
	Meld Sport (JPN) Ch. 1979	Northern Taste (CAN)
		Shadai Prima (JPN)
Reinamixa (FR) Gr. 1994	Linamix (FR) Gr. 1987	Mendez (FR)
		Lunadix (FR)
	Reine Margie (FR) Ch. 1981	Margouillat (FR)
		Reine Des Sables (FR)

LOOK HERE (GB) : Bay 2005

Hernando (FR) B. 1990	Niniski (USA) B. 1976	Nijinsky (CAN)
		Virginia Hills (USA)
	Whakilyric (USA) B. 1984	Miswaki (USA)
		Lyrism (USA)
Last Look (GB) Ch. 1995	Rainbow Quest (USA) B. 1981	Blushing Groom (FR)
		I Will Follow (USA)
	Derniere Danse (GB) B. 1987	Gay Mecene (USA)
		Dance Quest (FR)

NEW APPROACH (IRE) : Chesnut 2005

Galileo (IRE) B. 1998	Sadler's Wells (USA) B. 1981	Northern Dancer (CAN)
		Fairy Bridge (USA)
	Urban Sea (USA) Ch. 1989	Miswaki (USA)
		Allegretta (GB)
Park Express (IRE) Br. 1983	Ahonoora (GB) Ch. 1975	Lorenzaccio (GB)
		Helen Nichols (GB)
	Matcher (CAN) Br. 1966	Match (FR)
		Lachine (GB)

CONDUIT (IRE) : Chesnut 2005

Dalakhani (IRE) Gr. 2000	Darshaan (GB) Br. 1981	Shirley Heights (GB)
		Delsy (FR)
	Daltawa (IRE) Gr. 1989	Miswaki (USA)
		Damana (FR)
Well Head (IRE) B. 1989	Sadler's Wells (USA) B. 1981	Northern Dancer (CAN)
		Fairy Bridge (USA)
	River Dancer (IRE) B. 1983	Irish River (FR)
		Dancing Shadow (IRE)

SEA THE STARS (IRE)

Bay colt, foaled 6 April 2006
By Cape Cross (IRE) out of Urban Sea (USA) by Miswaki (USA)
Bred by Sunderland Holdings
Owned by Christopher Tsui
Trained by John M. Oxx at Currabeg, The Curragh, Co. Kildare.

2410309

Racing Record

Year	Timeform Annual Rating	Starts	Wins	2nd	3rd	4th	Prize Money
2008	109	3	2	-	-	1	£ 69,772
2009	140	6	6	-	-	-	£ 4,347,391

Principal Performances

2008 Won Beresford Stakes (G2) (2yo) Curragh (8f)
2009 Won 2000 Guineas Stakes (G1) (3yo colts & fillies) Newmarket (8f)
  Won Derby Stakes (G1) (3yo colts & fillies) Epsom (12f)
  Won Eclipse Stakes (G1) (3yo & upwards) Sandown (10f)
  Won International Stakes (G1) (3yo & upwards) York (10.4f)
  Won Irish Champion Stakes (G1) (3yo & upwards) Leopardstown (10f)
  Won Prix de l'Arc de Triomphe (G1) (3yo & upwards) Longchamp (12f)

*****

*I*n the words of Timeform's time-honoured definition of greatness, Sea The Stars was a racehorse 'of such superlative merit as to make him...far superior to the general run of classic winners'. He was certainly not 'the best horse I think we'll ever see' -an opinion voiced by Clare Balding on BBC TV. Clare was born in 1971, so missed Sea-Bird, Vaguely Noble and Nijinsky altogether and was still an infant when Mill Reef and Brigadier Gerard staked their claims to greatness during 1971-72. Tony Morris, the vastly experienced bloodstock correspondent for the Racing Post, wrote of Sea The Stars, 'I can't quite persuade myself that he would have beaten Sea-Bird...but I can believe... (he)... would have defeated every other great horse of my era...Vaguely Noble, Nijinsky, Mill Reef, Brigadier Gerard, Shergar and Dancing Brave.' Morris' carefully considered opinion carries a good deal more weight than that of

310

Clare Balding, who in common with many television sports pundits is over keen to insert as many 'greats' as possible into each programme. Brigadier Gerard would certainly have had too much speed for Sea The Stars over a mile. Could Sea The Stars have matched Dancing Brave's (p66) acceleration? Vaguely Noble was such a powerful and relentless galloper that even dual classic winner Sir Ivor could not get near enough to mount a challenge. The merit of Shergar is discussed on pages 18-19. Nijinsky is rated two pounds inferior and Mill Reef a pound better than Sea The Stars by Timeform in Racehorses of 1970 and 1971 respectively. This is a discussion that serves no real purpose and is only a matter of opinion. Surely it was enough just to enjoy the racehorse of 'superlative merit' that was Sea The Stars? The great colt was retired to the Aga Khan's Gilltown Stud at Kilcullen in County Kildare at a fee of €85,000. As a sire, Sea The Stars has made a sensational start with pattern winners My Titania (G3 Park S), Vazira (G3 Prix Vanteaux, G1 Prix Saint-Alary), Afternoon Sunlight (G3 1000 Guineas Trial S), Taghrooda (G1 Oaks S, King George VI & Queen Elizabeth S), Sea The Moon (G2 Union-Rennen, G1 Deutsches Derby), Zarshana (G3 Prix Minerve), Quasillo (G3 Bavarian Classic), All At Sea (LR Prix de Liancourt, Prix Zarkava) and Storm The Stars (G2 Great Voltigeur S, 2nd G1 Irish Derby, 3rd Derby S).

3110409

1920194

Above left: **SEA THE STARS** (Mick Kinane) wins the 2000 Guineas beating a good field that included Delegator (left), Rip Van Winkle, Lord Shanakill and Mastercraftsman. It was a first victory in this race for John Oxx and fourth for Kinane after Tirol (p104), Entrepreneur (p176) and King Of Kings (p188). Above right: **URBAN SEA** and Eric Saint-Martin won the 1993 Prix de l'Arc de Triomphe. She was a highly successful broodmare, her progeny including Black Sam Bellamy (1999, by Sadler's Wells – G1 Tattersalls Gold Cup), Galileo (p228), My Typhoon (2002, by Giant's Causeway – G1 Diana S) and listed placed Cherry Hinton (2002, by Green Desert, the dam of Bracelet (2011, by Montjeu – G1 Irish Oaks). Urban Sea descended from a good German family developed at Gestut Schlenderhan; her dam Allegretta (p211), a full-sister to Anno (1979 – G2 Deutsches St Leger), also produced King's Best (p210). Fifth dam Asterblute (1946, by Pharis) won the Deutsches Derby and Preis der Diana. Below right: A second English classic success for **SEA THE STARS** and Mick Kinane as they win the Derby beating four Aidan O'Brien trained colts, Fame And Glory (purple cap), Masterofthehorse (striped cap), Rip Van Winkle (left) and Golden Sword (blaze). It was a second Derby victory for **JOHN OXX** (below left) following Sinndar (p216) and third for Kinane, who had ridden Commander in Chief (p136) and Galileo. Mick Kinane (p137) retired at the end of the 2009 season.

1211809

GHANAATI (USA)

Bay filly, foaled 28 March 2006
By Giant's Causeway (USA) out of Sarayir (USA) by Mr Prospector (USA)
Bred by Shadwell Farm LLC
Owned by Hamdan Al-Maktoum
Trained by Barry W. Hills at Faringdon Place, Lambourn, Berkshire.

1310709

Racing Record

Year	Timeform Annual Rating	Starts	Wins	2nd	3rd	4th	Prize Money
2008	93	2	1	-	1	-	£ 4,584
2009	122	4	2	1	1	-	£ 457,128

Principal Performances

2009 Won 1000 Guineas Stakes (G1) (3yo fillies) Newmarket (8f)
      Won Coronation Stakes (G1) (3yo fillies) Royal Ascot (8f)
      3rd Sussex Stakes (G1) (3yo & upwards) Goodwood (8f)
      2nd Sun Chariot Stakes (G1) (3yo & upwards) (Fillies & mares) Newmarket (8f)

*****

G hanaati must surely be the first horse to win an English classic that had never raced on turf before. The filly went to Newmarket for the 1000 Guineas with her only racecourse experience being two poorly contested maiden events on the Polytrack at Kempton Park. In a market dominated by the odds-on Rainbow View, Ghanaati started at 20/1 and won decisively, following up with an even more impressive victory at Royal Ascot. After running well in defeat at Goodwood and Newmarket, she was retired to join her owner's broodmare band. Her first foal, Almuhalab (2011, by Dansili) has yet to win, but the second Alnashama (2012, by Dubawi) won a maiden race in 2015. Ghanaati was covered by Invincible Spirit at the Irish National Stud in 2015. Her dam Sarayir won the listed Oh So Sharp Stakes and also bred Mawatheeq (2005, by Danzig – G3 Cumberland Lodge S, 2nd G1 Champion S) and Rumoush (2007, by Rahy – LR Feilden S, 2nd G2 Park Hill S, 3rd G1 Oaks S). Sarayir was closely related to Nayef (1998, by Gulch – G1 Champion, International S, Prince of Wales's S, 2nd G1 King George VI & Queen Elizabeth S <see p223>) and a half-sister to Alwasmi (1984, by Northern Dancer – G3 John Porter S, 2nd G2 Jockey Club S), Nashwan (p96) and Unfuwain (p213). Their dam was the legendary

312

broodmare Height of Fashion (G2 Princess of Wales's S, G3 May Hill S, G3 Fillies' Mile), bred and raced by The Queen, but sold to Sheikh Hamdan in 1982 for whom she raced twice without success. Ghanaati's great grandam was The Queen's double classic winner Highclere (1971, by Queen's Hussar – G1 1000 Guineas, Prix de Diane), while her fifth dam Hypericum (1943, by Hyperion – 1000 Guineas), won the same classic for King George VI. This is also the family of another 1000 Guineas winner, Pebbles (p46).

0710709

Above and opposite: **GHANAATI** (Richard Hills) wins the 1000 Guineas beating Cuis Ghaire (check cap). This was the final English classic success for the jockey, who retired in March 2012.

1632000

1832894

2511881

Above left: **GIANT'S CAUSEWAY**, pictured here at Ascot with Mick Kinane, won five consecutive Group 1 races in 2000 including the Eclipse, Sussex and International Stakes. He has done well at stud siring Shamardal (4xG1 wins including Prix du Jockey-Club), Aragorn (G1 Breeders' Cup Mile), Eishin Apollon (G1 & £1,735,485 in Japan), Footstepsinthesand (p264) and Ghanaati. Above centre: **BARRY HILLS** won the last of his five English classics with Ghanaati following Enstone Spark (1000 Guineas 1978), Tap On Wood (2000 Guineas 1979), Moonax (p152) and Haafhd (p252). Other top-class horses trained by Hills include Rheingold (Prix de l'Arc de Triomphe), Dibidale (Irish & Yorkshire Oaks), Hawaiian Sound (Benson & Hedges Gold Cup), Cormorant Wood (Champion S), Distant Relative (Sussex S) Handsome Sailor (Nunthorpe S), Sure Blade (Queen Elizabeth II S), Royal Applause (Middle Park S), Storming Home (Champion S) and Gildoran (Ascot Gold Cup twice). Barry Hills retired in August 2011, handing over Faringdon Place to his son Charles. However, Barry's retirement proved short-lived as he took over Kingwood House Stables in Lambourn following the death of his eldest son John, in June 2014. Above right: **HER MAJESTY THE QUEEN** at Ascot after winning the Fillies' Mile with her Height Of Fashion, grandam of Ghanaati and the dam of the top-class colts Nashwan, Unfuwain and Nayef.

313

SARISKA (GB)

Bay filly, foaled 14 February 2006
By Pivotal (GB) out of Maycocks Bay (GB) by Muhtarram (USA)
Bred and owned by Lady Bamford
Trained by Michael L.W. Bell at Fitzroy Stables, Newmarket, Suffolk.

1615109

Racing Record

Year	Timeform Annual Rating	Starts	Wins	2nd	3rd	4th	Prize Money
2008	93	1	1	-	-	-	£ 4,857
2009	123	6	3	1	1	1	£ 618,677
2010	125	4	1	1	-	-	£ 105,190

Principal Performances

2009   Won Musidora Stakes (G3) (3yo fillies) York (10.4f)
        Won Oaks Stakes (G1) (3yo fillies) Epsom (12f)
        Won Irish Oaks Stakes (G1) (3yo fillies) Curragh (12f)
        2nd Yorkshire Oaks (G1) (Fillies & mares) York (12f)
        3rd Champion Stakes (G1) Newmarket (10f)
2010   Won Middleton Stakes (G2) (Fillies & mares) York (10.4f)
        2nd Coronation Cup (G1) Epsom (12f)

*****

S *ariska, so genuine and consistent in her classic season, unfortunately blotted her copybook at four-years-old. After winning at York and running very well at Epsom she refused to race in both subsequent starts and her retirement to stud was announced immediately with her first mating reported to be with Galileo (see p228). Maycocks Bay had other offspring that showed wayward tendencies. Her second foal, the listed winner Gull Wing (2004, by In The Wings) had refused to race on her last appearance at Doncaster and Zigato (2007, by Azamour) did not impress with his attitude either and it is to be hoped that Sariska does not pass on this trait to her own foals. Her first, Snow Moon (2012) has yet to race, Sariska foaled a colt by Frankel (p330) in 2015 and was then covered by*

314

Dubawi (p319). Maycocks Bay, a listed winner herself, was out of the unraced Beacon, a daughter of Mountain Lodge (1979, by Blakeney – G1 Irish St Leger). The fifth dam Eyewash (1946, by Blue Peter – Lancashire Oaks), bred several good winners including Sijui (1954, by Sayajirao – Fred Darling S), Collyria (1956, by Arctic Prince – Park Hill S) and Varinia (1963, by Charlottesville – Lingfield Oaks Trial S, 3rd Oaks S). Her dam All Moonshine (1941, by Bobsleigh), was a half-sister to Hyperion (p177) and dam of Mossborough (1947, by Nearco), the champion sire in Britain 1958. Sariska's half-sister Gull Wing is the dam of The Lark (2010, by Pivotal – G2 Park Hill S, 3rd G1 Oaks) and Eagle Top (2011, by Pivotal – G2 King Edward VII S, 2nd G1 King George VI & Queen Elizabeth S).

1411609

Above: **SARISKA** wins the Oaks beating Midday (rail) and High Heeled. This was a second English classic victory for jockey Jamie Spencer, who had previously won the St Leger on Brian Boru (p250), and first for owner/breeder **LADY CAROLE BAMFORD**'s (below left) Daylesford Stud at Moreton-in-Marsh in Gloucestershire. Below centre: **MICHAEL BELL** had his first Oaks success having won the Derby with Motivator (p270) in 2005.

1305115   1209114   0524296

Above right: **PIVOTAL**, pictured here with George Duffield up, was a top-class sprinter for Sir Mark Prescott's Heath House stables at Newmarket, winning the King's Stand and Nunthorpe Stakes. Pivotal has been a revelation since retiring to Cheveley Park Stud, siring the European classic winners Buzzword (Deutsches Derby), Halfway To Heaven and Saoire (both Irish 1000 Guineas), Falco (Poule d'Essai des Poulains) and Sariska. Other top level winners by Pivotal include Golden Apples (Yellow Ribbon S, Del Mar Oaks, Beverly D. S), Somnus (Prix de la Foret, Haydock Sprint Cup, Prix Maurice de Gheest), Peeress (Lockinge S, Sun Chariot S), Excellent Art (St James's Palace S), Kyllachy (G1 Nunthorpe S), Maarek (Prix de l'Abbaye), Immortal Verse (Coronation S, Prix Jacques Le Marois), Chorist (Pretty Polly S), Regal Parade (Haydock Sprint Cup, Prix Maurice de Gheest), Farhh (Champion S, Lockinge S), African Story (Dubai World Cup) and Queen's Jewel (Prix St-Alary).

MASTERY (GB)

Bay colt, foaled 25 February 2006
By Sulamani (IRE) out of Moyesii (USA) by Diesis (GB)
Bred by Darley
2008-March 2009: Owned by Hamdan Al-Maktoum and trained by
Mark S. Johnston at Kingsley House Stables, Middleham, Yorkshire
2009-10: Owned by Godolphin and trained by Saeed bin Suroor in Dubai and at Godolphin
Stables, Newmarket, Suffolk.

1315609

Racing Record

Year	Timeform Annual Rating	Starts	Wins	2nd	3rd	4th	Prize Money
2008	99	2	1	-	1	-	£ 4,780
2009	122	7	2	1	3	1	£ 809,415
2010	125	4	2	-	1	-	£ 840,653

Principal Performances

2009 Won Derby Italiano (G2) (3yo colts & fillies) Capannelle, Rome (11f)
      3rd Grand Prix de Paris (G1) (3yo colts & fillies) Longchamp (12f)
      2nd Great Voltigeur Stakes (G2) (3yo colts & geldings) York (12f)
      Won St Leger Stakes (G1) (3yo colts & fillies) Doncaster (14.6f)
2010 Won Floodlit Stakes (Listed Race) Kempton (12f Polytrack)
      Won Hong Kong Vase (G1) Sha Tin, Hong Kong (12f turf)

*****

*M*astery was transferred to the Godolphin operation after his first race as a three-year-old in *March 2009. The colt went on to win two classics and another Group 1 race in 2010 but cannot be considered any better than a below average winner of a poorly contested St Leger. It had been*

316

expected that Mastery would remain in training for 2011 but he was sold as a prospective stallion for export to Russia. His dam, a minor winner in France, has done well at stud, also producing Magic Tree (2002, by Timber Country), the dam of Mukhadram (2009, by Shamardal – G1 Eclipse S), Kirklees (2004, by Jade Robbery – G1 Gran Criterium) and Artisti (2005, by Cape Cross), the dam of Magic Artist (G3 Bavarian Classic, Premio Ambrosiano). Grandam Cherokee Rose (G1 Prix Maurice de Gheest, Haydock Sprint Cup) was a half-sister to Molesnes (1990, by Alleged – G1 Prix du Cadran). This is the family of Agar's Plough (1952, by Combat - Irish Oaks), the dam of Mesopotamia (1961, by Zarathustra – Railway & Chesham S) and fourth dam of Dance Machine (1982, by Green Dancer – Sweet Solera S), herself the dam of Halling (1991, by Diesis – G1 Eclipse S, International S).

2215609

Above: **MASTERY** (Ted Durcan) beats his better-fancied stablemate Kite Wood (no.4) (Frankie Dettori) to give Godolphin their fifth St Leger and first English classic success since Rule of Law (p262).

2615609

1517502

Above left: **SAEED BIN SUROOR** leads in his fifth St Leger winner for Godolphin following Classic Cliché (p162), Nedawi (p196), Mutafaweq (p208) and Rule of Law. For jockey **TED DURCAN** it was a first St Leger victory and second English classic after Light Shift (p292) in the 2007 Oaks. Above right: **SULAMANI** (1999, by Hernando) won the Prix du Jockey-Club (above) for the Niarchos Family in 2002 and five G1 races for Godolphin during 2003-4, including the International Stakes at York. Retired to Dalham Hall Stud at Newmarket and subsequently transferred to Haras du Logis in Normandy, Sulamani was not well supported by flat breeders. Mastery has been the only group class winner in Europe; in Brazil both Going Somewhere and Invictus won at G1 level. Sulamani now stands at Yorton Farm Stud near Welshpool as a National Hunt sire and has made a reasonable start in that role with Cash And Go (G1 Future Champions Novice H) and Rule The World (G2 Slaney Novice H) his best performers.

MAKFI (GB)

Bay colt, foaled 4 March 2007
By Dubawi (IRE) out of Dhelaal (GB) by Green Desert (USA)
Bred by Shadwell Estate Company Ltd.
Owned by Mathieu Offenstadt
Trained by Mikel Delzangles at Chantilly, Oise, France.

3411410

Racing Record

Year	Timeform Annual Rating	Starts	Wins	2nd	3rd	4th	Prize Money
2009	-	1	1	-	-	-	£ 11,650
2010	130	5	3	-	-	-	£ 573,072

Principal Performances

2010   Won Prix Djebel (G3) (3yo colts & geldings) Maisons-Laffitte (7f)
　　　 Won 2000 Guineas Stakes (G1) (3yo colts & fillies) Newmarket (8f)
　　　 Won Prix Jacques Le Marois (G1) Deauville (8f)

*****

*M*akfi, an unraced two-year-old from Marcus Tregoning's Lambourn yard, was culled by his breeder Sheikh Hamdan Al-Maktoum at Tattersalls Autumn Sales in Newmarket for 26,000 guineas. His new connections recouped nearly half of the purchase price when the colt won in late-November at Fontainebleau. Retired the winner of £584,722 in stakes, Makfi's owner enjoyed an even larger windfall when selling the colt for a reported £12m to Qatar sheikh, Fahad Al-Thani, to stand at his new Tweenhills Stud near Gloucester. Makfi has also shuttled to Westbury Stud at Karaka in New Zealand, standing at NZ$17,500, during the southern hemisphere breeding season. His offspring include Make Believe (G1 Poule d'Essai des Poulains), Maimara (G3 Prix de Lieurey), Cornwallville (LR Criterium de Languedoc) and Marky Mark (NZ-G1 Sires Produce S). It was announced during mid-October 2014 that Makfi would stand at the Aga Khan's Haras de Bonneval in Normandy for 2015. Dhelaal was unraced, but a half-sister to Alhaarth (1993, by Unfuwain – see p253). Their grandam

Green Valley (1967, by Val De Loir), also unraced, was dam of the top-class runner and stallion Green Dancer (1972, by Nijinsky – G1 Observer Gold Cup, Poule d'Essai des Poulains, Prix Lupin). This is the family of Sly Pola (1957, by Spy Song – Prix de l'Abbaye, Prix Robert Papin) and Authorised (p294).

3011410

Above: **MAKFI** wins a good renewal of the 2000 Guineas beating subsequent Group 1 winners Dick Turpin (Prix Jean Prat) and Canford Cliffs (Irish 2000 Guineas, St James's Palace S, Sussex S). At 33/1, Makfi was the longest priced winner of this classic since Bolkonski won for Henry Cecil in 1975.

2613404

© Unknown

0507209

Above left: **CHRISTOPHE LEMAIRE** won his second English classic on Makfi following Natagora (see p300) in the 1000 Guineas two years earlier. Above centre: Owner **MATHIEU OFFENSTADT**. Above right: **MIKEL DELZANGLES** was formerly assistant trainer to the late Jimmy Fitzgerald in Yorkshire and ten years with Alain de Royer-Dupre. Makfi was a first English classic winner for him.

Left: **DUBAWI** was the star of the solitary crop of the former Godolphin champion Dubai Millennium who died of grass sickness in April 2001. Dubawi won the Irish 2000 Guineas and Prix Jacques Le Marois for the same stable in 2005. He has done well at stud siring Monterosso and Prince Bishop (G1 Dubai World Cup), Lucky Nine (7xG1 wins in Singapore & Hong Kong), Secret Admirer (AUS-G1 Epsom H), Al Kazeem (Prince of Wales's S, Eclipse S), Akeed Mofeed (G1 Hong Kong Derby), Worthadd (G2 Derby Italiano), Hunter's Light (G1 Premio Roma, Jebel Hatta), Dubawi Heights (G1 Gamely S, Yellow Ribbon S), Poet's Voice (G1 Queen Elizabeth II S), Afsare (G2 Celebration Mile), Postponed (G1 King George VI & Queen Elizabeth S), Night Of Thunder (p360) and New Bay (G1 Prix du Jockey-Club). Dubawi stands at Dalham Hall Stud in Newmarket.
1619805

SPECIAL DUTY (GB)

Chesnut filly, foaled 12 February 2007
By Hennessy (USA) out of Quest To Peak (USA) by Distant View (USA)
Bred by Juddmonte Farms Limited
Owned by Khalid Abdullah
Trained by Christiane Head-Maarek at Chantilly, Oise, France.

2816209

Racing Record

Year	Timeform Annual Rating	Starts	Wins	2nd	3rd	4th	Prize Money
2009	118	4	2	2	-	-	£ 256,811
2010	113	6	2	-	1	-	£ 465,248

Principal Performances

2009   Won Prix Robert Papin (G2) (2yo colts & fillies) Maisons-Laffitte (5.5f)
       2nd Prix Morny (G1) (2yo colts & fillies) Deauville (6f)
       Won Cheveley Park Stakes (G1) (2yo fillies) Newmarket (6f)
2010   3rd Prix Imprudence (G3) (3yo fillies) Maisons-Laffitte (7f)
       Won 1000 Guineas Stakes (G1) (3yo fillies) Newmarket (8f)
       Won Poule d'Essai des Pouliches (G1) (3yo fillies) Longchamp (8f)

*****

*S*pecial Duty, unusually for a classic winner, let alone a double classic winner, was rated higher as a two-year-old by Timeform than she was at three. However, this filly was a very special dual classic winner, unique in that she was awarded both races in the steward's room. Raceform commented that 'she was slightly fortunate' to win the 1000 Guineas on the disqualification of Jacqueline Quest. They must have been using the wrong glasses as Special Duty was bumped and carried right by the 'winner' and despite this only beaten a nose; it would have been a complete injustice had she not been given the race. Special Duty returned injured after her next race and never recaptured her best form subsequently. Her first foal South Bank (2012, by Tapit), made her debut in the same Deauville listed race as her dam and like her, finished second. The once-raced maiden Quest To Peak was a full-sister to Sightseek (1999 – G1 Beldame S & $2.4m), out of the listed winner Viviana,

320

a grand-daughter of U.S. champion Chris Evert (1971, by Swoon's Son – G1 CCA Oaks ect.). This is the distinguished U.S. family of Chief's Crown (1982, by Danzig – G1 Travers S & $2.1m) and Etoile Montante (2000, by Miswaki – G1 Prix de la Foret).

2211710

Above: **SPECIAL DUTY** (Stephane Pasquier) was awarded the 1000 Guineas on the disqualification of Jacqueline Quest (green cap). Gile Na Greine (check cap) and Sent From Heaven (rail) finished third and fourth. It was the first time an English classic had been decided in the steward's room since 1980 when Nureyev was disqualified and the 2000 Guineas given to Known Fact (see p7).

Below: On this occasion luck is on the side of **SPECIAL DUTY** (Pasquier); Poule d'Essai des Pouliches first-past-the-post Liliside (left) was disqualified and placed sixth for causing interference to three other fillies. Special Duty, who had a clear run in the straight, was beaten a head. She was the first filly to win both classics since Ravinella (p82) in 1988, also trained by Christiane Head.

1605210

2010104

Left: **STEPHANE PASQUIER** was champion jockey in France in 2007 and rode his first English classic winner on Special Duty.
Right: **CHRISTIANE HEAD** had won the 1000 Guineas on three previous occasions with Ma Biche (p36), Ravinella & Hatoof (p122). Head has won most of the big races in France during a very successful training career which began in 1978.

0910104

SNOW FAIRY (IRE)

Bay filly, foaled 12 February 2007
By Intikhab (USA) out of Woodland Dream (IRE) by Charnwood Forest (IRE)
Bred by Windflower Overseas Holdings Incorporated
Owned by Anamoine Limited
Trained by Edward A.L. Dunlop at La Grange, Newmarket, Suffolk.

0814111

Racing Record

Year	Timeform Annual Rating	Starts	Wins	2nd	3rd	4th	Prize Money
2009	99	6	1	1	2	1	£ 15,083
2010	123	7	5	1	-	1	£ 2,075,374
2011	128	6	1	2	2	1	£ 1,459,263
2012	128	2	1	-	-	-	£ 362,083

Principal Performances

2010 Won Oaks Stakes (G1) (3yo fillies) Epsom (12f)
      Won Irish Oaks Stakes (G1) (3yo fillies) Curragh (12f)
      2nd Yorkshire Oaks (G1) (Fillies & mares) York (12f)
      4th St Leger Stakes (G1) (3yo colts & fillies) Doncaster (14.6f)
      Won Queen Elizabeth II Commemorative Cup (G1) Kyoto, Japan (11f turf)
      Won Hong Kong Cup (G1) Sha Tin, Hong Kong (10f turf)
2011 2nd Nassau Stakes (G1) (Fillies & mares) Goodwood (9.9f)
      2nd Irish Champion Stakes (G1) Leopardstown (10f)
      3rd Prix de l'Arc de Triomphe (G1) Longchamp (12f)
      3rd Champion Stakes (G1) Ascot (10f)
      Won Queen Elizabeth II Commemorative Cup (G1) Kyoto, Japan (11f turf)
2012 Won Irish Champion Stakes (G1) Leopardstown (10f)

S now Fairy was bought back by her breeder, Mrs Christina Patino for €1,800 at Tattersalls Ireland 2008 December Flat Sale. Racing for Mrs Patino's Anamoine Limited, the filly went on to win almost £4.7m in prize money. Snow Fairy suffered an injury in September 2012 when being prepared for the Prix de l'Arc de Triomphe and the decision was taken to retire her. Her first foal, a filly by her owner's stallion, Elusive Pimpernel (2007, by Elusive Quality – G3 Acomb & Craven S), was born in February 2015 and Snow Fairy was then covered by Irish National Stud stallion Palavicini. Woodland Dream, a minor winner in Ireland, was a half-sister to Big Bad Bob (2000, by Bob Back – LR Autumn S) and a great grand-daughter of Gay Fantasy (1981, by Troy). Sheer Audacity (1984), a sister to Gay Fantasy, was the dam of Oath (p206). This is the family of Palavicini (2002, by Giant's Causeway – G3 Strensall S) and Elusive Pimpernel, which both raced for Mrs Patino, and also the 2000 Guineas winner Mister Baileys (p144).

2412310

Above: **SNOW FAIRY** gives three times British champion jockey (2006, 2008-9) Ryan Moore his first English classic winner, beating the subsequently disqualified Meeznah (blaze) and Remember When (rail) in the Oaks.

2012410

3216013

Above left: **CHRISTINA PATINO**, whose horses usually race in the better known colours of Windflower Holdings, with her first English classic winner and **RYAN MOORE** after the Oaks at Epsom. Above right: **EDWARD DUNLOP** had been previously successful in the Oaks with Ouija Board (see p258). Other top-level winners trained by Dunlop include Lailani (Irish Oaks, Nassau S), Court Masterpiece (Prix de la Foret, Sussex S), Ta Rib (Poule d'Essai des Pouliches), Red Cadeaux (Hong Kong Vase), Iktamal (Haydock Sprint Cup) and Joshua Tree (Canadian International S).

WORKFORCE (GB)

Bay colt, foaled 14 March 2007
By King's Best (USA) out of Soviet Moon (IRE) by Sadler's Wells (USA)
Bred by Juddmonte Farms Limited
Owned by Khalid Abdullah
Trained by Sir Michael Stoute at Freemason Lodge, Newmarket, Suffolk.

1314111

Racing Record

Year	Timeform Annual Rating	Starts	Wins	2nd	3rd	4th	Prize Money
2009	106	1	1	-	-	-	£ 3,562
2010	133	4	2	1	-	-	£ 2,853,339
2011	130	4	1	2	-	-	£ 350,522

Principal Performances

2010 2nd Dante Stakes (G2) (3yo) York (10.4f)
      Won Derby Stakes (G1) (3yo colts & fillies) Epsom (12f)
      Won Prix de l'Arc de Triomphe (G1) Longchamp (12f)
2011 Won Brigadier Gerard Stakes (G3) Sandown (10f)
      2nd Eclipse Stakes (G1) Sandown (10f)
      2nd King George VI and Queen Elizabeth Stakes (G1) Ascot (12f)

*****

*W*orkforce was a very big yearling and did not go into training until June 2009. Within four months the colt was posting an impressive success in a maiden race at Goodwood. Workforce, an above average Derby winner and one of only six to go on to win the Prix de l'Arc de Triomphe, was retired to stud in Japan and stands at Shadai Farm in Hokkaido. Soviet Moon is an unraced full-sister to Brian Boru (p250), out of Eva Luna (G2 Park Hill S), a daughter of Oaks runner-up Media Luna (1981, by Star Appeal). The Derby winner's fourth dam Sounion (1961, by Vimy), was a half-sister to Lucyrowe (1966, by Crepello – Coronation S, Nassau S, Sun Chariot S), and herself the dam of Suni (1975, by Crepello – G3 Lingfield Oaks Trial S, 3rd G1 Oaks S).

1912610

0219106

Above left: **WORKFORCE** wins a third Derby for his owner Khalid Abdullah and first for jockey **RYAN MOORE** (above right) who was winning his second classic following Snow Fairy (p323) the day before. Prince Khalid's previous Derby winners were Quest For Fame (p106) and Commander in Chief (p136).

1509112

Left: **SIR MICHAEL STOUTE** has been champion trainer in Britain ten times between 1981-2009 and was winning a fifth Derby after Shergar (p18), Shahrastani (p68) Kris Kin (p248) and North Light (p260). Other English classic winners for Stoute have been Fair Salinia (1978) and Unite (p80) (Oaks); Shadeed (p60), Doyoun (p84), Golan (p222), Entrepreneur (p176) and King's Best (p210) (2000 Guineas) and Musical Bliss (p94) and Russian Rhythm (p244) (1000 Guineas). In 2008, Michael Stoute completed his full-hand of classics when Conduit (p306) won the St Leger after the trainer had suffered the frustration of saddling five runners-up. Other G1 winners for Stoute have included Shangamuzo and Estimate (Ascot Gold Cup), Opera House (Coronation Cup, Eclipse S, King George VI and Queen Elizabeth S), Kalanisi (Champion S), Shareef Dancer (Irish Derby), Singspiel (Coronation Cup, Japan Cup), Pilsudski (Eclipse S, Champion S), Marwell and Green Desert (July Cup), Ajdal (Nunthorpe S) and Zilzal (Sussex S, Queen Elizabeth II S).

0310210

Above: **WORKFORCE** and Ryan Moore beating Japanese challenger Nakayama Festa in the Prix de l'Arc de Triomphe.

SEA THE STARS (IRE) : Bay 2006

Cape Cross (IRE) B/br. 1994	Green Desert (USA) B. 1983	Danzig (USA)
		Foreign Courier (USA)
	Park Appeal (IRE) Br. 1982	Ahonoora (GB)
		Balidaress (IRE)
Urban Sea (USA) Ch. 1989	Miswaki (USA) Ch. 1978	Mr Prospector (USA)
		Hopespringseternal (USA)
	Allegretta (GB) Ch. 1978	Lombard (GER)
		Anatevka (GER)

GHANAATI (USA) : Bay 2006

Giant's Causeway (USA) Ch. 1997	Storm Cat (USA) B/br. 1983	Storm Bird (CAN)
		Terlingua (USA)
	Mariah's Storm (USA) B. 1991	Rahy (USA)
		Immense (USA)
Sarayir (USA) B. 1994	Mr Prospector (USA) B. 1970	Raise A Native (USA)
		Gold Digger (USA)
	Height of Fashion (FR) B. 1979	Bustino (GB)
		Highclere (GB)

SARISKA (GB) : Bay 2006

Pivotal (GB) Ch. 1993	Polar Falcon (USA) Br. 1987	Nureyev (USA)
		Marie d'Argonne (FR)
	Fearless Revival (GB) Ch. 1987	Cozzene (USA)
		Stufida (GB)
Maycocks Bay (GB) B. 1998	Muhtarram (USA) B. 1989	Alleged (USA)
		Ballet de France (USA)
	Beacon (GB) B. 1987	High Top (GB)
		Mountain Lodge (GB)

MASTERY (GB) : Bay 2006

Sulamani (IRE) B. 1999	Hernando (FR) B. 1990	Niniski (USA)
		Whakilyric (USA)
	Soul Dream (USA) B/br. 1990	Alleged (USA (USA)
		Normia (GB)
Moyesii (USA) B. 1997	Diesis (GB) Ch. 1980	Sharpen Up (GB)
		Doubly Sure (GB)
	Cherokee Rose (IRE) B. 1991	Dancing Brave (USA)
		Celtic Assembly (USA)

MAKFI (GB) : Bay 2007

Dubawi (IRE) B. 2002	Dubai Millennium (GB) B. 1996	Seeking The Gold (USA)
		Colorado Dancer (IRE)
	Zomaradah (GB) Br. 1995	Deploy (GB)
		Jawaher (IRE)
Dhelaal (GB) B. 2002	Green Desert (USA) B. 1983	Danzig (USA)
		Foreign Courier (USA)
	Irish Valley (USA) Ch. 1982	Irish River (FR)
		Green Valley (FR)

SPECIAL DUTY (GB) : Chesnut 2007

Hennessy (USA) Ch. 1993	Storm Cat (USA) B/br. 1983	Storm Bird (CAN)
		Terlingua (USA)
	Island Kitty (USA) Ch. 1976	Hawaii (SAF)
		T C Kitten (USA)
Quest To Peak (USA) B. 2002	Distant View (USA) Ch. 1991	Mr Prospector (USA)
		Seven Springs (USA)
	Viviana (USA) B. 1990	Nureyev (USA)
		Nijinsky Star (USA)

SNOW FAIRY (IRE) : Bay 2007

Intikhab (USA) B. 1994	Red Ransom (USA) B. 1987	Roberto (USA)
		Arabia (USA)
	Crafty Example (USA) B. 1987	Crafty Prospector (USA)
		Zienelle (USA)
Woodland Dream (IRE) Br. 2002	Charnwood Forest (IRE) B/br. 1992	Warning (GB)
		Dance of Leaves (GB)
	Fantasy Girl (IRE) Br. 1994	Marju (IRE)
		Persian Fantasy (GB)

WORKFORCE (GB) : Bay 2007

King's Best (USA) B. 1997	Kingmambo (USA) B. 1990	Mr Prospector (USA)
		Miesque (USA)
	Allegretta (GB) Ch. 1978	Lombard (GER)
		Anatevka (GER)
Soviet Moon (IRE) B. 2001	Sadler's Wells (USA) B. 1981	Northern Dancer (CAN)
		Fairy Bridge (USA)
	Eva Luna (USA) B. 1992	Alleged (USA)
		Media Luna (USA)

ARCTIC COSMOS (USA)

Bay colt, foaled 31 January 2007
By North Light (IRE) out of Fifth Avenue Doll (USA) by Marquetry (USA)
Bred by Sheridan and Iadora Farm
Owned by Rachel Hood and Robin J.H. Geffen
Trained by John H.M. Gosden at Clarehaven, Newmarket, Suffolk.

2317311

Racing Record

Year	Timeform Annual Rating	Starts	Wins	2nd	3rd	4th	Prize Money
2009	68	2	-	-	-	2	-
2010	123	6	3	1	2	-	£ 333,280
2011	117	2	-	1	-	1	£ 59,902
2012	114	4	1	-	-	-	£ 20,194

Principal Performances

2010 2nd King Edward VII Stakes (G2) (3yo colts & geldings) Royal Ascot (12f)
       3rd Gordon Stakes (G3) (3yo) Goodwood (12f)
       Won St Leger Stakes (G1) (3yo colts & fillies) Doncaster (14.6f)
2011 2nd Cumberland Lodge Stakes (G3) Ascot (12f)
       4th Canadian International (G1) Woodbine, Canada (12f turf)
2012 Won Magnolia Stakes (Listed Race) Kempton (10f Polytrack)

*****

A 47,000 guineas purchase at Tattersalls October Yearling Sales, Arctic Cosmos first showed signs of classic potential when placed at Royal Ascot and the colt showed further improvement to win at Doncaster fitted with blinkers for the first time. Arctic Cosmos fractured a cannon bone in training after the St Leger and was side-lined for a year before returning to action in October 2011. Unfortunately, Arctic Cosmos never recaptured his best form and finished last in his final three races, appearing as though all was not right with him. The jumping career being considered before the colt's St Leger victory was never really on afterwards, although one firm of so-called bookmakers had the cheek to quote him at a miserly 20/1 for the 2013 Champion Hurdle before Arctic Cosmos had even been schooled over hurdles! Ultimately he was retired to The Old Road Stud at Tallow in Co. Waterford where Arctic Cosmos stood at a fee of €1,500 in 2014. Arctic Cosmos descends from an undistinguished U.S. family. He is the first foal of his dam, who was at least tough and sound, winning ten times from fifty-three starts in minor company from two to six years of age. Fifth Avenue Doll was the only winner out of Allegro, a minor winner in 1989. The St Leger winner's third dam Dotsie Go (1968, by Clandestine), never did win in seven attempts but she bred five winners, including one at U.S. Grade 2 level.

1815710

Above: Twenty-two year old William Buick rides his first English classic winner on **ARCTIC COSMOS** beating Midas Touch (right), Corsica (red cap) and Snow Fairy (left, see p322). It was the first time since Touching Wood (p34) won the same race in 1982 that an English classic had been won by a horse wearing blinkers.

2008114

1309114

1309114

Above left: **WILLIAM BUICK**'s rise in the jockey's ranks has been meteoric from his first victory in September 2006 to champion apprentice in 2008 and classic winner in 2010. Above centre: President of the Racehorse Owners Association and elected Mayor of Newmarket in May 2014, **RACHEL HOOD**, co-owner of Arctic Cosmos, is married to **JOHN GOSDEN**. Gosden (right) is the son of the late John (Towser) Gosden, who trained at Lewes in Sussex and had charge of Derby winner Charlottown (1963, by Charlottesville) as a two-year-old before handing in his license through ill-health at the end of 1965. John Gosden, junior began as assistant to Vincent O'Brien in Ireland and Noel Murless at Newmarket, before moving to California, eventually beginning training on his own account in 1979. He returned to Newmarket in 1989 to train for Sheikh Mohammed at Stanley House, moving to Manton, Wiltshire for 2000 and back to Newmarket in 2007. John Gosden has trained winners of the 1000 Guineas (Lahan p212), Oaks (Taghrooda p366), Derby (Benny the Dip p184, Golden Horn p378), and four of the St Leger (Shantou p174, Lucarno p296, Arctic Cosmos and Masked Marvel p338). Gosden was champion trainer in Britain during 2012.

FRANKEL (GB)

Bay colt, foaled 11 February 2008
By Galileo (IRE) out of Kind (IRE) by Danehill (USA)
Bred by Juddmonte Farms Limited
Owned by Khalid Abdullah
Trained by Sir Henry Cecil at Warren Place, Newmarket, Suffolk.

1011011

Racing Record

Year	Timeform Annual Rating	Starts	Wins	2nd	3rd	4th	Prize Money
2010	133	4	4	-	-	-	£ 266,474
2011	143	5	5	-	-	-	£ 1,106,235
2012	147	5	5	-	-	-	£ 1,625,592

Principal Performances

2010   Won Royal Lodge Stakes (G2) (2yo colts & geldings) Ascot (8f)
       Won Dewhurst Stakes (G1) (2yo colts & fillies) Newmarket (7f)
2011   Won Greenham Stakes (G3) (3yo) Newbury (7f)
       Won 2000 Guineas Stakes (G1) (3yo colts & fillies) Newmarket (8f)
       Won St James's Palace Stakes (G1) (3yo colts) Royal Ascot (8f)
       Won Sussex Stakes (G1) Goodwood (8f)
       Won Queen Elizabeth II Stakes (G1) Ascot (8f)
2012   Won Lockinge Stakes (G1) Newbury (8f)
       Won Queen Anne Stakes (G1) Royal Ascot (8f)
       Won Sussex Stakes (G1) Goodwood (8f)
       Won International Stakes (G1) York (10.4f)
       Won Champion Stakes (G1) Ascot (10f)

*****

*T*imeform rate Frankel as the best horse to race on the flat since they began publishing ratings in 1947. Yet the rather timid way the horse was campaigned left many frustrated that Frankel wasn't given the chance to show what he could do on the even bigger stages available. Brilliant *victories in the 2000 Guineas and Sussex Stakes drew comparisons with Brigadier Gerard (rated 141 by Timeform in 1971). Unfortunately the bold route taken by that great horse's owner and trainer was not repeated with Frankel. An opportunity to test the colt at ten furlongs on ideal ground in the 2011 Champion Stakes was passed up in favour of a bloodless victory in the Queen Elizabeth II Stakes. When the chance of running four-year-old Frankel in the ten-furlong Prince of Wales's Stakes, or the Eclipse Stakes, was also ignored, it became obvious that there was no intention to try him over twelve furlongs in the King George VI and Queen Elizabeth Stakes at the end of July. Instead a further pointless procession was preferred at Goodwood where Frankel duly won a second Sussex Stakes by a wide margin, proving nothing that we didn't already know. Frankel was retired to his owner's Banstead Manor Stud at Cheveley, Newmarket, the unbeaten winner of fourteen races, commanding a covering fee of £125,000 and valued at over £100m. Sir Henry Cecil (who seemed more intent on ensuring that Frankel retired unbeaten than realising his full potential) was quoted as saying that 'it's not my fault ... that other horses are inferior'. However, it must be said that Cecil and Frankel deserved each other, they are two legends of the turf. The stakes placed winner Rockfest (1979, by Stage Door Johnny), great grandam of Frankel, was a private purchase by Juddmonte in 1983 when the bloodstock of John Hay Whitney was dispersed. Grandam Rainbow Lake (G3 Lancashire Oaks) was also the dam of Powerscourt (2000, by Sadler's Wells – G1 Tattersalls Gold Cup, Arlington Million, G2 Great Voltigeur S). Frankel's dam Kind won twice at listed level and has also bred Bullet Train (2007, by Sadler's Wells - G3 Derby Trial S) and Noble Mission (2009, by Galileo – G1 Tattersalls Gold Cup, GP de Saint-Cloud, Champion S).*

2110911

Above: Nobody had seen anything like it since Tudor Minstrel won the 2000 Guineas by eight lengths in 1947. **FRANKEL** 'only' wins by six lengths but had been at least ten lengths clear before halfway. It was a first and to date only English classic for Irish jockey **TOM QUEALLY** (below centre) and the twenty-fifth and last for Sir Henry Cecil, who died after a long illness in June 2013. Khalid Abdullah had previously won this classic with Known Fact (see p6), Dancing Brave (p66) and Zafonic (p134). At 2/1 on, Frankel was the shortest priced winner since Colombo started at 7/2 on in 1934. Below: **FRANKEL** finally steps up in distance and wins the International Stakes by seven lengths from Farhh (right) and St Nicholas Abbey. One of the largest crowds of recent years turned up at York to see Frankel and approach roads were jammed for miles around. The traffic situation was made worse than it need have been by only one gate being opened into the main car-park and no traffic control off the A1036 onto the racecourse approach road. York racecourse management may have had a highly profitable day but hardly shone otherwise and many first-time racegoers may well have decided that it was a first and last time.

2715512

BLUE BUNTING (USA)

Grey filly, foaled 20 March 2008
By Dynaformer (USA) out of Miarixa (FR) by Linamix (FR)
Bred by B.M. Kelley
Owned by Godolphin
Trained by Mahmood Al Zarooni at Moulton Paddocks, Newmarket, Suffolk.

0311411

Racing Record

Year	Timeform Annual Rating	Starts	Wins	2nd	3rd	4th	Prize Money
2010	101	3	2	1	-	-	£ 18,779
2011	122	5	3	-	-	1	£ 626,783

Principal Performances

2010 Won E.B.F. Montrose Fillies' Stakes (Listed Race) (2yo) Newmarket (8f)
2011 Won 1000 Guineas Stakes (G1) (3yo fillies) Newmarket (8f)
        4th Oaks Stakes (G1) (3yo fillies) Epsom (12f)
        Won Irish Oaks Stakes (G1) (3yo fillies) Curragh (12f)
        Won Yorkshire Oaks (G1) (Fillies & mares) York (12f)

*****

B lue Bunting was purchased for Godolphin at the Fasig-Tipton Saratoga Sales by Anthony Stroud for $200,000. The filly's two-year-old performances were useful but some way from making her a leading hope for the classics. Godolphin seemed to possess a much stronger classic candidate in the unbeaten White Moonstone, but when she fell by the wayside it was Blue Bunting who lined up at Newmarket for the 1000 Guineas as a 16/1 outsider. Her stamina and a great ride from Frankie Dettori gained the victory there, but at Epsom Dettori was caught out by the modest pace and too far behind when the pace quickened could never peg back the leaders. Compensation soon came in the Oaks' at the Curragh and York and it was decided to keep Blue Bunting in training for another year. Unfortunately she was injured in training during February 2012 and the decision made to retire her. Blue Bunting's first mating was with Godolphin's Dubai World Cup winner Street Cry. Unraced Miarixa was out of listed winner Mrs Arkada (3rd G1 Prix Saint-Alary). This is the family of Miss Satamixa (1992, by Linamix – G1 Prix Jacques le Marois).

1711311

Above: Racing into a strong headwind **BLUE BUNTING** (Frankie Dettori) stays-on better than Together (left) to win the 1000 Guineas. It was a third success in this classic for both the jockey and Godolphin following Cape Verdi (see p190) and Kazzia (p234).

0105111

Right: **FRANKIE DETTORI** performs his trademark 'flying dismount' after winning his fourteenth English classic on Blue Bunting. His other victories were on Balanchine (p150), Moonshell (p158) and Kazzia in the Oaks; Classic Cliché (p162), Shantou (p174), Scorpion (p274), Sixties Icon (p284) and Conduit (p306) in the St Leger; Mark of Esteem (p166) and Island Sands (p198) (2000 Guineas); Authorized (p294) in the Derby. Other top-class winners ridden by Dettori include Lammtarra (King George VI & Queen Elizabeth S, Prix de l'Arc de Triomphe), Daylami (Coronation Cup, Eclipse S, King George VI & Queen Elizabeth S, Breeders' Cup Turf), Sakhee (Prix de l'Arc de Triomphe), Dubai Millennium (Dubai World Cup), Swain (Coronation Cup, King George VI & Queen Elizabeth S), Ramonti (Sussex S, Queen Elizabeth II S) and Refuse To Bend (Eclipse S). Dettori's long association with Godolphin ended in 2012 and he is currently contracted to Sheikh Joaan Al Thani. Frankie Dettori was born in Milan on December 15, 1970 and was apprenticed to Luca Cumani at Bedford House Stables in Newmarket. He has been champion jockey in Britain on three occasions, 1994-5 and 2004, but is probably best remembered for being the only jockey to ride all seven winners on a seven-race card, performing that feat at Ascot on September 28, 1996.

1111411

2815811

Above left: **BLUE BUNTING** in the winner's circle at Newmarket with Sheikh Mohammed and his wife Princess Haya, **FRANKIE DETTORI** and **MAHMOOD AL ZAROONI** (right). This was a first English classic winner for Dubai-born Al Zarooni in his second season training for Godolphin. Above right: Victory in the Yorkshire Oaks for Dettori and BLUE BUNTING beating Vita Nova.

DANCING RAIN (IRE)

Chesnut filly, foaled 24 April 2008
By Danehill Dancer (IRE) out of Rain Flower (IRE) by Indian Ridge (GB)
Bred by Swettenham Stud
Owned by Martin J. & Lee A. Taylor
Trained by William Haggas at Somerville Lodge, Newmarket, Suffolk.

0512111

Racing Record

Year	Timeform Annual Rating	Starts	Wins	2nd	3rd	4th	Prize Money
2010	78	1	-	1	-	-	£ 850
2011	120	7	4	1	-	-	£ 542,870
2012	112	2	-	-	1	-	£ 28,784

Principal Performances

2011 Won Oaks Stakes (G1) (3yo fillies) Epsom (12f)
      Won Preis der Diana-Deutsches Stuten-Derby (G1) (3yo fillies) Dusseldorf (11f)
      Won British Champions Fillies and Mares Stakes (G2) Ascot (12f)
2012 3rd British Champions Fillies and Mares Stakes (G2) Ascot (12f)

*****

2011 saw the introduction into British racing of the Qipco Challenge Series, an ill-conceived and poorly implemented idea that drags together certain G1 and G2 classed races, awarding points for performance to supposedly arrive at a champion horse in each distance range. Part of the tacky preliminaries to each race involve the jockeys standing next to a flag depicting the owner's racing colours which each jockey is already wearing. Why not have the owners and trainers standing by the flag as well, in order to complete the ridicule? This was in the first years followed by a poor quality recording of what was presumably intended to be 'dramatic' music crashing out over the PA as the horses went to the start, in 2015 this has been played as the winner returns to unsaddle. All this would *be just about bearable for racing traditionalists had the long-established autumn racing programme not been butchered to accommodate a Champions Day to give the series a supposedly rousing finale at Ascot in late-October; too late some say, surely St Leger day would have been a far better choice? A remodelled St Leger, still for three-year-olds but over twelve furlongs, could have been the main race and would have revived the last classic. Instead, the Champion Stakes, previously run over the straight ten furlongs at Newmarket and a unique Group 1 race in the world, was switched to become the highlight of Champions Day, making it just another ten furlong race run around a right-hand bend, an exact copy of the Prince of Wales's Stakes run at Ascot in June. The relocation and all too frequent renaming of various long-established races is yet another example of the almost total disregard for British racing's rich history and heritage by the new generation of racing administrators. Qipco Champions Day was modelled on the Breeders' Cup in America, where they use a series of unimaginative and overlong race names and it was decided to follow the same pattern for Champions Day. This involved yet more renaming of existing races and saddling them with lengthy monikers such as the 'Qipco British Champions Fillies and Mares Stakes', presumably just in case any dimwit was unsure what the race was all about. Apparently, the Princess Royal Stakes, Jockey Club Cup and Diadem Stakes were not considered grand enough names to be used for Champions Day, although according to my dictionary a diadem is a crown worn as a sign of sovereignty. What was wrong with honouring The Jockey Club or the Princess Royal at what is supposed to be the flagship meeting of the year? So-called 'Champions Day' has been run on soft or heavy ground on three of the four years it has been staged. It cannot be too long before it is waterlogged off altogether; some might think that no more than the people whose brainstorm it was deserve.*

1812111

Above: **DANCING RAIN** benefits from an inspired ride from John Murtagh to win the Oaks beating Wonder Of Wonders (centre), Izzi Top (white cap) and Blue Bunting (left, see p333). Below left: **JOHN MURTAGH** and **WILLIAM** and **MAUREEN HAGGAS** in the winner's circle with their first Oaks winner. Maureen had broken her right leg when thrown by Dancing Rain during a starting stalls drill at Newmarket a month before the Oaks.

© George Selwyn

0312113

Above right: **DANCING RAIN** carrying her first foal by Frankel due in February 2014 is sold at the 2013 Tattersalls December Sales in Newmarket to a bid of 4m guineas by John Ferguson acting on behalf of Sheikh Mohammed Al-Maktoum. It was then the second-highest price ever achieved for a broodmare at auction in Europe. Dancing Rain, a €200,000 yearling purchase, was out of the unraced Rain Flower, a three-quarters sister to Derby winner Dr Devious (p126).

335

POUR MOI (IRE)

Bay colt, foaled 10 January 2008
By Montjeu (IRE) out of Gwynn (IRE) by Darshaan (GB)
Bred by Lynch Bages Limited
Owned by Mrs John Magnier, Michael Tabor and Derrick Smith
Trained by Andre Fabre at Chantilly, Oise, France.

0612311

Racing Record

Year	Timeform Annual Rating	Starts	Wins	2nd	3rd	4th	Prize Money
2010	-	2	1	-	-	-	£ 15,044
2011	125	3	2	-	1	-	£ 783,849

Principal Performances

2011 3rd Prix La Force (G3) (3yo) Longchamp (10.5f)
      Won Prix Greffulhe (G2) (3yo colts & fillies) Saint-Cloud (10f)
      Won Derby Stakes (G1) (3yo colts & fillies) Epsom (12f)

*****

*P*our Moi has been called 'the Derby winner who rose without trace'. Even following an impressive victory in the Prix Greffulhe the colt was still available at odds of 25/1 for Epsom, eventually starting as the 4/1 second favourite behind The Queen's Carlton House. Following his sensational success in the Derby, coming from last to first in the straight and still three lengths behind entering the final furlong, Pour Moi was rested with the Prix de l'Arc de Triomphe in mind. During training in late-August, Pour Moi suffered a severe over-reach to his near-fore which necessitated his retirement to Coolmore Stud at Fethard in County Tipperary. He was the first Derby winner not to run again since Secreto (see p50) in 1984 and only the seventh since Galcador in 1950. The other four being Crepello (1957), Psidium (1961), Morston (1973) and Golden Fleece (p30) in 1982. Pour Moi comes from an excellent family; his dam was unraced and before the Derby winner had bred Gagnoa (2005, by Sadler's Wells – G3 Prix Penelope, 2nd Prix de Diane, 3rd Irish Oaks). Gwynn's dam Victoress was a minor winner out of the successful broodmare Royal Statute (1969, by Northern Dancer), dam of

336

Konafa (1973, by Damascus – 2ⁿᵈ G1 1000 Guineas), and Akureyri (1978, by Buckpasser – G1 Fountain of Youth S). This is the family of Bosra Sham (p168), her full-brother Hector Protector and half-brother Shanghai (1989, by Procida), both winners of the classic Poule d'Essai des Poulains, as well as Snow Bride (p98) and Lammtarra (p160).

1212311

Above: A dramatic late run by **POUR MOI** wins the first Derby for a French-trained horse since Empery in 1976. Treasure Beach (striped sleeves) finishes second and Carlton House (black cap) third. This was the first English classic success for nineteen-year-old **MICKAEL BARZALONA** (below right) and third Derby for the Coolmore stallion Montjeu, who died in March 2012. Pour Moi was the second Derby winner to race in the colours of **SUSAN MAGNIER** (below centre) following Galileo (p228) and Ruler Of The World (p356) made it three in 2013.

2230303   © Trevor Jones   2912311

Above left: **ANDRE FABRE** was winning his first Derby and fifth English classic following Toulon (p120), Zafonic (p134), Intrepidity (p138) and Pennekamp (p154). Fabre was born on 9 December 1945 and was a leading jump-jockey in France winning more than 250 races including the Grand Steeple Chase de Paris at Auteuil. He has been the dominant trainer in France for almost thirty years being leading trainer twenty-six times between 1987 and 2014. Top-class winners trained by Fabre include Trempolino (Prix de l'Arc de Triomphe), Jolypha (Prix de Diane, Prix Vermeille), Tel Quel (Champion S), Peintre Celebre (Prix du Jockey-Club, Prix de l'Arc de Triomphe), Soviet Star (July Cup, Sussex S, Prix du Moulin), Carnegie (Prix de l'Arc de Triomphe, Grand Prix de Saint-Cloud), Lope De Vega (Poule d'Essai des Poulains, Prix du Jockey-Club), Sunshack (Prix Royal-Oak, Coronation Cup), Arcangues (Prix d'Ispahan, Breeders Cup Classic), Golden Lilac (Poule d'Essai des Pouliches, Prix de Diane), Banks Hill (Prix Jacques Le Marois), Subotica (Grand Prix de Paris, Prix de l'Arc de Triomphe), In The Wings (Coronation Cup, Grand Prix de Saint-Cloud), Intello (Prix du Jockey-Club), Hurricane Run (Irish Derby, King George VI & Queen Elizabeth S), Manduro (Prince of Wales's S), Winged Love (Irish Derby), Wemyss Bight (Irish Oaks), Shirocco (Coronation Cup, Breeders Cup Turf), Swain (Coronation Cup) and Sagamix and Rail Link (both Prix de l'Arc de Triomphe).

MASKED MARVEL (GB)

Bay colt, foaled 6 March 2008
By Montjeu (IRE) out of Waldmark (GER) by Mark of Esteem (IRE)
Bred by Newsells Park Stud, Royston, Hertfordshire
Owned by Bjorn E. Nielsen
Trained by John H.M. Gosden at Clarehaven, Newmarket, Suffolk.

3110912

Racing Record

Year	Timeform Annual Rating	Starts	Wins	2nd	3rd	4th	Prize Money
2010	88	2	1	-	-	-	£ 4,749
2011	126	6	3	-	-	-	£ 352,993
2012	115	5	-	-	1	1	£ 35,228
2013	-	5	-	1	1	-	£ 28,846
2014	-	3	-	-	-	-	£ 645

Principal Performances

2011 Won Cocked Hat Stakes (Listed Race) (3yo colts & geldings) Goodwood (11f)
      Won Bahrain Trophy (G3) (3yo) Newmarket (13f)
      Won St Leger Stakes (G1) (3yo colts & fillies) Doncaster (14.6f)
2012 3rd Diamond Jubilee Coronation Cup (G1) Epsom (12f)
2013 3rd Bacardi Hills Stakes (G2) Randwick, Australia (10f turf)

*****

*M*asked Marvel was bought by Bjorn Nielsen's racing manager Jeremy Brummit for €260,000 at the Deauville August Yearling Sales. The colt was always held in high regard by his trainer and was stepped up into group company on only his second start. After his St Leger victory Masked Marvel looked sure to do well in the cup races as a four-year-old but his form deteriorated after a promising third at Epsom and at the end of the season he was sold to race in Australia. Trained by Robert Hickmott, Masked Marvel failed to win 'down under' but was placed in two stakes races. Waldmark, a minor winner and group placed, descends from a good German family and since Masked Marvel has *bred Waldlerche (2009, by Monsun - G3 Prix Penelope) and Waldnah (2012, by New Approach – LR Dallmayr Coupe Lukull). The grandam Wurftaube won four group races including the G2 Deutsches St Leger and is the dam of Waldpark (2008, by Dubawi – G1 Deutsches Derby) and Waldjagd (2007, by Observatory) a group placed winner, sold at Tattersalls 2010 December Sales for 320,000 guineas. Great-grandam Wurfbahn (1987, by Frontal) was the dam of Wurfscheibe (2002, by Tiger Hill), a winner three times at Group 3 level in Germany. On 14 November 2014 it was announced that Masked Marvel had been purchased to stand at Haras d'Etreham in Normandy as a jumps stallion for 2015.*

1916211

Above: A second consecutive St Leger success for jockey William Buick and John Gosden as **MASKED MARVEL** beats Brown Panther and Sea Moon (left), breaking the track record in the process.

Below: Owner **BJORN NIELSEN** (left), **JOHN GOSDEN** and **WILLIAM BUICK** in the winner's circle with Masked Marvel after the St Leger. This was Gosden's fourth St Leger and sixth English classic success (see p329). For William Buick, who won the same race on Arctic Cosmos (p328), it was a second English classic victory. During November 2014 it was announced that Buick was quitting his position as stable-jockey to John Gosden to join Godolphin's private trainer, Charlie Appleby, a decision that cost him the ride on the outstanding 2015 Derby winner Golden Horn as well as a French classic on Star Of Seville.

3616211

CAMELOT (GB)

Bay colt, foaled 5 March 2009
By Montjeu (IRE) out of Tarfah (USA) by Kingmambo (USA)
Bred by Sheikh Abdulla bin Isa Al-Khalifa
Owned by Derrick Smith, Mrs John Magnier and Michael Tabor
Trained by Aidan P. O'Brien at Ballydoyle, Cashel, Co. Tipperary.

2618111

Racing Record

Year	Timeform Annual Rating	Starts	Wins	2nd	3rd	4th	Prize Money
2011	117	2	2	-	-	-	£ 141,679
2012	128	5	3	1	-	-	£ 1,687,337
2013	125	3	1	1	-	1	£ 97,552

Principal Performances

2011   Won Racing Post Trophy (G1) (2yo colts & fillies) Doncaster (8f) (photo above)
2012   Won 2000 Guineas Stakes (G1) (3yo colts & fillies) Newmarket (8f)
      Won Derby Stakes (G1) (3yo colts & fillies) Epsom (12f)
      Won Irish Derby Stakes (G1) (3yo colts & fillies) Curragh (12f)
      2nd St Leger Stakes (G1) (3yo colts & fillies) Doncaster (14.6f)
2013   Won Mooresbridge Stakes (G3) Curragh (10f)
      2nd Tattersalls Gold Cup (G1) Curragh (10.5f)

*****

*W*hen Camelot was defeated in his bid for Triple Crown glory it virtually extinguished all hope of a revival for the St Leger in its present form. Ironically the colt was not beaten by the extended distance of the last classic, but by a combination of bad luck in running, jockey error and the first signs of temperament problems. There also exists the possibility that Camelot may have been accidentally struck over the head by another jockey's whip as Joseph O'Brien searched for room to make his final run. Whatever caused the defeat, it will certainly discourage owners and trainers of future candidates from attempting the Triple Crown of the 2000 Guineas, Derby and St Leger which has not been achieved since Nijinsky in 1970 and before that by Bahram in 1935 and Rock Sand in 1903.The difficulty of winning three classics at a distance range of eight to an extended fourteen furlongs can be understood by realising that Camelot was the first since Giacometti in 1974 to be placed in all three, let

340

alone win them. Since 1945 only five colts have done so, Sayajirao (1947, won the St Leger after placing in the 2000 Guineas and Derby), Nagami (1958, third in all three races) and Nijinsky were the other three. The time may have come to take a fresh look at the distance over which the St Leger is run and possibly the Derby too. This topic is discussed further in the essay on Bob's Return (p140) and in the Introduction. Camelot's defeat in the St Leger denied Aidan O'Brien the unique feat of training the winner of all five English classics in one season. As a four-year-old Camelot had a disappointing season and was retired to Coolmore Stud at Fethard in County Tipperary. The stallion stood at Coolmore Australia for the 2014 southern hemisphere breeding season before returning to Ireland. Camelot is the second foal of Tarfah (G3 Dahlia S), a daughter of Fickle (LR Virginia S) and descending in the tail-female line from Seventh Bride (1966, by Royal Record – Princess Royal S), the dam of Polygamy (1971, by Reform - G1 Oaks S, 2nd 1000 Guineas) and Camelot's fourth dam One Over Parr (1972, by Reform – G3 Cheshire & Lancashire Oaks) for Louis Freedman's Cliveden Stud.

1911012

Above: **CAMELOT** and Joseph O'Brien win the 2000 Guineas beating French Fifteen (Oliver Peslier). This was a first English classic victory for the eighteen year old jockey, son of the trainer, who was winning his sixth 2000 Guineas following King of Kings (see p188), Rock of Gibraltar (p232), Footstepsinthesand (p264), George Washington (p276) and Henrythenavigator (p298). This was the third English classic in succession to fall to a son of the Coolmore stallion Montjeu.

Below: Nine runners, the smallest field since 1907 and **CAMELOT** (Joseph O'Brien) wins by an eased-down five lengths to set up dreams of the Triple Crown. This was the first time that a father and son trainer/jockey combination had won the Derby at Epsom

3112212

HOMECOMING QUEEN (IRE)

Bay filly, foaled 23 April 2009
By Holy Roman Emperor (IRE) ex Lagrion (USA) by Diesis (GB)
Bred by Tower Bloodstock
Owned by Mrs John Magnier, Michael Tabor and Derrick Smith
Trained by Aidan P. O'Brien at Ballydoyle, Cashel, Co. Tipperary.

© Peter Mooney

Racing Record

Year	Timeform Annual Rating	Starts	Wins	2nd	3rd	4th	Prize Money
2011	105	11	2	1	2	1	£ 39,466
2012	120	5	2	-	-	1	£ 246,742

Principal Performances

2011 2nd CL Weld Park Stakes (G3) (2yo fillies) Curragh (7f)
     Won Lanwades & Staffordstown Studs S. (Listed Race) (2yo fillies) Curragh (8f)
2012 Won 1000 Guineas Trial Stakes (G3) (3yo fillies) Leopardstown (7f)
     Won 1000 Guineas Stakes (G1) (3yo fillies) Newmarket (8f)
     4th Irish 1000 Guineas Stakes (G1) (3yo fillies) Curragh (8f)

*****

*H*omecoming Queen seemed thoroughly exposed during the course of a very busy first season as over a stone below classic winning standard in an ordinary year. The only encouraging thing that could be said about her was that the filly showed much improved form when racing on soft or heavy ground. As luck would have it, this is exactly what Homecoming Queen encountered when she posted an astonishing nine lengths victory in the 1000 Guineas. She reverted to her former undistinguished form in two subsequent races and was retired in June. It was announced that her first mate would be Coolmore's top stallion Galileo. The unraced Lagrion was a full-sister to Pure Genius (1986 – 2nd G1 Middle Park S) and before Homecoming Queen had bred Dylan Thomas (2003, by Danehill – G1 Irish Derby, Prix Ganay, King George VI & Queen Elizabeth S, Prix de l'Arc de Triomphe), a colt that narrowly came off third best in the pulsating finish for the 2006 Derby (p283). Other siblings were Queen's Logic (1999, by Grand Lodge – G1 Cheveley Park S), herself dam of Lady of

342

the Desert (2007, G2 Lowther S, Diadem S) and Remember When (2007, by Danehill Dancer – 2nd G1 Oaks S, 4th Irish 1000 Guineas), the dam of Wedding Vow (2012, by Galileo – G2 Kilboy Estate S). Their dam Wrap It Up was very moderate on the racecourse, but a half-sister to Gift Wrapped (1977, by Wolver Hollow – G3 Lingfield Oaks Trial), the dam of Reach (1982, by Kris – G2 Royal Lodge S) and Wrapping (1986, by Kris – 2nd G1 Oaks d'Italia), herself the dam of Papering (1993, by Shaadi – G2 Premio Lydia Tesio, 2nd G1 Prix Vermeille, Yorkshire Oaks). The great grandam, the durable Doc Nan (1963, by Francis S), was not particularly talented but won ten minor races from fifty-eight starts in the U.S.

0111312

Above: A dismal day of rain and bad light, weather which deteriorated further during a thirty minute delay caused by a fatal stalls accident. A 25/1 outsider, the longest priced winner since On The House in 1982 (see p26), **HOMECOMING QUEEN** (Ryan Moore) makes all the running and draws away from her field to win the 1000 Guineas by the widest margin since Mayonaise was judged to have won by twenty lengths in 1859. The only similar winning margin in recent times was in 1970 when Humble Duty and Lester Piggott strolled home by seven lengths. The hooded Starscope (blaze) finishes second and the winner's stable-companion Maybe (striped sleeves) third. Ryan Moore said afterwards 'when all you can hear is the commentator, you know you are a long way clear.'

1407105

0605312

Above left: **AIDAN O'BRIEN** won his second 1000 Guineas with Homecoming Queen following Virginia Waters (see p266) in 2005. O'Brien has been the dominant trainer in Ireland for almost two decades, being champion trainer there on sixteen occasions.

Above right: Heavy rain is falling as part-owner **DERRICK SMITH** (left) leads in his filly and **RYAN MOORE**. In the background is another part-owner, **MICHAEL TABOR**. Three times champion jockey in Britain (2006, 2008-9), Ryan Moore was winning his third English classic after Snow Fairy (p322) and Workforce (p324) in the Oaks and Derby of 2010.

343

ARCTIC COSMOS (USA) : Bay 2007

		Danehill (USA) B. 1986	Danzig (USA)
	North Light (IRE) B. 2001		Razyana (USA)
		Sought Out (IRE) B. 1988	Rainbow Quest (USA)
			Edinburgh (GB)
	Fifth Avenue Doll (USA) B. 1998	Marquetry (USA) Ch. 1987	Conquistador Cielo (USA)
			Regent's Walk (CAN)
		Allego (USA) B/br. 1985	Alleged (USA)
			Dotsie Go (USA)

FRANKEL (GB) : Bay 2008

		Sadler's Wells (USA) B. 1981	Northern Dancer (CAN)
	Galileo (IRE) B. 1998		Fairy Bridge (USA)
		Urban Sea (USA) Ch. 1989	Miswaki (USA)
			Allegretta (GB)
	Kind (IRE) B. 2001	Danehill (USA) B. 1986	Danzig (USA)
			Razyana (USA)
		Rainbow Lake (GB) B. 1990	Rainbow Quest (USA)
			Rockfest (USA)

BLUE BUNTING (USA) : Grey 2008

		Roberto (USA) B. 1969	Hail To Reason (USA)
	Dynaformer (USA) B/br. 1985		Bramalea (USA)
		Andover Way (USA) B/br. 1978	His Majesty (USA)
			On The Trail (USA)
	Miarixa (FR) Gr. 2001	Linamix (FR) Gr. 1987	Mendez (FR)
			Lunadix (FR)
		Mrs Arkada (FR) B. 1991	Akarad (FR)
			Mrs Annie (FR)

DANCING RAIN (IRE) : Chesnut 2008

		Danehill (USA) B. 1986	Danzig (USA)
	Danehill Dancer (IRE) B. 1993		Razyana (USA)
		Mira Adonde (USA) B/br. 1986	Sharpen Up (GB)
			Lettre d'Amour (USA)
	Rain Flower (IRE) Ch. 1997	Indian Ridge (IRE) Ch. 1985	Ahonoora (GB)
			Hillbrow (GB)
		Rose of Jericho (USA) B. 1984	Alleged (USA)
			Rose Red (USA)

POUR MOI (IRE) : Bay 2008

	Montjeu (IRE) B. 1996	Sadler's Wells (USA) B. 1981	Northern Dancer (CAN)
			Fairy Bridge (USA)
		Floripedes (FR) B. 1985	Top Ville (IRE)
			Toute Cy (FR)
	Gwynn (IRE) B. 1997	Darshaan (GB) Br. 1981	Shirley Heights (GB)
			Delsy (FR)
		Victoress (USA) B. 1984	Conquistador Cielo (USA)
			Royal Statute (USA)

MASKED MARVEL (GB) : Bay 2008

	Montjeu (IRE) B. 1996	Sadler's Wells (USA) B. 1981	Northern Dancer (CAN)
			Fairy Bridge (USA)
		Floripedes (FR) B. 1985	Top Ville (IRE)
			Toute Cy (FR)
	Waldmark (GER) Ch. 2000	Mark of Esteem (IRE) B. 1993	Darshaan (GB)
			Homage (GB)
		Wurftaube (GER) Ch. 1993	Acatenango (GER)
			Wurfbahn (GER)

CAMELOT (GB) : Bay 2009

	Montjeu (IRE) B. 1996	Sadler's Wells (USA) B. 1981	Northern Dancer (CAN)
			Fairy Bridge (USA)
		Floripedes (FR) B. 1985	Top Ville (IRE)
			Toute Cy (FR)
	Tarfah (USA) B. 2001	Kingmambo (USA) B. 1990	Mr Prospector (USA)
			Miesque (USA)
		Fickle (GB) B. 1996	Danehill (USA)
			Fade (GB)

HOMECOMING QUEEN (IRE) : Bay 2009

	Holy Roman Emperor (IRE) B. 2004	Danehill (USA) B. 1986	Danzig (USA)
			Razyana (USA)
		L'On Vite (USA) B. 1986	Secretariat (USA)
			Fanfreluche (USA)
	Lagrion (USA) Ch. 1989	Diesis (GB) Ch. 1980	Sharpen Up (GB)
			Doubly Sure (GB)
		Wrap It Up (IRE) Ch. 1979	Mount Hagen (FR)
			Doc Nan (USA)

WAS (IRE)

Bay filly, foaled 11 May 2009
By Galileo (IRE) out of Alluring Park (IRE) by Green Desert (USA)
Bred by Lodge Park Stud, Freshford, Co. Kilkenny
Owned by Derrick Smith, Mrs John Magnier and Michael Tabor
Trained by Aidan P. O'Brien at Ballydoyle, Cashel, Co. Tipperary.

2811812

Racing Record

Year	Timeform Annual Rating	Starts	Wins	2nd	3rd	4th	Prize Money
2011	88	1	1	-	-	-	£ 10,112
2012	117	6	1	-	3	1	£ 276,917
2013	112	2	-	1	-	1	£ 32,358

Principal Performances

2012 3rd Blue Wind Stakes (G3) (Fillies & mares) Naas (10f)
     Won Oaks Stakes (G1) (3yo fillies) Epsom (12f)
     4th Irish Oaks Stakes (G1) (3yo fillies) Curragh (12f)
     3rd Nassau Stakes (G1) (Fillies & mares) Goodwood (9.9f)
     3rd Yorkshire Oaks (G1) (Fillies & mares) York (12f)
2013 2nd Pretty Polly Stakes (G1) (Fillies & mares) Curragh (10f)

*****

The yearling filly purchased at Tattersalls October Sales in Newmarket and the top-priced lot overall at 1.2m guineas, was given the uninspiring name of Was. It rather begs the question 'Was what?' Nevertheless, her name did not stop Was becoming a classic winner, even if a lucky and low-rated one by Timeform. Was failed to confirm the form of her Oaks victory in four subsequent races in 2012, finishing behind the extremely unfortunate Oaks third The Fugue, at both Goodwood and York. Surprisingly kept in training at four, Was went close to a second Group 1 victory at the Curragh in late-June but was not seen on a racecourse again. Her dam Alluring Park was a listed placed winner and also bred Janood (2008, by Medicean – LR Washington Singer S) and Al Naamah (2012, by Galileo –

2nd G3 Prix Cleopatre). The grandam Park Express (G1 Irish Champion S, G2 Nassau S), was a great success on the racecourse and at stud, producing Shinko Forest (1993, by Green Desert), a Group 1 winner in Japan, Dazzling Park (1996, by Warning – G3 Matron S) and New Approach (see p304).

2211812

Above and opposite: **WAS** is kept clear of trouble by James Heffernan in a slowly-run race and wins the Oaks beating Shirocco Star (white cap) and the unlucky and fast-finishing The Fugue (left).

0106312

1309114

1429197

Above left: **JAMES HEFFERNAN** and part-owner **MICHAEL TABOR** (left) in the winner's circle with Was after the Oaks. It was a first English classic victory for Heffernan (above right).

Centre: **DERRICK SMITH**'s colours were first carried to English classic success by his 2000 Guineas winner Camelot (p340), also a double Derby winner at both Epsom and the Curragh. A St Leger followed for Smith in 2013 with Leading Light (p358) and a second Derby victory was provided by Australia (p368) in 2014.

Right: The July Cup winner **GREEN DESERT** was a very successful stallion, his best progeny including Invincible Spirit (Sprint Cup), Desert Prince (Irish 2000 Guineas), Oasis Dream (Nunthorpe S) and Cape Cross (Lockinge S). Green Desert was put down during early-September 2015 at Nunnery Stud.

1919695

ENCKE (USA)

Bay colt, foaled 24 February 2009
By Kingmambo (USA) out of Shawanda (IRE) by Sinndar (IRE)
Bred by Darley
Owned by Godolphin
2011-12 Trained by Mahmood Al-Zarooni and in
2013-14 by Charles Appleby at Moulton Paddocks, Newmarket, Suffolk.

0614712

Racing Record

Year	Timeform Annual Rating	Starts	Wins	2nd	3rd	4th	Prize Money
2011	99	2	1	1	-	-	£ 7,389
2012	123	4	2	1	1	-	£ 348,585
2013	-	0	-	-	-	-	-
2014	119	3	-	1	2	-	£ 41,856

Principal Performances

2012   2nd Gordon Stakes (G3) (3yo) Goodwood (12f)
      3rd Great Voltigeur Stakes (G2) (3yo colts & geldings) York (12f)
      Won St Leger Stakes (G1) (3yo colts & fillies) Doncaster (14.6f)
2014   2nd Glorious Stakes (G3) Goodwood (12f)
      3rd Irish St Leger Stakes (G1) (3yo & upwards) Curragh (14f)
      3rd Cumberland Lodge Stakes (G3) Ascot (12f)

*****

O n 22 April 2013 it was revealed that eleven horses trained under the Godolphin banner at their Moulton Paddocks stables by Mahmood Al-Zarooni had tested positive for anabolic steroids, a drug not permitted under the rules of racing in Britain. Al-Zarooni later admitted administering the drug to four other horses, making a total of fifteen. The horses, which included the unbeaten Certify, at the time ante-post favourite for the 1000 Guineas, were banned from racing in Britain for a period of six months. The head of Godolphin, Sheikh Mohammed Al-Maktoum and his racing manager Simon Crisford denied any knowledge of the use of drugs and Al-Zarooni effectively took all the blame. He was banned from racing for eight years and disappeared back to Dubai after stating that 'it was my responsibility to be aware of the rules and regulations around banned substances'. At the time the use of anabolic steroids was permitted in Dubai and it appeared from this statement that Al-Zarooni was claiming to be unaware they were a banned substance in Britain. Simon Crisford called it 'a dark day for Godolphin' and confirmed that Sheikh Mohammed had ordered 'an urgent review of all our procedures and controls'. On 20 May 2013, a further seven Godolphin horses, including Encke, were added to the list of horses which had tested positive for anabolic steroids and were also banned from racing for six months. A spokesman for the British Horseracing Authority stated that Encke had passed drugs tests before and after the St Leger and 'we can be certain... (Encke)...was not under the benefits of substances at the time of his classic victory'. Encke returned from his racing ban in 2014, but failed to confirm the merit of his St Leger defeat of Camelot (p340) and suffered a fatal injury in training on 14 October of the same year. Shawanda was bought privately by Darley after winning the Irish Oaks and Prix Vermeille for her breeder, the Aga Khan. This is the family of Shareta (2008, by Sinndar – G1 Yorkshire Oaks, Prix Vermeille) and Sharaya (1980, by Youth – G1 Prix Vermeille).

2616312

0716512

Above left: **ENCKE** foils Camelot's bid for the Triple Crown and beats the 2000 Guineas and Derby winner in the St Leger. Above right: **MAHMOOD AL-ZAROONI** (below right) leads in his first St Leger and second English classic winner following Blue Bunting (p332). Below left: **MICKAEL BARZALONA** rode his second English classic winner after Pour Moi (p336) in the Derby of 2011.

Below centre: Racing manager **SIMON CRISFORD** resigned from Godolphin during February 2014 and began training from stables in Newmarket in January 2015.

1206111

0610114

2211411

DAWN APPROACH (IRE)

Chesnut colt, foaled 23 April 2010 by
New Approach (IRE) out of Hymn of the Dawn (USA) by Phone Trick (USA)
Bred by James S. Bolger
2012: Owned by Mrs James S. Bolger
September 2012-2013: Owned by Godolphin
Trained by James S. Bolger at Glebe House, Coolcullen, Co. Carlow.

2717612

Racing Record

Year	Timeform Annual Rating	Starts	Wins	2nd	3rd	4th	Prize Money
2012	126	6	6	-	-	-	£ 366,188
2013	132	6	2	1	-	1	£ 560,592

Principal Performances

2012   Won Rochestown Stakes (Listed Race) (2yo colts & geldings) Naas (6f)
        Won Coventry Stakes (G2) (2yo) Royal Ascot (6f)
        Won National Stakes (G1) (2yo colts & fillies) Curragh (7f)
        Won Dewhurst Stakes (G1) (2yo colts & fillies) Newmarket (7f) (photo above)
2013   Won 2000 Guineas Stakes (G1) (3yo colts & fillies) Newmarket (8f)
        Won St James's Palace Stakes (G1) (3yo colts) Royal Ascot (8f)
        2nd Sussex Stakes (G1) (3yo & upwards) Goodwood (8f)
        4th Queen Elizabeth II Stakes (G1) (3yo & upwards) Ascot (8f)

*****

'*...p* *ulled very hard for his head...an extraordinary performance, which can have had few precedents in a major race...forfeited his chance by expending too much energy fighting his jockey'. Do these words from Timeform's Racehorses of 2008 sound familiar? They should, because the performance was repeated five years later in all except one important respect, by a first-crop son of the horse referred to above, in exactly the same race, ridden by the same jockey and conditioned by the same trainer. These quotes are taken from the essay on New Approach, who despite his headstrong* *antics was good enough to win the Derby. Dawn Approach too, fought his jockey from early in the race, plunging and throwing his head around, until the exhausted Kevin Manning, who was forced wide and could never find the cover he needed to relax Dawn Approach, allowed the colt to have his way. In a move reminiscent of another hard-pulling doubtful stayer, Tudor Minstrel in 1947, Dawn Approach strode into the lead down the hill to Tattenham Corner. Passing the three furlong marker it was apparent that Dawn Approach had beaten himself and Manning eased off when all hope was gone, eventually finishing last. Like Tudor Minstrel, Dawn Approach had his moments afterwards, but the brilliance had gone. A last gasp win at Royal Ascot was followed by a narrow defeat at Goodwood. After two further reverses, Dawn Approach retired to Kildangan Stud at Monasterevin in County Kildare at a fee of €35,000 for 2014. Hymn of the Dawn was purchased by James Bolger as a foal at Keeneland for $18,000 and proved virtually useless on the racecourse but has also bred Dawn Approach's full-brother Herald The Dawn (2013 – G2 Futurity S). The grandam Colonial Debut also failed to win a race but was out of a winning daughter of Kittiwake (1968, by Sea-Bird), the dam of Miss Oceana (1981, by Alydar – G1 Acorn S), Kitwood (1989, by Nureyev – G1 Prix Jean Prat) and Larida (1979, by Northern Dancer), the dam of Magic of Life (1985, by Seattle Slew – G1 Coronation S).*

3411413

Above: With his main rival Toronado running below form, **DAWN APPROACH** has a relatively easy task to win the 2000 Guineas by five lengths from Glory Awaits (blinkers) and Van Der Neer (left). It was a first victory in this classic for both jockey Kevin Manning and his father-in-law, **JAMES BOLGER** (below left). They had together previously won the 1000 Guineas with Finsceal Beo (see p288) and the Derby with New Approach (p304). Bolger had won the Oaks in 1991 with Jet Ski Lady (p118). Below centre: **KEVIN MANNING** celebrates as Dawn Approach is led into the winner's circle after the 2000 Guineas.

2008115   1011513   1806213

Above right: **DAWN APPROACH** (Kevin Manning) holds the challenge of a back-to-form Toronado (Richard Hughes) and wins the St James's Palace Stakes by a short-head. The placings were to be reversed at Goodwood in the next duel between the two best milers of their generation.

SKY LANTERN (IRE)

Grey filly, foaled 27 January 2010
By Red Clubs (IRE) ex Shawanni (GB) by Shareef Dancer (USA)
Bred by Tally-Ho Stud, Mullingar, Co. Westmeath
Owned by Ben Keswick
2012-13: Trained by Richard Hannon and 2014 by Richard Hannon, Jr. at East Everleigh
Stables, Marlborough.

0410214

Racing Record

Year	Timeform Annual Rating	Starts	Wins	2nd	3rd	4th	Prize Money
2012	112	6	3	2	-	-	£ 166,822
2013	122	7	3	2	-	-	£ 625,044
2014	110	3	-	-	-	-	£ 12,011

Principal Performances

2012   Won E.B.F. Sprint Stakes (Listed Race) (2yo fillies) Naas (6f)
     2nd Sweet Solera Stakes (G3) (2yo fillies) Newmarket (7f)
     2nd Prestige Stakes (G3) (2yo fillies) Goodwood (7f)
     Won Moyglare Stud Stakes (G1) (2yo fillies) Curragh (7f)
2013   2nd Nell Gwyn Stakes (G3) (3yo fillies) Newmarket (7f)
     Won 1000 Guineas Stakes (G1) (3yo fillies) Newmarket (8f)
     Won Coronation Stakes (G1) (3yo fillies) Royal Ascot (8f)
     2nd Falmouth Stakes (G1) (Fillies & mares) Newmarket (8f)
     Won Sun Chariot Stakes (G1) (Fillies & mares) Newmarket (8f)

*****

*D*uring the running of the 2013 Falmouth Stakes Sky Lantern was carried virtually across the whole width of the course by Elusive Kate, ridden by William Buick, and beaten by a neck. Although Sky Lantern was also struck across the head by Buick's whip, the stewards at Newmarket

352

inexplicably failed to disqualify Elusive Kate and the result was subsequently confirmed after an appeal by the connections of Sky Lantern. When such a blatant case of preventing another horse from winning a race is allowed to go unpunished it makes one wonder how long it will be before an accident caused by this kind of riding will severely injure a jockey, a horse or both. The current rules virtually encourage bad jockeyship; there is no incentive for jockeys to keep their horses running in a straight line because they know that unless they actually bring another horse down they will keep the race. We have gone from the ridiculous (Royal Gait, Ascot Gold Cup 1988) to the dangerous. Shawanni, a minor winner, had previously bred Shanty Star (2000, by Hector Protector – G3 Queen's Vase) and Arctic (2007, by Shamardal - G3 Round Tower S) for Darley before being culled in 2007. Sky Lantern was retired after her last race in October 2014 and it was announced on 16 November that her first mating will be with Dubawi (p319).

3611613

Above: A long overdue first English classic for jockey **RICHARD HUGHES** (below right) as he wins the 200th running of the 1000 Guineas on **SKY LANTERN** beating Just The Judge.

1207113   2232804   3014202

Above left: **RICHARD HANNON** trained his last classic winner before handing over to his son, Richard Jr. (centre) at the end of 2013. During a career that started in 1970, Hannon was four times champion trainer in Britain (1992, 2010-11-13) and saddled three winners of the 2000 Guineas, Mon Fils (1972), Don't Forget Me (p76) and Tirol (p104). Amongst the other 4,145 winners trained by Hannon were Lyric Fantasy (G1 Nunthorpe S), Assessor (G1 Prix Royal-Oak), Canford Cliffs, Toronado and Reel Buddy (all G1 Sussex S), Olympic Glory (G1 Queen Elizabeth II S) and Mr Brooks (G1 July Cup).

TALENT (GB)

Chestnut filly, foaled 25 February 2010
By New Approach (IRE) out of Prowess (IRE) by Peintre Celebre (USA)
Bred by Ashbrittle Stud & Mark H. Dixon
Owned by James L. Rowsell & Mark H. Dixon
Trained by Ralph Beckett at Kimpton Down Stables, Andover, Hants.

0417713

Racing Record

Year	Timeform Annual Rating	Starts	Wins	2nd	3rd	4th	Prize Money
2012	83	2	1	-	1	-	£ 6,276
2013	116	5	2	1	1	-	£ 450,438
2014	111	4	-	-	1	1	£ 32,483

Principal Performances

2013 Won Pretty Polly Stakes (Listed Race) (3yo fillies) Newmarket (10f)
      Won Oaks Stakes (G1) (3yo fillies) Epsom (12f)
      2nd St Leger Stakes (G1) (3yo colts & fillies) Doncaster (14.6f)
      3rd British Champions Fillies & Mares Stakes (G1) Ascot (12f)
2014 3rd Lancashire Oaks Stakes (G2) (3yo+) (Fillies & mares) Haydock (11.9f)

*****

*T*alent was one of the first crop of foals of the 2008 Derby winner New Approach (p304), which
also included Dawn Approach (p350), and the filly posted a good victory in the Oaks but was
beaten on all three subsequent starts in her classic year and is rated as a poor Oaks winner. Kept in
training for a further season, Talent disappointed and failed to win again. Her retirement was
announced in late-August and the filly joined her dam at the owners' Ashbrittle Stud at Wellington in
Somerset. Prowess was a listed placed winner out of Yawl (G3 Rockfel S), herself the best produce of
Oaks winner Bireme (p10), a half-sister to Anchor (1966, by Major Portion – Nell Gwyn S), Fluke (1967,
by Grey Sovereign – Jersey & Duke of York S), Buoy (1970, by Aureole – G1 Coronation Cup, 2nd G1 St
Leger) and Balinger (1976, by Welsh Pageant – G3 Queen Alexandra S). This family was founded on

the mare Felucca (1941, by Nearco) at Dick Hollingsworth's Arches Hall Stud and descends through Kyak (1953, by Big Game – Park Hill S) and her daughter Ripeck (1959, by Ribot), the fourth dam of Talent. This is also the family of two winners of the Group 2 King Edward VII Stakes, Mariner (1964, by Acropolis) and Sea Anchor (1972, by Alcide), as well as Bindaree (1994, by Roselier – G3 Grand National Steeple Chase).

1312513

Above: **TALENT** (Richard Hughes) winning the Oaks Stakes beating her stable companion Secret Gesture. The Lark (rail) finishes third ahead of Moth (left). This was the second English classic success of the season for Hughes, following Sky Lantern (p352). Ralph Beckett became the first trainer to saddle the winner and runner-up in the Oaks since Noel Murless did so with Altesse Royale and Maina in 1971.

3012413

© George Selwyn

Left: **RALPH BECKETT** is congratulated by **RICHARD HUGHES** after winning his second Oaks. Beckett had been previously successful with Look Here (p302) in 2008. This was the second and last English classic winner ridden by Hughes, who was champion jockey in Britain during 2012 for total winners ridden in the calendar year. Richard Hughes retired from the saddle at the end of July 2015 to start training from Danebury Place at Stockton in Hampshire. Right: **JAMES ROWSELL** and **MARK DIXON** (right) with the Oaks trophy.

Left: **PEINTRE CELEBRE,** with Olivier Peslier after winning the Prix de l'Arc de Triomphe in 1997, also won the Prix du Jockey-Club and Grand Prix de Paris. Peintre Celebre was injured in training early in 1998 and retired to Coolmore Stud in Co. Tipperary. For such a brilliant racehorse, he has proved a disappointing sire, his best progeny being Pride (Champion S, HK Gold Cup), Collection (Hong Kong Derby, HK Gold Cup), Helene Mascot (HK Classic Mile, Hong Kong Derby), Vallee Enchantee (HK Vase), Mighty High (Champions & Chater Cup), Byword (Prince of Wales's S), Bentley Biscuit (3xG1 in Australia) and Castledale (Santa Anita Derby, Breeders Cup Mile).

2032097

RULER OF THE WORLD (IRE)

Chesnut colt, foaled 17 March 2010
By Galileo (IRE) out of Love Me True (USA) by Kingmambo (USA)
Bred by Southern Bloodstock
Owned by Mrs John Magnier, Michael Tabor and Derrick Smith
Trained by Aidan P. O'Brien at Ballydoyle, Cashel, Co. Tipperary.

1409214

Racing Record

Year	Timeform Annual Rating	Starts	Wins	2nd	3rd	4th	Prize Money
2012	-	0	-	-	-	-	-
2013	128	7	3	1	1	-	£ 1,008,493
2014	126	4	1	-	-	-	£ 61,750

Principal Performances

2013   Won Chester Vase (G3) (3yo colts & geldings) Chester (12.3f)
      Won Derby Stakes (G1) (3yo colts & fillies) Epsom (12f)
      2nd Prix Niel (G2) (3yo colts & fillies) Longchamp (11.9f)
      3rd Champion Stakes (G1) (3yo & upwards) Ascot (10f)
2014   Won Prix Foy (G2) (4yo & upwards) Longchamp (11.9f)

*****

*R*uler Of The World, unraced as a two-year-old, improved with every race in his classic season, apart from a disappointing performance on ground probably too firm for him when unplaced in the Irish Derby. Ruler Of The World was unlucky not to win the Prix Niel when having to be switched inside the final furlong, finishing strongly and only beaten by a short-head. His best performance came in late-October at Ascot when a close third behind two top-class older horses in the Champion Stakes. On 26 March 2014 it was revealed that Sheikh Joaan Al-Thani had bought a 50% stake in Ruler Of The World and that the colt would race in 2014 as a partnership of Al Shaqab Racing and his three previous owners. After running poorly in the 2014 Champion Stakes it was announced six days later on 24

October that Ruler Of The World had been retired to Coolmore Stud at Fethard in County Tipperary due to the recurrence of a muscle injury to his hind quarters. His dam Love Me True had been bought for Coolmore for $1.35m as a yearling and has also bred multiple Group 1 winner Duke of Marmalade (2004, by Danehill – G1 King George VI & Queen Elizabeth S) and Giovanni Canaletto (2012, by Galileo – 3rd G1 Irish Derby, 4th Derby S). She descends from a successful U.S. family, that of two winners of the Group 1 Belmont Stakes, A.P. Indy (1989, by Seattle Slew) and Lemon Drop Kid (1996, by Kingmambo), as well as Summer Squall (1987, by Storm Bird – G1 Preakness S). In Europe this family has produced Wolfhound (1989, by Nureyev – G1 Prix de la Foret), a colt out of Ruler Of The World's great grandam Lassie Dear (1974, by Buckpasser).

1212813

Above: **RULER OF THE WORLD** (Ryan Moore), one of five runners in the race from Aidan O'Brien's Ballydoyle Stables but rejected by stable-jockey Joseph O'Brien, wins the Derby from Libertarian (left), Galileo Rock (hooped cap) and Battle Of Marengo (striped sleeves). Hot favourite Dawn Approach (extreme right) had spoiled his chance by fighting his jockey and finishes last.

3212713

3112713

Above left: **JOHN MAGNIER** of Coolmore and **AIDAN O'BRIEN** greeting **RYAN MOORE** and Ruler Of The World after the Derby. It was a fourth victory in this classic for the trainer after Galileo (p228), High Chaparral (p238) and Camelot (p340). Ruler Of The World became only the fourth horse since 1950 to win the Derby after being unraced at two following Phil Drake (1955), Morston (1973) and Commander In Chief (p136).

Above right: Ryan Moore is led in on his second Derby winner by part-owners **DERRICK SMITH** (holding the rein) and **MICHAEL TABOR** (right). This was Moore's fourth English classic success since 2010 following Snow Fairy (p322), Homecoming Queen (p342) and Workforce (p324). Ruler Of The World was the first horse to win the Derby wearing cheek pieces and the first since the blinkered Aboyeur in 1913 to win wearing headgear, excepting sheepskin nosebands.

357

LEADING LIGHT (IRE)

Bay colt, foaled 6 March 2010
By Montjeu (IRE) out of Dance Parade (USA) by Gone West (USA)
Bred by Lynch-Bages Limited
Owned by Derrick Smith, Mrs John Magnier and Michael Tabor
Trained by Aidan P. O'Brien at Ballydoyle, Cashel, Co. Tipperary.

0616313

Racing Record

Year	Timeform Annual Rating	Starts	Wins	2nd	3rd	4th	Prize Money
2012	88	2	1	-	-	1	£ 8,042
2013	121	5	4	-	-	-	£ 425,069
2014	125	5	3	1	-	-	£ 327,871

Principal Performances

2013 Won Gallinule Stakes (G3) (3yo) Curragh (10f)
Won Queen's Vase (G3) (3yo) Royal Ascot (16f)
Won St Leger Stakes (G1) (3yo colts & fillies) Doncaster (14.6f)
2014 Won Vintage Crop Stakes (G3) Navan (14f)
Won Gold Cup (G1) (4yo & upwards) Royal Ascot (20f)
Won Irish St Leger Trial Stakes (G3) (3yo & upwards) Curragh (14f)
2nd Irish St Leger Stakes (G1) (3yo & upwards) Curragh (14f)

*****

A fter being given a reality check by Leading Light's performance when supplemented into the 2013 Prix de l'Arc de Triomphe for €100,000, his connections resisted the temptation to chase rainbows over twelve furlongs in 2014 and were rewarded with an Ascot Gold Cup and two G3 victories. Unfortunately the colt suffered career ending injuries during a race at Ascot in mid-October and his retirement to Coolmore's Grange Stud at a fee of €4.5k for 2015 was announced by Aidan

O'Brien the following week. The incident which apparently caused the injuries to *Leading Light* happened when the Pat Smullen ridden *Forgotten Rules* (an appropriate name if ever there was one), the eventual winner, hung sharply to his right, seriously hampering and almost bringing down *Leading Light*. The knock-on effect virtually put paid to the chances of three other horses. The current B.H.A. rules on interference were discussed on p352-3 over the incident involving *Sky Lantern* at Newmarket in July 2013, when the stewards decided the transgression was not serious enough to disqualify *Elusive Kate*. This 2014 Ascot incident resulted in the loss to racing of one of its top horses *Leading Light* and the potential for more serious accidents to occur, such as the death of a rider or horse, will remain until the interference rules are tightened up, encouraging jockeys to keep their horses running straight. As most things in racing nowadays are driven by the motive of boosting bookmaker profit, how do they benefit from the first past the post keeping the race 99.9% of the time? There must be something in it for them. Might it be linked to keeping the timing of races right in the off-course betting shops? A steward's inquiry normally means a delay in the announcement of the result and betting shop punters, not knowing if they have won or lost, miss a race or two while waiting. It is very noticeable how early runners are assembled at the start over the last few seasons, so the race is off exactly on time, which means race timing in the shops runs to schedule and punters are never given time to reflect on their losses before the next is due off. The whole thing stinks to high heaven – racing should not be run for bookmakers and racing should not be in the position of having to run it for bookmakers. The current way in which the bookmaker's contribution to racing is calculated, on profit rather than turnover, is to blame. Bookmakers sponsor whole days at minor tracks for presumably a few hundred pounds and fill the card with handicaps for bad horses, more death traps for punters. Bookmakers decide in what order races are run and the programme always finishes with a tricky handicap so punters have little chance of retrieving losses. Somebody even managed to dream up a nice twenty-plus runner handicap to finish off Champions Day at Ascot so that bookmakers could make even more money! *Leading Light* was a 520,000 guineas yearling purchase for a Coolmore partnership at Tattersalls October Sales. *Dance Parade* was a good racemare winning the G2 Queen Mary and G3 Fred Darling Stakes and has also bred *Castles In The Air* (2005, by Oasis Dream – 5 races & £91,389). Her dam, listed winner *River Jig*, was from the family of U.S. champion *Round Table* (1954, by Princequillo), the 1958 Horse of the Year and also a highly successful sire, his winners including *Baldric* (1961 – 2000 Guineas and Champion S) and *Artaius* (1974, Eclipse and Sussex S).

2216313   2008214   © Steven Cargill

Above left: **LEADING LIGHT** (Joseph O'Brien) wins the St Leger beating Talent (p354) and Galileo Rock, a colt that had previously been third in the Derby and second in the Irish Derby. This was the twentieth English classic winner trained by Aidan O'Brien since his first, King Of Kings (p188), won the 2000 Guineas in 1998.

Above centre: **JOSEPH O'BRIEN** rode his first St Leger winner on Leading Light; the six-foot tall jockey, who cannot scale under nine stone, was winning his third English classic following the 2000 Guineas and Derby on Camelot (p340) in 2012. O'Brien was champion jockey in Ireland for the second successive year in 2013 with a record 136 winners, beating Mick Kinane's total of 115 set in 1993.

Above right: **LEADING LIGHT** and Joseph O'Brien winning the Ascot Gold Cup beating Estimate (centre) and Misunited (left), becoming the first English classic winner to win the Royal Ascot showpiece since Classic Cliché in 1996 (p162).

NIGHT OF THUNDER (IRE)

Chesnut colt, foaled 12 March 2011
By Dubawi (IRE) out of Forest Storm (GB) by Galileo (IRE)
Bred by Frank Dunne
2013-14: Owned by Saeed Manana   2015: Owned by Godolphin
2013: Trained by Richard Hannon and 2014-15 by Richard Hannon, Jr.
at East Everleigh Stables, Marlborough, Wiltshire.

1409414

Racing Record

Year	Timeform Annual Rating	Starts	Wins	2nd	3rd	4th	Prize Money
2013	110	2	2	-	-	-	£ 19,070
2014	127	6	1	3	1	-	£ 631,318
2015	123* (19 Sept)	3	1	-	-	-	£ 221,973

Principal Performances

2013   Won Doncaster Stakes (Listed Race) (2yo) Doncaster (6f)
2014   Won 2000 Guineas Stakes (G1) (3yo colts & fillies) Newmarket (8f)
    2nd St James's Palace Stakes (G1) (3yo colts) Royal Ascot (8f)
    3rd Prix du Moulin de Longchamp (G1) (3yo & upwards) Longchamp (8f)
    2nd Queen Elizabeth II Stakes (G1) (3yo & upwards) Ascot 8f
2015   Won Lockinge Stakes (G1) (4yo & upwards) Newbury (8f)

*****

*B*eaten four lengths by the outstanding three-year-old miler Kingman in the Greenham Stakes, Night Of Thunder, rejected by the stable jockey, turned around that result and beat Kingman by half-a-length in the 2000 Guineas three weeks later, despite swerving across virtually the whole width of Newmarket, a manoeuvre that must have cost both momentum and ground. What conclusions can be drawn from this result, as on all other form it should be the name of Kingman headlined at the top of this page? As the classic was run, it cannot be denied that Kingman had every chance to win had he *been good enough on the day. Subsequent results suggest that Kingman ran about two lengths below his best at Newmarket and with the benefit of hindsight perhaps his jockey would have done better to have tracked over from his far side draw to race with the larger stands side group. A 32,000 guineas yearling purchase at Tattersalls, Night Of Thunder is the only foal of the listed placed winner Forest Storm, who died in 2012, tracing through grandam Quiet Storm, also a listed placed winner, to the Irish 1000 Guineas winner Forest Flower (1984, by Green Forest). Kept in training for 2015, Night Of Thunder rewarded his connections with a second Group 1 victory, but following disappointing runs at Royal Ascot and Goodwood the colt's retirement to Kildangan Stud was announced on 17 August.*

© Ed Byrne

Above: **NIGHT OF THUNDER** (Kieren Fallon) wins the 2000 Guineas beating hot favourite Kingman (no.5). Third place goes to subsequent Derby winner Australia (p368) and Shifting Power (no.11) finishes fourth. With the leading horses finishing the whole width of the course apart, unsatisfactory finishes like this are occasionally inevitable if racecourse management position the starting stalls in the middle of the track. When questioned about this practise, a Newmarket official rather lamely replied that it was done to minimise the chance of interference. Kingman proved to be by far the best miler in the 2000 Guineas field and it is to be regretted that he was possibly denied his chance of winning because he raced on the 'wrong' side of the course.

2511214

1710114

1605315

Above left: **KIEREN FALLON** had not ridden an English classic winner since Alexandrova (p280) eight years before and at forty-nine years old his riding career had seemed in terminal decline. In contrast, **RICHARD HANNON, Jr** (right) trained a classic winner at the very first opportunity after taking over from his father at the end of 2013. Above centre: Most of the best horses owned by **SAEED MANANA** have been trained by Clive Brittain including Warrsan (G1 Coronation Cup twice) and Luso (G1 Derby Italiano). Night Of Thunder gave the Dubai-born owner his first English classic victory. Above right: **NIGHT OF THUNDER** wins the Lockinge Stakes with jockey James Doyle wearing the colours of the colt's new owner Godolphin.

361

WAS (IRE) : Bay 2009

		Sadler's Wells (USA) B. 1981	Northern Dancer (CAN)
Galileo (IRE) B. 1998			Fairy Bridge (USA)
		Urban Sea (USA) Ch. 1989	Miswaki (USA)
			Allegretta (GB)
Alluring Park (IRE) B. 1999		Green Desert (USA) B. 1983	Danzig (USA)
			Foreign Courier (USA)
		Park Express (IRE) Br. 1983	Ahonoora (GB)
			Matcher (CAN)

ENCKE (USA) : Bay 2009

		Mr Prospector (USA) B. 1970	Raise A Native (USA)
Kingmambo (USA) B. 1990			Gold Digger (USA)
		Miesque (USA) B. 1984	Nureyev (USA)
			Pasadoble (USA)
Shawanda (IRE) B. 2002		Sinndar (IRE) B. 1997	Grand Lodge (USA)
			Sinntara (IRE)
		Shamawna (IRE) B. 1989	Darshaan (GB)
			Shamsana (USA)

DAWN APPROACH (IRE) : Chesnut 2010

		Galileo (IRE) B. 1998	Northern Dancer (CAN)
New Approach (IRE) Ch. 2005			Urban Sea (USA)
		Park Express (IRE) Br. 1983	Ahonoora (GB)
			Matcher (CAN)
Hymn of The Dawn (USA) B. 1999		Phone Trick (USA) B. 1982	Clever Trick (USA)
			Over The Phone (USA)
		Colonial Debut (USA) B. 1994	Pleasant Colony (USA)
			Kittihawk Miss (USA)

SKY LANTERN (IRE) : Grey 2010

		Red Ransom (USA) B. 1987	Roberto (USA)
Red Clubs (IRE) Br. 2003			Arabia (USA)
		Two Clubs (GB) Br. 1996	First Trump (GB)
			Miss Cindy (GB)
Shawanni (GB) Gr. 1993		Shareef Dancer (USA) B. 1980	Northern Dancer (CAN)
			Sweet Alliance (USA)
		Negligent (GB) Gr. 1987	Ahonoora (GB)
			Negligence (GB)

TALENT (GB) : Chesnut 2010

	New Approach (IRE) Ch. 2005	Galileo (IRE) B. 1998	Sadler's Wells (USA)
			Urban Sea (USA)
		Park Express (IRE) Br. 1983	Ahonoora (GB)
			Matcher (CAN)
	Prowess (IRE) Ch. 2003	Peintre Celebre (USA) Ch. 1994	Nureyev (USA)
			Peinture Bleue (USA)
		Yawl (GB) B. 1990	Rainbow Quest (USA)
			Bireme (GB)

RULER OF THE WORLD (IRE) : Chesnut 2010

	Galileo (IRE) B. 1998	Sadler's Wells (USA) B. 1981	Northern Dancer (CAN)
			Fairy Bridge (USA)
		Urban Sea (USA) Ch. 1989	Miswaki (USA)
			Allegretta (GB)
	Love Me True (USA) Ch. 1998	Kingmambo (USA) B. 1990	Mr Prospector (USA)
			Miesque (USA)
		Lassie's Lady (USA) B. 1981	Alydar (USA)
			Lassie Dear (USA)

LEADING LIGHT (IRE) : Bay 2010

	Montjeu (IRE) B. 1996	Sadler's Wells (USA) B. 1981	Northern Dancer (CAN)
			Fairy Bridge (USA)
		Floripedes (FR) B. 1985	Top Ville (IRE)
			Toute Cy (FR)
	Dance Parade (USA) Ch. 1994	Gone West (USA) B. 1984	Mr Prospector (USA)
			Secrettame (USA)
		River Jig (USA) B. 1984	Irish River (FR)
			Baronova (USA)

NIGHT OF THUNDER (IRE) : Chesnut 2011

	Dubawi (IRE) B. 2002	Dubai Millennium (GB) B. 1996	Seeking The Gold (USA)
			Colorado Dancer (IRE)
		Zomaradah (GB) Br. 1995	Deploy (GB)
			Jawaher (IRE)
	Forest Storm (GB) Ch. 2006	Galileo (IRE) B. 1998	Sadler's Wells (USA)
			Urban Sea (USA)
		Quiet Storm (IRE) B. 2000	Desert Prince (IRE)
			Hertford Castle (GB)

MISS FRANCE (IRE)

Bay filly, foaled 23 March 2011
By Dansili (GB) ex Miss Tahiti (IRE) by Tirol (GB)
Bred by Dayton Investments Limited
Owned by Ballymore Thoroughbred Limited
Trained by Andre Fabre at Chantilly, Oise, France.

3111414

Racing Record

Year	Timeform Annual Rating	Starts	Wins	2nd	3rd	4th	Win Prize Money
2013	113	3	2	-	-	-	£ 34,473
2014	119	5	1	2	-	-	£ 358,684
2015	119* (19 Sept)	1	-	1	-	-	£ 8,062

Principal Performances

2013   Won Oh So Sharp Stakes (G3) (2yo fillies) Newmarket (7f)
2014   Won 1000 Guineas Stakes (G1) (3yo fillies) Newmarket (8f)
      2nd Prix Rothschild (G1) (3yo & upwards) (Fillies & mares) Deauville (8f)
      2nd Sun Chariot Stakes (G1) (Fillies & mares) Newmarket (8f)

*****

*B*allymore Thoroughbred Limited is a Dublin-based company with Diane Wildenstein, granddaughter of the late Daniel Wildenstein, owner of the English classic winners Flying Water (1973, by Habitat - 1000 Guineas), Pawneese (1973, by Carvin - Oaks) and Crow (1973, by Exbury – St Leger), listed as a director. Miss France is a descendent of what was formerly a moderate French family before the exploits of Miss Tahiti and her half-sister England's Legend (1997, by Lure – G1 Beverly D. S), were further enhanced by the classic victory of Miss France. Miss Tahiti's two foals before Miss France were both by Sadler's Wells, the listed placed triple winner, Maximum Security (1998) and Mer de Corail (1999 – LR Prix d'Automne, 2nd G3 Prix de Royaumont). Miss Tahiti has subsequently bred the unraced Miss Hawai (2000, by Peintre Celebre), dam of Beach Bunny (2005, by High Chaparral – LR Dance Design S, 2nd G1 Pretty Polly S), Malevitch (2001, by Exit To Nowhere), twice a winner in 2003 and Mission Secrete (2005, by Galileo), a minor winner in France.*

1111514

Above: **MISS FRANCE** wins the 1000 Guineas beating Lightning Thunder (rail) by a neck in an almost exact repeat of the finish of the Oh So Sharp Stakes the previous September when the distance between them had been a head. Ihtimal (no.5) finishes third and Manderley fourth. It was a first English classic victory for jockey **MAXIME GUYON** (below right) and a first in this race for trainer Andre Fabre.

2125199

1605310

Above: **DANSILI** was unlucky not to win a Group 1 race being placed second three times at that level. He's been a very successful stallion for Juddmonte Farms siring Rail Link (G1 Prix de l'Arc de Triomphe), Harbinger (King George VI & Queen Elizabeth S), Dank (G1 Breeders Cup Filly & Mare Turf), The Fugue (4xG1 including Prince of Wales's S) and Grand Marshall (G1 Sydney Cup). Miss France is his first English classic winner.

Right: **MISS TAHITI** was a classy performer for Andre Fabre and owner Daniel Wildenstein, winning the Prix Marcel Boussac and placing in both the Prix de Diane and Prix Vermeille.

2734595

365

TAGHROODA (GB)

Bay filly, foaled 27 January 2011
By Sea The Stars (IRE) out of Ezima (IRE) by Sadler's Wells (USA)
Bred by Shadwell Estate Company Limited
Owned by Hamdan Al-Maktoum
Trained by John H.M. Gosden at Clarehaven Stables, Newmarket, Suffolk.

2607114

Racing Record

Year	Timeform Annual Rating	Starts	Wins	2nd	3rd	4th	Prize Money
2013	92	1	1	-	-	-	£ 4,528
2014	127	5	3	1	1	-	£ 1,471,573

Principal Performances

2014   Won Pretty Polly Stakes (Listed Race) (3yo fillies) Newmarket (10f)
      Won Oaks Stakes (G1) (3yo fillies) Epsom (12f)
      Won King George VI and Queen Elizabeth Stakes (G1) Ascot (12f)
      2nd Yorkshire Oaks (G1) (3yo & upwards) (Fillies & mares) York (12f)
      3rd Prix de l'Arc de Triomphe (G1) (3yo & upwards) Longchamp (11.9f)

*****

*T*aghrooda became only the third three-year-old filly to win the King George VI and Queen Elizabeth Stakes, after Dahlia (1973) and Pawneese (1976), when following up her Oaks success with victory in the Ascot race. The "King George" was inaugurated in 1951 and the list of winners includes almost every middle-distance great of the last sixty years, only Sea-Bird and Sea The Stars being notable absentees. Surprise winners have been few and far between, unlike the Prix de l'Arc de Triomphe which has too frequently seen long-odds victors as well as unlucky losers, hampered while plotting a course through the usually large fields. Ideally placed in the middle of summer, so free of the soft or heavy going that often plagues the 'Arc' in October, the King George VI and Queen Elizabeth Stakes is truly the middle-distance championship race of Europe. After Australia (p368) had routed

366

Taghrooda's closest pursuers at Ascot, Telescope and Mukhadram, in the International Stakes at York, perhaps we should have been forewarned, but it still came as something of a shock when Taghrooda was beaten in the Yorkshire Oaks the following day. The filly was retired after the Prix de l'Arc de Triomphe to join her owner's stud and it was announced on 8 November that Taghrooda would be covered by Kingman (2011, by Invincible Spirit – G1 Irish 2000 Guineas, St James's Palace & Sussex S, Prix Jacques Le Marois) in 2015. Three times successful at listed level and Group 2 placed, Ezima descends from a very successful family developed by the Aga Khan. Her unraced dam Ezilla, was a full-sister to Ebaziya, also the winner of three Listed Races and Group 2 placed, as well as producing the top level winners Ebadiyla (1994, by Sadler's Wells – Irish Oaks, Prix Royal-Oak), Enzeli (1995, by Kahyasi – Ascot Gold Cup), Edabiya (1996, by Rainbow Quest – Moyglare Stud S) and Estimate (2009, by Monsun – Ascot Gold Cup). Ezima was purchased by Shadwell at Tattersalls 2008 December Sales for 320,000 guineas and Taghrooda is her second foal, followed by the unraced Maktaba (2012, by Dansili), a 2013 sister to Taghrooda and a 2014 filly by Raven's Pass. Ezima's first foal, by Tamayuz, died as a yearling.

0212214

Above: **TAGHROODA** wins The Oaks; Hamdan Al-Maktoum's second runner Tarfasha (black cap) finishes second ahead of Volume (rail). This was the first English classic victory for the owner since Ghanaati (p312) and a first in the Oaks for John Gosden.

2108214

2607714

Above left: Twice British champion jockey (2010-11), **PAUL HANAGAN** was in his second season as retained jockey for Hamdan Al-Maktoum when winning his first English classic on Taghrooda. Hanagan had previously ridden Wootton Bassett (Grand Criterium) and Mayson (July Cup) to Group 1 victories for trainer Richard Fahey and went on to win another on Mukhadram (Eclipse S) for Sheikh Hamdan in 2014. Above right: **TAGHROODA** and Paul Hanagan win the King George VI and Queen Elizabeth Stakes beating Telescope (right) and Sheikh Hamdan's second string Mukhadram.

AUSTRALIA (GB)

Chesnut colt, foaled 8 April 2011
By Galileo (IRE) out of Ouija Board (GB) by Cape Cross (IRE)
Bred by Stanley Estate and Stud Company
Owned by Derrick Smith, Mrs John Magnier, Michael Tabor and Teo Ah Khing
Trained by Aidan P. O'Brien at Ballydoyle, Cashel, Co. Tipperary.

2008214

Racing Record

Year	Timeform Annual Rating	Starts	Wins	2nd	3rd	4th	Prize Money
2013	116	3	2	1	-	-	£ 43,305
2014	132	5	3	1	1	-	£ 2,047,198

Principal Performances

2013 Won Breeders' Cup Juvenile Turf Trial Stakes (G3) (2yo) Leopardstown (8f)
2014 3rd 2000 Guineas Stakes (G1) (3yo colts & fillies) Newmarket (8f)
      Won Derby Stakes (G1) (3yo colts & fillies) Epsom (12f)
      Won Irish Derby Stakes (G1) (3yo colts & fillies) Curragh (12f)
      Won International Stakes (G1) (3yo & upwards) York (10f)
      2nd Irish Champion Stakes (G1) (3yo & upwards) Leopardstown (10f)

*****

*A*ustralia was purchased on behalf of a Coolmore partnership for 525,000 guineas at the Tattersalls October Yearling Sales. The fourth foal of Ouija Board became only the second Derby winner, after Lammtarra (p160), to be produced from a mating between Derby and Oaks winners. The colt was the subject of the usual spin from his trainer, 'we always thought he was the best horse we've ever had...doing things no two-year-old has ever done before'. Most listeners took Aidan O'Brien's announcement at York that after an outing in the Irish Champion Stakes Australia would take on the outstanding miler Kingman in the Queen Elizabeth II Stakes with a very large pinch of salt. Ultimately neither colt made it to Ascot, as Kingman was retired in September through illness and Coolmore *announced that Australia would not race again on 11 October, following a foot injury. The dual Derby winner is standing at Coolmore Stud at Fethard in County Tipperary, priced at €50,000 for 2015. Both Australia's sire Galileo (p228) and dam, Ouija Board (p258), appeared earlier in these pages. Ouija Board descends from a family developed at their Woodlands Stud by the present and past Earls of Derby and brought to wider public notice when Ouija Board's great grandam, the blind mare Samanda (1956, by Alycidon), was featured in Caroline Silver's book 'Classic Lives'. Australia is a half-brother to the gelded Voodoo Prince (2008, by Kingmambo), renamed Our Voodoo Prince when exported to Australia, where he is a winner at Group 3 level. There is more about this family on p259.*

0512614

Above: **AUSTRALIA** wins the Derby beating Kingston Hill (p370); it was jockey Joseph O'Brien's second victory in this classic following Camelot (p340), a fifth for Aidan O'Brien and an unprecedented third Derby in succession for the Ballydoyle trainer. This was also the fourth successive Derby victory for the Coolmore partnership of Derrick Smith, Susan Magnier and Michael Tabor.

Below: **JOSEPH O'BRIEN, TEO AH KHING** (2nd left), **MICHAEL TABOR** and **DERRICK SMITH** (right) with Australia in the winner's circle at York after the International Stakes. This was one of the last big-race winners ridden by O'Brien before it was revealed in early-April 2015 that due to increasing weight problems he would be replaced as the principal jockey for Coolmore's Ballydoyle Stables by Ryan Moore, although a serious injury suffered by Moore in early-July enabled O'Brien to resume his position for the remainder of the season.

2008914

KINGSTON HILL (GB)

Grey colt, foaled 15 January 2011
By Mastercraftsman (IRE) out of Audacieuse (GB) by Rainbow Quest (USA)
Bred by Ridgecourt Stud, Epsom, Surrey
Owned by Paul Smith
Trained by Roger Varian at Kremlin House Stables, Newmarket, Suffolk.

1309114

Racing Record

Year	Timeform Annual Rating	Starts	Wins	2nd	3rd	4th	Prize Money
2013	119	3	3	-	-	-	£ 176,927
2014	125	5	1	1	-	2	£ 927,352
2015	-	0	-	-	-	-	-

Principal Performances

2013   Won Autumn Stakes (G3) (2yo) Newmarket (8f)
        Won Racing Post Trophy (G1) (2yo colts & fillies) Doncaster (8f)
2014   2nd Derby Stakes (G1) (3yo colts & fillies) Epsom (12f)
        4th Eclipse Stakes (G1) (3yo & upwards) Sandown (10f)
        Won St Leger Stakes (G1) (3yo colts & fillies) Doncaster (14.6f)
        4th Prix de l'Arc de Triomphe (G1) (3yo & upwards) Longchamp (11.9f)

*****

*K*ingston Hill was a 70,000 guineas yearling purchase at Tattersalls in Newmarket and is owned by the son of Coolmore partner Derrick Smith. The colt is from the first crop of the Coolmore Stud stallion Mastercraftsman (G1 Irish 2000 Guineas, St James's Palace S). Audacieuse, who died in 2012, won the Group 3 Prix de Flore and was a half-sister to Waiter's Dream (2008, by Oasis Dream – G3 Acomb S) and listed winner Lord Jim (1992, by Kahyasi). The grandam Sarah Georgina was a minor winner at two, her only season to race, and a half-sister to Danseuse du Soir (1988, by Thatching – G1 Poule d'Essai des Pouliches, Prix de la Foret, G2 Prix Robert Papin), the dam of Jumbajukiba (2003, by Barathea – G3 Solonaway S twice, Gladness S, Minstrel S) and Scintillo (2005, by Fantastic Light – G1 Gran Criterium, G2 Grand Prix de Chantilly, G3 Winter Derby). Kingston Hill's fifth dam Relicia (1967,

370

by Relko), was a half-sister to the unraced Ardneasken (1964, by Right Royal), the dam of Warpath (1969, by Sovereign Path – Doonside Cup) and Dakota (1971, by Stupendous – G3 St Simon S, Ebor H). Even further back in the tail-female line is Daring Miss (1939, by Felicitation), the dam of the brothers Gay Time (1949, by Rockefella – Richmond S, Solario S, 2ⁿᵈ Derby S, King George VI & Queen Elizabeth S) and Elopement (1951 – Hardwicke S, 2ⁿᵈ St Leger S, 4ᵗʰ Derby S). Kingston Hill was kept in training as a four-year-old but injured his near foreleg during late-March and a further injury to the same limb in early-July eventually caused the colt's retirement to Coolmore Stud, an official announcement finally coming in mid-September, after rumours had been circulating for several weeks.

1309714

Above: **KINGSTON HILL** (Andrea Atzeni) wins the St Leger beating Romsdal. This was a first English classic victory for owner, trainer and jockey.

1309114

1309214

Above left: **PAUL SMITH** has had horses in training at Kremlin House since 2007 but Kingston Hill was his first big winner. Above right: **ANDREA ATZENI** and **ROGER VARIAN** with the St Leger trophy. Below: The sire and dam of Kingston Hill, **MASTERCRAFTSMAN** and **AUDACIEUSE** (left).

3229200

2010309

GLENEAGLES (IRE)

Bay colt, foaled 12 January 2012
By Galileo (IRE) out of You'resothrilling (USA) by Storm Cat (USA)
Bred by You'resothrilling Syndicate
Owned by Michael Tabor, Derrick Smith and Mrs John Magnier
Trained by Aidan P. O'Brien at Ballydoyle, Cashel, Co. Tipperary.

0205415

Racing Record

Year	Timeform Annual Rating	Starts	Wins	2nd	3rd	4th	Prize Money
2014	113	6	4	-	1	1	£ 271,771
2015	129* (19 Sept)	3	3	-	-	-	£ 647,579

Principal Performances

2014   Won Tyros Stakes (G3) (2yo) Leopardstown (7f)
      Won E.B.F. Futurity Stakes (G2) (2yo) Curragh (7f)
      Won Vincent O'Brien National Stakes (G1) (2yo colts & fillies) Curragh (7f)
      3rd Prix Jean-Luc Lagardere (Grand Criterium) (G1) (2yo colts & fillies) Longchamp (7f)
2015   Won 2000 Guineas Stakes (G1) (3yo colts & fillies) Newmarket (8f)
      Won Irish 2000 Guineas Stakes (G1) (3yo colts & fillies) Curragh (8f)
      Won St James's Palace Stakes (G1) (3yo colts) Royal Ascot (8f)

*****

*G*leneagles' grandam Mariah's Storm, a multiple graded stakes winner in the U.S., was purchased by John Magnier of Coolmore for $2.9m at the 1996 Keeneland November Sale. At the time of the sale, the mare was carrying a colt by Storm Cat which was named Giant's Causeway (p313). Returned to Storm Cat on six further occasions, Mariah's Storm foaled the stakes placed winners Freud (1998), Roar of the Tiger (1999) and Tumblebrutus (2001), as well as You'resothrilling (G2 Cherry Hinton S). Gleneagles' year-older sister Marvellous won the Irish 1000 Guineas for Coolmore and Aidan O'Brien in 2014, but subsequently disappointed in both the English and Irish Oaks. Their great grandam

Immense (1979, by Roberto) was a minor stakes winner in the U.S. and a half-sister to champion Dearly Precious (1973, by Dr Fager – G1 Acorn & Spinaway S). Panoramic (1987, by Rainbow Quest), a half-brother to Mariah's Storm, won the Group 2 Prix d'Harcourt. After his third 2015 Group 1 success at Royal Ascot, Gleneagles was the subject of a will-he-won't-he-run saga, reminiscent of some Ballydoyle trained horses in a previous era. His next scheduled race was intended to be in Goodwood's Sussex Stakes at the end of July, but his name was missing from the final declarations without his trainer even waiting to ascertain the state of the ground on the day. Aidan O'Brien had previously stated that the colt needed a sound surface. The going at Goodwood was described as 'good' by Timeform, leading to speculation that a confrontation with top older miler Solow (2010, by Singspiel) was deliberately avoided. A match-up against the very good Derby winner Golden Horn was also declined at York, the good to soft ground being cited as the reason, although Gleneagles did make an appearance in the pre-parade ring. A rather puzzling decision was taken to declare for the ten furlongs Irish Champion Stakes (the Dublin weather forecast predicted practically no chance of Gleneagles obtaining his preferred fast ground) in preference to the next day's Prix du Moulin over a mile, where in the end the going was very soft and Aidan O'Brien would undoubtedly have withdrawn the colt again. With Gleneagles' next target said to be the Breeders' Cup Classic over ten furlongs on dirt, rather than the more logical Breeders' Cup Mile on turf, we can only wait and see, but experience suggests the last may have been seen of the 2000 Guineas winner on a racecourse.

0205215

Above and opposite: **GLENEAGLES** (Ryan Moore) wins the 2000 Guineas beating Territories (blue colours) and Ivawood (left). It was a first victory in this classic for the jockey and enabled Aidan O'Brien to equal the record of Malton based trainer John Scott, who trained seven 2000 Guineas winners between 1842 and 1862.

0205715

2305315

Above left: **RYAN MOORE** and co-owner **MICHAEL TABOR** in the winner's circle with Gleneagles after the 2000 Guineas. Above right: Another Guineas for **GLENEAGLES**, the eighth horse to complete the double since 1969; Ryan Moore brings the colt through late to beat Endless Drama and Ivawood (rail) at the Curragh.

LEGATISSIMO (IRE)

Bay filly, foaled 22 April 2012
By Danehill Dancer (IRE) out of Yummy Mummy (GB) by Montjeu (IRE)
Bred by Newsells Park Stud, Royston, Hertfordshire
Owned by Michael Tabor, Derrick Smith and Mrs John Magnier
Trained by David Wachman at Longfield Stables, Goolds Cross, Co. Tipperary.

0305115

Racing Record

Year	Timeform Annual Rating	Starts	Wins	2nd	3rd	4th	Prize Money
2014	-	3	1	1	-	-	£ 17,404
2015	122* (19 Sept)	7	4	2	-	1	£ 875,180

Principal Performances

2014 2nd Flame of Tara E.B.F. Stakes (Listed Race) (2yo fillies) Curragh (8f)
2015 4th 1000 Guineas Trial Stakes (G3) (3yo fillies) Leopardstown (7f)
     Won E.B.F. Victor McCalmont Memorial Stakes (Listed Race) Gowran Park (9.5f)
     Won 1000 Guineas Stakes (G1) (3yo fillies) Newmarket (8f)
     2nd Oaks Stakes (G1) (3yo fillies) Epsom (12f)
     2nd Pretty Polly Stakes (G1) (Fillies & mares) Curragh (10f)
     Won Nassau Stakes (G1) (Fillies & mares) Goodwood (10f)
     Won Matron Stakes (G1) (Fillies & mares) Leopardstown (8f)

*****

*L*egatissimo, a 350,000 guineas yearling purchase at Tattersalls October Sales in Newmarket on behalf of a Coolmore partnership, trained on to become a good winner of the 1000 Guineas, surely unfortunate not to add the Oaks to her record and again beaten only a whisker, once more looking unlucky, in the Pretty Polly Stakes. Yummy Mummy, a minor winner in Ireland, is a full-sister

374

to Epsom Derby runner-up Fame And Glory (2006 – G1 Irish Derby, Ascot Gold Cup) and has also bred successful stayer Another Cocktail (2010, by Dalakhani) and Royal Battalion (2011, by Sea The Stars), a winner over hurdles. Legatissimo is Yummy Mummy's third foal and the mare has a yearling filly by Redoubte's Choice and visited Shamardal in 2015. Grandam Gryada was a minor winner and group placed at two-years-old, while her dam Grimpola (1982, by Windwurf - G2 Arag-Schwarzgold-Rennen) was second in the Preis der Diana (German Oaks). This is also the family of Gonbarda (2002, by Lando - G1 Deutschland Preis, Preis von Europa), herself the dam of Farhh (2008, by Pivotal - G1 Lockinge & Champion S).

0305415

Above: **LEGATISSIMO** wins the 1000 Guineas beating compatriot Lucida, the pair well clear of their rivals, who were headed by the non-staying champion two-year-old filly Tiggy Wiggy, her run proving yet again that top sprinters can almost, but not quite, stay the Newmarket Rowley mile when conditions are not testing. This victory completed a 2015 Guineas double for jockey Ryan Moore and owners Michael Tabor, Susan Magnier and Derrick Smith, who had won the 2000 Guineas with Gleneagles the previous afternoon.

0305115

0305715

0108615

Above left: **DAVID WACHMAN** won his first English classic with Legatissimo. Wachman, who is married to Katie Magnier, daughter of John and Susan Magnier of Coolmore Stud, has trained other top level winners in Britain, France and Ireland including Damson (Phoenix S), Again (Moyglare Stud S, Irish 1000 Guineas), Bushranger (Prix Morny, Middle Park S) and Sudirman (Phoenix S). Above centre: **RYAN MOORE** returns to the winner's circle on Legatissimo after the 1000 Guineas, a second victory in this classic for the jockey following Homecoming Queen (p342) in 2012 and his sixth English classic overall. Above right: **LEGATISSIMO** returns to winning ways in the Nassau Stakes at Goodwood ridden by Wayne Lordan, who came in for the ride when Moore was sidelined after sustaining a severe neck injury in a starting stalls accident at Newmarket in July.

QUALIFY (IRE)

Bay filly, foaled 22 April 2012
By Fastnet Rock (AUS) out of Perihelion (IRE) by Galileo (IRE)
Bred by Whisperview Trading Limited
Owned by Mrs Chantal Consuelo Regalado-Gonzalez
Trained by Aidan P. O'Brien at Ballydoyle, Cashel, Co. Tipperary.

0506215

Racing Record

Year	Timeform Annual Rating	Starts	Wins	2nd	3rd	4th	Prize Money
2014	104	7	2	-	1	1	£ 51,300
2015	114* (19 Sept)	4	1	-	-	-	£ 264,885

Principal Performances

2014   3rd Silver Flash Stakes (G3) (2yo fillies) Leopardstown (7f)
        Won Park Stakes (G3) (2yo fillies) Curragh (7f)
2015   Won Oaks Stakes (G1) (3yo fillies) Epsom (12f)

*****

*A*fter showing useful form as a two-year-old, but not that of a potential classic winner, Qualify started at a short-priced 12/1 for the 1000 Guineas but performed dismally, finishing a tailed-off last. A better effort followed in the Irish equivalent but the filly's tenth place, seven lengths behind the winner, merely seemed to confirm her 2014 Timeform rating. With the champion Australian sprinter Fastnet Rock as her sire it hardly seemed likely that Qualify would improve stepped up to twelve furlongs, but her dam's stout breeding prevailed and Qualify ran on bravely to catch 1000 Guineas winner Legatissimo on the line. She was the first top level winner in Europe for her sire. Qualify's winning grandam Medicosma descended from a successful Juddmonte family and herself bred six winners. Great grandam Media Luna (1981, by Star Appeal) finished second in the Oaks behind Circus Plume (p53) and bred six winners including Eva Luna (1992, by Alleged – G3 Park Hill S), the dam of

Moon Search (1999, by Rainbow Quest – G2 Prix de Royallieu), Brian Boru (p250) and Sea Moon (2008, by Beat Hollow – G2 Great Voltigeur S, Hardwicke S, 3rd G1 St Leger S). Eva Luna also bred the unraced Soviet Moon (2001, by Sadler's Wells), dam of Derby and Prix de l'Arc de Triomphe winner Workforce (p324).

0506415

Above: **QUALIFY** and Colm O'Donoghue head the unlucky favourite Legatissimo (centre) in the last stride to win the Oaks with Lady Of Dubai (no.7) in third place. At 50/1 Qualify was longest-priced winner of this classic since Jet Ski Lady in 1991. Trainer Aidan O'Brien's joy at landing his fifth Oaks would have been somewhat qualified after the Epsom stewards fined him £3,000 because his three runners were late saddling.

0506115

0017908

Above left: **COLM O'DONOGHUE** returns to the winner's circle on Qualify after recording his first victory in an English classic. Above right: **PERIHELION**, pictured here with John Murtagh in the saddle, was bred by Aidan and Anne-Marie O'Brien, with Anne-Marie's father, Joe Crowley, under their Whisperview Trading banner, and raced in the colours of Anne-Marie. The filly won her maiden and was second in the Group 2 Park Hill Stakes. Perihelion has done well at stud foaling the winners Satellite (2011, by Danehill Dancer) and Shogun (2013, by Fastnet Rock), as well as Qualify.

GOLDEN HORN (GB)

Bay/brown colt, foaled 27 March 2012
By Cape Cross (IRE) out of Fleche d'Or (GB) by Dubai Destination (USA)
Bred by Hascombe and Valiant Studs, Newmarket, Suffolk
Owned by Anthony E. Oppenheimer
Trained by John H.M. Gosden at Clarehaven Stables, Newmarket, Suffolk.

0407115

Racing Record

Year	Timeform Annual Rating	Starts	Wins	2nd	3rd	4th	Prize Money
2014	107	1	1	-	-	-	£ 6,469
2015	133* (19 Sept)	6	5	1	-	-	£ 1,871,300

Principal Performances

2015 Won Feilden Stakes (Listed Race) (3yo) Newmarket (9f)
Won Dante Stakes (G2) (3yo) York (10.4f)
Won Derby Stakes (G1) (3yo colts & fillies) Epsom (12f)
Won Eclipse Stakes (G1) (3yo & upwards) Sandown (10f)
2nd International Stakes (G1) (3yo & upwards) York (10.4f)
Won Irish Champion Stakes (G1) (3yo & upwards) Leopardstown (10f)

*****

*D*espite holding serious reservations about his unbeaten colt staying the Derby distance Anthony Oppenheimer decided to stump up the late entry fee and was rewarded five days later when Golden Horn won the greatest classic in the world. Oppenheimer had unfortunately sold the unraced Fleche d'Or, in foal to Champs Elysees (2003, by Danehill), at Tattersalls 2012 December Sales to Harry McCalmont of Norelands Stud in County Kilkenny for 62,000 guineas. The resulting filly was sold by Norelands as a yearling at Goffs Orby Sale for €150k. Golden Horn is the second foal of Fleche d'Or after the useful Eastern Belle (2011, by Champs Elysees – LR Ballymacoll Stud S). Fleche d'Or has since bred a filly by Acclamation in 2014 and after a barren year is in foal to Shamardal in 2015. Anthony Oppenheimer did however have the luck to retain Golden Horn when the colt failed to reach *his reserve of 190,000 guineas at Tattersalls as a yearling. Grandam, listed winner Nuryana, bred ten winners including Mystic Knight (1993, by Caerleon – G3 Lingfield Derby Trial S), Rebecca Sharp (1994, by Machiavellian – G1 Coronation S) and Hidden Hope (2001, by Daylami – LR Cheshire Oaks). Great grandam Loralane (1977, by Habitat) was a minor winner and a half-sister to On The House (p26). Through Tessa Gillian (1950, by Nearco – 2nd 1000 Guineas), sixth dam of Golden Horn, this family traces back in direct female line to the celebrated runner and broodmare, Mumtaz Mahal (1921, by The Tetrarch – Nunthorpe S). It is only of academic interest after so many years but the 1923 edition of The Bloodstock Breeders Review p50-51, quotes an article published in the Sporting Chronicle of that year which suggested that the pedigree of Mumtaz Mahal's tenth dam Spitfire (1800, by Beningbrough) may have been 'invented' after the mare entered stud at Newmarket in 1806. Certainly two male siblings were regarded at the time as 'half-bred', their breeder, the Reverend Percival of Acomb, sold them as such and they both won races restricted to 'half-breds'. It would seem that somewhere in the mists of time Spitfire managed to leave her plebeian ancestry behind! Golden Horn's unbeaten run came to an end in controversial circumstances at York in mid-August. The gelding Dick Doughtywylie, reportedly often used as a lead-horse for Golden Horn in his work, was supplemented to provide the same service for the International Stakes. Unfortunately the two jockeys, Frankie Dettori and Robert Havlin, seemed to go out with no other plan than Dick Doughtywylie would lead. Golden Horn became upset when his work-mate, who had been slow leaving the stalls, went past him and he was prevented by Dettori from tucking in behind as usual, with the result that too much energy was expended early and the colt had nothing left to repel the challenge of Arabian Queen in the last furlong. John Gosden stated afterwards that granted hindsight they would have done things differently. Sadly there is no second chance in horse racing; it has to be done right the first time. Strong rumour has it that Golden Horn will retire to The National Stud at Newmarket when his racing days are over and become the first Derby winner to stand there since Shaamit in 1997.*

Right: Frankie Dettori and John Gosden win their second Derby as £75k supplementary entry **GOLDEN HORN** beats stable companion and subsequent Irish Derby winner, Jack Hobbs. Gosden had previously won this classic with Benny The Dip (p184) and Dettori on Authorized (p294) in 2007. The 2015 Derby should not be left without mentioning the excessively loud music broadcast over the public address and presumably intended to be dramatic, with which the assembled thousands on Epsom Downs had their ears assaulted shortly before the running of the race. This kind of mindless nonsense should have no place in horse racing, a sport essentially dramatic in itself and not requiring any artificial build-up.

0606815

1405115

ANTHONY OPPENHEIMER (left) bred Golden Horn at his Hascombe and Valiant Studs.

Right: **GOLDEN HORN** and Dettori beating the 2014 Prix du Jockey Club and Irish Champion Stakes winner, The Grey Gatsby, in Sandown's Eclipse Stakes.

0407415

379

SIMPLE VERSE (IRE)

Bay filly, foaled 5 March 2012
By Duke of Marmalade (IRE) out of Guantanamera (IRE) by Sadler's Wells (USA)
Bred by Barronstown Stud, Grange Con, Co. Wicklow
Owned by Qatar Racing Ltd/Sheikh Suhaim Al Thani/M. Al Kubaisi
Trained by Ralph Beckett at Kimpton Down Stables, Andover, Hampshire.

1209115

Racing Record

Year	Timeform Annual Rating	Starts	Wins	2nd	3rd	4th	Prize Money
2014	-	0	-	-	-	-	-
2015	119* (19 Sept)	7	4	2	1	-	£ 470,374

Principal Performances

2015 Won Lillie Langtry Stakes (G3) (Fillies & mares) Goodwood (12f)
      Won St Leger Stakes (G1) (3yo colts & fillies) Doncaster (14.6f)

*****

*S*imple Verse was a €240,000 yearling purchase and the fourth foal of the unraced Guantanamera, who was out of the listed placed winner Bluffing. Great grandam Instinctive Move (1981, by Nijinsky) was a minor winner and a half-sister to Law Society (1982, by Alleged – G1 Irish Derby S, G2 National S, G3 Chester Vase, 2nd G1 Dewhurst S), a colt that finished a distant runner-up behind Slip Anchor (p62) in the Derby at Epsom. Guantanamera had previously bred the winning brothers Lord Jim (2009, by Holy Roman Emperor) and Maxentius (2010 – 3rd G2 Superlative S). Simple Verse showed much improved form when winning at Goodwood in late-July and the decision was taken to supplement her for £70,000 into the St Leger, where the filly courageously survived a bumping and boring match with the runner-up Bondi Beach, but was subsequently disqualified by the stewards and her jockey suspended. Ralph Beckett appealed against the decision and Simple Verse was reinstated as a classic winner at the hearing held eleven days later. It was a verdict that seemed thoroughly justified as the original disqualification had looked harsh under the current rules.*

1209615

Above: A literal battle-royal between two brave horses goes narrowly in favour of **SIMPLE VERSE** (no.8) but the positions were reversed at the subsequent steward's inquiry and the St Leger victory awarded to Bondi Beach and Colm O'Donoghue, a decision later revised at an appeal hearing. It was a second successive victory in this classic for jockey **ANDREA ATZENI** (below right) following Kingston Hill (p370) and a third English classic for **RALPH BECKETT** (below left, with Fahad Al Thani of Qatar Racing), who had previously won the Oaks with Look Here (p302) and Talent (p354). This would have been the first time a St Leger winner had been disqualified since 1789, when the colt Zanga was stood down for jostling in favour of Earl Fitzwilliam's filly Pewett (1786, by Tandem).

1209115

2008114

SIMPLE VERSE (IRE) : Bay 2012			
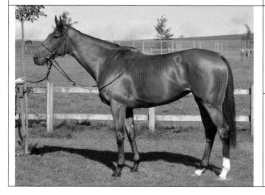	Duke of Marmalade (IRE) B. 2004	Danehill (USA) B. 1986	Danzig (USA)
			Razyana (USA)
		Love Me True (USA) Ch. 1998	Kingmambo (USA)
			Lassie's Lady (USA)
	Guantanamera (IRE) B. 2004	Sadler's Wells (USA) B. 1981	Northern Dancer (CAN)
			Fairy Bridge (USA)
		Bluffing (IRE) B. 1992	Darshaan (GB)
			Instinctive Move (USA)

MISS FRANCE (IRE) : Bay 2011

Dansili (GB) B. 1996	Danehill (USA) B. 1986	Danzig (USA)
		Razyana (USA)
	Hasili (IRE) B. 1991	Kahyasi (IRE)
		Kerali (GB)
Miss Tahiti (IRE) Br. 1993	Tirol (IRE) Br. 1987	Thatching (IRE)
		Alpine Niece (GB)
	Mini Luthe (FR) B. 1982	Luthier (FR)
		Minifer (GB)

TAGHROODA (GB) : Bay 2011

Sea The Stars (IRE) B. 2006	Cape Cross (IRE) B/br. 1994	Green Desert (USA)
		Park Appeal (IRE)
	Urban Sea (USA) Ch. 1989	Miswaki (USA)
		Allegretta (GB)
Ezima (IRE) B. 2004	Sadler's Wells (USA) B. 1981	Northern Dancer (CAN)
		Fairy Bridge (USA)
	Ezilla (IRE) B. 1997	Darshaan (GB)
		Ezana (IRE)

AUSTRALIA (GB) : Chesnut 2011

Galileo (IRE) B. 1998	Sadler's Wells (USA) B. 1981	Northern Dancer (CAN)
		Fairy Bridge (USA)
	Urban Sea (USA) Ch. 1989	Miswaki (USA)
		Allegretta (GB)
Ouija Board (GB) B. 2001	Cape Cross (IRE) B/br. 1994	Green Desert (USA)
		Park Appeal (IRE)
	Selection Board (GB) B. 1982	Welsh Pageant (FR)
		Ouija (GB)

KINGSTON HILL (GB) : Grey 2011

Mastercraftsman (IRE) Gr. 2006	Danehill Dancer (IRE) B. 1993	Danehill (USA)
		Mira Adonde (USA)
	Starlight Dreams (USA) Gr. 1995	Black Tie Affair (IRE)
		Reves Celeste (USA)
Audacieuse (GB) B. 1997	Rainbow Quest (USA) B. 1981	Blushing Groom (FR)
		I Will Follow (USA)
	Sarah Georgina (IRE) B. 1987	Persian Bold (IRE)
		Dance By Night (GB)

GLENEAGLES (IRE) : Bay 2012

Galileo (IRE) B. 1998	Sadler's Wells (USA) B. 1981	Northern Dancer (CAN)
		Fairy Bridge (USA)
	Urban Sea (USA) Ch. 1989	Miswaki (USA)
		Allegretta (GB)
You'resothrilling (USA) B/br. 2005	Storm Cat (USA) B/br. 1983	Storm Bird (CAN)
		Terlingua (USA)
	Mariah's Storm (USA) B. 1991	Rahy (USA)
		Immense (USA)

LEGATISSIMO (IRE) : Bay 2012

Danehill Dancer (IRE) B. 1993	Danehill (USA) B. 1986	Danzig (USA)
		Razyana (USA)
	Mira Adonde (USA) B/br. 1986	Sharpen Up (GB)
		Lettre d'Amour (USA)
Yummy Mummy (GB) B. 2005	Montjeu (IRE) B. 1996	Sadler's Wells (USA)
		Floripedes (FR)
	Gryada (GB) B. 1993	Shirley Heights (GB)
		Grimpola (GER)

QUALIFY (IRE) : Bay 2012

Fastnet Rock (AUS) B. 2001	Danehill (USA) B. 1986	Danzig (USA)
		Razyana (USA)
	Piccadilly Circus (AUS) B. 1995	Royal Academy (USA)
		Gatana (AUS)
Perihelion (IRE) Ch. 2005	Galileo (IRE) B. 1998	Sadler's Wells (USA)
		Urban Sea (USA)
	Medicosma (USA) Ch. 1986	The Minstrel (CAN)
		Media Luna (GB)

GOLDEN HORN (GB) : B/br. 2012

Cape Cross (IRE) B/br. 1994	Green Desert (USA) B. 1983	Danzig (USA)
		Foreign Courier (USA)
	Park Appeal (IRE) Br. 1982	Ahonoora (GB)
		Balidaress (IRE)
Fleche d'Or (GB) B. 2006	Dubai Destination (USA) B. 1999	Kingmambo (USA)
		Mysterial (USA)
	Nuryana (GB) B. 1984	Nureyev (USA)
		Loralane (GB)

ERRATA & ADDENDA

Bireme : p10, was also half-sister to Kedge (1964, by Petition – Hackwood S).

Midway Lady : p64, was sister to Capias (1991 – LR Leicester Mercury S, 2nd G3 Jockey Club Cup, 2nd G3 Curragh Cup) and half-sister to Heavenly Calm (1994, by Diesis – LR Prix de Thiberville).

Nashwan : p96, his dam was a three-parts sister to Burghclere (1977, by Busted), the dam of Wind In Her Hair (1991, by Alzao – G1 Aral Pokal, 2nd G1 Oaks S, 3rd G1 Yorkshire Oaks), herself dam of the outstanding Japanese runner and sire Deep Impact (2002, by Sunday Silence), twice Horse of the Year in Japan. Height of Fashion also bred Sarayir (1994, by Mr Prospector – LR Oh So Sharp S, the dam of Ghanaati <p312>).

Clive Brittain : p115, announced on 3 September that he was retiring from training at the end of 2015. Clive had held a training license since 1972, moving to his Carlburg Stables on the Bury Road at Newmarket in 1975 after three years at Pegasus Stables on Snailwell Road. Apart from his six English classic winners, Brittain also trained Jupiter Island (G1 Japan Cup), Sikeston (G2 Queen Anne S & three G1 races in Italy), Hailsham & Luso (both G1 Derby Italiano), Terimon (G1 International S, 2nd G1 Derby S), User Friendly (G1 Irish Oaks, 2nd G1 Prix de l'Arc de Triomphe), Ivanka & Teggiano (both G1 Fillies' Mile), Crimplene (G1 Irish 1000 Guineas, Coronation S, Nassau S), Warrsan (G1 Coronation Cup twice), Var (G1 Prix de l'Abbaye), Rizeena (G1 Coronation S) and Sayyedati (G1 Sussex S, Prix Jacques Le Marois).

Dr Devious : p126, his winning daughter Countess Sybil (1998, ex Countess Candy by Great Nephew) is the dam of Air Pilot (2009, by Zamindar – G3 International S, Curragh; LR James Seymour S).

Commander in Chief : p136, his winning full-sister Totality (1991) finished 2nd in the G3 Lancashire Oaks.

Lady Carla : p170, was also dam of the minor winner Prairie Hawk (2005, by Hawk Wing).

King Of Kings : p188, was sire of Queen Of Queens (2004, AUS-G3 S.A. Oaks, 4th AUS-G1 Australian Oaks).

Galileo : p228, Minding (2013, G1 Moyglare Stud S), Order of St George (2012, G1 Irish St Leger S) and Mondialiste (2010, Can-G1 Woodbine Mile S).

Rock of Gibraltar : p233, Prince Gibraltar also won the G1 Grosser Preis von Baden at Baden-Baden 2015.

Footstepsinthesand : p264, is sire of Living The Life (2010, US-G2 Presque Isle Downs Masters S).

Motivator : p270, Treve (2010) won the G1 Grand Prix de Saint-Cloud in 2015.

Cockney Rebel : p286, moves to Haras du Thenney at Saint-Pierre Azif in Normandy for 2016.

New Approach : p304, is sire of Connecticut (2011, TUR-G2 International Bosphorus Cup, Veliefendi).

Sea The Stars : p310, is sire of Cloth Of Stars (2013, G3 Prix des Chenes).

Gleneagles : p372, his full-sister Coolmore (2013) won the G3 Park Stakes at the Curragh.

APPENDIX

1000 GUINEAS 1950-2015 WINNER	YEAR	TIMEFORM ANNUAL RATING	RATINGS TOTAL	AVERAGE RATING OF WINNERS	10 YEAR AV
Camaree	1950	122	122	122.00	
Belle of All	1951	124	246	123.00	
Zabara	1952	128	374	124.67	
Happy Laughter	1953	126	500	125.00	
Festoon	1954	122	622	124.40	
Meld	1955	128	750	125.00	
Honeylight	1956	130	880	125.71	
Rose Royale	1957	129	1009	126.12	
Bella Paola	1958	131	1140	126.67	
Petite Etoile	1959	134	1274	127.40	127.40
Never Too Late II	1960	128	1402	127.45	
Sweet Solera	1961	127	1529	127.42	
Abermaid	1962	124	1653	127.15	
Hula Dancer	1963	133	1786	127.57	
Pourparler	1964	116	1902	126.80	
Night Off	1965	113	2015	125.94	
Glad Rags	1966	117	2132	125.41	
Fleet	1967	123	2255	125.28	
Caergwrle	1968	115	2370	124.74	
Full Dress II	1969	115	2485	124.25	121.10
Humble Duty	1970	127	2612	124.38	
Altesse Royale	1971	126	2738	124.45	
Waterloo	1972	116	2854	124.09	
Mysterious	1973	127	2981	124.21	
Highclere	1974	129	3110	124.40	
Nocturnal Spree	1975	121	3231	124.27	
Flying Water	1976	120	3351	124.11	
Mrs McArdy	1977	123	3474	124.07	
Enstone Spark	1978	119	3593	123.90	
One In A Million	1979	125	3718	123.93	123.30
Quick As Lightning	1980	123	3841	123.90	
Fairy Footsteps	1981	123	3964	123.87	
On The House	1982	125	4089	123.91	
Ma Biche	1983	125	4214	123.94	
Pebbles	1984	124	4338	123.94	
Oh So Sharp	1985	131	4469	124.14	
Midway Lady	1986	126	4595	124.19	
Miesque	1987	131	4726	124.37	
Ravinella	1988	121	4847	124.28	
Musical Bliss	1989	117	4964	124.10	124.60
Salsabil	1990	130	5094	124.24	
Shadayid	1991	122	5216	124.19	
Hatoof	1992	120	5336	124.09	
Sayyedati	1993	122	5458	124.05	
Las Meninas	1994	115	5573	123.84	
Harayir	1995	119	5692	123.74	
Bosra Sham	1996	132	5824	123.91	
Sleepytime	1997	121	5945	123.85	
Cape Verdi	1998	126	6071	123.90	

	1999	117	6188	123.76	122.40
Wince	1999	117	6188	123.76	122.40
Lahan	2000	117	6305	123.63	
Ameerat	2001	116	6421	123.48	
Kazzia	2002	121	6542	123.43	
Russian Rhythm	2003	123	6665	123.43	
Attraction	2004	125	6790	123.45	
Virginia Waters	2005	116	6906	123.32	
Speciosa	2006	115	7021	123.18	
Finsceal Beo	2007	123	7144	123.17	
Natagora	2008	116	7260	123.05	
Ghanaati	2009	122	7382	123.03	119.40
Special Duty	2010	113	7495	122.87	
Blue Bunting	2011	122	7617	122.85	
Homecoming Queen	2012	120	7737	122.81	
Sky Lantern	2013	122	7859	122.80	
Miss France	2014	119	7978	122.74	
Legatissimo	2015	122*			

2000 GUINEAS 1950-2015 WINNER	YEAR	TIMEFORM ANNUAL RATING	RATINGS TOTAL	AVERAGE RATING OF WINNERS	10 YEAR AV
Palestine	1950	133	133	133.00	
Ki Ming	1951	134	267	133.50	
Thunderhead II	1952	133	400	133.33	
Nearula	1953	131	531	132.75	
Darius	1954	129	660	132.00	
Our Babu	1955	129	789	131.50	
Gilles de Retz	1956	132	921	131.57	
Crepello	1957	136	1057	132.12	
Pall Mall	1958	128	1185	131.67	
Taboun	1959	128	1313	131.30	131.30
Martial	1960	131	1444	131.27	
Rockavon	1961	120	1564	130.33	
Privy Councillor	1962	125	1689	129.92	
Only For Life	1963	126	1815	129.64	
Baldric II	1964	131	1946	129.73	
Niksar	1965	123	2069	129.31	
Kashmir II	1966	125	2194	129.06	
Royal Palace	1967	131	2325	129.17	
Sir Ivor	1968	135	2460	129.47	
Right Tack	1969	131	2591	129.55	127.80
Nijinsky	1970	138	2729	129.95	
Brigadier Gerard	1971	141	2870	130.45	
High Top	1972	129	2999	130.39	
Mon Fils	1973	124	3123	130.12	
Nonoalco	1974	131	3254	130.16	
Bolkonski	1975	134	3388	130.31	
Wollow	1976	132	3520	130.37	
Nebbiolo	1977	125	3645	130.18	
Roland Gardens	1978	122	3767	129.90	
Tap On Wood	1979	130	3897	129.90	130.60
Known Fact	1980	135	4032	130.06	
To-Agori-Mou	1981	133	4165	130.16	
Zino	1982	127	4292	130.06	
Lomond	1983	128	4420	130.00	

El Gran Senor	1984	136	4556	130.17	
Shadeed	1985	135	4691	130.31	
Dancing Brave	1986	140	4831	130.57	
Don't Forget Me	1987	127	4958	130.47	
Doyoun	1988	124	5082	130.31	
Nashwan	1989	135	5217	130.42	132.00
Tirol	1990	127	5344	130.34	
Mystiko	1991	124	5468	130.19	
Rodrigo de Triano	1992	130	5598	130.19	
Zafonic	1993	130	5728	130.18	
Mister Baileys	1994	123	5851	130.02	
Pennekamp	1995	130	5981	130.02	
Mark of Esteem	1996	137	6118	130.17	
Entrepreneur	1997	123	6241	130.02	
King of Kings	1998	125	6366	129.92	
Island Sands	1999	122	6488	129.76	127.10
King's Best	2000	132	6620	129.80	
Golan	2001	125	6745	129.71	
Rock of Gibraltar	2002	133	6878	129.77	
Refuse To Bend	2003	124	7002	129.67	
Haafhd	2004	129	7131	129.65	
Footstepsinthesand	2005	120	7251	129.48	
George Washington	2006	133	7384	129.54	
Cockney Rebel	2007	127	7511	129.50	
Henrythenavigator	2008	131	7642	129.52	
Sea The Stars	2009	140	7782	129.70	129.40
Makfi	2010	130	7912	129.70	
Frankel	2011	143	8055	129.92	
Camelot	2012	128	8183	129.89	
Dawn Approach	2013	132	8315	129.92	
Night Of Thunder	2014	127	8442	129.88	
Gleneagles	2015	129*			

THE OAKS 1950-2015 WINNER	YEAR	TIMEFORM ANNUAL RATING	RATINGS TOTAL	AVERAGE RATING OF WINNERS	10 YEAR AV
Asmena	1950	118	118	118.00	
Neasham Belle	1951	124	242	121.00	
Frieze	1952	126	368	122.67	
Ambiguity	1953	118	486	121.50	
Sun Cap	1954	122	608	121.60	
Meld	1955	128	736	122.67	
Sicarelle	1956	128	864	123.43	
Carrozza	1957	120	984	123.00	
Bella Paola	1958	131	1115	123.89	
Petite Etoile	1959	134	1249	124.90	124.90
Never Too Late II	1960	128	1377	125.18	
Sweet Solera	1961	127	1504	125.33	
Monade	1962	129	1633	125.62	
Noblesse	1963	133	1766	126.14	
Homeward Bound	1964	126	1892	126.13	
Long Look	1965	112	2004	125.25	
Valoris	1966	120	2124	124.94	
Pia	1967	116	2240	124.44	
La Lagune	1968	125	2365	124.47	

Sleeping Partner	1969	120	2485	124.25	123.60
Lupe	1970	121	2606	124.10	
Altesse Royale	1971	126	2732	124.18	
Ginevra	1972	122	2854	124.09	
Mysterious	1973	127	2981	124.21	
Polygamy	1974	120	3101	124.04	
Juliette Marny	1975	123	3224	124.00	
Pawneese	1976	131	3355	124.26	
Dunfermline	1977	133	3488	124.57	
Fair Salinia	1978	125	3613	124.59	
Scintillate	1979	119	3732	124.40	124.70
Bireme	1980	127	3859	124.48	
Blue Wind	1981	127	3986	124.56	
Time Charter	1982	131	4117	124.76	
Sun Princess	1983	130	4247	124.91	
Circus Plume	1984	124	4371	124.89	
Oh So Sharp	1985	131	4502	125.06	
Midway Lady	1986	126	4628	125.08	
Unite	1987	126	4754	125.11	
Diminuendo	1988	126	4880	125.13	
Snow Bride	1989	121	5001	125.02	126.90
Salsabil	1990	130	5131	125.15	
Jet Ski Lady	1991	122	5253	125.07	
User Friendly	1992	128	5381	125.14	
Intrepidity	1993	124	5505	125.11	
Balanchine	1994	131	5636	125.24	
Moonshell	1995	117	5753	125.07	
Lady Carla	1996	122	5875	125.00	
Reams of Verse	1997	121	5996	124.92	
Shahtoush	1998	120	6116	124.82	
Ramruma	1999	123	6239	124.78	124.00
Love Divine	2000	120	6359	124.69	
Imagine	2001	119	6478	124.58	
Kazzia	2002	121	6599	124.51	
Casual Look	2003	114	6713	124.31	
Ouija Board	2004	125	6838	124.33	
Eswarah	2005	117	6955	124.20	
Alexandrova	2006	123	7078	124.18	
Light Shift	2007	121	7199	124.12	
Look Here	2008	123	7322	124.10	
Sariska	2009	123	7445	124.08	120.60
Snow Fairy	2010	123	7568	124.07	
Dancing Rain	2011	120	7688	124.00	
Was	2012	117	7805	123.89	
Talent	2013	116	7921	123.77	
Taghrooda	2014	127	8048	123.82	
Qualify	2015	114*			

THE DERBY 1950-2015 WINNER	YEAR	TIMEFORM ANNUAL RATING	RATINGS TOTAL	AVERAGE RATING OF WINNERS	10 YEAR AV
Galcador	1950	133	133	133.00	
Arctic Prince	1951	135	268	134.00	
Tulyar	1952	134	402	134.00	
Pinza	1953	137	539	134.75	

Never Say Die	1954	137	676	135.20	
Phil Drake	1955	132	808	134.67	
Lavandin	1956	128	936	133.71	
Crepello	1957	136	1072	134.00	
Hard Ridden	1958	131	1203	133.67	
Parthia	1959	132	1335	133.50	133.50
St Paddy	1960	133	1468	133.45	
Psidium	1961	130	1598	133.17	
Larkspur	1962	128	1726	132.77	
Relko	1963	136	1862	133.00	
Santa Claus	1964	133	1995	133.00	
Sea-Bird II	1965	145	2140	133.75	
Charlottown	1966	127	2267	133.35	
Royal Palace	1967	131	2398	133.22	
Sir Ivor	1968	135	2533	133.32	
Blakeney	1969	123	2656	132.80	132.10
Nijinsky	1970	138	2794	133.05	
Mill Reef	1971	141	2935	133.41	
Roberto	1972	131	3066	133.30	
Morston	1973	125	3191	132.96	
Snow Knight	1974	125	3316	132.64	
Grundy	1975	137	3453	132.81	
Empery	1976	128	3581	132.63	
The Minstrel	1977	135	3716	132.71	
Shirley Heights	1978	130	3846	132.62	
Troy	1979	137	3983	132.77	132.70
Henbit	1980	130	4113	132.68	
Shergar	1981	140	4253	132.91	
Golden Fleece	1982	133	4386	132.91	
Teenoso	1983	132	4518	132.88	
Secreto	1984	128	4646	132.74	
Slip Anchor	1985	136	4782	132.83	
Shahrastani	1986	135	4917	132.89	
Reference Point	1987	139	5056	133.05	
Kahyasi	1988	130	5186	132.97	
Nashwan	1989	135	5321	133.02	133.80
Quest For Fame	1990	127	5448	132.88	
Generous	1991	139	5587	133.02	
Dr Devious	1992	127	5714	132.88	
Commander in Chief	1993	128	5842	132.77	
Erhaab	1994	127	5969	132.64	
Lammtarra	1995	134	6103	132.67	
Shaamit	1996	127	6230	132.55	
Benny the Dip	1997	127	6357	132.44	
High-Rise	1998	130	6487	132.39	
Oath	1999	125	6612	132.24	129.10
Sinndar	2000	134	6746	132.27	
Galileo	2001	134	6880	132.31	
High Chaparral	2002	130	7010	132.26	
Kris Kin	2003	126	7136	132.15	
North Light	2004	126	7262	132.04	
Motivator	2005	131	7393	132.02	
Sir Percy	2006	129	7522	131.96	
Authorized	2007	133	7655	131.98	

New Approach	2008	132	7787	131.98	
Sea The Stars	2009	140	7927	132.12	131.50
Workforce	2010	133	8060	132.13	
Pour Moi	2011	125	8185	132.02	
Camelot	2012	128	8313	131.95	
Ruler of the World	2013	128	8441	131.89	
Australia	2014	132	8573	131.89	
Golden Horn	2015	133*			

THE ST LEGER 1950-2015 WINNER	YEAR	TIMEFORM ANNUAL RATING	RATINGS TOTAL	AVERAGE RATING OF WINNERS	10 YEAR AV
Scratch	1950	134	134	134.00	
Talma II	1951	130	264	132.00	
Tulyar	1952	134	398	132.67	
Premonition	1953	130	528	132.00	
Never Say Die	1954	137	665	133.00	
Meld	1955	128	793	132.17	
Cambremer	1956	129	922	131.71	
Ballymoss	1957	132	1054	131.75	
Alcide	1958	135	1189	132.11	
Cantelo	1959	129	1318	131.80	131.80
St Paddy	1960	133	1451	131.91	
Aurelius	1961	127	1578	131.50	
Hethersett	1962	134	1712	131.69	
Ragusa	1963	137	1849	132.07	
Indiana	1964	129	1978	131.87	
Provoke	1965	130	2108	131.75	
Sodium	1966	128	2236	131.53	
Ribocco	1967	129	2365	131.39	
Ribero	1968	126	2491	131.11	
Intermezzo	1969	124	2615	130.75	129.70
Nijinsky	1970	138	2753	131.10	
Athens Wood	1971	126	2879	130.86	
Boucher	1972	124	3003	130.57	
Peleid	1973	125	3128	130.33	
Bustino	1974	130	3258	130.32	
Bruni	1975	132	3390	130.38	
Crow	1976	134	3524	130.52	
Dunfermline	1977	133	3657	130.61	
Julio Mariner	1978	127	3784	130.48	
Son of Love	1979	126	3910	130.33	129.50
Light Cavalry	1980	128	4038	130.26	
Cut Above	1981	130	4168	130.25	
Touching Wood	1982	127	4295	130.15	
Sun Princess	1983	130	4425	130.15	
Commanche Run	1984	129	4554	130.11	
Oh So Sharp	1985	131	4685	130.14	
Moon Madness	1986	128	4813	130.08	
Reference Point	1987	139	4952	130.32	
Minster Son	1988	130	5082	130.31	
Michelozzo	1989	127	5209	130.22	129.90
Snurge	1990	130	5339	130.22	
Toulon	1991	125	5464	130.10	
User Friendly	1992	128	5592	130.05	

Bob's Return	1993	123	5715	129.89	
Moonax	1994	121	5836	129.69	
Classic Cliché	1995	120	5956	129.48	
Shantou	1996	124	6080	129.36	
Silver Patriarch	1997	125	6205	129.27	
Nedawi	1998	124	6329	129.16	
Mutafaweq	1999	129	6458	129.16	124.90
Millenary	2000	122	6580	129.02	
Milan	2001	129	6709	129.02	
Bollin Eric	2002	125	6834	128.94	
Brian Boru	2003	124	6958	128.85	
Rule of Law	2004	125	7083	128.78	
Scorpion	2005	126	7209	128.73	
Sixties Icon	2006	125	7334	128.67	
Lucarno	2007	121	7455	128.53	
Conduit	2008	130	7585	128.56	
Mastery	2009	122	7707	128.45	124.90
Arctic Cosmos	2010	123	7830	128.36	
Masked Marvel	2011	126	7956	128.32	
Encke	2012	123	8079	128.24	
Leading Light	2013	121	8200	128.12	
Kingston Hill	2014	125	8325	128.08	
Simple Verse	2015	119*			

* The ratings for the 2015 classic winners were as at 19 September 2015

PRIX ROYAL-OAK 1950-2014 WINNER	YEAR	TIMEFORM ANNUAL RATING	RATINGS TOTAL	AVERAGE RATING OF WINNERS
Pan	1950	126	126	126.00
Stymphale	1951	126	252	126.00
Feu du Diable	1952	124	376	125.33
Buisson d'Or	1953	126	502	125.50
Sica Boy	1954	132	634	126.80
Macip	1955	126	760	126.67
Arabian*	1956	No rating	760	126.67
Scot II	1957	131	891	127.29
Wallaby II	1958	126	1017	127.12
Vamour	1959	127	1144	127.11
Puissant Chef	1960	132	1276	127.60
Match III	1961	129	1405	127.73
Sicilian Prince	1962	126	1531	127.58
Relko	1963	136	1667	128.23
Barbieri	1964	129	1796	128.29
Reliance	1965	137	1933	128.87
Vasco de Gama	1966	125	2058	128.62
Samos III	1967	125	2183	128.41
Dhaudevi	1968	127	2310	128.33
Le Chouan	1969	123	2433	128.05
Sassafras	1970	135	2568	128.40
Bourbon	1971	129	2697	128.43
Pleben	1972	127	2824	128.36
Lady Berry	1973	121	2945	128.04
Busiris	1974	126	3071	127.96
Henry le Balafre	1975	125	3196	127.84

Exceller	1976	129	3325	127.88
Rex Magna	1977	129	3454	127.93
Brave Johnny	1978	124	3578	127.79
Niniski **	1979	125	3703	127.69
Gold River	1980	125	3828	127.60
Ardross	1981	131	3959	127.71
Denel	1982	126	4085	127.66
Old Country	1983	122	4207	127.48
Agent Double	1984	122	4329	127.32
Mersey	1985	116	4445	127.00
El Cuite	1986	123	4568	126.89
Royal Gait	1987	120	4688	126.70
Star Lift	1988	122	4810	126.58
Top Sunrise	1989	122	4932	126.46
Braashee***	1990	118	+ 116.5	
Indian Queen***		115	5048.5	126.21
Turgeon	1991	119	5167.5	126.04
Assessor	1992	118	5285.5	125.85
Raintrap	1993	122	5407.5	125.76
Moonax	1994	121	5528.5	125.65
Sunshack	1995	122	5650.5	125.57
Red Roses Story	1996	118	5768.5	125.40
Ebadiyla	1997	122	5890.5	125.33
Tiraaz	1998	115	6005.5	125.11
Amilynx	1999	121	6126.5	125.03
Amilynx	2000	126	6252.5	125.05
Vinnie Roe	2001	126	6378.5	125.07
Mr Dinos	2002	117	6495.5	124.91
Westerner	2003	121	6616.5	124.84
Westerner	2004	123	6739.5	124.81
Alcazar	2005	118	6857.5	124.68
Montare	2006	116	6973.5	124.53
Allegretto	2007	118	7091.5	124.41
Yeats	2008	128	7219.5	124.47
Ask	2009	126	7345.5	124.50
Gentoo	2010	119	7464.5	124.41
Be Fabulous	2011	116	7580.5	124.27
Les Beaufs	2012	114	7694.5	124.10
Tac de Boistron	2013	119	7814.5	124.04
Tac de Boistron	2014	124	7938.5	124.03

* Arabian was not included in Racehorses of 1956
** Race was opened to horses above the age of three for the first time in 1979
*** In 1990 Braashee and Indian Queen dead-heated – an average has been taken of their ratings

IRISH ST LEGER 1950-2014 WINNER	YEAR	TIMEFORM ANNUAL RATING	RATINGS TOTAL	AVERAGE RATING OF WINNERS
Morning Madam	1950	106	106	106.00
Do Well*	1951	No rating	106	106.00
Judicate	1952	120	226	113.00
Sea Charger	1953	129	355	118.33
Zarathustra**	1954	?	355	118.33
Diamond Slipper	1955	122	477	119.25
Magnetic North	1956	118	595	119.00

Ommeyad	1957	116	711	118.50
Royal Highway	1958	117	828	118.29
Barclay	1959	122	950	118.75
Lynchris	1960	127	1077	119.67
Vimadee	1961	120	1197	119.70
Arctic Vale	1962	117	1314	119.45
Christmas Island	1963	120	1434	119.50
Biscayne	1964	123	1557	119.77
Craighouse	1965	123	1680	120.00
White Gloves	1966	117	1797	119.80
Dan Kano	1967	115	1912	119.50
Giolla Mear	1968	113	2025	119.12
Reindeer	1969	119	2144	119.11
Allangrange	1970	126	2270	119.47
Parnell	1971	124	2394	119.70
Pidget	1972	120	2514	119.71
Conor Pass	1973	111	2625	119.32
Mistigri	1974	121	2746	119.39
Caucasus	1975	127	2873	119.71
Meneval	1976	128	3001	120.04
Transworld	1977	121	3122	120.08
M-Lolshan	1978	125	3247	120.26
Niniski	1979	125	3372	120.43
Gonzales	1980	120	3492	120.41
Protection Racket	1981	122	3614	120.47
Touching Wood	1982	127	3741	120.68
Mountain Lodge ***	1983	120	3861	120.66
Opale	1984	117	3978	120.55
Leading Counsel	1985	122	4100	120.59
Authaal	1986	118	4218	120.51
Eurobird	1987	118	4336	120.44
Dark Lomond	1988	122	4458	120.49
Petite Ile	1989	121	4579	120.50
Ibn Bey	1990	126	4705	120.64
Turgeon	1991	119	4824	120.60
Mashaallah	1992	123	4947	120.66
Vintage Crop	1993	125	5072	120.76
Vintage Crop	1994	121	5193	120.77
Strategic Choice	1995	122	5315	120.70
Oscar Schindler	1996	127	5442	120.93
Oscar Schindler	1997	127	5569	121.07
Kayf Tara	1998	126	5695	121.17
Kayf Tara	1999	130	5825	121.35
Arctic Owl	2000	122	5947	121.37
Vinnie Roe	2001	126	6073	121.46
Vinnie Roe	2002	126	6199	121.55
Vinnie Roe	2003	125	6324	121.62
Vinnie Roe	2004	128	6452	121.74
Collier Hill	2005	120	6572	121.70
Kastoria	2006	124	6696	121.75
Yeats	2007	126	6822	121.82
Septimus	2008	129	6951	121.95
Alandi	2009	121	7072	121.93
Sans Frontieres	2010	125	7197	121.98

Duncan****	2011	121	+ 121	
Jukebox Jury****		121	7318	121.97
Royal Diamond	2012	117	7435	121.89
Voleuse de Coeurs	2013	122	7557	121.89
Brown Panther	2014	123	7680	121.90

* Do Well was not included in Racehorses of 1951
** Zarathustra was too unreliable to be given a rating in Racehorses of 1954
*** Race opened to horses above the age of three for the first time in 1983
**** In 2011 Duncan and Jukebox Jury dead-heated – they were both rated 121 in Racehorses of 2011

INDEX

This index contains references to the principal subjects featured in the text. Page numbers in italics denote photographs.

HORSE INDEX

N.B. To keep the index within reasonable limits, only Group Race winners in England, Ireland and France and other notable horses have been included.

399

402

407

RACE INDEX

N.B. Only current Group 1 races in England and the French and Irish classics have been included, although some might consider the Prix Vermeille, Prix Royal-Oak and the Irish St Leger no longer as classics.